1978

SOURCEBOOK ON PROBATION, PAROLE AND PARDONS

Third Edition, Fifth Printing, 1975

SOURCEBOOK ON PROBATION, PAROLE AND PARDONS

By

CHARLES L. NEWMAN

Head
Center for Law Enforcement and Corrections
College of Human Development
The Pennsylvania State University

CHARLES C THOMAS • PUBLISHER
Springfield • Illinois • U.S.A.

Published and Distributed Throughout the World by

CHARLES C THOMAS • PUBLISHER
Bannerstone House
301-327 East Lawrence Avenue, Springfield, Illinois, U.S.A.

ISBN 0-398-01396-9

Library of Congress Catalog Card Number: 68-296823

First Edition, 1958
Second Edition, 1964
Third Edition, First Printing, 1968
Third Edition, Second Printing, 1970
Third Edition, Third Printing, 1972
Third Edition, Fourth Printing, 1973
Third Edition, Fifth Printing, 1975

With THOMAS BOOKS *careful attention is given to all details of manufacturing and design. It is the Publisher's desire to present books that are satisfactory as to their physical qualities and artistic possibilities and appropriate for their particular use.* THOMAS BOOKS *will be true to those laws of quality that assure a good name and good will.*

Printed in the United States of America
R-1

**Dedicated to Those
Who Seek to Improve
The Lot of Their
Fellow Men . . .**

**and to My Wife,
Della**

Introduction to the Third Edition

IN the decade since the publication of the First Edition of this *Sourcebook,* significant developments have occurred in the United States which have had impact upon the administration of justice in general and on probation and parole in particular. Increasingly there are indications that those who view the field now see it as a system needing total integration. There is a growing consensus that the correctional system consists of both institutional and field services, an idea that the First Edition of this volume attempted to introduce. Moreover, there is a growing recognition by the ancillary services of mental health and vocational rehabilitation that they, too, have a part in the restoration of the offender, both to and in the community.

The significant contribution of the President's Commission on Law Enforcement and the Administration of Justice represents another forward step in the administration of justice. The recentness of their reports precludes any immediate evaluation of consequences either upon the correctional establishment, the courts, law enforcement or the public. It seems entirely reasonable, however, to predict that the new body of knowledge which has been generated by the Commission and the public concern which has been elicited by the reports, along with the several recent landmark U.S. Supreme Court decisions, as well as the public clamor for a reduction of "crime in the streets," will leave significant impressions upon the administration of justice system.

At the time that the First Edition was prepared, the involvement of the university sector in relation to the administration of justice was limited and had no significant impact either upon the correctional field or upon public policy matters affecting the administration of justice. That situation has changed remarkably, in terms of the number of university programs involved in preparation of personnel for the field and in terms of the production of data which can be utilized by institutions and field services alike in gaining understanding of the correctional client and the effectiveness of services related to these programs.

Many problems still remain unsolved, not least among which is the continuing deficit of adequate numbers of personnel with the appropriate educational preparation and training to carry out the mission of the administration of justice. Hopefully, the work of the Joint Commission on Correctional Manpower and Training will provide some insights on solving the manpower problem in corrections. Adequate funding continues to be a problem, even though the total dollar appropriation to the correctional field has increased remarkably in the past decade.

In the continuing search for effective techniques, the field of corrections, as well as the other human services areas, has tended to respond to fads. Unfortunately, in the search for new ideas, old ideas are left untried and unfulfilled. Perhaps in time the "ultimate" cure will be found. In the meantime, however, we shall have to continue attempts to deal with each offender as an individual, adjusting his time in the community or in the institution to his capacity to control and direct his behavior toward socially acceptable channels. I suspect that the accomplishment of that objective is, in the final analysis, the "ultimate" cure.

As in prior editions, the materials in this book represent both writings from my own and other sources. The responsibility for the selection of materials is my own. I continue to express my grateful appreciation to the authors and publishers who graciously permitted the use of their materials in this Third Edition.

CHARLES L. NEWMAN

Introduction to the Second Edition

SINCE the first edition of this *Sourcebook* was published in 1958, developments have occurred which have had a significant impact on probation and parole. While these services are viewed and administered in many different ways, there are indications that they are increasingly viewed as integral parts of the total correctional process.

Probation and parole associations have, in steadily increasing numbers, changed their names to include "corrections" and to deemphasize the past separateness of probation, parole, and institution personnel. The National Probation and Parole Association changed its name to the National Council on Crime and Delinquency to emphasize the problems with which we are all concerned rather than only two of the methods for dealing with these problems. The NCCD had, in fact, already extended its range of consultation, survey, standard setting, and information service to all other phases of correction. The NCCD, however, continues to promote probation and parole as the two most effective and economical methods for dealing with the majority of offenders within the community and for identifying those offenders who require rehabilitation within the controls of an institution.

One of the most significant developments—spearheaded by federal legislation, the NCCD's Advisory Council of Judges, the National Conference of State Trial Judges, and the National Council of Juvenile Court Judges—has been the movement to provide training for judges. As federal, state, and local judges have gathered formally to examine the information and knowledge which must be available to them to make individualization fact rather than fiction in court decisions, the work of capable probation and parole officers and parole boards has found new respect in the minds of the judges.

A concomitant development has been the recognition that specialized training for probation and parole work is mandatory where common sense and an ability to work with people were not long ago considered sufficient by many employers in the court and correctional agencies. This recognition has increased the demands for short-term institutes for personnel who have not had the benefit of professional training, and more universities than ever before are offering such institutes. The accrediting agency for graduate schools of social work, the Council on Social Work Education, has made a special study of the social work training needs in corrections and has developed a project to give leadership in meeting these needs. This *Sourcebook* by Professor Charles L. Newman will continue to provide valuable information for the officer and professional-in-training, as well as for the professional in need of refreshing.

Hopefully the thirst for training in corrections and the movement toward professionalism in probation and parole will require another edition of this publication within a very few years. At that time, we would hope to report more progress in the following areas, where only a beginning has been made: new short-term methods and techniques for probation and parole services for misdemeanants; increased application of group work and community organization methods in probation and parole; movement of the jail into the correctional complex as a short-term treatment institution; the development of intake criteria and controls for adult detention; extension of diagnostic services to all juvenile, family, and criminal courts through regional detention-diagnostic centers to replace the old concepts of the local detention home and county jail; improved knowledge, techniques, and sentencing laws for dealing with dangerous offenders apart from those who are not dangerous; more alternatives to institutional treatment, with halfway houses and residential centers playing even more important roles in advance of confinement.

The millennium will have arrived when neither state nor federal agencies will increase the capacity of their institution systems until steps have been taken through standard setting, subsidy, or direct operation to bring probation, parole, and other forms of community services up to the maximum level of use and performance.

MILTON G. RECTOR, *Director*
National Council on Crime and Delinquency

Introduction to the First Edition

THE terms *probation, parole,* and *pardon* have meanings and usages which can be separately defined and identified. In the public eye, however, they are used interchangeably, and unfortunately quite frequently with the connotation that the law-violator is being allowed to "get away" with "something."

It is difficult to say where the greatest confusion lies: in the differentiation between the usages of probation, parole, and pardons, or, in the appreciation of the underlying correctional philosophy involved in probation and parole, and the concept of social justice involved in the pardon.

Historically, pardon is by far the oldest. Absolute in its initial form, it later was transposed so that the focus included certain conditions which, in essence, changed pardon from the means of expunging guilt, to the recognition that guilt existed but that the penalty should be mitigated. From these roots, then, came the *conditional pardon,* and later, the parole.

The origin of probation remains in some dispute. It contains elements of the conditional pardon, in that requirements for incarceration are withheld conditional to the meeting of certain behavioral requirements, yet different because it does not involve imprisonment as may be the case in conditional pardon.

In this book, materials in the probation, parole, and pardons areas are surveyed. Although basically intended as a text for college courses in criminology and corrections, it should also have utility as a basic manual for in-service training of probation and parole workers. Moreover, it should provide basic material for the general reader who has more than a casual interest in the areas concerned.

No attempt has been made to make this volume an encyclopedia. There are many excellent books which have been devoted solely to counseling techniques, interviewing, case record preparation, and the like. Certainly the reader who wishes to have a more thorough knowledge of such materials will have to seek beyond the confines of these covers. What I have attempted, however, is to prepare a volume, drawing materials from the most authoritative sources, which will have practical applied value to the person who is or will be faced with the day-to-day function of probation and parole supervision.

But man does not live by bread alone, and the probation or parole officer needs to know that which is beyond his everyday, utilitarian needs. Thus, also are included materials which cover the historical developments in probation, parole, and pardons, as well as a glimpse of the practices outside the United States.

We must recognize at the outset that this book has certain biases, and it is only fair that the reader be alerted before delving into the contents. The assumption is carried throughout this book that probation and parole are a part of the correctional cycle, which begins with the arresting officer and ends with the final release from prison or from parole, and the community.

The obvious conclusion is, then, that neither probation nor parole will be any more effective than the weakest element in the cycle. That is to say, where the court does not make proper dispositions in its assignment of probation, we cannot but assume that the success of probation will be seriously handicapped. When the prison does not prepare the inmate for community living, then parole, by itself, is faced with a most difficult, and often impossible task. When the community is unwilling to accept the probationer or parolee after he has been "treated" and pronounced "cured," then the tasks of these services are made immeasurably more complex. When the police continue to "pick up" a parolee on suspicion for every unsolved crime, regardless of the possibility that he may not have been involved, because he has a "record," then the invitation is to repeated law violation.

Simply stated, the success of probation and parole can be measured partly by the effectiveness of its personnel, and partly by the quality of services rendered and attitudes maintained by the auxiliary correctional services, law enforcement, and the public.

Another bias refers to the professional identification of the probation and parole officer. There are strong proponents for the argument that probation and parole officers are, and *should be,* social workers (and generally in the more restricted sense, caseworkers). Others argue with equal strength that this is not the case. We do not spend much time considering whether probation and parole are social work or something else. The duality between the aim of social control (expressed as the protection of society) and of social treatment (which is the necessity for rehabilitation of the law violator) is presented in a plaguing enigma in probation and parole work. Whatever methods are employed by the agent, whether they are labelled *casework, counseling, vocational rehabilitation,* or something else, the dual aim must be met. And, insofar as society is concerned, the primacy of interest is directed to its own protection. It must be recognized, however, that the protection of society is vested in the rehabilitation of the offender as well as through strict authoritarian surveillance.

Another bias is presented. Specifically, it states that the techniques of treatment involved in probation and parole work are basically the same, although the clientele may differ with the relation to their previous experience in antisocial behavior and/or institutionalization. The day may arrive when, on the basis of sound selective techniques, probation will be granted to only those individuals who would best profit from noninstitutionalized reeducation. The day may also arrive when all prisoners released from prison will be placed under parole supervision to assist in the process of readjustment from institution to community life. But until that time arrives, we can assume that there are a great many more likenesses between probationers and parolees than there are differences.

CHARLES L. NEWMAN

Contents

SOURCEBOOK ON PROBATION, PAROLE AND PARDONS

Chapter One

The Beginnings of Probation

THE emergence of a method called *probation* during the last half of the nineteenth century marked a definite advance in the disposition and treatment of law violators. As a system, it began as a legal device for alleviating the harshness of punishment and preventing the contamination of the criminal novice in the unsavory atmosphere of the prison. Over the years, the concept has been expanded far beyond that envisioned by its founders.

But in parts of the country, probation has grown without sound guidance or definite direction, with resultant inadequacies and abuse. Since its administration has remained primarily with the trial courts, it is essentially local in character.

In this chapter, we trace the development of probation. What are the precursors of probation? Is it a social invention of American design, or are its roots in English common law? In the following selections, two opposing points of view are presented. The reader can then make up his own mind, based on the respective arguments presented.

THE ORIGINS OF PROBATION: FROM COMMON LAW ROOTS*

Several attempts have been made to trace the legal origins of probation to medieval and early modern European law. The precedents found in this period of legal history, however, generally relate to the suspension of punishment subject to good behavior rather than to probation as such, that is, a *combination* of the conditional suspension of punishment and the personal supervision of the released offender during a trial period. There can be little doubt that there has not been any continuous process of historical development linking early Continental instances of the use of the conditional suspension of punishment with contemporary

* Reprinted in part by permission of the United Nations. Department of Social Affairs: *Probation and Related Measures,* 1951, pp. 16-26. Footnotes are omitted.

probation. Probation as it is known today has been derived from the practical extension of the English common law, and an analysis of the legal origins of probation must therefore be principally concerned with England and America.

In England and in the United States of America, probation developed out of various methods for the conditional suspension of punishment. Generally speaking, the court practices in question were inaugurated, or adopted from previously existing practices, as attempts to avoid the mechanical application of the harsh and cruel precepts of a rigorous, repressive criminal law. Among these Anglo-American judicial expedients which have been mentioned as direct precursors of probation are the so-called benefit of clergy, the judicial reprieve, the release of an offender on his own recognizance, provisional "filing" of a case, and other legal devices for the suspension of either the imposition or the execution of sentence. With a view to a full understanding of the legal origins of probation, it is necessary to review briefly the nature of the practices.

The Benefit of Clergy

The so-called benefit of clergy was a special plea of devious origin, by virtue of which certain categories of offenders could—after conviction but before judgment—claim exemption from, or mitigation of, punishment. In practice, it was primarily a device to avoid capital punishment. The importance of this plea in the criminal proceedings of the eighteenth and early nineteenth centuries is beyond any doubt: "According to the common practice in England of working out modern improvements through antiquated forms, this exemption was made the means of modifying the severity of the criminal law." It is, however, extremely doubtful that this device had any direct influence on the later development of the suspension of sentence or of any other immediate precursor of probation.

The Judicial Reprieve

The judicial reprieve was a temporary suspension, by the court, of either the imposition or the execution of a sentence. It was used for specific purposes, such as to permit a convicted person to apply for a pardon, or under circumstances wherein the judge was not satisfied with the verdict or wherein the evidence was suspicious. Although this measure involved only a temporary stay of imposition or execution of sentence, it did lead, in some cases, to an abandonment of prosecution. It does not appear, however, that in England this device was ever extended to embrace what is now termed an *indefinite suspension of sentence,* particularly in cases which presented no peculiar reason—arising from the lack of or limitations on procedure—for withholding execution of sentence. On the other hand, there is, no doubt, more than a modicum of good reason in tracing the later pretensions of American courts to a power of indefinite suspension of sentence back to this early practice of reprieve in the English courts.

The Recognizance

The *recognizance* is a legal device deeply embedded in English law. It originated as a measure of preventive justice, and as such it consists in obliging those persons, whom there is a probable ground to suspect of future misbehavior, to stipulate with and to give full assurance to the public that such offense as is apprehended shall not happen. . . . This "assurance to the public" is given by entering into a recognizance or bond (with or without sureties) creating a debt to the State which becomes enforceable, however, only when the specified conditions are not observed. The recognizance is entered into for a specified period of time.

At an early date, the use of the principle of the recognizance (or binding-over) was also extended to actual offenders arraigned before the criminal courts. The device came to be used both to insure the appearance of an offender before the court at a future date when called upon, and as a disposition (or part thereof) in the case of convicted offenders. With the passing of time, the recognizance came to be used almost exclusively with reference to criminal proceedings rather than as a measure of preventive justice. It should be noted, however, that the recognizance, when used in connection with persons arraigned before criminal courts, does not lose its character as a measure of preventive justice but is actually designed to insure the future lawful behavior of the offender or, as Blackstone said, "must be understood rather as a caution against the repetition of the offense, than (as) any immediate pain or punishment."

For centuries the courts of England on occasion bound over and released minor offenders on their own recognizance, *with* or *without sureties*. Similarly, instances of this practice can be found in the records of the American colonies. During the first half of the nineteenth century, this device was adopted with increasing frequency, particularly in the case of youthful and petty offenders, the imprisonment of whom did not appear to be warranted. The practice seems to have been common in New England (particularly Massachusetts) at the time, and it was to be found also in other jurisdictions of the United States of America.

The device of binding-over was used extensively and imaginatively by Judge Peter Oxenbridge Thacher during his term of office (1823-1843) in the Municipal Court of Boston, and the practices developed by him were of particular significance in the later development of probation in Massachusetts. The earliest recorded case in this connection is the case of *Commonwealth v. Chase* (1830). In Judge Thacher's opinion, we find in this case a clear statement of the nature of the practice of binding-over as employed by him:

> The indictment against Jerusha Chase was found at the January term of this court, 1830. She pleaded guilty to the same, and sentence would have been pronounced at that time, but upon the application of her friends, and with the consent of the attorney of the commonwealth, she was permitted, upon her recognizance for her appearance in this court whenever she should be called for, to go at large. It has sometimes been practiced in this court, in cases of peculiar interest, and in the hope that the party would avoid the commission of any offense afterwards, to discharge him on a recognizance of this description. The effect is, that no sentence will ever be pronounced against him, if he shall behave himself well afterwards, and avoid any further violation of the law. . . .

In 1836, the Commonwealth of Massachusetts, as part of a general revision of its statutory law, gave legislative recognition to the practice of release upon recognizance, *with sureties*, at any stage of the proceedings, insofar as it applied to petty offenders in the lower courts. In the report of the commissioners charged with the revision of the statutory law of the Commonwealth, the commissioners formulated the theoretical basis of this alteration in the law relating to the punishment of petty offenders, as follows:

> This alteration consists in the discretionary power proposed to be given to the courts and magistrates, before whom this class of offenders may be brought, to discharge them, if they have any friends who will give satisfactory security for their future good behavior, for a reasonable time. When such sureties can be obtained, it can hardly fail to operate as powerful check upon the conduct of the party, who is thus upon his good behavior. And if his character and habits are such that no one will consent to be sponsor for him, it must forcibly impress on his mind the value of a good character, while it deprives him of all ground of just complaint of the severity of the law, or the magistrate.

It is significant to compare this formulation of the theory underlying the use of release on recognizance with a British formulation of the second half of the nineteenth century. In a book published in 1877, Edward William Cox, Recorder of Portsmouth, specifically described the release of offenders on their own recognizance, with sureties, as a "substitute for punishment," and he noted that, while the conduct of the released offenders was proper, no further action was taken. In particular, he was strongly motivated by the desire to avoid the demoralizing and contaminating influence of short terms of imprisonment, especially in the case of first and juvenile offenders. As for the *rationale* of the use of the recognizances, with sureties, he says, "The suspension only of the judgment, the knowledge that if he (the offender) offends he may yet be punished—the hold which his bail thus has upon him, to a great extent guarantee that if there is in him an inclination to redeem himself he will return to a life of honesty."

Provisional Release on Bail

It has been noted in the preceding paragraphs that the device of releasing an offender on his own recognizance (binding-over) may be used *with* or *without sureties*. Conversely, the device of sureties (or bail) may be employed with or without simultaneously binding-over the defendant on his own recognizance. The significance of the device of sureties, when combined with the recognizance, as a precursor of probation, has already been discussed; it remains to be pointed out, however, that both in England and in the United States of America the device of bail as such (*i.e.*, when not used in conjunction with the recognizance) has similarly been of major historical significance in the evolution of probation, namely, as a device for the provisional suspension of punishment in relation to rudimentary probation practices.

Binding-over, Bail, and the Origins of Probation

It has been noted above that the recognizance is essentially a preventive rather than a punitive measure of dealing with actual or potential offenders. In the early nineteenth century the increased use of this device was motivated, no doubt, to a considerable extent by considerations of mercy; in this respect the device was one of the measures employed to reduce the hardships involved in the mechanical application of a rigorous criminal law. The rehabilitative object of the measure—that is, the prevention of crime by the restoration of the offender as a law-abiding member of society—was, however, always present. Nevertheless, during this era the device came to be applied with an increasing realization of its rehabilitative potentialities, and came to be accompanied by increasingly effective safeguards and aids in the form of the personal supervision of, and assistance to, the released offender during the trial period. It should further be noted that the recognizance has always contained the germs of supervision—it involves the conditional suspension of punishment, and some vigilance is required to ascertain whether the conditions concerned are being compiled with.

It is clear that the provisional release of offenders in the charge of sureties similarly contained the germs of probationary supervision (irrespective of whether this device was combined with the recognizance). In view of their financial interest in the conduct of the provisionally released offender, sureties are bound to try to insure the good behavior of the offender through personal supervision, assistance, or influence. The deliberate use, by the courts, of the salutary influence of sureties on offenders released conditionally, either on their own recognizance or on bail, indeed seems to have been in a very real sense the first rudimentary stage in the development of probation.

The Provisional "Filing" of Cases

The practice of provisionally "filing" a case seems to have been peculiar to Massachusetts. This device consisted of the suspension of the imposition of sentence when, "after verdict of guilty in a criminal case . . . the Court is satisfied that, by reason of extenuating circumstances, or of the pendency of a question of law in a like case before a higher court, or other sufficient reason, public justice does not require an immediate sentence. . . ." The use of this procedure was subject to the consent of the defendant and of the prosecuting attorney, and the suspension was made subject to such conditions as the court in its discretion might impose. The order that a case be laid on file was not equivalent to a final judgment but left it within the power of the court to take action on the case at any time, upon motion of either party.

The Suspension of Sentences at Common Law

By way of summary, it may be noted that there existed during the nineteenth century and earlier, several legal devices which enabled the English and the American courts to suspend either the imposition of sentence (recognizance to keep peace or to be of good behavior and to appear for judgment when called upon, provisional release on bail, the provisional "filing of a case," and the judicial reprieve) or the execution of sentence (also the judicial reprieve). That these devices existed, and allowed *at least* for the temporary suspension of sentence for *specific purposes,* is beyond any doubt. The question whether the English and American courts possess, at common law, an inherent power to suspend sentence *indefinitely* is, however, more problematic.

In analyzing the question of an inherent judicial power to suspend sentence *indefinitely,* it is necessary to distinguish clearly between the use of the special devices of the recognizance and bail, on the one hand, and other devices used for the provisional suspension of punishment on the other hand. Prior to statutory provisions to this effect, the courts both in England and in the

United States of America *did,* in fact, engage in the suspension of the imposition of sentence when releasing offenders on their own recognizances, and took no further action with regard to the infliction of punishment if the condition of good behavior was complied with. Similarly, this procedure was followed, prior to statutory authorization, in at least two of the other countries of the British Commonwealth: New England and Canada. Both in England and in certain jurisdictions of the United States of America (notably Massachusetts), the conditional suspension of the imposition of sentence, with the ultimate release of the offender from all punishment in case of good behavior, was practiced (without statutory authorization) also in relation to the provisional release of offenders on bail.

For all practical purposes it may be said that—beyond the relatively circumscribed practice of suspending the imposition of a sentence by means of releasing an offender on a recognizance and/or bail—the English courts *did not* assume the existence of an inherent common law power to suspend sentence indefinitely. In the United States of America, however, a variety of practices developed, with a tendency to extend the suspension of sentence beyond the employment of the recognizance and/or bail. In particular, this involved the suspension of the imposition or of the execution of sentence on the basis of the common law precedent of the judicial reprieve. With the increasing use of the conditional suspension of punishment, with or without some sort of probationary supervision, courts in different jurisdictions adopted contradictory points of view on the question of the existence, at common law, of an inherent judicial power of indefinite suspension of sentence. While some held that the courts had such a power, others rejected this view arguing either that the conditions justifying the recognition of such a power in England did not obtain in the United States, or that the indefinite suspension of sentence by the court constituted an encroachment on the executive prerogative of pardon and reprieve, and thus infringed upon the doctrine of the separation of powers.

The United States Supreme Court finally expressed itself on the issue in question in the so-called *Killits* case. The late Chief

Justice White decided that the English common law did not give the federal courts the power to suspend sentence indefinitely.

> It is true that, owing to the want of power in common law courts to grant new trials and to the absence of a right to review convictions in a higher court, it is we think, to be conceded: (a) that both suspensions of sentence and suspensions of the enforcement of sentence, temporary in character, were often resorted to on grounds of error or miscarriage of justice which under our system would be corrected either by new trials or by the exercise of the power to review; (b) that not infrequently, where the suspension either of the imposition of a sentence or of its execution was made for the purpose of enabling a pardon to be sought or bestowed, by a failure to further proceed in the criminal cause in the future, although no pardon had been sought or obtained, the punishment fixed by law was escaped. But neither of these conditions serves to convert the mere exercise of a judicial discretion to temporarily suspend for the accomplishment of a purpose contemplated by law into the existence of an arbitrary judicial power to permanently refuse to enforce the law.

With reference to the decision in the *Killits* case, the Attorney General's Survey concludes as follows:

> For practical purposes it may be said that this decision served to explode the erroneous belief that had grown up in some States. . . . It may be concluded, therefore, that there is no historical warrant in the English common law for the claim that American courts have an inherent power to suspend sentence indefinitely. Where this power has been asserted, it has been based on a misconception of English authorities or recognized because it tempered the criminal law with mercy and had grown as a local practice.

It should be noted that the Court's decision in the *Killits* case did not seek to invalidate the practice of releasing offenders on their own recognizances but instead referred to "the fact that common law courts possessed the power by recognizances to secure good behavior, that is, to enforce the law. . . ." This fact did not, however, afford support for "the proposition that those courts possessed the arbitrary discretion to permanently decline to enforce the law."

From the point of view of the development of probation as a distinct method for the treatment of offenders, the extent to which the judicial devices in which it had its historical origins, were, in fact, extralegal and not warranted by the English common law, is of small significance. The important point is that these devices developed, and could in fact only develop, in a system of common law jurisdiction which is flexible enough to allow for the gradual adjustment of existing practices to new needs and new objectives. In England this process of adjustment was more conservative, and it is probable that the courts stayed within their common law powers; in any case, the legality of the devices used for the conditional suspension of punishment, in relation to early pre-statutory probation practices, was never challenged in England, in Canada, or in New Zealand. In the United States of America, the courts overstepped their common law powers, and the resulting diversity and confusion of principles and authorities necessitated the authoritative revision of the legal bases of the practices that developed. Nevertheless, came the definitive explosion of the doctrine of an inherent judicial power to suspend any part of the administration of criminal justice, and when public opinion had already been fully prepared for this new method for the treatment of offenders. Consequently, the final rejection by the Supreme Court of the doctrine of a common law judicial power of indefinite suspension of sentence actually served as a stimulus for the enactment of statutes expressly authorizing the suspension of sentence and probation.

THE ORIGINS OF PROBATION: STATUTORY ROOTS*

Probation, both in conception and development, is America's distinctive contribution to progressive penology. I would like to make a point of the phrase, "distinctively American," because some of the textbooks go to great lengths to trace its origins to British common law and to what Dean Roscoe Pound calls "the received ideals" of Continental legal systems. In this, they are wrong. The development of probation has been entirely statutory, certainly so insofar as the system is an expression of *planned*

---

* Reprinted in part by permission of the National Probation and Parole Association. Edmond Fitzgerald: The presentence investigation. *NPPA Journal*, 2(No. 4):321-323, Oct. 1956. Footnotes are omitted.

state policy. Probation in America is characterized principally not by affinities with, but by deliberate divergences from, the common law and European precedents in general.

One of the interesting things to observe over the span of the century is the degree to which our entire philosophy of criminal law—and not merely that phase of it represented by probation—is moving farther and farther away from Old World antecedents as the years go on. In the older countries, when there still was some political and economic stability, the identifying hallmark of the legal philosophy could be described as reverence for precedent and for time-honored institutions and resistance to radical change. In England the historical record is one of a legal system slowly and cautiously adapting itself to the changing needs and talents of the people. It took them a long time, for example, to relax the lengthy syllabus of excessively punitive sanctions which were applied even to minor offenders until comparatively recent times. The death penalty or mutilation was provided until well into the nineteenth century for some offenses that would today be considered trivial. It is typical of the British that the moderation of the penal statutes, when this finally came about, resulted from the slow momentum of unfolding history rather than from the initiative of Parliament or of any specific man or movement.

It is true that the momentum has been helped along here and there by the venalities of rules (e.g., Bentham's *Principles of Morals and Legislation*), or by the barbs of satirists (e.g., Jonathan Swift's *Drapier's Letters* and its influence on the repeal of a whole series of penal laws aimed not so much at crime control as at suppression of civil liberties). But, in the main, the record shows that for the Englishman the pragmatic test sufficed: if his laws worked somehow and if they did not bother him personally, he was not interested in seeing how they worked and he was not disposed to tamper with them overmuch. And similarly on the Continent.

In America, by contrast, the tendency was—and is—not to regard tradition as necessarily sacred. We have never been interested in preserving the *status quo,* except to maintain our "inalienable rights" and our constitutional freedoms. This is perhaps inevitable in a policy which has grown as rapidly as ours. The pace of economic expansion, of receding frontiers, of polyglot population increase, of proliferating technology, has made it difficult for governmental forms to keep abreast. It is not surprising, therefore, that legislative policy, in penal no less than in other spheres, has been determined more by the utilitarian needs of the growing community than by precedent or tradition. And probation is nothing if not utilitarian.

The generally accepted definition of *probation,* as applied to adult offenders at any rate, is about as follows: a form of disposition under which a court suspends either the sentence or execution of the judgment of sentence or selected offenders, releasing them conditionally on good behavior, under prescribed terms and rules and subject to the control, guidance, and assistance of the court as exercised through officers appointed to supervise them. The essence of the system is the conditional suspension of sentence *plus* supervision of all the activities of the defendant (probationer) for the period of the suspension. It was in America that the combination was first set in motion, by the judges of the Boston Municipal Court in cooperation with John Augustus. It was accomplished, in the beginning, not in any continuous process of historical development arising out of early British or Continental use of the conditional suspension, but rather in an ingenious departure from, or distortion of, the precedents.

For many years and in several jurisdictions in the United States, the courts proceeded on the theory that there was an inherent power at common law to suspend sentences on convicted criminals indefinitely. The fact is, however, that apart from a relatively circumscribed practice of invoking the procedures known as "benefit of clergy" and "judicial reprieve," the British courts had never assumed or claimed any such inherent power. In actuality, both benefit of clergy and judicial reprieve were little more than artifices to avoid imposition of full legal process; they were employed principally to delay or avert punishment in cases where the courts felt the prescribed penalty for the given offense to be either "out of order" or excessive for the particular individual convicted. In that sense, the devices were negative rather than positive. Both were used in the Colonies for some years but were found to be of uneven or unsatisfactory application. They were later practically abandoned as the American courts began to confer upon themselves the right to make positive suspensions for fixed periods, by which is meant purposeful suspensions with the stated or implicit objective of regeneration and with definite or determinate time limits. Thus, benefit of clergy and judicial reprieve fell into complete disuse after probation emerged as an accepted legal system.

This acceptance of probation did not come about quietly or automatically. Throughout the latter part of the nineteenth century and well into the twentieth, judges and lawyers had considerable difficulty in reconciling the system with the existing scheme of things, mainly because of the absence of established legal and procedural precedents. A number of appeals arose, for instance, in various states out of the question as to whether placements on probation represented a judicial invasion of the executive's pardoning prerogative under the "separation of powers" doctrine. The New York Court of Appeals, in ruling on an appeal from a suspension of sentence and grant of probation in 1894, upheld the trial court's action over the prosecutor's appeal but stated that its opinion "must not be understood as conferring any new power, because the power to suspend was inherent in all Superior Courts of criminal jurisdiction at common law." This decision was later discovered to be based largely on a misconstruction, if not indeed misquotation, of a famous passage in Lord Hale's *Pleas of the Crown,* describing a practice which had grown up under British law. Chief Justice White, of the United States Supreme Court, commenting on the decision, referred to the misquotation from Lord Hale as "complete error," stating that in a diligent examination of *Pleas of the Crown* he found no passage containing the clauses cited by the New York Court of Appeals.

Chief Justice White thus demolished any lingering theory of common law antecedents for probation. As a consequence, its further development had to be entirely statutory; in the past fifty years, hundreds of enabling laws have been passed, providing for probation service of either statewide or local coverage.

One by-product of what might be called the "illegitimate"

origins of probation is that while its philosophy and objectives have always met with ready acceptance, its methods have not—at any rate not to the same extent. Notwithstanding that broad definitions of rules and procedures have often been enunciated, legislatively and otherwise, their testing and refinement was a long, difficult, and not always completely understood experimental process. Not until the Supreme Court review of probation's policies and practices in the momentous *Williams* decision did these finally achieve constitutional acceptability, so to speak. The *Williams* case, then, is epochal in the sense that it became the agent through which the husky hundred-year-old probation infant was "legitimatized."

Chapter Two

The Origins of Parole and Conditional Pardons

IN the nineteenth century, the trend in penal philosophy shifted from one of punishment to that of reformation of the individual. The history of parole is inextricably a part of that movement. The reformers of the eighteenth and nineteenth centuries sowed the seeds from which sprang the reformatory idea. Subsequently, the parole movement was born.

The foundations of modern parole, then, are to be found in the progression from strict imprisonment, to freedom within limited areas, to liberation with conditions (either conditional pardon or ticket-of-leave), followed by restoration of liberty.

Parole, as it functions today, is difficult to define in terms of a single precise concept. It is an integral part of the total correctional process. As such, it is a method of selectively releasing offenders from institutions, under supervision in the community, whereby the community is afforded continuing protection while the offender is making his adjustment and beginning his contribution to society.

Early parole practices, however, were closely associated with the colonizing of newly inhabited areas, as well as with the relocation of the offender in the community from which he came prior to imprisonment. In the beginning, supervision was limited to occasional surveillance. The concept of *treatment* developed slowly and to this day has not received total public acceptance.

In this chapter, we consider the diverse roots from which parole has developed.

THE ORIGINS OF PAROLE*

A number of false beliefs exist regarding parole and its administration, and at least two of these current misconceptions have

* Reprinted in part by permission of the New York State Division of Parole. From *Manual for Parole Officers*, 1953, pp. 1-19. Footnotes are omitted.

so little basis in fact that it is difficult to understand their widespread acceptance. There is, for example, the popular conception that parole developed from the Australian system of ticket-of-leave. The other equally fallacious belief is that rules and regulations of parole now in operation are those originated by members of boards of parole or administrators of parole.

Parole is the conditional release of an individual from a penal or correctional institution, after he has served part of the sentence imposed upon him. Parole did not develop from any specific source or experiment but is an outgrowth of a number of independent measures: the conditional pardon, the apprenticeship by indenture, the transportation of criminals to America and Australia, the English and Irish experiences with the system of ticket-of-leave, and the work of American prison reformers during the nineteenth century.

Conditional Pardons and Transportation to America

The transportation of criminals to the American colonies began early in the seventeenth century. The precedent for this removal of criminals from England can be found in a law passed in 1597 providing for the banishment "beyond the seas of rogues" who appeared to be dangerous. As early as 1617, the Privy Council passed an order granting reprieves and stays of execution to persons convicted of robbery who were strong enough to be employed in service beyond the seas.

The transportation of criminals to America was backed and supported by the London, Virginia, and Massachusetts Companies, and similar organizations. At the time the plan was proposed, acute economic conditions prevailed in England. Unemployment was widespread. Taxes, particularly for the relief of the poor, were high and the English labor market was overcrowded. In spite of the existing situation, there were groups in England who opposed colonization, although the insistent demands for labor in the American colonies could not be met. It was in an effort to avoid antagonizing these groups, and at the same time to satisfy the need for labor in the Colonies, that the Government devised the plan to transport convicted felons to America. The plan was presented to the King, and he approved the proposal to grant reprieves and stays of execution to the convicted felons who were physically able to be employed in service.

The procedure which was developed to select individuals to be recommended to the King was somewhat similar to the present-day methods followed by prison officials in recommending to the governor or parole boards in various states, the names of prisoners whose minimum terms are to be decreased by compensation or commutation allowance for good conduct and for work willingly performed.

In England, lists of names were compiled by court officials and signed by the judge or frequently by the mayor and recorder. The lists were then presented to the Secretary of State. In cases wherein a death sentence had been imposed, a stay of execution was automatically granted until the King had reviewed the recommendation made by the judge. The pardons granted by the King were written in Latin and accompanied by a docket in English, giving the name of the prisoner and his crime; in some instances, a statement was added giving the reason why clemency had been granted.

In the beginning, no specific conditions were imposed upon those receiving such pardons. However, a number of those pardoned had evaded transportation or had returned to England prior to the expiration of their term, and it was found necessary to impose certain restrictions upon the individuals to whom these pardons were granted. It was about 1655 that the form of pardon was amended to include specific conditions and to provide for the nullification of the pardon if the recipient failed to abide by the conditions imposed.

Transportation to America

During the early days of transportation, the Government paid to each contractor a fee of approximately five pounds for each prisoner transported. However, under the provisions of a law enacted in 1717, this procedure was discontinued and the contractor or shipmaster was given "property in the service" of the prisoner until the expiration of the full term. Once a prisoner was delivered to the contractor or shipmaster, the Government took no further interest in his welfare or behavior unless he violated the conditions of the pardon by returning to England prior to the expiration of his sentence.

Upon arrival of the pardoned felons in the Colonies, their services were sold to the highest bidder and the shipmaster then transferred the "property in service" agreement to the new master. The felon thereupon was no longer referred to as a criminal but became an indentured servant.

The system of indenture dates back to the Statute of Artifices enacted in 1562, and originally it had no relation to persons convicted of crime. Blackstone defined apprentices as "another species of servants who were usually bound out for a term of years by deed indenture." The contract of indenture was written on a large sheet of paper, the halves separated by a wavy or jagged line called an indent. The master and the apprentice or his guardian signed the form, thereby agreeing to conform with the conditions specified. Van Doren, in his biography of Benjamin Franklin, quotes the conditions imposed upon Franklin in 1718 when, at the age of twelve, he became indentured to his brother:

> . . . During which term the said apprentice his master faithfully shall or will serve, his secrets keep, his lawful demands everywhere gladly do. He shall do no damage to his said master nor see it done to others, but to his power shall let or forthwith give notice to his said master of the same. The goods of his said master he shall not waste, nor the same without license of him to give or lend. Hurt to his said master he shall not do, cause or procure to be done. He shall neither buy nor sell without his master's license. Taverns, inns or alehouses he shall not haunt. At cards or dice tables or any other unlawful game he shall not play. Matrimony he shall not contract nor from the services of his master day or night absent himself but in all things as an honest faithful apprentice shall and will demean and behave himself toward said master all during said term.

This indenture bears a similarity to the procedure now followed by parole boards in this country. Like the indentured servant, a prisoner conditionally released on parole agrees in writing to accept certain conditions included on the release form, which is signed by the members of the parole board and the prisoner. Even some of the conditions imposed today on conditionally released prisoners are similar to those included on the indenture agreement.

Transportation was, of course, terminated by the Revolutionary War, but for some time before this the Colonists had vigorously protested against the importation of criminals. A tax was levied on each poor disabled individual or felon received in the Colonies, but even the imposition of the tax did not end the practice.

Bentham, in reviewing criminal laws, comments that transportation had all the defects punishment can have and none of the qualities it might have; that under the transportation system, bondage was added to banishment but the convict who was able to offer the shipmaster a sum larger than that offered by an American colonist could procure his liberty at the first port of call en route to America.

Transportation to Australia

The termination of the Revolutionary War ended transportation to America, but England did not repeal her transportation law. Judges continued to impose sentences of transportation, and the places of detention for prisoners awaiting transportation became overcrowded. Some attempt was made to relieve the situation by granting pardons freely but, when a serious outbreak of crime occurred, the public demanded that the transportation law be enforced.

The Pitt government had no interest in the rehabilitation of criminals. However, faced with a crime wave and the unsanitary conditions and overcrowding in the criminal detention quarters, the Government recognized the need for some immediate action. Australia had been discovered by Captain Cook in 1770, and the Government deliberated whether to use this land as a refuge for the thousands of American Royalists who had returned to England and were starving, or to establish Australia as a new colony for the reception of transported felons.

In 1787, the King announced that Australia was to be used for convict settlement and in May, 1787 the first fleet sailed, arriving at Botany Bay on January 18, 1788.

A different procedure was followed by the Government in dealing with prisoners transported to Australia than had previously been followed in transporting prisoners to America. All the expense incurred was met by the Government; the criminals transported did not become indentured servants but remained prisoners under the control of the Government, which assumed responsibility for their behavior and welfare.

More conservative writers like Ives admit that the system of transportation had some value. He stated he believed transportation was, to some extent, "the wisest method of dealing with major criminals." O'Brien asserts, "It afforded an army of more than one hundred thousand persons a fresh start with real possibilities of rehabilitation."

No unbiased account of the history of transportation to Australia has been published. Authors who have dealt with this subject have dilated upon the primitive conditions which prevailed and the horrors which existed at Norfolk Island, Port Arthur, and the other penal settlements. The murders resulting from the sadistic treatment accorded to prisoners have been stressed, and there are even accounts of prisoners who escaped and later practiced cannibalism.

The first governor of the penal settlement was given "property in service" for all felons under his supervision. He inaugurated the plan of assigning prisoners to the free settlers and, when this transfer became effective, the settler or new custodian took over the "property in service" agreement.

From the days of Henry VIII, power to pardon felons could not be delegated to any individual without statutory authority. In 1790 a special enabling act gave to the governors of the penal settlements power to remit sentences of transported prisoners. The first governor of Australia received instructions from the Government regarding the emancipation and discharge from servitude of prisoners whose conduct and work records indicated they were worthy to receive a grant of land. At first, these prisoners receive an absolute pardon but later a new form of conditional pardon was instituted which became known as ticket-of-leave. This ticket-of-leave was merely a declaration signed by the governor or his secretary, dispensing a convict from attendance at government work and enabling him, on condition of supporting himself, to seek employment within a specified district. No provision was made for his supervision by the government, the ticket merely stating:

> It is His Excellency, the Governor's pleasure to dispense with the government work of...... tried at...... convicted of...... and to permit...... to employ...... (off government stores) in any lawful occupation with the district of...... for his own advantage during good behavior or until His Excellency's further pleasure shall be made known.

This type of permit also took its origin from the Statute of Artifices which provided that a servant, having lawfully terminated his employment, must be given a testimonial by his master. This testimonial gave the servant license to depart from the master and liberty to work elsewhere. No employer could legally accept anyone for service unless this testimonial or certificate of availability was produced.

Until 1811, tickets-of-leave were freely granted to prisoners for good conduct, meritorious service, or for the purpose of marriage. In 1811 a policy was adopted requiring that prisoners serve specific periods of time before being eligible to receive tickets-of-leave. This procedure, however, was not strictly adhered to until 1821, when a regular scale was formulated. Those who had a sentence of seven years could obtain a ticket-of-leave after serving four years; those with sentences of fourteen years, after serving six years; and those with life sentences, after serving eight years.

Great stress has been placed upon the experience of Alexander Maconochie, who was assigned as Governor of Norfolk Island in 1840. He devised new methods of treating prisoners, but his experiments were limited to the prisoners confined in Norfolk; the success he achieved can hardly be attributed to the entire Australian system.

Maconochie said that in Van Dieman's Island he had "witnessed the dreadful state of depravity" to which the men in the public gangs had sunk, and the idea occurred to him that these conditions arose from the state of slavery to which the prisoners had been reduced. He originated the experiment of granting marks as a form of wages by which the state of slavery might be obviated and whereby the act of punishment would not be eliminated. He brought his proposed plan to the attention of the House of Commons in 1837, three years prior to his appointment as Governor of Norfolk.

He proposed that the duration of the sentence be measured by labor and good conduct within a minimum of time; that the labor thus required be represented by marks proportional to the original sentence, the prisoner to earn these marks in penal servitude before discharge. Marks were to be credited day-by-day to the convict, according to the amount of work accomplished. Maconochie, however, remained at Norfolk Island for a period of only four years and while his ideas were progressive and his experiments successful, his term of office was so limited that his achievements did not have any revolutionary effect on the system of transportation.

With the increase of free settlers, Australian colonists began to protest the Government's use of the land for what they termed "a dumping ground for criminals." Although there were other reasons, the contributing factor in the decision of the Government to terminate transportation to Australia was the threat of the colonists to revolt.

Prior to the decision to terminate transportation, some effort had been made to alleviate some of the caustic criticism of the system by careful selection of the prisoners to be transported to Australia. The proposal was made that prisoners would first have to undergo a period of training and discipline in penal servitude in England before transportation was effected. It was planned that this training period would cover a period of eighteen months. However, the experiment of selection was a failure, but it did mark the beginning of the utilization of trained and experienced individuals who were made responsible for the selection of the prisoners who had profited by the training program.

Three prison commissioners were appointed to accomplish the selection. The membership of this group may have established the precedent followed by American prison reformers in creating boards of parole consisting of three members.

The final termination of transportation to Australia did not occur until 1867, although opposition to the plan had been expressed as early as 1812.

England's Experience With Ticket-of-leave

In America, as early as 1817, provisions had been made for the reduction of sentences by allowances for satisfactory work and conduct. The English Penal Servitude Act of 1853, governing prisoners convicted in England and Ireland, substituted imprisonment for transportation. By this Act, prisoners who received sentences of fourteen years or less were committed to prison, but the judge was granted permissive power to order the transportation or imprisonment of individuals who had received terms of more than fourteen years. This law also specified the length of time prisoners were required to serve before becoming eligible for conditional release on ticket-of-leave.

Those who had sentences exceeding seven years but not more than ten years became eligible for ticket-of-leave after they had served four years and not more than six years. Prisoners who had sentences of more than ten years but less than fifteen were required to serve at least six but not more than eight years, and those with sentences of fifteen years or more were required to serve not less than six nor more than ten years. America did not develop the use of the indeterminate sentence until nearly a quarter of a century after English enactment of the Act of 1853.

The Act of 1853 related to conditional release and gave legal status to the system of ticket-of-leave. It provided:

> It shall be lawful for Her Majesty by an order in writing under the hand and seal of one of Her Majesty's principal secretaries of State, to grant to any convict now under sentence of transportation, or who may hereafter be sentenced to transportation, or to any punishment substituted for transportation, by this Act, a license to be at large in the United Kingdom and the Channel Islands, or in such part thereof respectively as in such license shall be expressed, during such portions of his or her term of transportation or imprisonment, and upon such conditions in all respects as to Her Majesty shall deem fit; and that it shall be lawful for Her Majesty to revoke or alter such license by a like order at Her Majesty's pleasure.
>
> So long as such license shall continue in force and unrevoked, such convict shall not be liable to be imprisoned or transported by reason of his or her sentence, but shall be allowed to go and remain at large according to the terms of such license.
>
> Provided always, that if it shall please Her Majesty to revoke

any such license as aforesaid, it shall be lawful for one of Her Majesty's principal secretaries of State, by warrant under his hand and seal, to signify to anyone of the Police Magistrates of the Metropolis that such license has been revoked, and to require such Magistrate to issue his warrant under his hand and seal for the apprehension of the convict to whom such license was granted, and such Magistrate shall issue his warrant accordingly and such warrant shall and may be executed by the constable to whom the same shall be delivered, for that purpose in any part of the United Kingdom or in the Isles of Jersey, Guernsey, Alderney or Sark, and shall have the same force and effect in all the said places as if the same had been originally issued or subsequently endorsed by a Justice of the Peace or Magistrate or other lawful authority having jurisdiction in the place where the same shall be executed, and such convict, when apprehended under such warrant, shall be brought, as soon as he conveniently may be, before the Magistrate by whom the said warrant shall have been issued or some other Magistrate of the same Court, and such Magistrate shall thereupon make out his warrant under his hand and seal, for the recommitment of such convict to the prison or place of confinement from which he was released by virtue of the said license, and such convict shall be so recommitted accordingly, and shall thereupon be remitted to his or her original sentence, and shall undergo the residue thereof as if no such license had been granted.

The following conditions were endorsed on the license of every convict liberated on a ticket-of-leave in England:

1. The power of revoking or altering the license of a convict will most certainly be exercised in the case of misconduct.
2. If, therefore, he wishes to retain the privilege, which by his good behavior under penal discipline he has obtained, he must prove by his subsequent conduct that he is really worthy of Her Majesty's clemency.
3. To produce a forfeiture of the license, it is by no means necessary that the holder should be convicted of any new offense. If he associates with notoriously bad characters, leads an idle or dissolute life, or has no visible means of obtaining an honest livelihood etc., it will be assumed that he is about to relapse into crime, and he will be at once apprehended and recommitted to prison under his original sentence.

The British public accepted that, in compliance with the provisions of the law, the programs followed in the prisons would be reformative and that prisoners selected for release on ticket-of-leave represented definite proof of having profited by the training and, therefore, their conditional release would not be incompatible with the welfare of society.

Long before the termination of transportation, it had been recognized that the experiment followed in Australia of releasing prisoners on ticket-of-leave without further supervision was a serious mistake. However, this knowledge did not prevent a repetition of the procedure. The public had assumed that the Home Office planned to enforce the conditions imposed upon prisoners on ticket-of-leave during the first two years after the enactment of the Servitude Act of 1853. The outbreak of serious crimes which occurred within the next three years was attributed to the lack of supervision accorded the released prisoners. A campaign of criticism was carried on, and ticket-of-leave men were blamed for most of the crimes committed. The public became convinced that the ticket-of-leave system was not only a menace to public safety but was an absolute failure.

The public was vociferous in its demands for action to correct the misuse of tickets-of-leave. A select committee was appointed to hold hearings and, at one of the meetings, a representative of the Home Office testified that no efforts had been made to develop any plan for the supervision of ticket-of-leave men after release. The Home Office had merely accepted that ticket-of-leave men were prisoners who had completed their sentences. The head of the London police admitted that he had also misinterpreted the provisions of the Act of 1853 and had, in fact, issued orders to the police that they were not to interfere with ticket-of-leave men.

Representatives of other law-enforcing agencies asserted that it was not possible to identify ticket-of-leave men because no report on the convicts was furnished them by the officials granting the ticket and because the ticket-of-leave men had destroyed their licenses to be at large as a means of avoiding apprehension and identification. The only result of these hearings was the adoption of a resolution by the Select Committee:

1. That the system of license to be at large, or ticket-of-leave, has been in operation too short a time to enable the committee

to form a clear and decided opinion either as to the effect which it had already produced or to its probable ultimate workings.

2. That the system appears to be founded upon a principle, wise and just in itself: that of enabling a convict to obtain by continued good conduct, while undergoing punishment, the remission of a portion of this sentence upon the expressed condition, however, that in case of subsequent misconduct, he should serve the residue of the original term specified in the original sentence.
3. That to render this system of ticket-of-leave, adopted both for the reformation of offenders and the interest of the public, the conditions endorsed on the ticket-of-leave ought to be enforced more strongly than appears to have been hitherto the case.
4. That every convict on his release with a ticket-of-leave ought to be reported to the police of the town or district to which he is sent.

A series of prison riots occurred in the English prisons in 1862. Coupled with another serious crime wave, this again focused attention on the administration of prisons and the ticket-of-leave system. The public again demanded that effective measures be taken to change the administration of prisons and correct the weaknesses of the ticket-of-leave system. Although the intent of the Act of 1853 had been to make prisons reformative in character, this objective had not been achieved. No real labor was performed in the prisons, discipline was lax, and the prison officials—apprehensive of the dangerous convicts—freely granted credit for good conduct to make prisoners eligible for release at the earliest possible date.

The House of Commons was petitioned to bring the situation to the attention of the Queen, who appointed a Royal Commission. At the public hearings held by the commission, it was discovered that during the seven years since 1856, when the Select Committee had adopted its resolution, no system had been put into operation to supervise prisoners after their release. The fact that no understanding or cooperative agreement existed between the Home Office and the law-enforcing agencies was also brought out. The head of the London police openly admitted that until a few minutes prior to his appearance before the Royal Commission he had never seen a ticket-of-leave and had no knowledge of the conditions endorsed thereon.

Individuals who favored supervision by the police and those who opposed it appeared before the commission. Ticket-of-leave men testified that they objected to reporting to the police because the latter were considered their "special enemies who dogged them and informed their employers of their criminal status." These criminals stated that they would be forced to steal or starve if supervised by the police, as no employer would hire them if aware of their criminal record. The police testified that if a ticket-of-leave man were required to report to the police in each community he visited, the need for watching would cease. They urged that the system of irregular supervision be abolished and that some uniform procedure with prescribed rules and regulations be established.

The Royal Commission in its report stressed the unreformative programs in operation in the prisons which rendered the prisoners unprepared for freedom. They also expressed the opinion that a large proportion of the prisoners released on ticket-of-leave had given no reliable proof of their reformation prior to release. The commission strongly urged that England adopt the system followed in the prisons of Ireland.

As a result of the report of the Royal Commission, the services of the police were used for supervision and later a number of Prisoner's Aid Societies, supported partly by the Government, were established. These agencies followed the methods of supervising prisoners which had proved effective in Ireland.

The Irish System of Ticket-of-leave

Sir William Crofton became head of the Irish prison system in 1854, one year after the enactment of the Servitude Act. He accepted the idea that the intent of the law was to make penal institutions something more than places of safekeeping, and that the programs in the prisons should be designed toward reformation and tickets-of-leave granted only to prisoners who gave visible evidence of definite achievement and change of attitude.

The Irish convict system, under Crofton's administration, became famous for its three stages of penal servitude, particularly the second stage where classification was governed by marks obtained for good conduct and achievement in education and industry. So-called indeterminate prisons were also utilized, where conditions were made as nearly normal as possible and where no more restraint was exercised over the inmates than was necessary to maintain order.

The administrators of the Irish system maintained that its success was due to the cooperation extended by the convict toward his own amendment and to his conviction sooner or later that the system, however penal in its character, was designed for his benefit and that stringent regulations imposed for his supervision after release rendered a vocation of crime unprofitable and hazardous to follow. The form of ticket-of-leave issued in Ireland was slightly different from the one used in England. Known as Form E, the Irish form reads:

> Number of Convict's Book .... Order of License to be a convict made under Statute 27 and 28 Victoria, Chapter 47, Dublin Castle .... day of .... 18.... Her Majesty is graciously pleased to grant to .... of .... who was convicted of burglary first degree, at .... the .... thereupon sentenced to be kept in penal servitude for the term of .... and is now confined in the .... Convict Prison, Her Royal license to be at large from the day of his liberation under this order, during the remaining portion of said time of penal servitude, unless the said .... shall before the expiration of the said time be convicted of some indictable offense within the United Kingdom, in which case such license will be immediately forfeited by law, or unless it shall please Her Majesty sooner, to revoke or alter such license. This license is given subject to the conditions endorsed upon the same. Upon the breach of any of which it will be liable to be revoked whether such breach is followed by conviction or not, and Her Majesty hereby orders that the said .... be set at liberty within thirty days from the date of this order.

The ticket-of-leave was signed by the Chief Secretary of the Lord Lieutenant of Ireland and imposed the following conditions:

1. The holder shall preserve this license and produce it when called upon to do so by a magistrate or police officer.
2. He shall abstain from any violation of the law.
3. He shall not habitually associate with notoriously bad characters, such as reported thieves and prostitutes.

4. He shall not lead an idle and dissolute life, without means of obtaining an honest livelihood.

   If the license is forfeited or revoked in consequence of a conviction of any felony, he will be liable to undergo a term of penal servitude equal to that portion of his term of ...... years, which remains unexpired when his license was granted, viz., the term of .... years .... months.

Each ticket-of-leave man was further instructed as follows:

> Each convict coming to reside in Dublin City or in the County of Dublin will, within three days after his arrival, report himself at the Police Office, Exchange Court, Dublin, where he will receive instructions as to his further reporting himself.
>
> Each convict, residing in the provinces, will report himself to the constabulary station of his locality within three days after his arrival and subsequently on the first of each month.
>
> A convict must not change his locality without notifying the change to his constabulary in order that his registration may be changed to the locality to which he is about to proceed.
>
> Any infringement of these rules by the convict will cause to be assumed that he is leading an idle, irregular life and thereby entail a revocation of his license.

A description of the convicted man granted a ticket-of-leave was fully outlined on the back of the form.

Ticket-of-leave men residing in rural districts were supervised entirely by the police, but those residing in Dublin were supervised by a civilian employee who had the title of Inspector of Released Prisoners. He worked cooperatively with the police, but it was his responsibility to secure employment for the ticket-of-leave men. He required them to report at stated intervals and visited their homes every two weeks and also verified their employment. The problem of hounding by the police, which had been stressed at the hearings before the Select Committee and the Royal Commission in London, did not arise in Ireland. It was accepted that conditionally released prisoners would inform their employers of their criminal record and if they failed to do so, the head of the police was responsible for this action. Many of the problems being discussed by present-day parole executives confronted the administrators of the Irish system, and they adopted their policies to meet the needs. Contrary to the experience in

England, the Irish system of ticket-of-leave had the confidence and support of both the public and the convicted criminal.

Prisoner's Aid Societies

In England and Ireland after 1864, the Prisoner's Aid Society was established, the Government contributing a share of funds equal to the sum raised by the society for its work. This society employed agents who devoted their full time to the supervision of released prisoners, and whose duties were outlined as follows:

1. To visit the local prisoners weekly or oftener, if ordered by the Honorable Secretary and to take his instruction as to dealing with the cases selected for aid.
2. To visit local employers of labor, taking every opportunity of seeing and becoming personally acquainted with foreman and other officials explaining to them the objectives of the Society and endeavoring to secure their cooperation.
3. To see the prisoner at the jail and accompany him to the railway station when needed, and to provide board and lodging for him for a limited time.
4. To visit constantly all persons under the care of the Society so long as they were unemployed and after employment is found.
5. To enter daily in a journal all parties seen and places visited and to submit the journal to the Committee at the monthly meeting.
6. To expend, under the direction of the Honorable Secretary, the money of all ticket-of-leave men under his supervision and to lose no opportunity of procuring suitable employment for them.

Developments in the United States

By 1865, the Crofton system had been widely publicized in America, and prison reformers who were critical of the conditions existing in our prisons suggested the adoption of new methods based on the Crofton plan. Although there were some critics of the Irish system, little attention was given to their opposition, and American reformers continually enunciated the need for new types of prison programs to provide for the grading of criminals, according to the degree of their reformation, and the use of the mark system as a check on their progress and restraint against disorder.

Propagandists for the Crofton system, however, did not believe in the adoption of the ticket-of-leave and specifically stated that "no ticket-of-leave system will ever be made acceptable and proper in the United States." Their attitude was apparently based on the conception that it would be un-American to place any individual under police supervision, and they did not believe that any form of supervision would be effective. A letter written by Crofton in 1874, in reply to an inquiry sent him by the Secretary of the New York Prison Association, may have been responsible for a change in their viewpoint. In his communication, Crofton stressed that the police of Ireland were permitted to delegate competent individuals in the community to act as custodians for ticket-of-leave men. He suggested that America follow the practice of having prisoners about to be released name a "next friend" to whom they would be willing to make their reports, a person "likely to befriend them," and then to arrange with competent persons for supervision of a friendly character to the well-doer but at the same time of a nature to restrain the evil disposed by compelling the released prisoners to observe the conditions upon which they have been liberated.

At the time the propaganda was being carried on for the adoption of the Crofton plan, the Elmira Reformatory in New York State was being constructed. Because of the widespread interest in prison programs, it would logically be assumed that before the new institution was opened, a suitable plan or organization would have been developed and necessary legislation enacted, or at least suggested by the board of managers of the state government.

Elmira Reformatory was formally opened in July of 1876 and had been operating for almost a year before its first superintendent, Z. E. Brockway, drafted a measure establishing a definite policy.

Prior to his appointment to Elmira Reformatory, Mr. Brockway had been head of the House of Correction in Detroit and, while there, had drafted an indeterminate sentence law. His proposed measure outlined the following special features for the Elmira system:

1. An indeterminate or indefinite sentence, the length of time served to be dependent upon the behavior and capacity of the prisoner, within statutory limitation.
2. The status and privileges accorded to the prisoner, as in the Crofton plan, were to be determined by his behavior and progress.
3. Education was to be compulsory.
4. Provision was made for the release on parole of carefully selected prisoners.

Although no novel idea was included in the organization and administrative plan for Elmira, in its operation the system combined principles, the validity of which had been recognized separately.

The acceptance of the indeterminate sentence is so general today that it is difficult to comprehend why it should have become a serious controversial issue. The movement to substitute the indeterminate or reformative sentence for the fixed or definite term began in England early in the nineteenth century.

As early as 1839, George Combs, a Scottish philosopher, visited America to lecture; it was he who suggested the idea of a sentencing board, the indeterminate sentence, parole, and what later became the basis for the system under which modern boards of parole function. In one of his lectures, he said:

> If the principles which I advocate shall ever be adopted, the sentence of the criminal judge, on conviction of a crime, would simply be one of finding the individual has committed a certain offense and is not fit to live in society, and therefore granting warrant for his transmission to a penitentiary to be there confined, instructed, and employed until liberated in due course of law.
>
> The process of liberation would then become one of the greatest importance. There should be official inspectors of penitentiaries invested with some of the powers of a court, sitting at regular intervals and proceeding according to fixed rules. They should be authorized to receive applications for liberation at all their sessions and to grant the prayer of them on being satisfied that such a thorough change had been effected in the mental condition of the prisoner that he might safely be permitted to resume his place in society.
>
> Until this conviction was produced upon examination of his dis-

position, of his attainment, in knowledge of his acquired skills or some useful employment, of his habits of industry, and, in short, of his general qualifications to provide for his own support, to restrain his criminal propensities from committing abuses and to act the part of a useful citizen, he should be retained as an inmate of a penitentiary.

The vital principle of the indeterminate sentence was that no prisoner would be paroled until he was fit for freedom. Those who campaigned for the adoption of the indeterminate sentence recognized that in itself it had no mystic power but that its real strength was in the reformatory agencies—labor, education, and religion. It was also recognized that the indeterminate sentence placed in the hands of competent prison officials a tool which could be effectively used.

The main opposition to the enactment of indeterminate sentence laws came from the judges who were unwilling to relinquish their traditional privilege of fixing the time prisoners must serve. Despite their opposition, however, the law was enacted and provisions were also made for the parole of prisoners. At the beginning of the twentieth century, twenty-six states had adopted these measures.

The Elmira Reformatory and the Inception of Parole

Parole originated at the Elmira Reformatory and hence the procedures as they were initiated may have some historical interest. Before being considered for parole, each inmate was required to maintain a good record of conduct for a period of twelve months. He was expected to have gained the confidence of the superintendent and the managers and, before being released, he was required to present suitable plans for permanent employment. When his release had been approved, he was given a new suit of clothing and sufficient funds to reach his destination and to pay his immediate expenses. The superintendent then interviewed him on the day of his release and instructed him to proceed to his employment and remain there, if practicable, for at least six months. He was required to report to a guardian on his arrival and write directly to the superintendent notifying him that he had done so.

One of the conditions of his parole was that he must report on the first of every month to his guardian and report his situation and conduct. The guardian's report and certification by the parolee's employer as to his wages were transmitted to the superintendent of Elmira. A record was kept of all paroled men who were required to report for a minimum period of six months. It was the belief that a longer period under supervision would be discouraging to the average paroled man.

According to the philosophy of the reformatory officials, it was considered preferable to have the paroled prisoner return to the place from which he was committed or the place of his usual habitation, on the basis that "recuperation from a damaged reputation and recovery of public confidence are easiest in the community where the misconduct occurred." The employer and the parole supervisor were "always made fully acquainted with all the facts, this for the sake of honesty, safety, and for the salutary mutuality of the confidential relations involved." Paroled prisoners were not permitted to conceal or deny their history. Monthly reports certified by the employer and supervisor were required. The officials considered the chief of the local police—"not the average policeman in the great cities, nor indeed a religious or philanthropical organization or private individual"—the most satisfactory individual to supervise paroled prisoners.

American prison reformers were aware of the conditions under which prisoners conditionally released from institutions in England and Ireland were granted their liberation. Although for the most part the same restrictions were enforced, certain new procedures were developed in the supervision of released prisoners in this country.

One of the first institutions for juvenile delinquents was established in New York State in 1820. An Indenturing Committee of three members was appointed, and they adopted the policy of requiring written reports from the sponsors and the children who were released from the institution.

Early in the history of prisons in the United States, one of the major considerations of penologists and the public was centered in the problems presented by discharged prisoners. Prisoner's Aid

Societies were established early in the nineteenth century to give needed relief to prisoners discharged from the institutions and to aid them in securing employment. Each prisoner who was given assistance by one of these societies was required to submit written reports to the society covering his progress, behavior, earnings, and savings. This policy of requiring written reports from prisoners was later adopted by the officials at the Elmira Reformatory.

With the great stress placed upon reformation, and the knowledge of England's experience with ticket-of-leave men, it should have been obvious that if the new system was to be given a fair trial, prison programs would have to be revolutionized. Ignoring this important factor in the treatment of criminals, state after state proceeded to enact indeterminate sentence and parole laws, and the abuse of them became widespread.

No thought was given to the training of prisoners toward their future adjustment in the community, and both prison administrators and inmates soon accepted the idea that reformed or unreformed, allowance of time for good behavior was automatic and release at the earliest possible date was a right rather than a privilege. After release, supervision was either nonexistent or totally inadequate if it was required. The result was a duplication of the English experience.

Every charge that had been made against the operation of the early English system of ticket-of-leave was leveled against the administration of parole in the United States.

It has been only within the past two decades that drastic action has been taken by a number of states to render prison reform and parole effective parts of the state system of correctional care. It is now recognized that parole can be an effective method of community protection and at the same time offer constructive aid to released prisoners. To achieve these objectives, however, the system must be adequately financed, nonpolitical in operation, and supported by public trust and confidence.

Chapter Three

The Legal Rights of Prisoners

THE institution of pardon and the practice of pardoning long antedated the prison system. Evidence of this appears in Mosaic law, the Vedic law of India, and elsewhere. In England, the use of executive clemency seems to have grown out of the conflict between the King and the nobles who threatened his power. Although loosely recognized among his predecessors, it was William the Conqueror who brought to England the view that the pardoning power was the exclusive prerogative of the King. The main exception to this practice was the "benefit of clergy," which had been built up by the church in its system of canon law.

Many of the early English legal writers admitted the necessity of pardons as long as justice was exercised as it was. Recall that in the seventeenth century there were some three hundred crimes which were designated as felonies and that as felonies, where "clergy" could not be pleaded, the punishment was death. The judge had no alternative: he could condemn to death, or he could reprieve. Beccaria argued that as punishments became more mild, there would be less necessity for pardons. And so it has been.

The English practice of pardon was followed by the American colonies. In the establishment of Colonial charters, the pardoning power was vested in the royal representative.

Following the liberation of the Colonies from England, the pardoning power was vested in different officials in the various states.

The administration of the machinery of pardons in the United States today continues to be confused and not infrequently inequitably maintained. The major study of pardons continues to be among the Attorney General's *Survey of Release Procedures* (five volumes) 1939-1940. Over two decades later, the report, insofar as pardons are concerned, remains substantially correct.

Are pardons being abused? The true functions of pardons are still misunderstood in many quarters. Pardon as a legal device for tempering justice with mercy and for righting the wrongs of justice should be forever preserved. It is not, however, a substitute for parole, nor a reward for exemplary conduct exhibited by one under penal servitude.

Closely associated with the pardon is the topic of the legal rights of prisoners. Strangely, the statutes of many states are silent on the matter of rights of convicted felons. Needless to say, the general public is even more confused by many of the popular misconceptions regarding the "loss of citizenship" and "civil rights."

LEGAL RIGHTS OF PRISONERS*

No asset in our cultural heritage has been more precious than the sense of justice and the methods by which we have traditionally sought to fulfill it. We have accepted as a rudimentary necessity of social control the fair testing of man's legal guilt of crime. The struggles of democratic revolution in England and on the Continent have erected a bulwark of procedures to assure a full protection against wrongful conviction, so that innocent suspects might not be accursed as criminals. In this country the legal rights with which history has endowed the accused have persevered more or less intact through the vicissitudes of recurrent emergencies and hysteria.

The critical observer of our culture is confronted with a strikingly different picture in our methods of dealing with convicted criminals. For the accused, there is regularity and uniformity assured through the rule of law but, once convicted, offenders are handled under a veritable chaos of procedures, philosophies, and objectives. In sentencing and treatment, one finds an administrative hegemony little restrained by legal or due process conceptions. This contrast between a well-defined legal ordering of trial and a poorly defined administrative system of sentencing and treatment appears to be rooted largely in the differing historical evolution of each. The modern correctional sanctions, together with their supporting theories and procedures, have developed in

* Reprinted by permission of the American Academy of Political and Social Science. Paul W. Tappan: The legal rights of prisoners. The *Annals*, *293*:99-111, May 1954. Footnotes are omitted.

the main subsequent to that renaissance of criminal law in which our basic ideals of justice were molded.

The old retributive penology was predicated on the view that the proven criminal was an "outlaw" without legal rights. Not only might he be subjected to the crudest penalties, but he lost his citizenship (if not his life), his identity of person, and his property. The historical development of a legal due process to protect those accused of crime did not substantially alter the nature of punishments inflicted on those convicted. Religious, moral, and political conceptions established little refuge for the criminal, once his guilt was established. However, humanistic influences, particularly during the nineteenth century, came to alleviate some of the barbarism in the treatment of offenders—to provide extenuations, exceptions, and escapes from the full rigor of punishment. There has been a gradual and considerable change in modern penology under the impact of social humanitarianism, of behavioral sciences and permissive philosophy, and of diverse other cultural influences. Correctional treatment has been swayed by new and often conflicting ideologies of individualization, rehabilitation, social protection, and social reform. But the changes have occurred for the most part administratively, with little relation to conceptions of due process and the rule of law that had developed during the eighteenth century and before. In an age of reliance upon administrative judgment and process, we have deprecated the restriction of executive authority by law. As in other areas of governance, we have looked, often with dewy-eyed expectancy, to the expert, though with great uncertainty in the field of corrections as to what constitutes expertness. We have sought abstract, loosely defined goals, with a minimum of direction or control by law over the authorities charged with the treatment of the criminal.

Thus it is that, as we look to the legal rights of prisoners in the United States, we find—in vivid contrast to the substantive law of crimes and to the law of evidence and procedure—that there are broad penumbrae of vague legal specifications and areas of deep shade where the law is wholly silent. Rights of citizenship and of person and property attaching to the criminal have not been clearly defined by constitution or statute. The convict generally has the right to appeal from conviction and to protection against cruel and unusual punishments but, as we shall note in more detail below, even these protections are limited and vary in practice. Certain other rights and restrictions are established by law in some jurisdictions, but there is no consistency in the matter.

Loss of Rights

There are four main ways in which ordinary political or civil rights of the individual may be taken away as a direct or indirect consequence of criminal conviction.

Civil-death Statutes

Special statutes may attach the status of civil death to the offender, usually on the basis of a sentence to life imprisonment or death. Civil-death statutes survive today in some seventeen jurisdictions, though the meaning of the term is far from uniform in these states. It has been held that the convict who is civilly dead cannot sue to enforce his rights in court. The seriousness of this restriction is discussed briefly at a later point. In several of these states, offenders under life sentence are specifically prohibited from exercising rights to contract or to sell or inherit property. In some states, property is distributed after conviction of the offender as though he were actually dead. In others, it may pass at once under a will, though it is unlikely that this could result in the absence of a statute specifically so providing. Ordinary political rights to vote, hold office, testify, or act as juror are extinguished.

Civil-death statutes are among the most primitive survivals in our system of penalties. It appears clear that where certain rights should be taken from the felon, this ought to be done in specific terms rather than under a civil-death law.

Suspended Rights

Rights may be suspended during a term of imprisonment less than life. Nine of the states with civil-death statutes and one other provide for the general suspension of rights during imprisonment short of a life term. Where no such statutes exist, it appears that convicts can sue but that, where rights are suspended, they cannot—though they may be sued and can defend against an action. The right to hold public office or positions of honor or trust is suspended during imprisonment in several states, though a majority of jurisdictions provide for actual forfeiture persisting after incarceration rather than mere suspension. The right to testify is suspended as a matter of convenience in most jurisdictions, but a number of states provide that the offender's deposition may be taken in prison.

Permanent Deprivations

Conviction of a felony, generally, or of specified crimes involving "moral turpitude" may result in the absolute loss of certain rights. Commonly, these statutory provisions establish the deprivations on conviction coupled with imprisonment, and one must look to the provisions on restoration of rights to determine whether the conviction terminates rights or whether imprisonment merely suspends them. The laws are neither consistent nor clear in this matter. It appears from the statutes that there is not mere suspension but full deprivation (unless and until there is a subsequent restoration by pardon or other means) of the right to vote in at least thirty-five states. In a majority of states, there is also actual forfeiture of public office and positions of trust. A few states disqualify the felon for jury duty.

Marital rights and status present a somewhat peculiar problem. Rights of cohabitation are suspended universally. In other respects, policy varies extensively. In several jurisdictions, life imprisonment involving civil death automatically terminates the marriage, without the necessity for any legal action. In others, the spouse must secure a decree even though the prisoner is civilly dead. In thirty-six states, conviction for a felony, coupled with imprisonment, is a ground for divorce; if a divorce is granted, pardon does not restore conjugal rights. In some jurisdictions, the felon's children can be given to adoption without his consent.

Deprivation by Commissions or Boards

Conviction may be the basis of action by a licensing agency or professional board to deprive the offender of certain rights, usually those of employment. This is an indirect method of determining his rights. In the fields of civil service regulations for governmental employment, licensing and revocation of license for certain professions and other occupations, and rights of compensation for injury or other wrongs and of residence within the United States, deprivations may often be determined by commissions of boards rather than by courts of criminal law.

State statutes commonly list some of the following who may be deprived of their occupations as a result of their conviction of an infamous crime: accountants, barbers, civil engineers, detectives, automobile operators, embalmers, hairdressers, junk dealers, real estate brokers, liquor store owners, pawnbrokers, pharmacists, midwives, naturopaths, nurses, veterinarians, chiropodists, chiropractors, dentists, physicians, surgeons, and lawyers. It is the general rule that a licensing agency, court, or governmental department may refuse to issue or may revoke a license or permit in such occupations where it is shown that the offender has been convicted of a felony, a crime involving moral turpitude, or an offense specifically designated as a basis of exclusion. Where revocation has occurred, the offender generally has a right to appeal to a court for review, as provided by statute. He may have a similar right to appeal if a license is denied him. The power to issue or revoke is a specialized administrative one, however, and the courts will not generally overrule the decision of an agency without a clear showing of gross abuse of discretion.

It may be noted that there is some provision limiting or postponing the exercise of civil or personal rights directly or indirectly (as, for example, by tolling the statutes of limitations) in every state. Since the deprivations that we have mentioned are derived to a large extent from the common law, it is probable that some losses of rights are drawn from tradition in jurisdictions where there are no express statutory provisions therefor.

Restoration of Rights

We have summarized briefly the general patterns relating to the suspension or deprivation of rights entailed by criminal conviction. It is apparent that the existing structures have developed crescively and differentially throughout the country over a period of time. There has been nothing uniform or systematic in the philosophy or objectives by which the rules have developed. And there has been little effort to assure a regulatory due process of law to protect either the offender or the public. In practice, two or more of the methods described above are employed in most jurisdictions in denying or limiting offenders' rights, and the restrictions differ considerably in nature, as we have noted. Commonly it is impossible to determine from the statutes alone whether particular rights are lost, suspended, or retained by the offender.

Further confusion arises from the variation in practice as to the restoration of rights forfeited or suspended. There appear to be several patterns by which rights may be restored: (1) Restoration may occur automatically, by operation of law, upon discharge from imprisonment or from parole. (2) An ordinary executive pardon may restore some or all rights automatically, or particular rights may need to be specified in the pardon. (3) Some form of special action of certification, as provided by statute, may be required.

State Pardon

The most prevalent method of restoring civil rights that have been denied as a consequence of conviction is through pardon by the state. Some or all rights removed may be restored either by pardon or by some similar form of executive or legislative clemency in thirty-seven states. In ten of those noted, only the suffrage is restored by pardon, but in one of these (Rhode Island) the voting privilege may not be restored where conviction was for perjury or an infamous crime. Two others (Nevada and Virginia) prohibit the subsequent holding of office or positions of trust. A minority rule, prevailing in at least five jurisdictions, requires that the pardon must provide specifically for the restoration of any rights that the executive may wish to return. It should be noted, moreover, that in certain situations, rights lost may not be restored even by a full and unconditional pardon. Thus, property interests that have been vested in others cannot be returned. Pardoned offenders who have been rendered civilly dead are most likely to have suffered permanent loss of property rights, of course. Also, where a spouse has exercised the privilege of divorce from the offender, the convict cannot regain connubial rights through a pardon. The writer has noted elsewhere his opinion that pardon is a poor device for restoring civil or other rights.*

Enforcement of Franchise Loss

Enforcement of provisions for the deprivation of the franchise and other political rights, when they are not automatically restored upon release from imprisonment, is generally of a quite superficial nature. Unless a special investigation is made into voting frauds, for example, the police and FBI files are not ordinarily consulted to determine whether men have been convicted of crimes. There are laws in most if not all jurisdictions, however, designating illegal registration or voting and the usurping of office as crimes; such laws undoubtedly act as some deterrent. When an offender moves into a jurisdiction where his prior conviction or incarceration raises a bar to certain civil rights, he may wrongfully but unknowingly exercise the rights that he has lost without being discovered. It has been held that where the defendant honestly believed that his rights had been restored by a pardon, he was improperly convicted of willful and knowing violation.

Automatic Restoration

The most liberal, least discriminating method of restoring lost rights is to return them automatically upon completion of sentence. Wisconsin provides for automatic restoration when the offender serves out his term or otherwise satisfies the sentence of the court. Somewhat similarly, Ohio law restores forfeited rights to all prisoners who have served their maximum terms or who are

---

* "While in theory pardon is an act of executive clemency, to be used sparingly in instances where innocence has been shown subsequent to conviction or where some other injustice has been worked, actually in many jurisdictions the pardoning power is often used by the chief executive of the state as a substitute for parole and in this connection may be badly misused. It does not make sense or justice to grant restoration of civil rights either generally or by specific provision through the governor's pardon and to withhold these rights from those released on parole or discharged at the expiration of sentence. The effect is to make restoration a matter of gubernatorial leniency rather than a considered policy of correctional rehabilitation. Other methods, therefore, are desirable to restore the offender to the normal rights and duties of the citizen in the community."

granted final release by the Pardon and Parole Commission. In Colorado, rights may be restored either by pardon or service of a full term, and in Kansas "citizenship" is restored after the governor commutes sentence or after prisoners are discharged from supervision. In several jurisdictions a time factor or some other element is introduced into this sort of provision. Thus, Missouri law releases from disabilities prisoners who have received good time allowances and who have lived in the community without further offense for a period of two years. In South Dakota the criminal discharged from the penitentiary with a clear record of good conduct is restored to full rights. Tennessee restores rights automatically after six months or three years, depending on the offense involved, except for infamous crimes, where a court action is required. Several states apply a rule of restoration to probationers comparable to the principle recommended by the Model Act of the National Probation and Parole Association. Delaware allows the striking of the verdict or plea of guilty from the record when a probationer has complied with all conditions of his probation. Idaho and Illinois provide, somewhat less liberally, for the restoration of civil rights upon completion of the probation period. In Oregon the probationer or parolee may exercise all civil rights that are not "political," presumably voting and holding office.

Certification

A more selective approach to restoration has been established in several jurisdictions where some form of certification is required for the purpose. A California law of 1944 provides that any felon released from a state institution may apply for a certificate of rehabilitation and a pardon after completing his sentence or parole period with satisfactory behavior. The certificate restores most civil rights. In New York a certificate of good conduct may be granted by the parole board, upon application of the offender, after he has conducted himself satisfactorily for five years after suspension of sentence, release on parole or termination of sentence. This certificate ends disabilities that were created by conviction. Certificates of good conduct are also issued in Colorado, Minnesota, Ohio (at the Women's Reformatory), and Wyoming. In these states, however, certification is by the warden of the institution and, on the basis of that action, the governor will restore civil rights in Minnesota and Ohio and may do so in Colorado and Wyoming.

Restoration of Licenses

Finally, where licenses or permits to practice certain occupations or professions are taken away by special boards or commissions, such privilege is ordinarily not restored merely by pardon or by certification of the sort noted above. These deprivations represent the effort of an occupational group to protect itself and the general public against dangers that may be threatened by the criminal. Once an agency has withdrawn a privilege, it must itself act positively to restore it and may refuse to do so, depending on the law and the rules under which it operates. In order to force its favorable action, it must generally be shown in court that the agency has abused its discretion.

Rights Generally Retained

We have discussed above some of the rights that are lost as a consequence of criminal conviction or imprisonment and how these rights may be regained. Our penal system also provides specifically for the prisoner's retention of some rights of person and property, generally so that he may be protected from excessive abuse. As we have noted, the tendency has been to avoid or mitigate the harsh consequences that historically have attached to civil death and to imprisonment. There are serious problems involved, however, in the lack of consistent policy and even more in finding means by which to make these rights real in practice.

As to property rights, it is the general rule that the prisoner may sue. However, as indicated above, where rights are generally suspended, the inmate cannot sue. This is a serious restriction on his power to secure remedy for injuries or wrongs that may have been done him during imprisonment. It is generally held, however, that the prisoner may be sued and can, therefore, defend such action. Moreover, except where statutes specifically provide to the contrary, it appears to be the rule that the prisoner may contract and may take, hold, convey, or inherit property. In several jurisdictions, provision is made for the appointment of trustees to care for the prisoner's property until his release. In thirty states, there are provisions suspending the statutes of limitation during imprisonment, so that inmates who cannot sue while imprisoned may have their action after release. In at least twenty-eight states the laws make some provisions against forfeitures so that the historical consequences of attainder and corruption of blood may be avoided.

Protections and Remedies for the Offender

One form of protection for the convicted offender is the provision against cruel and unusual punishments that may be found in the eighth amendment of the Federal Constitution and in those constitutions of all states except Connecticut and Vermont. Presumably, the infliction of cruel punishments would also be in violation of the due process clause of the fourteenth amendment. Seven of the states establish in their constitutions the principle that punishment should be proportioned to the offense. Unfortunately these general provisions do not inform at all concretely as to what should be considered cruel. They are generally interpreted to refer to the kind rather than the amount of punishment, but conceptions of excessive cruelty vary. In nine states, specific laws prohibit corporal punishment, and, in some other states, restrictions are imposed on the forms or conditions of its employment. Such practices as whipping and striking, showering, tying up, and using the straitjacket, gag, or thumbscrew are prohibited in a few states. Only one jurisdiction (Louisiana) prohibits solitary confinement, and many states provide specifically for its use—some with severe dietary restrictions to accompany it. The Attorney General's Survey in 1939 observed that solitary segregation was being used in all but four prisons of the United States. The report also noted that at least twenty-six prisons were employing some form of corporal punishment; probably many more were, but it is difficult to secure valid information on this sort of question. It appears that constitutional and statutory provisions are of limited utility in protecting the committing offender, mainly because we have found it difficult to define what is improper and because enforcement of a good policy is extremely difficult. Perhaps sound practice depends more on the good sense and humaneness of individual wardens than anything else.

Legal Remedies

The legal remedies available to the prisoner against wrongs occurring to him during confinement are injunctions, habeas corpus writs, and civil suits for damages. Unfortunately, these are by no means always adequate. As Samuel Widdifield has noted:

> . . . it has been held that disciplinary punishment is peremptory and not subject to review except where there has been gross excess. The problem of proof may be a difficult one to surmount. In states where the prisoner has been declared civilly dead or has had his civil rights suspended, access to the courts may be impossible. Further, the prisoner may not be permitted to see a lawyer, or may not be able to afford one, in order to be made aware of his rights. Most objectionable, the prison officials may do everything they can to prevent a prisoner from asserting his rights.

The remedy of injunction is ordinarily not allowed unless it can be clearly shown that irremediable injury to property or personal rights is threatened. The writ of habeas corpus, however, may be used to rectify mistreatment under both state and federal practice. Its effectiveness has been limited by the holding that recourse to federal process can only be had after state remedies are exhausted. The record in Illinois reveals that the state courts can effectively prevent such remedies over an extended period of time, and it has recently been held that the federal courts will provide remedy where the state has failed to do so.

A civil suit for damages sustained is a somewhat inadequate remedy, not only because it is not designed to prevent injury initially but also because in a number of jurisdictions, as we have seen, the prisoner cannot sue until after his discharge from incarceration. The difficulties of proof are greatly increased, of course, when this is the case. There is a federal civil rights statute that may be invoked for wrongs sustained, either under state or federal imprisonment. A few states have similar laws. Actions brought under such statutes must be taken against the warden or his staff, however, since state governments are protected from suit.

The courts have generally held that it is the duty of prison officials to exercise reasonable care to protect the life and health of the prisoner. There have been very few such suits successfully pursued, however.

Criminal action may be directed against those responsible for prison mistreatment or neglect of duty under the federal civil rights law and under special criminal statutes in some thirty-four states. These provide generally for fines or jail terms. Difficulty of access to the courts and of mustering proof may account for the small number of such cases successfully prosecuted.

Rights as Affected by Federal Law

Some special comment must be made on civil rights as they are affected by federal law. For the most part, United States statutes do not provide for the loss of either citizenship or civil rights. Most such rights derive from state constitutions and laws rather than federal, and their deprivation occurs, therefore, through the jurisdictional power of the state. Hence, a federal conviction of a crime or imprisonment in a federal institution may result in loss of political and other rights by reason of the specific legal provisions for the deprivation of such rights in the particular state, even though the conviction was not had in a state court. Restoration of rights also depends upon state law, but it too may be affected by federal action: Presidential pardon, while it does not itself confer or restore any rights, generally removes the effect of conviction and imprisonment so that the individual may regain his privileges either with or without further action by the state, depending upon its legal provisions on restoration. As under state practice, federal actions of clemency may be specifically denominated as "pardons to restore civil rights" where they are not based upon innocence. Naturally, only federal pardons may be granted for federal offenses, and state pardons for state crimes. It should be noted that, in accordance with the principle involved here, civil and other deprivations that are auxiliary to the conviction are quite different in effect than are the major penalties imposed by the courts: A conviction or imprisonment in *any* state or in the federal courts may result in loss of rights in another jurisdiction in accordance with its laws. Similarly a pardon or other device of clemency employed by an appropriate executive has effects elsewhere that depend upon the laws of the jurisdiction where the offender attempts to assert his rights.

As a partial exception to the generalizations made above, it should be noted that there are some limited provisions in the laws of the United States for a direct denial of rights. Loss of citizenship or nationality may result from a court-martial conviction for desertion in time of war or from a charge of treason, of attempting to overthrow the government by force, or of bearing arms against the United States.

Beyond these provisions, the law disqualifies individuals from holding federal office or position of trust if they are convicted of treason, inciting rebellion, conspiracy to violate civil rights of any citizen, bribery, mutilation, or falsification of public records; this also applies to government employees who receive compensation for rendering service to any person in relation to a matter in which the United States is interested before any government department.

Deportation and Loss of Citizenship

On a somewhat different footing are the provisions for deportation of aliens on the basis of criminal conviction: the deprivation of the privilege of domicile. The Immigation Act of 1917 makes provision for the deportation of undesirable aliens upon the directive of the Attorney General where it can be shown that they have been convicted of crimes involving moral turpitude. An order of deportation may be appealed to the Board of Immigration Appeals or attacked by a writ of habeas corpus if the alien is in custody and can show that his hearing was not fair, that the evidence was not substantial, that the order exceeded the Attorney General's authority, or that the accused has been held unreasonably long. Also, in accordance with provisions of law in the jurisdiction where such convictions occurred, an unconditional pardon may preclude deportation by blotting out guilt. In at least one jurisdiction (Pennsylvania), completion of the prison term is sufficient to accomplish this result. In a recent year, a governor of

New York State granted forty-eight pardons to aliens whose prison terms had expired but who had remained liable to deportation, some of them for a number of years.

Save for the exceptional offenses we have noted, the native does not lose his citizenship through law violations. When he does sustain such loss, he becomes a stateless person but this does not necessitate his deportation. However, it has been held that when a native here has become a citizen of another country, though he did not intend to abandon his United States citizenship, he may be deprived of the latter and refused admission to the United States as an alien, even if no crime was involved. Under our immigration laws the criminal alien may be excluded or deported for fraudulent admission. The noncriminal alien who is admitted may be deported for the subsequent commission of crimes involving moral turpitude and, if he has been issued a certificate of citizenship, may be deprived thereof.

A Reasonable Approach

It is not proposed in this text to deal elaborately with solutions to the problems of civil rights. Our purpose is merely to describe summarily the present confused condition of these matters. In conclusion, however, it may not be inappropriate to comment on the principles involved and what may be a reasonable social and penological approach. The deprivation of "civil rights" may be conceived to be either an auxiliary punishment in itself or the incidental consequence of conviction and sentence, not intended to be specifically punitive but merely protective of public interests and of official convenience. Such a distinction as this appears unimportant to the offender: he may well consider these losses to be a part of the vindictive punishments that society exacts. And, in fact, deprivation of civil rights does appear very frequently to reflect retributive sentiments rather than any real need for community protection. The risk of repeated crime to which society is continuously subject from released offenders is patently greater than the possible consequences of their exercise of the rights that are generally removed.

Deprivation of the right to vote, to hold public office, or to act as juror during a period of incarceration is quite clearly a matter of convenience, if not necessity. Loss of the right to practice one's business or profession or to assume a position of trust, even after release from imprisonment, may often be more a matter of public protection than of retribution. However, when the right to vote, to act as juror or to testify, to hold office or trust, to practice in an occupation of one's training and choice is denied—to probationers, to parolees, to those who have completed their sentences and been discharged, and even to those who have been pardoned—the gratuitously punitive element is great. In such instances, it appears that more mischief than benefit may commonly be worked, for the restrictions imposed do more to prevent rehabilitation than they do to protect the public.

The customary forms of deprivations of civil rights, it is submitted, are not for the most part sound as auxiliary punishments. Except for the deprivation of occupational privileges (including the holding of public office), these deprivations do little or nothing to repress crime. This is not to deny that auxiliary punishments—such as restitution—may serve an obviously useful purpose, but the losses of civil rights are not, for the most part, of comparable utility.

Some General Principles

In the light of what we have written, the following principles are submitted.

1. The ordinary forms of deprivations that we have discussed are not appropriate as auxiliary punishments, for they serve little purpose in deterring crime or incapacitating criminals. Put differently, they are not appropriate measures under a penology that would eschew punishments exacted for their own sake or designed to brand the offender as infamous or outlaw.

2. As a matter of public and official convenience, it is desirable during imprisonment to limit the criminal's freedom to act as juror or serve in public office, perhaps to vote (though no great harm would result, it seems, from prisoners' use of absentee ballots). The principle of convenience is restricted, obviously, to the period of actual incarceration. Moreover, though some con-

siderable inconvenience may be involved, it is desirable to *permit* the exercise of certain important privileges such as the right to sue and to receive and convey property, real and personal. The right to sue for wrongs done to the prisoner or his property is of special importance. If the offender is not allowed direct access to the courts for such purposes, he should at least be permitted to enjoy these rights through a representative.

3. Aside from periods of incarceration, it may be desirable to protect public interests by prohibiting the exercise of certain ordinary rights for some period of time, such as the privileges of occupation and office. It appears, however, that a finer discrimination should be employed in serving this objective. Some balance must be struck between the measures of threat to community welfare, on the one side, and on the other both the intrinsic value of maximizing personal freedom under a system of democratic justice and the utility of encouraging the sound exercise of rights in helping individuals to become responsible citizens. For the most part, aside from exceptions that have been noted, the civil and property rights lost through conviction raise small problem of social danger. It appears that the law should not provide flatly for denial of civil and political rights to those who are on probation or parole. Limited and special provision might well be made, however, for the denial during the period of sentence of (1) certain political rights (particularly the holding of office) to those who have committed atrocious political offenses and of (2) certain occupational privileges to those who have illegally exploited their occupations. There appears to be no excessive hazard, however, in the English rule that leaves full rights with those who are selected for probation. And there is merit in assisting the rehabilitation of the parolee by restoring all rights to him. There is also some danger, of course, but prison release must involve risk in any event.

4. Justice demands an end to penalties. So does rehabilitation. No principle is more clear, perhaps, than this: Upon completion of his sentence, if not before, the offender should be fully restored to his rights. If any of these deprivations is so significant penologically that it should persist beyond the court's sentence to prison or probation, it should be elevated to the status of a primary and independent sanction, specifically designed to accomplish ap-

propriate correctional goals of deterrence, incapacitation, or rehabilitation. In that way, such a deprivation would receive the special focus of attention required in adjusting penalty both to the offense and the offender. Possibly the grafting politician, the corrupt judge, or the purveyor of illicit medication, for example, should not be permitted ever again to ply his trade. Restrictions of this sort have major impact on the offender, however, comparable to that of imprisonment, and often of even greater seriousness to the individual involved. The employment of a permanent or long-persistent sanction of this sort should be based on quite specific categories of offense and on judicial discrimination as to those individual offenders for whom the sanction appears to be necessary as a matter of public protection. Unfortunately, it has not been possible under our system to control the actions of licensing agencies in accordance with sound principles of justice; but, so far as legal deprivations and the behavior of courts are concerned, we can eradicate from current practice such obsolete residuals as civil death and blanket deprivations based on conviction or sentence, and such unnecessarily complicated forms of restoration as pardon and certificates of good conduct.

In this entire area of the incidental deprivation of rights and their restoration, we can liberalize practice greatly with very little threat to the public and with considerable advantage in maintaining a legitimate measure of self-respect on the part of the offender. Wisconsin law seems reasonable in this respect.

THE PARDONING POWER*

The substantive criminal law—concerning itself with the technical problem of what act combined with what mental state is necessary to constitute any of the various crimes in our criminal jurisprudence—has been aptly described as "an island of technicality in a sea of discretion." Thus, before trial, the police have broad discretion as to whether to arrest, and the prosecutor as to whether to prosecute, and if so, for what crime. After conviction, the trial judge (or, less frequently, the trial jury) has discretion as

* Reprinted by permission of the American Academy of Political and Social Science. Austin W. Scott, Jr.: The pardoning power, The *Annals, 284*:95-100, Nov. 1952. Footnotes are omitted.

to what sentence, within limits, to impose or whether to suspend sentence and place on probation; the parole board has discretion as to the duration of penal treatment; and the pardoning authorities have discretion as to the use of the pardon power.

The technical and inflexible nature of the problem of guilt or innocence of crime (inherited largely from the historical fact that in England, when the criminal law was being developed, so many crimes were punishable by death) makes desirable the placing of a good deal of discretion in the groups concerned with criminal law enforcement: police, prosecutors, judges, juries, parole boards, and pardon authorities. If this discretion is taken away from any one of these groups, the burden becomes correspondingly greater on the others to make wise use of their discretionary powers.

Thus in capital cases, it has in the past been not uncommon to deprive judges or juries of their normal discretion as to sentence by making the death sentence mandatory. The trend in recent years has been, if not to abolish capital punishment, at least to abolish the mandatory death sentence. Accompanying this movement has been something of a decline in the importance of the pardon power in capital cases. But as long as capital punishment continues, power to pardon in capital cases is bound to remain an important element in the administration of criminal justice.

The broad power vested in pardon officials to pardon, to commute sentences, and to grant reprieves, applies, of course, to many crimes other than capital crimes. In this section, however, we shall limit ourselves to a consideration of these powers in relation to capital cases where the death penalty has been imposed.

Who May Exercise Pardon Powers

All civilized countries make use of some form of the pardon power to give flexibility to the administration of justice in criminal cases. In England, this power historically is vested in the Crown. But in the United States it is vested in the People, who can delegate the power to whomever they please. As a matter of practice, the People have found it most convenient to give the power to the executive branch of the government. Thus, under the Constitution of the United States, the pardon power in federal cases has been delegated to the President; and practically all the state constitutions have delegated this power in state criminal cases to the governor, either alone or in conjunction with advisers.

A large majority of state constitutions originally gave the power to pardon to the governor alone. The more recent trend has been toward putting more power in the hands of a board. Simplifying matters somewhat, we find that today there are three different arrangements among the states. First, in about one-quarter of the states, the executive pardon power is vested in the governor alone; some of these states, however, furnish a pardon attorney to aid the governor in these cases. Second, about half the states have provided for advisory boards whose function is to hold hearings in pardon applications and to make recommendations to the governor, who alone may make the final decision; in practice, the governor usually adopts the recommendations of the board. Third, in about a quarter of the states, there are boards which, instead of acting simply in an advisory capacity, have the final decision about pardons; in all these states, however, the governor is a member of the board.

Types of Pardons in Capital Cases

In discussing the power to pardon in cases where the death penalty has been imposed, it will be well to consider separately three different types of executive clemency: (1) full pardon, (2) commutation of sentence to imprisonment for life or a term of years, and (3) reprieve, or stay of execution.

Full Pardon

In only a rare case does one sentenced to death for crime receive a full pardon. Usually the best he can hope for is a commutation of his sentence to life imprisonment. But there is one type of case, fortunately quite rare in capital cases, where justice demands a full pardon—namely, where subsequent events prove that the convicted person is innocent.

There is some dispute as to how often innocent persons are convicted of serious crimes. Some enthusiasts assert that the many procedural safeguards which are afforded criminal defendants in this country—the right to a jury trial, to counsel, to be informed of the charge, to call witnesses, the privilege against self-incrimination, for instance—make it impossible to convict an innocent person. The District Attorney for New York County reports that only 3 out of 27,288 persons convicted of felony in that county during the years 1938 to 1949 were later shown to be innocent.

On the other hand, Professor Edwin M. Borchard, in his book, *Convicting the Innocent,* has collected and discussed at length sixty-five cases of innocent persons convicted of crime, mostly in this country, of which twenty-nine were murder cases. He says that these sixty-five cases were chosen from a much larger number.

Borchard's cases show that innocent persons are sometimes convicted of crime in mistaken identification by the victim, who is often emotionally disturbed by his experience; sometimes on erroneous inferences drawn from circumstantial evidence; sometimes on the basis of perjured testimony of hostile witnesses. Prosecutors, expected by the public to produce convictions, are seldom as impartial as they are ideally supposed to be, although they do not often stoop so low as to use perjured testimony intentionally against the defendant or to suppress evidence favorable to him. Public pressure for revenge sometimes leads juries to convict innocent persons. If the jury learns that an accused person has been convicted of an earlier crime, his chances of being convicted of this later crime are considerably enhanced, so much so that he often refuses to testify in his own behalf for fear the jury will learn of his former conviction.

Thus it is clear that for one reason or another an innocent defendant is sometimes convicted and sentenced to death, a fact which obviously constitutes one of the strongest reasons for abolishing capital punishment. In such a case, it is only right that the defendant be given a full pardon. It seems odd, but in most cases of innocence established some time after conviction, a pardon is the only effective way to rectify the wrong since courts generally have no power to grant new trials because of newly discovered evidence after a relatively short period of time following conviction.

Commutation of Sentence

Commutation is the substitution of a lighter for a heavier punishment. Unlike pardon, it does not mean forgiveness and does not effect a restoration of civil rights. Most state constitutions specifically include in the pardoning power the power to grant commutations. In those states whose constitutions do not specifically so provide, it is held that such a power is included in the grant of the pardoning power, for the reason that the greater power (to pardon) necessarily includes the lesser power (to commute).

The power to commute sentences is exercised in a great many cases other than death cases, usually to make eligible for parole a prisoner whose term has not expired. Here we shall consider the power only as used to avoid the death sentence, an important but far less common use of commutation. In practice, the power is generally exercised by commuting death sentences to life imprisonment, although occasionally the sentence is reduced to imprisonment of a term of years.

To prevent the arbitrary or dishonest exercise of the pardoning power by pardon authorities, most of the states require regular annual or biennial reports to the legislature by pardon authorities concerning the granting of pardons, commutations, and reprieves. A study of these reports gives us some indication as to the reasons why commutations are granted in practice. Often the recommendation of the judge who tried the case, the district attorney who prosecuted it, or the state supreme court which reviewed it, is emphasized. Frequently the fact that, of several joint participants in the crime, only one received the death sentence (particularly if this one was not the moving spirit behind the commission of the crime) is given as a reason for commuting the sentence to life imprisonment.

Sometimes the evidence against the defendant, although sufficient to sustain a conviction, is conflicting or is based on circumstantial evidence alone, in which cases the pardon authorities may decide to commute the death sentence. Commutations (or even occasionally full pardons) are sometimes granted because of prior promises made by prosecutors, which the state feels bound to honor, of lighter punishment or immunity in return for turning state's evidence. Sometimes there are extenuating circumstances which do not affect the technical legal question of guilt or innocence of a capital crime but which do call for the exercise of mercy.

Other reasons have been given as well, including such matters as the youth of the condemned person, the evil influence exercised over him by his stronger or older companions, his good prison record, or the fact that this was his first offense. At times the reasons are suggested very vaguely—"because of the peculiar circumstances of the crime" or "because it is considered that justice will be satisfied without the taking of this man's life."

Factors Influencing Pardon Officials

Without doubt, there are motivating forces which lead pardon officials to grant pardons or commutations but which are not given as reasons for acting. At times the condemned man is a member of a group which exercises great pressure on pardon officials to grant clemency; conversely, the victim of the crime may be a member of a group which just as vigorously opposes clemency. Politics is an important factor, too, especially where the governor alone exercises the pardoning power without being insulated by a board of pardons. As an elected official, he is not impervious to the display of public opinion for or against a condemned prisoner.

An interesting question arises as to how the governor's private views of capital punishment affect his commutation of death sentences. We may expect, for instance, that one who strongly disapproves of such punishment would be more prone to commute death sentences than would others. A number of years ago, the Governor of Oklahoma announced his view that the death penalty was legalized murder and stated that he would commute all death sentences to life imprisonment. The Oklahoma Criminal Court of Appeals thereupon denounced the governor's position in angry tones, stating that the law forbade him to "allow his scruples to influence him in the least." But since it is uniformly held that the exercise of discretion by pardon officials is a matter not to be reviewed or interfered with by the courts, it is difficult to see how, as a practical manner, there can be any effective way of preventing pardon authorities from letting their views on capital punishment influence their decisions on commutations of death sentences.

Extent of Commutation

One last problem is the extent to which pardoning officials have in fact exercised their power to commute death sentences. Figures are not directly available on a national basis as to the number of cases where the death penalty was imposed but sentence was commuted. However, we can learn something by comparing the number of prisoners received by federal and state prisons each year under sentence of death with the number of prisoners executed at these same prisons during the same period. Those not executed must have either received commutation, died (either naturally or by suicide), escaped, or had their cases reversed by a higher court. The latter three possibilities are not very common, however.

For the seven years, 1940 to1946 inclusive, 771 condemned prisoners were received, of which number 587 were executed. Most of the 184 unaccounted for undoubtedly received commutations. It would seem, then, that, taking the country as a whole, commutations are granted in about 20 to 25 per cent of the cases where the penalty is imposed. This statement is somewhat confirmed by the earlier assertion of the Select Committee on Capital Punishment that "over a given period, the percentage of death sentences carried out to execution is 71.9 in the United States."

Statistics are available in some of the individual states as to the numerical relationship between those executed and those whose sentences were commuted. Thus in New York from 1920 to 1936, there were 252 executions and 83 commutations. In New Jersey from 1907 to 1937 there were 119 persons electrocuted and 27 granted commutation. Texas granted 7 commutations out of 64 cases in the four years 1947 to 1951.

It seems safe to say that, of the many persons who are convicted of crimes whose maximum punishment is death, comparatively few receive a death sentence. Of those who are sentenced to die, most are executed, but about one in four or five obtains a commutation to life imprisonment.

Reprieve

A reprieve in the case of one sentenced to death is merely a postponement of execution. In general, the power to pardon carries with it the power to reprieve, whether or not the reprieve is expressly mentioned in the constitution among the other forms of clemency. While reprieves are sometimes granted in noncapital cases, they are most important in capital cases, to stay execution of death.

The reports of pardon authorities indicate a variety of different reasons for granting reprieves in capital cases. They are often granted—as of course they should be if the law does not provide for an automatic stay of execution—pending the appeal of the case to a higher court or to allow the condemned man to apply to the United States Supreme Court for certiorari or to allow him to pursue other procedural remedies in the courts. If newly discovered evidence bearing on the case is found, reprieve should be granted a woman prisoner who is pregnant. It is a well-settled rule of law that an insane person cannot be executed, so reprieves are often granted to determine the question of insanity, and, if insanity is found, to postpone execution until sanity is regained. Reprieves are sometimes granted for less important reasons, such as the fact that the date of execution is a holiday or a Sunday or the prisoner's birthday.

Conclusion

Pardon authorities are given broad and almost unrestricted discretion over pardons, commutations, and reprieves. This fact is one of the elements of strength in the proper administration of criminal justice. But it has sometimes led to abuse, especially in those states where one man has the final determination over clemency. Unscrupulous governors may build up their political careers by using the pardoning power to please people with political influence. Others, more honest, are influenced by the effect of their decisions on the electorate, rather than by the merits of the particular case.

While the discretion of pardon authorities is so broad that there exists no definite standard by which to determine whether the discretion is being abused, yet some situations have arisen which clearly show an abuse of discretion. The most notorious of these cases is that of a former Governor of Oklahoma, who was impeached because he frequently exercised his power to pardon, not on the merits of the case but rather as an accommodation for friends or for personal financial rewards.

In spite of occasional abuse, however, it seems obvious that the power to pardon is a necessary part of American criminal jurisprudence in capital as well as noncapital cases. As long as a conviction cannot be reversed after a period of time for newly discovered evidence proving the defendant's innocence, we need the power to pardon for innocence. There will always be cases of technical guilt but, because of extenuating circumstances, comparatively little moral fault. The pardon power, in other words, is necessary in cases where the strict legal rules of guilt and innocence have produced harsh or unjust results. Doubtless the administration of the pardoning power can be improved, as the Attorney General's *Survey of Release Procedures,* including pardon has concluded. But the power to pardon will continue to play an important part in the ultimate disposition of capital cases as long as capital punishment remains with us.

WHY PARDON? A REEXAMINATION*

The question may be raised whether the ancient institution has not outlived its usefulness. Is there any valid reason why pardon should be retained? Are not judicial review and modern release procedures such as parole sufficient to do all that pardon ever did —and do it better?

To a large extent, the answer must be *yes.* Much, and in some states most, of what is being done under the governor's pardoning power could and should be done either by the courts or by a parole board. There remains a valid field for the pardoning power to occupy, but it is a much more restricted field than it occupies today.

This is perhaps the most important conclusion which this sur-

---

* Reprinted in part by permission. United States Attorney General's *Survey of Release Procedures,* 3:296-300, 1940. Footnotes are omitted.

vey of pardon has to offer. Let us therefore state it emphatically and in detail. The exercise of the pardoning power should be restricted from two sides.

1. *Criminal procedure should be liberalized so as to permit reversal of a conviction where new evidence is found indicating that the defendant was innocent.* A pardon granted on the ground of innocence is an anomaly at best. Anglo-American law has been peculiarly indifferent to this problem. Continental law has gone much further in permitting judicial reconsideration of such cases. Obviously, this is the only logical and satisfactory way to handle the problem. An innocent man who has been wrongly convicted is entitled to vindication, by reversal of the erroneous conviction. To pardon him for being innocent is irony. What is more, it creates confusion in determining the proper effect to be given to a pardon.

The objection to permitting such reversal, of course, is that it would render the law uncertain if there were not a time after which a case was closed and the judgment final. It may be conceded that some limits must be drawn, but the fact remains that the right of appellate review is much more restricted in this regard in most American states than it is in most Continental countries.

2. *All releases on condition of good behavior and under supervision should be under the parole law, and not by conditional pardon.* This is the legitimate field of parole. There is no reason for having similar types of releases granted by two different agencies. Furthermore, the parole organization has better facilities for determining when a prisoner should be so released and for supervising him thereafter. Even where the parole law is inadequate, the proper approach is to strengthen it rather than to handle the problem by conditional pardon or other forms of executive clemency.

This would mean the almost total elimination of conditional pardons. Special situations may arise from time to time when certain conditions may properly be attached to a pardon, but the use of conditional pardon as a regular procedure, in lieu of parole, should be abandoned. Even the states having no separate parole system, and where parole rests legally upon the governor's clemency power, should enact a parole law resting upon the state's power to punish criminals and rehabilitate socially dangerous persons, wholly divorced from the governor's power to grant clemency.

To the same end, the parole laws should be liberalized so as to give the parole board full discretion for paroling any prisoner it deems worthy. This means repealing all restrictions in the parole statutes making certain classes of prisoners ineligible for parole. The primary reason why conditional pardon, commutation, reprieve, and other forms of executive clemency have been so extensively used to effect conditional release has been to cover cases not eligible for parole. The big mistake made by those who think we should be hard-boiled about parole is in forgetting that while they may bar the door against release on parole, the back door of executive clemency always remains open. The result is that restrictions written into the parole laws by those who do not think that certain kinds of criminals should be turned loose on parole—murderers, rapists, second offenders, or those who have not served a certain portion of their sentences—too often defeat their own objective. The convicts we refuse to release on parole are released on indefinite furloughs, on conditional pardons, or other types of releases under which there are much less actual supervision and control than under parole.

Of course, taking all restrictions out of the parole law and vesting the parole board with unrestricted power to determine when and to whom parole should be granted means giving the board a degree of power which could be easily abused. The answer, however, must be to safeguard the capability and honesty of the board rather than to cut down its power by arbitrary restrictions. Granting parole is necessarily a matter of individualized consideration of each case. The board should be so constituted as to guarantee that its decisions will be based upon careful, scientific investigation and capable honest judgment. In short, the answer to defects in the parole system is a better parole system, not less parole.

If such reforms were adopted, what would be left for executive clemency? Enough. It would still be needed for the same general purposes for which it has been used historically—to take care of cases where the legal rules have produced a harsh, unjust, or popularly unacceptable result, or where, for politic reasons, the rule of law should be set aside. Such cases will continue to arise under any legal system. A criminal code can only define antisocial conduct in general terms. It can never take into account all the special circumstances which may be involved in a given case. The safety valve will remain necessary. To imagine that the reforms we have suggested would remove all necessity for the intervention of a pardoning power would be as naive as the notion of the French revolutionists that the introduction of the jury system would make justice perfect and pardon unnecessary.

We may enumerate some of the situations which will continue to arise, in which pardon may be proper.

1. Political upheavals and emergencies, wherein pardon may be necessary to pacify a revolution-torn country or to unite a country for war.
2. Calm second judgment after a period of war hysteria, during which persons were given very severe sentences for political offenses later realized to have been very minor or upon evidence later felt to be insufficient.
3. Similarly, changed public opinion after a period of severe penalties against certain conduct which is later looked upon as much less criminal, or as no crime at all. Prohibition is a recent example. The present severity against kidnappers may give rise to cases which future judgment may recommend for clemency.
4. Cases "where punishment would do more harm than good," to quote Bentham, as in certain cases of sedition, conspiracy, or acts of public disorder.
5. Technical violations leading to hard results. We can mention at least one example—where the legal "principal" in a crime may be only a comparatively innocent hireling while the brains of the plot is legally guilty only as an accessory.
6. Cases where pardon is necessary to uphold the good faith of the state, as where a criminal has been promised immunity for turning state's evidence.
7. Cases of later proved innocence or of mitigating circumstances. Although we have recommended liberalizing ju-

dicial procedure so that most of these cases could be handled by proceedings to reverse the conviction, probably some restrictions will necessarily be retained upon the right to such judicial review, and cases may still arise in which such review is impossible, though innocence is clearly probable.

8. Applications for reprieve or commutation, especially in death sentence cases. Here, too, liberalization of judicial procedure should permit reprieves to be granted by the courts. But while there is a somewhat less logical reason for retaining this power in the executive than can be found for most of the other examples listed above, this last recourse to the governor is a benevolent power which we shall probably want to retain and it will no doubt continue to be a major part of the pardoning power.

ORGANIZATION OF PARDON ADMINISTRATION*

The obvious political implications and considerations involved in most of the valid grounds for pardon indicate the propriety of retaining this power in the hands of the chief executive. The objection that this takes too much of the governor's time from more important matters of state is true today—when executive clemency is used in so many states as a regular and normal release procedure, handling cases which should be left to a competent parole board—but it should not be true if pardon were restricted to the exceptional cases as we have recommended. In the Federal Government, where this distinction is observed, there is no undue press of pardon cases burdening the President.

This does not mean that it would not be helpful to have a pardon official or board to assist the governor in this function. A board would seem preferable to one official, for the determination of whether clemency should be granted would usually involve considerations of policy upon which it would be well for the governor to have the views of other executive officials of his administration, rather than a pardon attorney or other official who too often may be merely a kind of secretary.

---

* Reprinted in part by permission. United States Attorney General's *Survey of Release Procedures,* 3:302-308, 1940. Footnotes are omitted.

In most states the board might properly be composed of such other executive officers as the attorney general and the secretary of state. The attorney general should be included because many of the cases will probably involve legal implications.

Prison and parole officials should not be members of this board. Considerations relevant in ordinary release procedures should not be interpolated into the deliberations, and if the viewpoint of penal authorities were introduced into clemency hearings, it would promote exactly the situation we have tried to rectify—the usurpation by the executive clemency power of the field belonging to parole and penology generally. Even such major penal officials as the head of a department of correction or of public welfare should therefore have no place on the pardon board.

It would be helpful for the board to have a secretary or pardon attorney devoting all or a substantial part of his time to his duties as such. Certainly in the larger states this would be necessary. His duties might be patterned after those of the pardon attorney of the United States.

The board may or may not be given some power beyond merely advising the governor. Three main alternatives are suggested:

1. All applications must be brought before the board, but the governor may, after obtaining the board's views, take any action he wishes.
2. The governor must obtain the board's consent and cannot grant a pardon over the unfavorable action of the board.
3. The ultimate pardoning power is in the board itself, of which the governor is only one member. The governor may have only one vote, as any other member, or he may have a veto power.

It seems unnecessary to go beyond the first method. This subjects the governor's action to control which is sufficient to exert powerful pressure against abuse, and yet is respectful and leaves full responsibility resting very directly upon his own shoulders.

Vesting the pardoning power in a board, of which the governor is only one member with one vote, scatters responsibility so that it may be difficult for the public to place the blame for abuse of the pardon power.

Of course, it should be mandatory for the governor to report regularly to the legislature all cases of clemency granted. This publicity, together with the requirement that he first submit all cases to the board, would seem to place sufficient checks upon the governor to make abuse unlikely.

Procedure

Pardon procedure should be (1) simple, (2) thorough, (3) public, (4) free of charge, and (5) adversary rather than ex parte in nature.

By a *simple procedure* is meant one which the average prisoner is able to handle without the aid of a lawyer. Of course, important or difficult cases probably will require a lawyer, and certainly the right to counsel in all cases should be allowed.

By a *thorough procedure* is meant one in which the final decision is reached not merely upon allegations stated in the prisoner's petition, or in court records, or upon recommendations of the trial judge, prosecutor, or interested citizens, but upon a careful investigation of the case. The pardoning authorities should have available at least one officer to make such investigations.

Not every phase of the procedure can be public, but it is proper that a right to public hearing be granted, in which the whole case may be subjected to the full light of publicity.

The granting of clemency in proper cases is a matter of public interest, and not of interest to the prisoner alone. There is, therefore, no reason for charging the cost to him. The right to apply should be free of charge. The practice of one state, of charging ten dollars for the privilege of applying for clemency, is not to be commended.

By *adversary proceedings* is meant a procedure in which the State is regularly represented at any public hearings.

Application

The regulations found in most states concerning the manner in which executive clemency may be applied for are usually designed to accomplish two aims: (1) to bring applications before the pardoning authorities in an orderly manner, with at least a minimum of the necessary facts in the case to permit intelligent disposition and (2) to provide notice to the prosecuting officials and to the public generally of the fact that clemency is being applied for.

While the first of these is a wholly proper purpose, in many states too much reliance seems to be placed upon it. It is proper to demand that the petitioner state the grounds upon which he asks for clemency, but such statements can never be sufficient to decide the case. The elaborate requirements found in some states, therefore, of affidavits of the trial judge and prosecutor and others; transcripts of the evidence in the criminal trial, and even copies of the indictment, verdict, and judgment; prison records; statements of the prosecuting witness and members of the jury—all these are still inadequate and unreliable. No multiplication of such documents will enable the board to reach a sound result merely upon the papers in the case. A personal investigation by the board itself is necessary, and for this reason it is indispensable that the board have at its command the services of an investigator to assemble the facts.

Public notice of the fact that application has been made is a wholesome requirement. Unfortunately, no method of accomplishing this purpose adequate for modern society has been devised. The requirement still found in some states that such notice be posted in the courthouse was effective in the horse-and-buggy days, but it is practically negligible in effect today. Not much better is the usual requirement of publication in a newspaper. This problem of official public notice is, of course, not peculiar to pardon cases; it arises in numerous other situations. It is, however, probably somewhat more acute here than in other connections. Building contractors have a business interest in keeping themselves informed of advertisements for bids for public work; the same is more or less true of tax sales, and so forth. But no one has any specific interest in contesting pardon applications. The victim of the crime may feel an interest, but he will probably not make it a point to read newspaper advertisements of pardon applications for years after the crime.

Perhaps the laggard law will eventually adopt modern publicity devices such as the radio to replace outmoded methods like posting in the courthouse or publishing a small notice in an obscure journal.

One aid to publicity is to have pardon hearings held at regular stated times. This, in itself, does not give notice of the specific cases to be heard, but it is of some value.

Limitations on Repeated Applications

Surprisingly few states have placed any restrictions on the right to petition for clemency again and again. In New Jersey a convict whose petition for clemency has once been refused must wait two years before petitioning again; and in Florida, Georgia, Nebraska, and Utah, he must wait one year. In all other states, he can petition every six months or even more often.

Apparently, pardon boards in most states have not felt that this privilege was being abused, even though many of them hear applications for parole as well as for pardon and may have a high percentage of all the prison inmates applying for one or the other at a single session.

Investigation

As already said, in all too many states, the pardoning authorities do not have the benefit of any personal investigation of the cases coming before them, but rely entirely upon the papers in their files. Only a few states have an investigator available. In states where pardon and parole administration are combined, the parole staff is available for pardon cases. The catch is that parole investigations are often inadequate, too. Moreover, as we have pointed out, pardon should be restricted to cases requiring a different sort of investigation from that used in parole.

Hearings

A formal, public hearing should be a prerequisite to the granting of any pardon or commutation. This is granted in most of the states where a pardon board exists.

Applicants should not only be permitted but requested to be present, and should have the right to present any relevant evidence. The pardon board should have power to subpoena witnesses and take testimony under oath. If cases which should be handled by parole are excluded from executive clemency, the remaining cases are likely to be of greater importance than is now generally the case, and so will probably require more elaborate consideration.

Attorneys should be permitted to appear before the board on behalf of an applicant, as is true now in about half the states where formal pardon hearings are held. However, it seems undesirable to permit attorneys to appear without the prisoner himself. The objections sometimes made that permitting prisoners to appear before the pardon board disrupts prison discipline and unduly influences the board members in his favor are without foundation. Very often the prisoner's personal appearance is unfavorable and influences the board to refuse clemency.

It is most important that the State be made a party to all pardon cases, and that it be represented at the hearings by the attorney general or a member of his staff, who should oppose the granting of the petition where that course seems proper. Merely notifying the prosecutor who tried the criminal case and permitting him to be present if he wishes is not sufficient to protect the public's interest. What is needed is a statutory provision providing for the presence of the attorney general or a member of his staff. The mere knowledge that the State will be thus represented should contribute considerably to reduce unfounded applications.

Function of the Board

It is vain to insist that the board should in no case undertake to act as a court of review but should confine itself to a consideration only of matters which "properly bear upon the propriety of extending clemency." Necessarily the board will act more or less as a court of review, not only in cases where the claim is innocence but in most other cases as well. Of course, the sort of cross-examining of the witnesses about the facts of the crime in which lawyers on the board are prone to indulge is usually rather irrelevant, especially where there is no claim that the applicant is innocent. We have pointed out that the rigidity of the law or the fallibility of evidence sometimes demands the complement of the pardoning power to achieve justice. Pardon is a corrective measure in such cases, and the board in determining whether the penalty should be dispensed with or mitigated is necessarily performing a function which is quasi-judicial at least.

Decisions

While hearings should be public, decisions obviously should be arrived at in closed session. In some states, such session is held immediately after the hearing; in others, several days later. Where a great mass of cases is handled at one session, it is almost compulsory to dispose of them at once, lest the members forget the facts and circumstances involved. If cases properly belonging to parole were excluded, a plethora of pardon cases would be unlikely, and it would probably be better to allow some days for reflection between the hearing and the board's decision.

PAROLE REVOCATION PROCEDURE*

The layman and most courts look upon parole as a gift to the convict, an act of leniency on the part of the executive, frequently given as a reward for good behavior in prison. But parole is actually much more than an act of leniency. It is one of a number of criminological devices, including probation, conditional pardon, and parole, which, though differing in various details, have in common the goal of protection of society through the rehabilitation of the criminal. The parolee is required to live up to a rigid code of conduct which is intended to aid him in his readjustment to a socially acceptable and useful life. Revocation acts as a sanction to insure that, if the parolee (by violation of the conditions imposed upon him) shows that he is either unwilling to cooperate with the effort to rehabilitate him or otherwise unready for release, he will be returned to the prison to serve the remainder of his sentence. At the same time, the threat of capricious or arbitrary recommitment does not encourage either cooperation or the success of the process of rehabilitation. The procedural steps in parole must therefore be analyzed with the objectives of simplicity, celerity, and protection against arbitrary action in mind.

---

* Reprinted by permission of the Harvard Law Review Association (copyright 1951). Parole revocation procedures, *Harvard Law Review, 65*:309-319, Dec. 1951. Footnotes are omitted.

Constitutional Considerations

The existence of this sanction of revocation raises the question whether there are any constitutional limitations on its exercise. Several courts have specifically stated that the rights of the parolee are statutory only and are not protected by the due process provision of the Constitution. In stating this, the federal courts have relied upon the dictum by Mr. Justice Cardozo in a 1935 hearing where the Court required a hearing for the revocation of probation, basing its decision on a statute and refusing to accept the petitioner's contention that such a hearing was a constitutional right. But in 1941, the Circuit Court of Appeals for the Sixth Circuit, relying specifically on the fourteenth amendment, reversed a refusal of habeus corpus where the prisoner had been denied notice or opportunity to be heard in the revocation of a conditional pardon. The majority view that no constitutional problem exists has been justified by one or more of the following arguments: (1) that parole is a mere act of grace on the part of the executive, conferring no rights on the parolee and subject to withdrawal at any time; (2) that the parole is a contract between sovereign and convict in which the latter agrees to certain conditions, one of which may be revocation at the will of the granter without hearing or notice; (3) that the parolee remains in the custody of the warden of the prison or the parole board and revocation is a mere change in the form of this custody which does not require special protection; and (4) that the parolee was given full constitutional protection at the time of the original trial.

The first of these theories has received the widest acceptance. But, while the actual granting of the parole may be an act of grace, the parolee is thus given a certain liberty which should be accorded some protection. The contract theory depends upon the power of the convict to accept parole or conditional release. The Supreme Court, speaking through Mr. Justice Holmes in *Biddle v. Perovich* (274 U.S. 480) denied such a power to accept or reject a change in the form of his confinement. Since parole is a part of the reform system, it is difficult to find an option here when none exists with regard to accepting the sentence after conviction. The third theory seems to ignore the inherent difference between custody involved in imprisonment in a cell and "custody" as applied to a person who is at liberty in the world. A few courts have used a variation of the custody theory in saying that the violation is an "escape" from custody and that the parolee who has violated parole is nothing more than a fugitive from justice. This argument assumes that there has been a violation, which is the very question on which the parolee claims a right to a hearing.

The theory that the rights of the parolee were given full protection at the original trial is the strongest. Stated so boldly, the theory depends upon the postulate that revocation does not increase punishment. In fact, once his parole is revoked, the parolee may be forced to serve the maximum sentence undiminished by the time spent on parole. In addition, his conduct is considerably restricted while on parole: he must report periodically to a parole officer; he cannot leave the state to which he is sent on release without permission; he may be denied the privilege of driving a car; he may not use intoxicating liquors; he may be subject to a curfew; he may not marry without special permission from the parole authorities. This is not the freedom of the ordinary citizen. The addition of these years of restriction to the maximum punishment of the court sentence is thus potentially an increase in punishment. A few courts have met this objection by considering the risk of additional punishment without a contemporaneous hearing as being included in the original sentence.

Since the parole system is provided for in the statutes, along with the specific penalties for crimes, these courts argue that the legislature and trial court intended it as a part of the punishment which can be imposed for violations of criminal statutes. Though the last argument might justify the statement that there is no constitutional right to protection of the parolee on revocation, there is some question as to whether the legislature or sentencing court in fact contemplated that the parole system with the risk of additional punishment would be included in the original sentence of the court. Certainly the legislature did not intend to give the parole board or executive the power to revoke and thus increase punishment on mere whim.

It may be plausibly contended that the interest in continuing the parolee's liberty is strong enough to require a regular judicial proceeding before revocation. Even if the circumscribed nature and penal context of his freedom reduce somewhat the constitutional protection required, the minimal protection against the danger of arbitrary or capricious actions should not be eliminated. The question remains as to what specific procedure is required to give this protection.

Procedural Requirements

Arrest

The first step is that of arresting the alleged violator. The federal law provides that the warrant for arrest may be issued by either the board of parole as a whole or by any member thereof. Before the 1948 codification and revision, the statute provided that this should be done only on the basis of "reliable information." It may be argued that the omission of these words from the revised section 4205 indicated an intent that the warrant may issue without such information. But since the avowed intention of the revisers was to codify existing law, eliminating inconsistent or obsolete provisions, such a substantial change seems unintended. Furthermore, federal courts have said that the issuance of a warrant without any information would constitute forbidden arbitrary action. There appears to be no constitutional right to have the arrest based on "reliable information." Although the fourth amendment requires that people "be secure in their persons . . . against unreasonable . . . seizures . . . and no Warrants shall issue, but upon probable cause, supported by Oath or affirmation," at the time of its adoption such release procedures as paroles were not recognized. The fourth amendment was therefore probably originally intended to refer to persons who were being taken into custody for the first time. The retaking of a person who is already under the obligation to serve a sentence may differ enough to prevent application of the amendment, or, if the amendment applied, to give unreasonableness and probable cause a milder meaning in this context. The due process clause would not prevent speedy investigations of alleged parole violations, but it should protect against arbitrary action.

The warrant may be issued at any time within the term of the maximum sentence of the parolee, for this purpose treating parole time as service of the sentence. The courts have interpreted this as meaning the absolute maximum of the sentence imposed, good conduct time being forfeited by violation of the parole conditions. The running of the maximum sentence is suspended during service of a sentence for another crime. Sometimes the warrant, although issued within the maximum term, is not put into execution by an arrest until after that term has run. Courts have generally upheld such action on the ground that upon violation of a condition and the issuance of a warrant for his arrest the violator becomes a fugitive from justice and cannot claim to be serving his sentence. Where the cause of such delay is action on the part of the parolee in absenting himself from the jurisdiction of the board the suspension of execution may be justified. But protection of society demands that there be no unnecessary delay in recapturing the violator. Also the parolee should be given a chance to exculpate himself as soon as possible. Delay may deprive him of evidence which would otherwise prove him innocent of violation. Since the period of delay does not count on his sentence, it increases the duration of effective restraint where the parolee materially complies with all but one condition of parole.

Hearing

After the arrest, the next step is to decide whether a violation has occurred. Here the federal statute provides that the parolee shall be given "an opportunity to appear before the Board, a member thereof, or an examiner designated by the Board." A large number of states have similar provisions. State courts have required hearings in the absence of provisions in the parole statutes or release instruments denying the right to a hearing. The federal court in *Fleenor v. Hammond* (116 F.2d 982) went beyond this point to say that there is a constitutional right to a hearing which no provisions in a release instrument can take away. That statutory provisions would also be ineffective to deny a hearing is suggested by the Michigan Supreme Court in *People v. Moore* (62 Mich. 496; 29 N.W. 80), which held unconstitutional a statutory provision allowing the violator of a conditional pardon to be held without preliminary examination before a magistrate or notice of charges pending a hearing on the question of violation. These cases represent the minority, but the preferable point of view.*

Some federal and state courts have said that the "hearing" need be only of the most summary nature. This hardly satisfied the demands of the situation. There is no requirement of a jury trial, except where there is in issue the identity of the parolee and the arrested person. Administrative convenience demands something less than a full trial with the attendant technical delays, for the board could not give careful consideration to the many cases before it without resort to some informality in the hearing. Also in the informal proceeding, the board may be able to get a clearer view of the true psychology of the parolee which will supply helpful clues to effecting his ultimate adjustment to society, and the parolee is able to discuss his problem and see for himself the error of his conduct. All of these advantages further the rehabilitation of the parolee.

But the undesirability of a formal trial on revocations of parole does not mean that some of the procedural requirements may not carry over into the informal hearing. The parolee should be entitled to notice of the charges against him so that he may meet such charges at the hearing without being required to prepare a full justification of every action and an accounting of every minute of time spent on parole. Connected with this should be the right on the part of the parolee to present evidence as to the truth of the charges, and perhaps as to the proper disposition of the case. While this may not involve the technical rules of a judicial trial, the parolee should be allowed to examine accusing witnesses either at the hearing or by interrogatories before the hearing. The right to representation by counsel was denied by the Fifth Circuit in *Hiatt v. Compagna* (178 F.2d 42; 340 U.S. 880), following a board of parole ruling excluding counsel from the hearing, but was recognized by the District of Columbia Circuit. The argument that counsel may unduly complicate the hearing and lead to

---

* The revocation of parole may be compared to the deportation of an alien. Although the alien is not entitled to a jury trial on deportation, he is entitled to a "fair hearing."

a variation from the desired information makes the unlikely assumption that the mere presence of a lawyer would be sufficient to overthrow the established custom of informal hearings. It should be realized that the parolee may not be equipped to present all the facts of his case in the best manner, and presumably the board can act most effectively in effecting rehabilitation when all of the facts are placed before it. The presence of a lawyer trained in dealing with facts and presenting them clearly should be of aid to both parolee and the board. Throughout the hearing, the two objectives of speedy confinement of the violator and protection of the innocent parolee against unfair treatment must be balanced.

Judicial Review

The third step in the procedure is judicial review of the revocation. The question of revocation is one of discretion on the part of the parole board, which is presumably composed of men who, as experts in criminology and penology, are better equipped than the courts to determine whether return to prison is in the best interests of society and the parolee. Not every violation of parole need lead to reconfinement. A minor violation by one who is making an honest effort to reform may lead only to the imposition of a stricter code of conduct for some period. On the other hand, a minor violation by a parolee who gives no indication of attempting to cooperate with the parole authorities should be followed by immediate return to prison. In view of this situation the courts have wisely refrained from reviewing the facts or merits of the decision other than to correct abuses of discretion on the part of the parole board such as issuance of a warrant without any information to substantiate claim of violation, or the revocation of parole without any hearing or without some essential elements of a hearing. This limited type of review gives protection against arbitrary and capricious action and at the same time leaves the board free to make the ultimate decisions as to the question of policy involved.

Application of the Administrative Procedure Act

It has been argued that since the Federal Board of Parole is an administrative agency, it should be governed by the Administrative Procedure Act (APA) which would require the elements of notice, right to present evidence and right to counsel discussed above, and possibly judicial review. It would seem on the fact of the statute that the parole revocation hearing comes within the area of administrative ajudication under sections 2 and 5. But section 7(a) provides that "nothing in this Act shall be deemed to supersede the conduct of specified classes of proceedings in whole or in part by or before boards or other officers specially provided for by or designated pursuant to statute." The reports of the Senate and House Judiciary Committees say that the language was not intended to create a loophole for an agency to escape the requirements of the Act, but to exclude only those proceedings held before persons of a peculiar competence who would contribute something more than would the trial examiners provided for by the Act. Since section 4207 of the Criminal Code provides for a revocation hearing before the board of parole, its members or examiners designated by the statute, it appears that the hearing is exempted from the application of the Act. In addition, the very nature of the question involved, the rehabilitation of the parolee and the protection of society, requires discretionary action by the specialized presiding officers. Furthermore, the need for a full understanding of the parolee and his problems may make it desirable to have the parole officer who has been closely connected with the investigation of the case sit as an examiner or advise the person hearing the case. Such procedure would not be possible under section 5(c) of the APA.

Conclusion

The majority of courts, rather than analyze the purposes of parole procedure and the requirements of due process, have merely relied on antiquated legal formulae in denying necessary protections to the parolee. Some have taken a more enlightened view, recognizing that the central purposes of the revocation of parole—protection of society and the rehabilitation of the parolee—can best be accomplished by a procedure which is speedy, sure, and fair to the alleged violator.

Chapter Four

Professional Preparation for Probation and Parole Personnel

THE idea that probation and parole officers are not merely agents of surveillance, but in large measure should be responsible for the rehabilitation of offenders, raises questions of qualifications and training for such personnel.

The issue has been raised frequently and argued heatedly by some that probation and parole are *social work practice* and, as such, require the specialized *professional* training offered by scores of social work schools across the country. Others, with equal conviction and perhaps superior evidence, have pointed out the vast differences which prevail between corrections and social work.

Correctional work is a highly specialized occupation, calling for special training and experience. Though some opinion today favors training of the probation counselor in casework with a psychiatric focus, it stands to reason that broad preparation relating to administration of justice—incorporating such areas as criminology, corrections, and law enforcement—is a vital underpinning of probation and parole work.

Educational requirements now vary considerably, but probation departments should insist on the officer-applicant having completed as the minimum requirement four years of undergraduate training in a college or university leading to a bachelor's degree with a major in corrections, vocational rehabilitation counseling, or social science sequence. Such training, however, is no substitute for such personal characteristics as integrity, tolerance, emotional maturity, initiative, tact, and the ability to work cooperatively and unselfishly with others.

The success of correctional field services is, in no small measure, determined by the quality of the supervision rendered. Unquestionably much of the current criticism of probation and parole should be confined to the inadequacies and inaptitudes of its practitioners rather than to the principles upon which probation is based. It is only with enhanced skill which comes through training and supervised experience that we can hope to raise the performance level and success of correctional practice.

EDUCATION AND TRAINING FOR CORRECTIONS*

One of the prime areas of national concern today relates to crime control and the development of competent personnel to staff our law-enforcement and corrections services.

In this section, I should like to consider several dimensions related to education for the field of corrections. First, I would suggest that education for corrections can be located as a discreet educational area rather than as a sector of sociology, law, psychology, psychiatry, or social work, governed exclusively by the educational models and principles generic to these fields. Admittedly, corrections is subsumed within the broader field of human welfare services which also includes education, medicine, religion, and law, all of which are directed to meet the needs of designated groups within society. Further, a field of practice for people with various professional skills, corrections is a consumer of the products of a number of disciplines and occupational groups which constitute its working parts. But corrections has a unique content as a professional area and, moreover, it contributes its own unique knowledge to the basic disciplines.

Lack of a Unified Field Concept

I do not believe that we have yet achieved a *unified* correctional field, as indicated by the fact that there is a very prominent tendency to view the offender, both juvenile and adult, from a succession of narrow and specialized perspectives among which can be found a police "view," a legal "view," a custodial "view," and a treatment "view." Each of these "views" is divergent, and each lacks a common denominator around which a coherent conception of the correctional process can be organized.

Please recognize that these statements represent generaliza-

* Reprinted from *The Quarterly*. Charles L. Newman: Educational issues and strategies for the field of corrections. *The Quarterly, 24:*(No. 1), Spring 1967.

tions: that police officials feel threatened by any viewpoint which presents the offender as other than an enemy of society; that lawyers act in terms of a classical interpretation of crime in which the law violator is seen as a free moral agent who must pay a suitable penalty for his crime; that social workers, psychologists, and psychiatrists are prone to believe that their task of dealing with human beings should not be affected or impeded by the setting in which they work; and that other specialists within the correctional field defend their domain with equal zeal. The prison officer, unable to find a professional identification, often falls prey to the public demand that the individual be held, with custody as an end in itself. The teacher, the chaplain, the librarian, the shop man, the farm director, and others who work within the correctional field all are chary about making a close identification with the field in which their skills are utilized.

Not only does this pose a serious problem for the field of corrections, but it also makes virtually impossible any discussion of education for the correctional field except in terms of the separate and identifiable groups which make up the professions and subprofessions of the field. Yet such compartmentalization actually defeats what we must ultimately achieve—and that is a unified correctional field.

There are some who will say that such unification is beyond achievement. I think that such conceptual and actual unification can and ultimately will be developed. But first, we are going to have to decide what it is that the correctional field is to accomplish: What are its social ends and purposes; which of the professional disciplines is to carry leadership responsibility; and which of the professional areas will provide the adjunct services? This means, first, that all persons who function within the correctional cycle must see a common purpose in their work. That common purpose is the restoration of the offender to the community with a somewhat more acceptable pattern of behavior than was indicated with his delinquent act. Secondly, this unification suggests a more common bond with the traditions of a larger society which bases its values upon the ultimate worth of the individual in society, regardless of the specific act which may have set the individual apart.

The lack of an integrated philosophy in the corrections field, the struggle to establish a dominant position as to method, and the competition between phases of the correctional cycle are not accidental occurrences, nor should they be naively interpreted as merely someone's inability to see things right. Nor is this a situation which can be resolved by simple discussion and persuasion. Part of our problem stems from the burden of history. But the largest share of the contemporary difficulty stems from a vacuum in leadership.

As a corollary to the confusion in the field of corrections, we find what is almost a situation of chaos in the variety of educational and training programs for personnel in the field of corrections. Training must be training "for something," and as long as we do not know what that "something" is, we cannot say what proper training should be. Some maintain the position that specialized education for corrections should not be developed since the correctional field has not created for itself a definitive philosophy. To my thinking, such a position is indefensible. The university, as the conventional educational center for the professions, has the responsibility not only to provide the setting for learning and to assist in the clarification of objectives for the field, but also to conceptualize training models which will support these objectives.

Any meaningful discussion of professional education for corrections cannot be in terms of the promotion of a single level or timing sequence. Rather, it is desirable that we think in terms of a continuum of learning opportunities to prepare the individuals to meet the needs of the field.

Post-entry Training

Irrespective of the type of educational preparation an individual may have before he seeks a position in a correctional agency, we may rightly assume that he comes with very little knowledge of the fundamental mechanics of agency operation. In the United States, probation and parole agencies and correctional institutions often provide an orientation period and an "apprenticeship," with the subsequent assignment of the new worker to an experienced officer who will continue the orientation process. Some of these programs are formally organized and can be quite valuable to the new worker, not only in terms of providing procedural information but also in terms of providing a general orientation to the philosophy and goals of the agency.

Obviously, some post-entry programs (or perhaps more properly "beginning service" training) are more effectively developed than others. All too frequently, however, the new employee is not given any meaningful instruction beyond an exposure to the "rule book" and is sent forth essentially as a free agent in an unsuspecting society. Elsewhere, departmental training programs are doing a fine job, not only in creating a professional image for personnel but also in instructing them in the basic mechanics of providing effective service to correctional clients and to the community. But in those instances where such beginning service preparation is not offered, the offender is deprived of the help of a well-informed agent.

I would presume that the new person entering the correctional field has the proper motivation to the field—and that he is not coming into the field in order to work out his own emotional problems through his caseload. Moreover, I would note here that neither education nor the lack of it assures us of a stable and emotionally mature individual—and that agency administrators and educators must be constantly alert to individuals who either initially, or eventually, show patterns of emotional behavior which make them unsuited to service in the correctional field.

The length of the post-entry training period will depend upon a variety of factors, not least among which is the ability and demonstrated capacity of the new worker. A coherent "core" program, however, must be established for all new staff. This core post-entry training program in correctional-field or institutional services should include an exposure to the various social resources of the community and region, agency visitation, an exposure to law-enforcement personnel and practices, and visits to correctional facilities for juveniles and adults in the region. Post-entry training continues throughout the individual's tenure in the agency, bringing him up-to-date on changes in agency policy and operation, as well as seeking out his thinking on proposed policy changes.

Staff Development

Over a period of a decade, some people have ten years of developing and growing experiences; others have only a few months experience repeated many times. Basically, the function of staff development programs, as a part of education for the correctional field, is to stretch the latent capacity of the individual worker so that (1) he can do a better job; (2) he can gain more job satisfaction through finding more effective and efficient ways of performing his job; and (3) he can move steadily, as his capacity warrants, into leadership and executive roles.

The university can play a major role in the development and operation of staff development *programs,* which take many forms. (Note the plural—we cannot have a *single program* to meet the needs of all staff since all are at different stages of development.) Many conventional academic courses will have value in the development of the career corrections worker. Special-purpose non-credit courses can also accomplish the upgrading goal.

As was indicated earlier, *post-entry training* involves not only a concentrated exposure to the mechanics of agency rules and practice but also an opportunity to identify with the community in which service is to be rendered. It must be structured in such a way as to enhance a unified view of the correctional process rather than to compartmentalize the individual in a single and unrealistic view of the totality.

Staff development supplements post-entry training. It is, again, structured to meet the needs of the individual for more effective job performance and the personal satisfaction which will ultimately evolve. I believe that the university can, and should, have an important role to play in the staff development process. Conferences, institutes, and workshops can all contribute to the development of the individual, and an opportunity to participate in such activities should be extended to all personnel at line and staff levels.

Pre-entry Education

Pre-entry education and training make up that aspect of professional preparation which involves the person seeking a career opportunity in the corrections field.

We are just beginning to recognize the problems which we are facing in the preparation of individuals for the correctional field. I do not believe that any academic area has a patent on the best method. Political science, psychology, sociology, and legal education leave much to be desired in their educational models. I think that a pattern of education which stresses applicational designs on a strong science base, coupled with practical experience, provides a better fit to needs of the correctional field. I do think that much of what has been taught on the graduate level (e.g., in social work) could be handled quite well by undergraduates, especially since the quality of undergraduate students has improved so markedly in recent years.

I believe that it is unrealistic in contemporary society—where an individual cannot afford the luxury of a protracted education without concern for eventual sources of financial income—that we do not provide a vocational base through which the basic human values are communicated. Thus, the place to begin and to intensify career preparation is in the undergraduate curriculum. We are living in a day of specialization—in an era of the specialist who is likely to become removed from the reality of the larger social plane of which he is unalterably a segment. Thus, while on the one hand we want to enhance an identification with a field of interest, we must guard against the possibility that this interest does not become a removal from the rest of the correctional community.

In keeping with this notion of professional specialization, I must reemphasize that there are *levels and degrees of intensive preparation.* One does not need four years of postgraduate training in medicine in order to do the highly necessary functions of a medical laboratory technician. Yet, one does need a type of intensive preparation based upon the specific definition of the role which the individual plays in the treatment process. Thus, any notion of professional education of the person for the field of corrections must be clearly tied to the role and responsibility that the individual will carry within the field. We are making some progress in that direction through the various standards which are being drawn for the field. But, in large measure, the role definition of the probation officer, the institutional worker, and the parole supervisor will have to come from the field.

Education creates preparation, but preparation must serve the needs of the field. Thus, this is a joint responsibility, shared by the field and the university, for creating an educational experience which will have both utilitarian and broad social value. We have seen a growing emergence of this pattern in all phases of education—in the social as well as the physical sciences. This is a healthy trend. It does not mean that the correctional field controls the direction of education, nor that education controls the field—but rather that they mutually recognize the joint responsibility for the preparation of people for their occupational mission and as community members.

Part of the issue today, in terms of what type of education is necessary, hinges upon the lack of agreement on the sensitivity of specific correctional roles. If the officer in the corrections field functions as a data collector, then he needs one level of training. If we view him essentially as an independent treatment person, with a great deal of decision-making responsibility, then a different intensification of training is necessary. If the institutional officer is a watchman, he needs different educational preparation than if he is a group therapist. This should lead us then to recognize that the content of preparation should be predicated upon the role definition and performance expectation of the corrections agent.

In keeping with the idea of levels of professional education and preparation, I strongly believe that there are some materials which cannot be adequately covered in the four-year period allotted to the undergraduate preparation of the individual. Admittedly, some individuals will lack either the inclination, ability, or interest to go beyond that point. Others will seek a more sensitive role in the structure of their profession and, as a consequence, will need more advanced training.

A Model for Corrections Education at the Four-year Level

In this educational model, it is assumed that the person entering the area of law enforcement and corrections needs a strong base (core content) which is parallel to that provided to students concerned with the social and behavioral science areas, except that the educational content must be organized in such a fashion as to give an applicational focus to content.

In order to assure the broadest coverage which the bachelor's degree denotes, it is vital that the following areas of content discussed below be included in the four-year curriculum.

1. *Organization of Government*
   This content area will be concerned with local, state, and national government, with particular emphasis upon the place of law in the operation of governmental activities. The content would also include a concern with the political structure of society and the role of government in economic activity, including a consideration of the sources and allocation of governmental finances; government as a controller; government as a provider; government as a regulator.
2. *Organization of Society*
   The content of this area should be related to an understanding of American society from a structural-functional frame of reference. In addition, consideration should be given to role, status, culture, class, community, neighborhood, mobility, social problems, race relations and minorities, historical antecedents of Western society, and deviance from a societal perspective.
3. *Organization of the Human Personality*
   The life cycle (conception through senescence) should be considered both from a biophysical and a social psychological perspective. Both normal and abnormal behavior, with special reference to the law violator, should be stressed.
4. *Communications Area*
   The content area should produce skills in written and verbal communication, public information, and report writing.
5. *Concept Formation*
   This area of content should provide an awareness of the logical processes, identification of problems, the scientific method, and the quantification and analysis of data.
6. *Clinical Processes Area*
   This area would provide technical skill in interviewing, treatment models related to the enhancement of social functioning,

control of deviant behavior and the role of the change agent, as well as the array and distribution of human welfare services.

7. *Administration of Justice*

   This content area should be concerned with the progression from arrest to release, crime-producing factors in society, the offender and his control, the rights of the individual under due process, and the correctional apparatus.

8. *Skill Areas*

   Strategically placed within the curriculum, there should be a series of practicum courses related to law enforcement, services of the correctional field, and institutional settings. The practicum, if properly designed, will reinforce the didactic classroom material and provide an opportunity for the individual to test, on an applied basis, the conceptual material he has learned. Each individual should have three different settings for practicum experiences so that he will have exposure to the full array of services within the administration of the justice cycle. Thus, the student will have an awareness and appreciation of those services which precede and/or follow the area of occupational interest and choice. Through the rotation, the individual will have a more professional relationship than he would if his exposure were limited to a single setting.

Conclusion

The challenge of the correctional field now, and in the future, is to restore the individual offender to a productive and law-abiding life.

The correctional field is predicated upon the essential humanitarian values which accept the worthwhileness of every individual. Many offenders do not demonstrate to the larger population that this image of worthwhileness is a correct one.

Thus, it is the mission of the correctional field to guide the offender into patterns of behavior which will restore him to social acceptability and a sense of personal worth. This is not a magical process. We have come to recognize that there are methods and skills needed to implement and accelerate the restorative process. This will not be possible until we have an adequate manpower pool of educated personnel to assist in the restoration, to provide the supervision, and to supply the leadership.

IN-SERVICE TRAINING*

As one of the social institutions specializing in "peoplework," the correctional agency is especially dependent on the quality of its staff if its programed activities are to have positive long-term effect. In-service training of existing agency staff must be the major device for creating a core of competent personnel during the current transitional phase of the professionalization of correctional practice. This thesis does not challenge the importance of preservice training because institutions of higher education are best equipped to provide the high level of prolonged and theoretical instruction essential to development of a correctional profession. Rather, this section assumes that the academic world is not prepared at present to provide the necessary quantity of competent personnel. Universities will have to expand programs for training correctional professionals at an unprecedented rate if personnel requirements are to be met. Fundamental issues have not been resolved.

In-service training has potentiality as a tool for correctional reform through performing functions we shall discuss under the terms *preservation of the agency's social system, development of staff sensitivity,* and *implementation of organizational change.*

The Correctional Agency as a Social System

The correctional agency is supposed to instill in its offender-clients an identification with the total social order and to reorient their attitudes into a more constructive and positive form. In striving to meet these responsibilities, the therapeutic-oriented agency is handicapped by inadequate facilities, insufficient operating budgets, mounting caseloads, and shortage of qualified personnel. The need for specialized training has increased with the awareness of the complexity of behavioral maladjustments and greater resolve in many agencies to improve treatment tactics.

---

* Reprinted from *Criminologica.* Elmer H. Johnson: In-service training: A key to correctional progress. *Criminologica, 4*(No. 3), Nov. 1966. Footnotes are omitted.

When the agency has been able to marshal the higher quality of resources and personnel necessary to meet its obligations, a more elaborate division of labor has created the need to systematize the relationships among staff members and between staff and offender-clients. Informal and personal arrangements have had to be supplanted by codes of formalized rules and deliberately created organizational plans implemented by specialized functionaries skilled in the techniques of bureaucratic administration. This trend has raised the problem of counteracting the formalistic impersonality favored by bureaucratic administration since correctional techniques require individualistic handling of the offender.

The flesh-and-blood human beings who man the bureaucratic structure interact under social and psychological conditions and face everyday situations which only approximate those assumed in abstraction when the formal organizational norms were established. Consequently, informal groupings emerge as a result of the workers' adjustments to the realities of daily situations and their efforts to achieve personal goals which may be distinct from (even conflicting with) formal organizational interests. The executive has the problem of minimizing the adverse effects of informal groups on agency operations. Hopefully, he may be able to enlist the informal groups as a force promoting the ultimate purposes of the agency.

The correctional agency has special urgency in its efforts to motivate its employees. The relationships initiated by staff members are intended to resocialize the offender through learning and internalization of prosocial norms. To initiate and sustain the resocialization process, the staff member must be sensitive to the social and psychological dynamics of interpersonal relationships, be capable of recognizing the offender as a unique and total personality, and be able to coordinate his efforts with other specialists brought together as a team with a particular division of labor. He serves as a behavioral model for clients and as the most immediate and direct symbol of the organization to which they are subject. The formal organization ideally represents a rational plan for mobilizing the talents of the staff to press offenders toward prosocial behavior. But the spontaneity and unpredictability of the dynamic resocialization process counterindicates suppression of the informal relationships developing among staff members and between staff and offenders.

The correctional agency is a social system in that ideological themes, roles, and statuses lend order to the interaction of the individuals comprising the collective whole. The behaviors of agency personnel are given continuity and predictability through persistence of an agency culture developed in the course of the experience of dealing with successive generations of offender-clients; of adjusting to the agency's external environment made up of political, social, and economic forces; and of developing routines of intrastaff cooperation.

The status system of the agency is a means of allocating the agency functions among personnel and provides incentives for effective membership in the work organization. The work functions of the various specialists on the staff are integrated with one another when the job roles press the job holders toward reciprocal behaviors converting individuals into a team.

The agency ideology provides its adherents with an intellectual orientation toward the behavior of themselves and of others within their social universe. The ideology colors the setting of specific goals to be implemented more effectively through changes in staff attitudes and the upgrading of staff competency through in-service training.

Traditionally, penological practice has been based on a punitive ideology which defines the criminal as a peril of life and property, probably incorrigible. In recent decades, another ideology has received increasing support as correction has felt the impact of concepts derived from social welfare, mental hygiene, and social science. The therapeutic ideology views the offender as a person of value with a potentiality for improvement. The focus of attention is upon his personal qualities and his social environment because the major objective is to modify the relationship between these two sets of variables as the means of reducing the criminality through various therapeutic approaches.

The punitive ideology favors the establishment of an authoritarian regime centralizing power at the apex of a high pyramid, symbolizing a sharply limited diffusion of decision-making authority. An authoritarian administration requires indoctrination of the staff in a code of specific rules and in a set of standardized procedures. Efforts to improve staff communication are devoted largely to minimizing the possibility of inaccurate reception of messages and instructions from the top management level. The therapeutic ideology demands individualization of techniques to fit the particular treatment problems posed by the offender-client and his environment. It requires the gaining of rapport with him to enlist his voluntary participation in the rehabilitative process. Compared with authoritarianism, greater permissiveness is granted the client and therapist. The greater diffusion of authority calls for a broader distribution of competence among staff members.

Preservation of the Social System

When any single element, or a set of elements, making up the agency environment is altered, a new permutation of relationships is created. The elements include superior authorities who assign responsibilities and allocate resources to the agency; the quality of agency leadership in terms of ideology, attitude toward reform, and managerial skill; functional relationships with allied agencies; degree of public concern with criminological issues; and the treatment amenability of offender-clients. In-service training is a tool for preserving the equilibrium of the agency's social system because it deals with staff efficiency, one of the common denominators for all elements.

Communication of Policy or Procedural Changes

Preservation of the agency's social system appears to imply conservatism in the use of training to counteract tendencies to upset the *status quo*. But even this use of training requires a recognition of the dynamic relationships among the elements of the agency's environment, with stability a matter of a moving equilibrium. "It takes all the running you can do, to keep in the same place," the Queen told Alice. However, when organizational and ideological change is the assigned goal for training, preservation of the fundamental order of agency activities is still necessary. Training sessions offer the opportunity to inform all parties of the new policies and procedures as a means of avoiding intra-staff conflicts. Communication of the larger significance of changes reassures personnel experiencing status anxiety and affords the basis for maintaining the cooperation essential to effective division of labor.

Readjustment of Division of Labor

Organizational efficiency requires an allocation of work functions to enable each specialist to integrate his efforts with those of other specialists. The agency itself can facilitate administrative disorganization when inconsistencies are incorporated within the employee role or between roles. The parole officer may be expected to maintain surveillance similar to a policeman and simultaneously follow social work practice in reintegrating the parolee into the fabric of community life. Factions of personnel may organize to support specialized goals against the interests of the agency as a whole. Job specialization itself may promote the formation of coalitions. By increasing awareness of the total organizational scheme, in-service training minimizes role conflicts. Furthermore, in the course of work, the employee will encounter unique problems not specifically within his task responsibilities. Over a period of time, the employee may perform tasks not his own in order to expedite handling of a particular case. These informal extensions of his duties may become habitual to the point of interference with the efficiency of the agency's division of labor. In-service training may bring these informal arrangements to light and bring about readjustments in routinized procedures for sake of greater organizational efficiency.

Countering of Bureaucratic Impersonality

The treatment of offenders within rehabilitation-oriented organizations raises the dilemma of organizational discipline versus individual initiative. Bureaucratic organization holds the promise of efficient application of specialized knowledge for more intensive diagnosis and treatment. Expensive personnel and facilities can be utilized more efficiently through rationally developed organization of procedures and occupational roles. However, rehabilitative treatment must be sensitive to the uniqueness of the offender as a person, of the relationship between his background and his behavior, and of the implication of his particular status with the social systems within which his past, present, and future behaviors occur.

The ultimate purposes of treatment are likely to be subverted if offenders are regimented into impersonal categories on the basis of superficial similarities among offenders lending themselves to routine handling when procedures become an end in themselves. Spontaneity in interaction is promoted by raising the staff members' ability to translate theoretical principles into personalized applications to everyday, unpredictable activities while taking advantage of agency resources through adjustment to organizational patterns.

Prevention of Employee Disciplinary Problems

The principle of individualization is applicable also to employee interrelationships. In-service training enhances competence of supervisors in preventing and handling employee disciplinary problems. The staff interactions during training are opportunities for diagnosing employees' potentiality for undisciplined behavior. By restimulating the work drive and clarifying the purposes of agency policies, training reduces the likelihood of employee infractions.

Easing of Employee Tensions

Disciplinary problems among employees are of unusual importance to a correctional agency whose major responsibility is to deal with maladjusted and sometimes hostile persons. To deal effectively with such clients, the staff member must be a behavioral model in self-control, maturity, and insights into oneself. Personal problems of staff members and intrastaff dissension can become destructive to the treatment program by substituting the staff member for the offender as a proper candidate for therapy. Prevention of employee disciplinary incidents involves sensitivity of supervisors to the emotional pressures exerted on correctional workers by their troubled clients and by the conflicts between organizational rules and the individual qualities of both client and staff member. Training sessions raise the employee's tolerance of emotional stress through ventilation, by increasing emotional support from peers, and by raising the employee's faith in his own competence.

Implementation of Organizational Change

Correctional reform involves introduction of fundamental changes to reduce discrepancies between generally accepted goals and existing practices. In-service training may be introduced in the final phase of externally stimulated penal reform. However, in-service training is particularly useful for implementing change stimulated by the agency itself.

Involvement of executives in the very activities to be changed calls for a remarkable degree of objectivity toward a program with which they feel personal identification. However, familiarity with current practices and the realities of correctional work, coupled with a resolve to initiate fundamental changes, places the executive in a favorable position to effect improvements of lasting significance because the changes are more likely to be consistent with the developmental history of the agency. The brand of reform advocated here would alter the agency's status-role system, extend adherence to a therapeutic ideology to the lower levels of staff, and raise the level of competence in the theories and practice of treatment tactics among personnel in direct contact with offenders.

Correctional reform indigenous to the agency has taken several approaches, not necessarily exclusive of one another. Humanitarianism has motivated the easing of the pains of confinement. Administrative procedures have been modernized. New forms of architecture have reduced the foreboding appearance of prisons and, less frequently, have sought to substitute psychological controls for physical restrictions. The adjustment of released prisoners has been promoted.

None of these approaches necessarily involves serious modification of the traditional correctional agency as a social system. These approaches are not specifically directed toward behavior change of offenders, ideological reorientation of staff, and restructuring of intrastaff and staff-offender relationships. There are correctional concepts which do involve these fundamental changes. The therapeutic community is an example of an approach directed toward creating an attitudinal climate whereby all social relationships between staff and inmates contribute to rehabilitation. This concept involves reshaping the social structure of the prison itself to negate the effects of confinement, of the punitive ideology, of the inmate social structure, and of the pathological aspects of bureaucratic organization. The Provo experiment is an example of a similar effort for probation.

In-service training comes into play after superior authorities have committed themselves to reform and have amassed the resources for bringing the proposed changes to fruition. This conception of training is consistent with the use of education as an agent for change. Although the school cannot create a new society independent of the other forces of change, it can contribute to the change process when the group controlling the school permits initiation of change. In-service training can be a vehicle for organizational change in the five respects to be discussed below.

Increasing Adherence to the New Ideology

A social system is an organization of ideas. Therefore, ideological change is basic to reform of the agency's social system. The brand of correctional reform advocated here emphasizes the importance of extending the identification of employees with a new ideology as a key to lasting change. In-service training serves this purpose because it is a means of promoting and facilitating the extent of communication between management and personnel, among staff members, and between agency and experts in allied fields. Training sessions become seminars wherein all persons participate in a common educational experience. Theoreticians and experts from other allied fields introduce new ideas and offer frames of reference to give significance to the discreet events of correctional practice. The employees contribute the empirical experiences of correctional work and give reality to discussions through their concern for concrete applications of the abstract ideas to which they are being exposed.

A climate for ideological change is created because the individual's scope of understanding of his experiences is extended.

The correctional worker is released from the trammels of tradition because he is exposed to unfamiliar ideas and familiar ideas are exposed to critical analysis. The difference itself induces change. The training sessions are implements for creating a tradition of learning, stimulating curiosity, and nurturing a quest for new and diverse knowledge. Furthermore, innovation is encouraged because the training inculcates an atmosphere of anticipation of change. If the employees expect something new, it is more likely to appear than if it is unforeseen and unheralded.

However, it is unrealistic to believe that the possibilities of ideological change are unlimited. The ultimate objectives of training are broken down into interim goals. Each interim goal is beyond present accomplishment but is within the grasp of the employees. As training proceeds through a series of interim goals, the scope of employee acceptance is broadened but never beyond the limits of the employees' expectations. Otherwise, varying degrees of resistance will be encountered to negate achievement of the ultimate goal.

Introduced for the sake of economic benefits, new procedures frequently imply acceptance of new ideas not envisaged by the innovator. Application of the procedure soon involves the agency in adjustments to these ideas. Then the way is open for in-service training to gain staff understanding of, and adherence to, the new ideology which inadvertently had been introduced.

Revision of the Role-status System

To stabilize the social system on the basis of a new status hierarchy and new role norms, the staff members would be oriented to the new organizational structure and the functional relationships pertinent to their particular place in that structure. By breaking down the total reform program into evolutionary stages, training can be planned to implement each stage in its turn. By interpretation of abstract principles into its concrete applications, the training sessions can be adapted to the empirical interests of the workers. The shock of change is reduced by revealing to each worker the benefits to the workers themselves accruing from the increased effectiveness of the agency program. Furthermore, shock is reduced when the worker realizes that the familiar ideas are incorporated within the new ideas to which he is being exposed. His new role is not as divergent from his previous role as he first had feared.

Minimization of Disturbance of Staff Relationships

Changes in the agency's status-role system upset familiar relationships and necessitate adjustment of the employee to new rules for ranking himself and his associates. Status anxiety is likely to be created when newcomers are introduced into the organization to perform new functions. The "older hands" will feel insecure because their familiarity with habitual routines is a lesser asset.

Because anxiety breeds on misinformation, a systematic explanation of the reasons for the changes is an appropriate antidote. Probably the employee already has been dissatisfied with the very conditions to be corrected. These conditions may have brought role conflicts and status anxieties of their own. His new status-role may free him to demonstrate initiative and imagination in ways previously forbidden.

Enlistment of Informal Staff Groups

Earlier we noted the importance of informal relationships in affording the spontaneity essential to support the resocialization process. In seeking to mobilize informal groups to support purposes of the formal organization, in-service training has precedence in that these groups are shaped indirectly by the personnel policies and procedures used in selecting employees from the wider range of persons who present themselves as job candidates. In this sense, the employees select their associates for congeniality groups from personnel who were previously selected according to skills, aptitudes, education, personal characteristics, and prior experience demand appropriate for achieving agency goals. In-service training goes beyond this situation to try to develop a closer affinity between informal and formal group interests.

To enlist the support of informal groups, two-way communication between the levels of the status hierarchy must be opened. The general objectives and treatment tactics have been determined, but there is plenty of latitude remaining for decision making in the details which must be worked out. By listening to subordinates, the administrator can correct the discrepancies between his abstract assumptions in policy making and the concrete realities faced in implementing policies. Because the individual employee has a chance to participate, there is a greater possibility that his daily activities will more closely correspond with the requirements set by the formal organization.

Raising Staff Competence

Competence for what purpose? What kinds of competence? What level of competence should be sought? How will the competence be brought to bear upon the recurrent problems characteristic of the agency's activities? Attempts to answer these difficult questions soon involve one in the study of the social system of the agency as it is and as it is hoped to be. Because in-service training must conform to the political principle of seeking the possible, study conclusions will vary with the particular opportunities available to the agency within its particular environment and its present state. It is useful to consider the level of competence one can realistically expect to achieve within a reasonable period of time.

The elementary level of competence is achieved through an orientation type of training. The new employee receives instruction in the functions and procedures of the agency to enable him to integrate his work within the total system of job positions. New employees, lacking of desired quality, will be upgraded when the tasks do not require extensive and prolonged instruction. Training sessions return the experienced employee's attention to the fundamental principles of his organization. Reexamination of the relationship between his tasks and the agency's purposes will serve as an intellectual refresher, restoring the zest of challenge to work which has become routine.

The intermediate level of competence calls for application of criminological principles to empirical practice, but at a level within the grasp of personnel unlikely to have more than a high school education. Emphasis is placed on concrete applications of theories.

The advanced level of competence implies that a substantial proportion of the staff has undergone intensive preservice training. Knowledge and skills already possessed are given new meanings through reassessment in the course of studying problems encountered by the agency. Common interests with allied academic disciplines are revealed through common study of problems by diverse specialists. This level of competence is the ultimate objective toward which the elementary and intermediate levels are interim stages.

Development of Sensitivity

Since all criminological practice entails to some degree the diversion of criminal behavior into socially approved channels, in-service training has the goal of enhancing the ability of the correctional worker to motivate the offender to change his behavior.

The worker-offender interactions take place within an environment made up of a host of visual and auditory stimuli which must be interpreted if meaningful behavior is to occur. Social behavior requires selection out for attention of only a fraction of the stimuli present in a situation. The criteria for selection affect what the actor perceives in a situation and how he evaluates what he selects for attention and action. Both the worker and the offender select a fraction of the stimuli according to the frame of reference each has brought to the situation. The frame of reference is made up of values, feelings, and assumptions which prestructure the observer's orientation to the situation. Rehabilitation is a process of reducing the discrepancies between the offender's frame of reference and the one the correctional worker has the duty to support.

Sensitivity, the capacity to respond to stimulation, is involved in two general ways. The worker must view the situation as the offender sees it if the worker is to contribute actively to creation of situations which move the offender from one form of conduct to another. The offender must be sensitized to the inadequacies of his habitual orientation to his social universe.

Psychology's conception of sensitivity centers on accuracy of perception. In this sense, sensitivity refers to a capacity to assess visual and auditory stimuli in a meaningful way. However, the perceptions must be integrated within an intellectual framework of concepts if observation is to result in knowledgeable assessment. For example, Korn and McCorkle imagine two professional criminologists assessing routine activities in a cell block. The first visitor is impressed favorably by a guard's close contacts with the inmates. The second visitor, more experienced in prison administration, soon detects evidence that the prisoners are manipulating the guard to conceal transgressions of prison rules. Because of more experience and theoretical insights, the second criminologist was able to select those aspects of the situation which were crucial to the task of inspection. His training had made him intellectually sensitive in his selection of crucial stimuli from the host of stimuli present in the cell block.

Social psychological sensitivity is synonymous with "empathy," "diagnostic skill," or "understanding others." Empathy implies an intuitive process whereby one is able to take the role of the other through "feeling" his situation. Diagnostic and therapeutic tasks require interpersonal understanding and skills which penetrate beyond superficialities to the covert meanings of behavior. Efficient task performance is complicated when the offender has undergone experiences and personality conditioning not shared personally by the correctional worker. Sociocultural and personality theories offer a framework for formal training of personnel as a means of increasing sensitivity to orientations the worker has not experienced personally.

Sensitivity toward self is a vital quality to be developed in the correctional worker because his own personality is a major ingredient of therapy. Through training, he is helped to build a mirror to see himself as an actor in a social system which encompasses interactions of staff members and offenders within the structure of correctional programs. He is sensitized to new modes of evaluating his own behavior through new awareness of the dynamics of the sociocultural environment within which his tasks are performed. By gaining insights into himself, the worker develops greater sensitivity toward others and greater effectiveness in interpersonal relationships.

In emphasizing the importance of in-service training, Giardini has drawn from his empirical experience in parole administration to offer practical principles which are appropriate for bringing this discussion to a close. The administrative heads must be convinced that in-service training is desirable. Training should encompass all members of the staff and should be formulated as much as possible by all members of the agency. It should be in continuous operation, at least in the sense of planning. It should be repeatedly reevaluated as to its aims, effectiveness, and results. It should be under competent leadership and carefully planned by experts in the behavioral sciences, educational methodology, and social administration. This latter point is consistent with a major theme of this section: that understanding of the agency as a social and ideological system is vital to effective use of in-service training as a tool for correctional progress.

THE PROBATION OFFICER AND HIS PERSONALITY*

We hold that the probation officer's personality, with the use he makes of it in helping his clients, is his most potent therapeutic tool. Those who agree with this proposition will necessarily include probation work among the helping arts. Its kinship with psychiatric and casework help will be assumed. Furthermore, those who agree with this proposition will see important implications for probation service in a statement on interpersonal relations recently appearing in the *Menninger Clinic Bulletin:* "The physician's personality is one of, if not *the* most potent therapeutic tool he can use." And they will appreciate a paraphrase of Somerset Maugham's insight as to the core problem of writing: "All the probation officer has to offer, when you come down to brass tacks, is himself."

We are not considering here such elements of probation work as procedures, practices, and regulations, but rather the more subjective elements—the intangibles, personal attributes, qualities of character—which are at the heart of a probation officer's service. The impatient or the overly scientific may turn away from this approach. For them, it may seem too elusive, not susceptible of scientific proof. Admittedly, discussion of qualifications for

---

* Reprinted by permission of *Federal Probation.* Edmund G. Burbank and Ernest W. Goldsborough: The probation officer's personality: A key factor in rehabilitation. *Federal Probation, 18*(No. 2):11-14, June 1954. Footnotes are omitted.

practicing an art partakes of the emotional, of imponderables. These are qualities that refuse to lend themselves to precise measurement or to yield to impatient urgings. We gladly admit the inconclusiveness and the uncertainties. But we believe that even though there are no precise formulae or systems of measurements for the development of healing personalities, the professionals who operate in our courts have, through the years, acquired a certain wisdom. While they cannot make silk purses out of sow's ears, they can make pretty good probation officers out of those who at first appear not too promising.

Previously we made some assumptions. The first is that personalities are capable of change, that is, probation officers are made and not born. The second is that knowledge and skill are available to help bring out the best in the personality of a probation officer. If there is agreement on these two assumptions, then it seems to us that the first problem confronting the court is to decide what it wants the probation officer to become and, second, how the office should be set up to achieve that end. We are concerned here with those two problems. We suspect it is easier to catalogue an acceptable list of personality attributes of a probation officer than to spell out how such attributes are developed. Always, in the field of rehabilitation, the important point is *how do you do it?*

Some Cardinal Qualities of Personality

Probation work, in common with the other healing arts, requires a mature and well-integrated personality. The overriding motive, the wider purpose, and the deepest plan of the probation officer will be reflected in his day-to-day achievements. Those achievements of the task, if properly done, will reflect an implicit faith in the capacity of his probationer to grow. The demands on an officer are great, for he is working with persons who almost always are playing a dangerous game. Yet, even while affirming the ultimate value of genuine personal integrity, we are bound to recognize that each officer will have weaknesses. The better part of integrity, as of wisdom, is to acknowledge weakness—to recognize and acknowledge our particular prejudices, defenses, blind spots, and areas of inadequate knowledge. Conceal or rationalize them as we will, they are bound to affect our job performance in one way or another. It is no sin to possess such weaknesses and limitations; the sin is denying them, unrepentantly inflicting them on others, and continuing to work with other human beings without first trying to discipline ourselves.

More specifically, the probation officer should have both maturity and integrity, which comprise five cardinal qualities of personality.

1. *The ability to form and sustain wholesome interpersonal relationships.* In probation work, the officer needs the capacity to identify with a wide range of people. He will work with the "white collar" criminal and the defective delinquent, the addict and the alcoholic, the homosexual and the homicidal. The degree to which the officer cares for what happens to his client, whatever the offense and whatever the cultural background, will be reflected in a thousand ways as he proceeds with his daily tasks —"The outer trend confirms the inner pattern." If the inner pattern of the probation officer is to confuse the delinquent deed with the whole life of the man committing it, the outer trend—the achieved result—will show a judgmental, intolerant probation officer. If the inner pattern of the officer is devotion to the cause of helping the offender to summon up his own vision of the better life, to muster his own strength to achieve that better life, then the outer trend—the achieved result—will show a probation officer with a healing personality.

2. *The ability to accept responsibility for the authority he carries.* This ability is not easily won. Many an adult is unwilling to face his infantile attitudes toward authority. He will not willingly yield to the rightful and inevitable demands which life with other people compels. Nor will he always give proper consideration to the impact his own authority has upon those subject to it. The probation officer who is an adult accepts authority as a condition of everyday living—a process of disciplining our individual impulses and desires for the mutual benefit of all. Probation signifies that the offender is out of tune with the social demands of the community. The probation officer who represents authority must use it firmly but tempered with judgment and understanding. If he has the proper measure of his own adequacy, he will not yield

to his own need to superimpose his power and control over one who is in his care. He will view his essential task as helping the probationer decide on a course of action.

Long ago, Galileo wrote: "You cannot teach a man anything; you can only help him to find it within himself." In keeping with this sage advice, the probation officer can help the probationer to find within himself the power and readiness to decide on a course of action, the power and readiness to use relationships constructively. The probationer will never accept a condition—or an officer—he cannot respect. He may kowtow and conform, but he will inwardly despise and rebel and will not grow in responsibility. We are aware of no more trenchant thinking on the conditions of personality change, whether applied to probation or parole officer, probationer or parolee, than is contained in the following excerpt:

> the individual personality and behavior pattern invariably and inevitably changes, if it changes at all, from the individual's own motivations, from his own choices, from his own efforts to attain his own satisfactions. No decisions made under duress or by somebody else are binding upon the individual when he is free. No behavior based upon fear is maintained when danger is past. The one absolutely indispensable foundation of any effort to correct unacceptable patterns of behavior, or to sustain new, acceptable patterns—which is the basic aim of (parole)—is that the responsibility for that behavior shall remain, always and throughout, with the individual. And the one essential skill required in the administration of a helping service directed to this end is the disciplined ability to develop and maintain a helping relationship in which the individual remains always free, and always obliged to accept and discharge—never to evade—his own responsibility for his own choices and judgements and their consequences. The only help which anyone can give to another person toward accepting new patterns of behavior is to afford the opportunity for clearly facing and steadily clarifying the available alternatives of action and their potential consequences, and to sustain the individual's strength to face the realities and to accept responsibility for the choices he does and must make.

3. *Ability to work with aggressive persons.* The probation officer, as has been well said, must have "strength and some immunity in facing extreme aggression and hostility because some responsibilities in this field include ability to meet hazardous situa-

tions where the awareness of the need as well as the ability to take calculated risks is essential."

The probation officer will not always find his charges obviously aggressive. Their hostility is revealed in more subtle ways. Real tears must be distinguished from crocodile tears. Scenes of rage or despair are often admirably staged. To acknowledge this does not in itself make it easier for the probation officer to do his job, but somehow he must learn to work with all types of aggression and maintain a high degree of objectivity and poise.

4. *Ability to work with other agencies and people.* The type of person who must be the star of the show is out of place in a probation office. This is true, first of all, because the key person is the probationer. It is in his power to use or abuse the proffered service. Secondly, probation work is too complicated and difficult to provide space for a prima donna. Those of us responsible for helping human beings need all of the assistance we can get. The diversity and perversity of human personality are so extensive that no one person and no one discipline has a cure-all. We can operate more effectively by pooling our resources of information and talent for the good of the probationer and the community.

5. *Ability to improve in performance.* This, of course, implies change for the probation officer as he works on the job. It is surely not unreasonable to expect and require this for the person who expects and requires change in his probationer. It is altogether too easy to see and stress the probationer's faults and shortcomings; not so easy to see or to discipline one's own. Yet it is elementary that there is no helping possible if the helper cannot distinguish his own emotions from those of the client. It is of great importance to be sure that rightful insistence upon the offender's assuming responsibility for his own conduct is not the product of an officer's own laziness; not an attempt to justify an officer's own indifference or unwillingness to reach out; not a community rationalization for niggardly supply of legitimate and essential probation services.

The great Roman writer Juvenal once asked a profound question which has echoed down the corridors of the history of government for two thousand years: "Who shall guard the guards themselves?" His question rephrased: Who shall help the helpers themselves? That question takes us to the second part of our inquiry. We have stated what in general the probation officer should become. Now we must examine how we might set up the office so that the probation officer has the best chance of becoming that kind of a person.

There is no need here to detail widely known and accepted principles which, when taken together, comprise a sound code of personnel practices. Standards and procedures for recruitment and for the payment of personnel are readily available. Optimum caseload and the proper allocation of time between presentence investigations and supervision of probationers are subjects of frequent discussion and written analysis. While these are aids to good performance on the job, in our judgment, there is need to dwell on questions which are too often begged. *Who helps the helper and how is it done?* Probation officers are not born with helping skill nor is it thrust upon them. It is acquired. It is acquired either in a professional school of social work or in in-service training. In any event, it is acquired in a probation office.

Atmosphere of the Court and Probation Office

The most important thing about a probation office is its spirit, its atmosphere, the morale of its staff. Its tone is set, above all, by the judge or the board of judges. We do not mean to be in contempt of court when we suggest, therefore, that the five cardinal qualities of a probation officer's personality apply equally to the judges. When the probation office, as an arm of the court, is viewed as a setting in which growth of skill and development of adult responsibility take place, no special wisdom is required to appreciate the importance of the breezes which blow from the judge's chambers. The memories of too many probation officers are filled with crosscurrents of unjudicial, antisocial attitudes of some judges. They recall vividly that Judge X had confidence in his probation officers, discussed cases with them freely, and, most important of all, relied on the probation officer's judgment. They recall Judge Y, a martinet, with contempt of probation and those who came within the jurisdiction of the court. Multiply Judge X and Judge Y two or three times to account for the larger board of judges and let your imagination paint the picture of the chaotic atmosphere of the probation office and the frustration of its officers.

The atmosphere of the probation office cannot be overstressed because it sets the condition in which a job is done by many people. A healthy court atmosphere implies high standards of probation performance. New officers, and old, in such a setting are expected to carry the type of responsibility which demonstrates increasingly their integrity and maturity. What we are saying is this: The atmosphere of a probation office reveals the degree of integration of purpose and, in the last analysis, the level of performance and effectiveness in discharging its responsibility to clientele and community. Who more than the judges are in a position to set the spirit of the court and its office? If they want it to be subject to improper political influences, it will be. If they want loyal, creative, competent personnel, the judges can do more than anyone else to insure it. Who helps the helper? Part of our answer is that the judges do.

The Probation Officer Can Always Learn

Mindful that an administrative chain is no stronger than its weakest links, the chief probation officer and supervisory staff are other links in the chain of those who help the helper. The function of supervisory staff is to assist the probation officer in evaluating the assets and liabilities of *his* personality as it relates to his role in helping his charges achieve acceptable changes in their behavior. The focus of supervision should be on the officer's learning and performance on the job.

What must he be required to learn? At the very least, these five abilities which we have already characterized as the mark of maturity and integrity of the probation officer.

First, he must move substantially beyond his former prejudices, defenses, blind spots, and limitations in order to enhance his ability to sustain wholesome interpersonal relationships.

Second, how he has used supervision should reveal his unmistakable attitude toward authority and dependency. The very attitudes which inhibit his use of supervision will invariably limit his capacity to help his charges.

Third, as with the probationer, an officer's attempt to examine his own weak spots is met with varying degrees of aggressive and subtle resistance. The probation officer must demonstrate his ability to understand and discipline his own aggression and resistance.

Fourth, no probation officer possesses the key which unlocks the door to any one man's problem. It is, therefore, essential to make use of all available knowledge and insights which other agencies in the community may possess from their contacts with the probationer.

Fifth, if the probation officer is not concerned about his level of performance and is unwilling or unable to make a different and more constructive use of supervision, then he is not the man for the job. Is the probation officer not concerned with helping a probationer begin to make constructive use of supervision? Does he not have to help him understand the problem with which he is struggling to accept and to conform to community standards? Is he not concerned with helping the probationer find a different and more satisfying solution to his way of life? Acceptable standards of performance are a rightful expectation of the court and the community. To demand acceptable performance from probation officers without helping them to achieve this end is just as false as placing a man on probation and allowing him to go it alone. We affirm there should be no probation without supervision for the probation officer. One needs help to achieve the degree of objectivity, maturity, and self-discipline necessary to help probationers.

It is in this spirit, we think, that Judge Elwood Melson is writing when he defines the responsibility of the court in these words:

> It is, I believe, to create those conditions and that atmosphere which, within the court's limitations, are most conducive to the production of change.
>
> Again, experience has taught me, and I believe will teach any other judge who is able and willing to learn, that there is nothing, absolutely nothing, which will better create the conditions and atmosphere most conducive to change, than the employment and the complete integration within the authority of his court, of a tech-

nically trained staff of skilled and thoroughly understanding probation officers working under trained, skilled supervision.

Not until this has been done, will the court have discharged its responsibility to the community.

For centuries, the Western world has known that man can be free only through mastery of himself—free, that is, to assume his inescapable responsibility for meeting the obligations of community living. Part of the challenge of our era is to provide the proper atmosphere and setting for probation officers to develop the kind of skill to become the persons who really help probationers to achieve more responsible behavior.

Chapter Five

Probation Investigation, Selection, and Revocation

THE primary purpose of a preliminary probation investigation is to aid the court in making an informed disposition of a case. When the court knows the offender's previous behavior, reasons for it, and circumstances surrounding it, the decision as to the type of treatment needed will be more easily determined. In a sense, probation investigation is analogous to the thorough medical diagnostic examination, in which the etiology and disposition of the illness are determined and therapy is recommended on the basis of evaluation of diagnostic material.

As a diagnosis is not discarded when treatment of an illness is initiated, so the preliminary probation investigation is used by the probation officer as a guide to supervision and, under other circumstances, by the prison classification and other authorities, and perhaps ultimately by the parole agent. It stands to reason that neither probation officers, prison correctional staff, nor the parole personnel can be expected to assist intelligently those under their supervision without adequate information as the basis for such advice and guidance.

Though in some jurisdictions the probation officer may make recommendations regarding the disposition of the case, it is the court which is vested with the power to impose probation or other form of treatment—likewise, the power to determine the conditions or requirements to be imposed on probationers. Sometimes conditions are pecuniary, in the form of restitution, the payment of fines or other assessments, or the support of dependents.

Statutory provisions regarding the duration of the probation period vary greatly from state to state. In some jurisdictions, it is assumed that the term of probation should be analogous to a period of incarceration and, as a consequence, the maximum term allowable for a particular offense is generally imposed. In other states, a maximum period, generally not exceeding five years of probation supervision, is assigned. Elsewhere, the probation period is apparently subject to no limit, and the assignment is made entirely at the discretion of the court.

It appears obvious then, that there is no uniformity in the probation period in the United States. Likewise, it can be assumed that there is an unevenness in the quality and type of investigation which precedes assignment of probation. Certainly, also, selection is based upon a multiplicity of factors, sometimes the least used among which is the offender's capacity to benefit from the period of community supervision. Yet there is no disagreement among those who are well informed in the probation field that the adjustment factor should be the one of prime consideration in the selection of individuals for probation.

Although there is no standard form for all preliminary probation investigations, the following outline provides a guide which should be useful to all persons concerned with the preparation of a report of investigation.

PRELIMINARY INVESTIGATION FOR PROBATION*

A. The Legal History of the Offender

1. *Offender's Previous Court and Institutional Record*
   Brief statements about police contacts and past offenses including mitigating and aggravating circumstances surrounding each offense, if such information is available. If previously imprisoned, how did offender behave during his incarceration according to institutional reports? If offender has been on probation or parole, state his reaction to such correctional treatment and recorded results as reported by probation and parole authorities.
2. *Statement of the Present Offense*
   State accurately dates, time, place, and manner in which the offense was committed. State whether offender has been in detention or on bail, for how many days and what amount. Information under this section will generally be obtained

* Reprinted by permission of the New York State Division of Probation. From *Manual for Probation Officers*, 5th ed., rev., 1945, pp. 128-133.

from court records, complainant, witnesses, codefendants, etc. Record offender's attitude toward, and behavior while in, detention.

3. *Statement of the Complainant*
   Describe complainant's attitude toward offense and offender, and feelings regarding disposition of the case.
4. *Statement of the Offender Concerning the Present Offense*
   Occasional use of offender's own words—when they typify his attitudes, education or otherwise individualize him—may be advisable.
5. *Mitigating and Aggravating Circumstances of the Offense*
   a. General. Was the offender a leader, a follower, or a "lone wolf" in the commission of crime? Was the offender intoxicated or under the influence of narcotics when crime was committed? Did offender resist arrest? If weapon was used in perpetration of crime, when, where, and why was it obtained? Has offender cooperated with the law-enforcing agency and to what extent? (Identification of confederates and assistance in recovering proceeds of the crime.) Does injured party fear reprisals because of the arrest?
   b. Crimes Against Property. Was there a series of crimes? Amount of property damaged or stolen? How much has been recovered and still remains unrecovered? What became of the stolen property? Was complainant insured? Was complainant reimbursed by surety company and to what extent?
   c. Crimes Against the Person. What is the extent of complainant's injuries? (Working time lost—expenses incurred by complainant—permanent injuries, etc.)
   d. Sex Offenses. Age, education, mental condition, religion, reputation, and chastity of complainant. Has complainant acquired a social disease or become pregnant? Has there been an offer of marriage and what are the attitudes of the parties involved toward each other and their situation? Other pertinent social data concerning complainant and complainant's family.

6. *Codefendants*

Record their dispositions by the court. Are codefendants friendly or antagonistic toward defendant?

B. OFFENDER'S SOCIAL HISTORY

1. *Early Life and Education*

Give date and place of birth. Vertify ages whenever necessary to determine court jurisdiction and disposition (i.e. eligibility for commitment to institutions with age restrictions). Describe outstanding events or circumstances in his early life such as separation, desertions, or divorce of parents; an unnatural home environment; placement in an orphanage, boarding home, or institution; early training and supervision of offender. Relationships between the offender, his parents, guardian, relatives, and companions. Attitudes and behavior of offender during early life. His reaction to various types of discipline. Information about children's court record may be placed in this section rather than under "legal history" on face sheet if so desired.

Information about offender's school attendance record, school behavior record, and school work record should be included in this section. What are reasons, if any, for his failure to make a school adjustment? What are opinions of the teachers who came in contact with him?

2. *Employment and Economic History*

Describe work habits, cooperation or lack of same, and types of work done. State and, if necessary, discuss reasons for changes in employment. What are employers' opinions of offender? If offender is unemployed, give reasons for same; describe efforts to secure work and attitudes concerning same. Include information about Army, Navy, Marine, Air Force, and Coast Guard service.

State all sources of income. State assets of offender both in real and personal property. Generally state obligations of offender. Degree of detail in this section will depend upon the type of case. If restitution or support payments may be expected, more detail will be needed to prove degree of financial ability to pay.

3. *Character, Habits, Associates and Leisure-time Activities*
   Record available information about offender's use of alcohol and narcotics, sex practices, and gambling. If excesses are noted which direct relationship to offender's criminal behavior, greater detail will be necessary. With what type of person does offender associate? How do offender's associates influence him? How does offender use leisure time (hobbies, types of reading and active membership in fraternal organizations)?
4. *Marital History*
   If offender is married, describe circumstances surrounding marriage (childhood romance, short courtship, premarital pregnancy, etc.), date and place, and by whom performed. Describe compatibility; for separations, divorces, and subsequent marriages, relate same information as required for the original marriage. Describe the role of each parent in raising the children and children's attitude toward offender.
5. *Religious Training and Observances*
   Faith, name, and address of church; name of priest, minister or rabbi. Describe offender's frequency of attendance and attitude toward the effect of religion. Is there a difference of religion in the home and how does it affect the family life?
6. *Mental and Physical Condition*
   Describe diseases which may have materially affected or limited in any way offender's normal physical and social development or future social adjustment. If offender has been examined by a psychologist or psychiatrist, give summary of report and give direct quotation of any recommendation made by these authorities. State when and by whom mental and/or physical examination was given.
7. *Offender's Family History*
   a. Wife and Children. Give brief history of wife and her role in offender's personality and social growth. Significant information about wife and children which has bearing upon the case. In abandonment and out-of-wedlock cases, give *verified* birth dates of children.
   b. Parental. Describe offender's father, giving age (year of

birth), occupation, personality, attitude toward offender, and any special characteristics which may have particularly affected offender and which bear upon his present situation. If convicted of a crime, give pertinent information concerning conviction. If deceased, give cause, circumstances, and date of death which may be important.

c. Maternal. Same information. (If offender raised by persons other than his parents, give above information regarding them.)

d. Brothers and Sisters. Pertinent information regarding their activities and attitudes toward offender. Behavior which has or may have some relationship to offender's behavior.

8. *Home and Neighborhood Background*

Describe type of home and neighborhood, length of residence in this home, its general cleanliness, adequacy and atmosphere (cheerful, drab, etc.), facilities in the neighborhood for social resources and recreational outlets. If present home is an elevation or decline in family standard, state causes and results.

9. *Community Attitude Toward the Offender*

Describe neighborhood and community attitude toward defendant and his offense, if obtainable.

C. OTHER INFORMATION

1. *Resources Available for Treatment*

Summarize pertinent findings of resources and agencies, which have attempted to aid offender, reported by the Social Service Exchange or Central Index; describe their impressions and prognosis if not included under another topical heading. Also describe any resources which are available as potentially constructive factors (job, interested relative, etc.).

2. *Summary of the Investigation*

This section should briefly sum up the situation (describe and analyze in an unbiased manner). It should contain both assets and liabilities in their relative weight and importance. This section should be a clear and honest picture of offender and should afford the court an opportunity to be aware of offender as a whole.

Recommendation by the probation officer should be based on the findings of the investigation. In his role as an unbiased third party, the probation officer's recommendation should be logical and have basis in the body of the report. (Investigation report to be signed by the probation officer who made the investigation and to be approved by chief probation officer.)

3. *Judgment of the Court*

   If this is included on face sheet, no repetition is necessary.

HIDDEN FACTORS IN PROBATION RECOMMENDATIONS*

Many of us can recall our school-day participation in "bull sessions" held in a back booth over beer mugs, from which we emerged with an exhilarating sense of having "really let our hair down" and of having done some mutual "soul searching" with our friends. Recently, I had the opportunity to enjoy a similarly rewarding and stimulating experience when I attended an informal bull session held by a group of probation officers whose primary function is to make a presentence investigation of adult candidates for probation in the criminal courts.

This group met for the express purpose of candidly inquiring into its collective conscience regarding some of the less obvious factors which may, under certain circumstances, consciously or unconsciously influence the probation officer's recommendation to the court in individual cases. The discussion turned around several rather disturbing questions which the group agreed were well worth a frank exploration.

As in any such bull session, no formal type of record was kept of the conversation, and the following highlights, based on my rough notes, can impart only some small flavor of the group's pattern of thought as it evolved through the spirited discussion. I found the experience enjoyable, provocative, and worth shar-

---

* Reprinted with permission from *Crime and Delinquency*. Chester H. Bartoo: Some hidden factors behind a probation officer's recommendations. *Crime and Delinquency,* 9(No. 3):276-281, July 1963.

ing with others in the correctional field who at times may have asked themselves questions similar to those that follow.

Tendency to Avoid Problems

Do we tend to recommend that probation be denied when a probationary plan would present knotty and complex problems that we prefer to avoid? The frankness called for and elicited from the group by this first question set the tone for the entire session. The group agreed that we may, in certain cases and under certain circumstances, be led into recommending denial of probation because of the complexity and immensity of the task we would have to face in working out a practical program as an alternative. This temptation to take the easy way out would probably be strongest in times of stress and heavy caseloads. As caseload demands become heavier and time more limited, we subconsciously become more aware of, and concerned over, the tremendous volume of time-consuming correspondence to other jurisdictions and institutions that would be necessary in order to work out and support a recommendation for probation. And when the defendant is a rather questionable risk for such a program in the first place, we often tend unconsciously to be moved more by "personal convenience" than we care to admit, and we find it more comfortable to rationalize our decision as based upon "other factors." The group concluded that, under stress, we should be particularly careful to watch for a hidden factor in our thinking, be cognizant of it if it is present, and make every effort to keep it from influencing our professional decisions.

In cases where the chance for success on probation is small, do we nevertheless tend to recommend the grant of probation to avoid conflict? The group considered this question somewhat similar to the first and agreed that the "comfort factor" might conceivably influence our thinking, especially when a dubious case for probation is being considered. Sometimes, when we know that our judges are strongly in favor of placing certain types of offenders on probation and when we are otherwise "on the fence" in our thinking, we may be swayed into recommending probation because it is more comfortable to conform than to take a more unpopular stand. Nevertheless, the group felt that a professional person usually tries conscientously to base his judgments on his training and experience and on the actual facts of the case in question. Few competent officers in the field are consistently "on the fencers"; most of them base their decisions on the facts of their investigation rather than on personal convenience or their desire for harmony.

Community Interest and Public Opinion

To what extent does consideration for "the best interests of the community" influence our recommendations? The best interests of the community as an influencing factor in our decisions was a topic that evoked considerable discussion. What exactly *are* the best interests of a community? Replies ranged from taxes to physical protection, but the group's general feeling was that anything in any way affecting the community was *ipso facto* a matter of community interest and concern. Since the probation officer is an employee as well as a member of the community and is charged with making decisions which, if implemented, will affect the community to some extent in every case, the community's best interests are involved in every recommendation he makes. The group agreed that our prime concern, therefore, must be for the protection of the community and only secondly for the best interests of the offender.

In connection with this topic, an interesting side discussion took place in which it was pointed out that new officers fresh from schools or training programs are often inclined to recommend probation in every case which offers some hope that the defendant's behavior and attitude might be favorably modified thereby. Often, they feel that the goal of rehabilitation serves the best interests of the community and justifies any risk that may be entailed in releasing the offender on probation. While more seasoned officers would agree that any program which offers some hope of rehabilitating the offender is worthwhile, they are more apt to evaluate carefully the degree of risk he may present to the community before recommending probation. For example, a program of counsel and psychotherapy admittedly might be valuable in the long-range treatment of a child molester or a serious narcotics offender and might be a sound enough reason for granting probation supervision combined with outpatient therapy. On the other hand, placing on probation an offender with such proclivities can be risky—especially in the early stage —before the therapy has become effective. While the benefits of treatment without the stigma of a prison commitment would seem the most desirable choice in terms of the defendant's own eventual welfare, the probation officer formulating his recommendation must not lose sight of his prime obligation to protect the community. Hence, the more seasoned officer might very well conclude that the crucial initial stage of a treatment program could be applied more safely in the controlled institutional setting of a state prison medical facility (to be followed up by a period of close parole supervision) rather than in the community through a grant of probation.

The group was genuinely disturbed over the apparent schism between the probation officer's training and his method of actual operation, and felt that this dichotomy needed to be resolved.

How and to what extent does currently expressed "public opinion" affect our recommendations in probation reports? This topic evoked some spirited discussion as to what "public opinion" really is. Someone pointed out that the opinions expressed by political speakers, newspapers, periodicals, radio, and television do not necessarily represent public opinion but may, on the contrary, be attempts to mold or influence it for private interests. In some areas of the world where the mass media are strictly under governmental control, it becomes almost impossible to determine true public opinion or to judge the extent to which the media do represent or have influenced the thinking of the people. In our communities, any of the media making a deliberate attempt to influence public thinking may in the end actually come to represent the thinking of large numbers of people who have accepted the imposed opinions as their own. The group concluded that the true opinion of a mass public is almost impossible to ascertain at any given time, but that it could be regarded as that which was currently expressed in the various mass media. If so, then publicly expressed opinion cannot help having some influence on our own thinking—although the group disagreed on the extent and direction of the influence. As an example, someone mentioned the editorial notice and supportive comment given a series of locally published articles which criticized the granting of probation in any narcotics case. Just how much influence these articles had on members of the group can be judged from some of their own comments which follow:

"We cannot call ourselves professionals if we allow ourselves to be pushed into decisions by the newspapers!"

"Being aware of what the public is reading or being told about our field is part of the necessary ongoing education of any professional person. However, we should seek to evaluate its validity and to take this into consideration in seeking to better our own public relations."

"Perhaps the correctional field needs to play a larger part in helping to mold public opinion. Mass media could be used for this purpose to present the public with what we are trying to accomplish."

"Because we deal with problem cases every day in our work, familiarity makes them seem less serious to us than to the public, which reads only about the spectacular aspects. Perhaps occasional public criticism will tend to keep us more alert and sharpen our own perspective."

"Our professional role does not justify our ignoring expressed public opinion; the challenge of differing concepts helps to keep our own thinking fluid and dynamic."

Our Own Attitudes

To what extent do our moral standards, codes of ethics, and attitudes influence our decision to recommend probation? The group felt that a person's own standards and codes inevitably color his judgment of others but that the professional worker is generally aware of this and must conscientiously make every effort to view and evaluate each of his clients as objectively as possible. The group, of course, was aware that mere recognition of one's own subjectivity is not in itself protection against complacency. Frequent self-review is necessary for every officer wishing to maintain his objectivity.

To what extent might conscious or unconscious identification with the defendant or his problems tend to influence our recom-

mendation? Some sort of identification always takes place in every officer-client relationship, but most professional workers are aware of this and make every effort to keep it under control. A certain amount of empathy can promote better understanding and enhance case insight, while a complete lack of identification with the client can make for an extremely rigid relationship and poor insight into the client. Equally undesirable is the other extreme, overidentification, an unconscious reaction formed for the most part by the less experienced investigators. Group members suggested that when a worker becomes conscious that he is overidentifying with his client, he should make every effort to compensate for it or, if he cannot, should even ask to be relieved of the particular case. If, on the other hand, he is not aware of his overidentification, he may have to wait until he discusses the case with others—when his overidentification will either become self-evident or be pointed out to him—before he can do anything about the situation.

To Avoid Severity of Penalty

Do we sometimes recommend probation for obviously dubious subjects because of the extreme severity of the alternative? In considering probation for somewhat questionable risks, the group was unanimous that a very severe legal penalty as the only alternative plays a very large part in our thinking. Cited as an example was a twenty-four-year-old defendant convicted of first-degree burglary and possessing a long sad history of failure in various youth treatment programs. Since the only alternative to probation in this case was a prison sentence of five years to life, most of the group agreed that they would be more likely to "stretch a point and take a greater risk" by recommending probation. If the alternative were less severe, however, they might well have felt inclined to recommend denial on the basis of other factors.

Consistent with the protection and best interests of the community, probation seeks to focus upon the individual offender and to determine what treatment approach might best aid in his eventual readjustment and reacceptance into the community. Hence, as part of this overall picture, the probation officer may properly consider the severity and possible effects of any alternative penal sentence to be served if probation is denied, as well as weigh the possible benefits to be derived if probation is granted.

The Offense

Is our recommendation for or against a grant of probation influenced by the nature and magnitude of the offense? The nature and magnitude of any offense are bound, at least in some degree, to influence the thinking of probation officers as well as the thinking of others, including legislators. For example, in most states, the magnitude of the theft determines the severity and type of punishment to be meted out, and even the court in which the offense will be adjudicated. In many states, too—particularly in California—such crimes as embezzlement of public funds and crimes of violence involving deadly weapons or bodily injury have moved the legislature to specifically prohibit the courts from granting probation to persons convicted of these offenses.

Thus, the group pointed out that when a person has been convicted of selling heroin to juveniles, for example, this fact in itself will militate against recommending probation, regardless of other factors in the case. To illustrate how the magnitude of an offense will often influence our thinking in individual cases, the group discussed a common offense, that of writing "bad" checks. All agreed that they would be much more likely to consider recommending probation if the offense involved one small check than if it involved a large number of checks amounting to many thousands of dollars.

Do we sometimes allow our recommendation to serve as a judgment of the defendant's offense rather than as an evaluation of the applicability of programs available to him and his situation? All of us have, at one time or another, been guilty of making a judgment as to the defendant's actual participation in some particular offense and of allowing this to color our recommendation (although some members differed on the extent to which this actually occurs). Several persons felt strongly that we passed judgments on guilt or innocence more frequently than we care to admit to ourselves and that we tend to be influenced by the extent of the defendant's participation in the offense. Even though a defendant might well profit from an institutional program, we are sometimes inclined to recommend a less practical probation program because we feel that he played a minor role in the actual offense, or because he "has not done anything bad enough as yet" to face what we believe is a harsher treatment! The reverse holds equally true, for instance, in cases involving a first offender convicted of selling narcotics to juveniles or in fairly large amounts: Even when a suitable probation program is available and the defendant has the capacity to profit from it, we are often strongly inclined to recommend denial of probation primarily because of the nature of the offense.

CONDITIONS OF PROBATION*

> The court has placed you on probation, believing that if you sincerely try to obey and live up to the conditions of your probation, your attitude and conduct will improve both to the benefit of the United States and of yourself.

After reading this pronouncement in the concluding paragraph of the federal probation system form entitled "Conditions of Probation," the newly selected probationer is asked to affix his signature to this paper beside that of the probation officer in order to signify a mutual acknowledgment of the terms of sentence. Thus is inaugurated a formal relationship between the court and the probationer. To the legalistic mind, this might appear to be a contractual one by virtue of both parties having entered into a fixed agreement; to those entertaining a custodial bent, it may indicate the establishment of an officer-ward relationship; while to others, it represents a supervisor-client relationship as found in social work.

Regardless of which of these contrasting viewpoints one accepts, it is agreed that serious and far-reaching responsibilities have been assumed by both parties. The probationer may be expected to initiate at once changes in his mode of life in order to bring about compliance with the agreement. In using this form of treatment, the court—in its attempt to correct the probationer's

---

* Reprinted in part by permission of *Federal Probation*. Richard F. Doyle: Conditions of probation: Their imposition and application. *Federal Probation, 17*(No. 3):19-22, Sept. 1953. Footnotes are omitted.

faulty social attitude and forestall his committing further anti-social acts—designates certain conditions of probation. But the court's obligation does not end with the imposition of these conditions, for its probation officers are required by statute to "use all suitable methods, not inconsistent with the conditions, imposed by the court to aid probationers and bring about improvements in their (probationers') conduct and condition."

Practices in Imposing Conditions of Probation

The purpose of this section is to cite practices followed by both federal and state courts in imposing conditions of probation and to offer comments in the hope of stimulating greater thought and care in their selection and application. Before discussing these practices, it would seem appropriate to comment briefly on the historical background of this form of sentence. The release of offenders by the court under specified conditions is not new, as it was used as early as the year 1820. At that time the magistrates of Warwickshire, England, adopted the expedient of passing sentence of imprisonment for one day upon a youthful offender on condition that he be returned to the care of his parents or master, "to be by him more carefully watched and supervised in the future." This enlightened attitude was not shared by most early courts, which in the main were governed by a spirit of revenge and desire to inflict punishment. Gradually, however, especially in Massachusetts, the birthplace of probation, courts took cognizance of the degradation that existed in the prisons and elected to spare a few selected offenders from this contamination. Usually this consideration was extended only to those individuals who had committed trivial offenses or to those the court wished to reward for service to the state. In more recent times, this negative approach has given way to a positive one whereby the courts expend untold effort in behalf of offenders through probation departments and diagnostic and guidance clinics, as well as various social agencies. This change of attitude created the need for the greatest of flexibility in imposing sentence, and probation offered the method for its fulfillment.

The response to this opportunity has not been gratifying, largely because of the indifferent attitude displayed by numerous courts, particularly the lesser courts by their slipshod, haphazard sentencing practices. Althogether too frequently sentences are passed intuitively without benefit of sufficient facts, and in many instances the offender is not supplied with adequate information as to the terms of this probation sentence. Yet compliance is expected by the court, and commitment may result when violations occur. In a comparatively recent case the Michigan Supreme Court ordered the freeing of a prisoner when it was shown that he had not been properly informed as to the terms of his probation by the sentencing court, which had institutionalized him after finding him guilty as a probation violator. The Federal Probation Act and a number of state statutes require that the probationer be furnished with a written statement of the conditions of his probation.

General Conditions of Probation

Many courts in their approach to the difficult problem of designating terms of probation adopt minimum requirements for all probation cases. These general conditions are more often than not conservative in tenor, as illustrated by the list used in the federal probation service. Consequently, little controversy ensues from their usage for, aside from the conditions restricting travel and requiring periodic reports, the probationer is not being asked to fulfill any obligations that are not normally expected of all law-abiding citizens. In a few instances in which the probationer is employed in a capacity such as a salesman, truck driver, or seaman, the restraint imposed upon his traveling might prove to be a handicap, as may the requiring of written reports from an illiterate or poorly educated person. Likewise, the required personal reporting to the probation office by an invalid or by one who lives at a considerable distance might prove burdensome. In such cases, these should be waived immediately; to insist on compliance to unreasonable terms will only result in disrespect for the entire probationary order.

Special Conditions of Probation

It is within the category of special conditions that one encounters the unusual and often undesirable factors. Probation statutes are liberal in character and enable courts to designate practically any term it chooses as long as the probationer's constitutional rights are not jeopardized.

Speaking of constitutional rights recalls to mind an episode that occurred in Detroit a few years ago when one of the local newspapers reported that a federal judge, in placing two young girls on probation, stipulated that they were not to have dates. This statement by the paper was entirely erroneous; but before it could be corrected it had been given nationwide circulation by both the press and radio, resulting in much protesting over the lack of understanding and inhumane treatment by the court. One person wrote directly to the President, proclaiming that the "sentence was unconstitutional in that it interfered with their unalienable right to life, liberty and the pursuit of happiness." To the writer's knowledge, this is the only time that the general public was bestirred from its apathy about the context of probationary terms.

Unrealistic Conditions

Strange as it may seem upon first thought, the very liberality of probation statutes sometimes works to the detriment of the probationer by permitting courts to stipulate unrealistic terms. As frequently happens, harm is done in an effort to help; and when this occurs it is invariably due to the court's lacking sufficient facts or to its desire to impose its own code of morals on the probationer. Charles H. Boswell in his article, "If I Were a Judge," points out that courts, particularly juvenile courts, rather frequently impose unreasonable terms:

> Any judge who believes that delinquent children in their middle and late teens should remain home after dark has forgotten his own adolescent years. Requiring youngsters to be home early every evening is only extending an invitation to youngsters to violate probation conditions. It is also unrealistic to expect to separate two boys who live next door to each other or to expect a seventeen-year-old boy to give up smoking when he has had the habit for two years. The condition of requiring youngsters to attend church is also frowned upon by probation officers. This kind of requirement tends to associate the church with punitive action. Of course, we all want youngsters to have religious experiences, but compulsory church attendance is not

the way to achieve that goal. In fact it is more likely to turn the youngster away from the church than it is to get him to seek the aid of church leaders of his volition.

Fine as a Condition

Perhaps the most commonly applied special conditions relate to a fine or restitution to the aggrieved party who has sustained a financial loss arising out of the offense. As a rule these are not objectionable, although there is a tendency on the part of a few courts to make the probationer "feel the sting of paying." If this severely taxes his capacity, hardship may result not only to him but to his family. One minor objection to the designation of these requirements may come from the probation officer who dislikes being cast in the role of a collector, but this is insignificant when viewed in the light of other factors.

Special Place of Residence

On occasions, it is found desirable to order the probationer to establish residence away from the community in which he is sentenced. In such cases, care should be exercised to insure adequate supervision so that harm may not come to the residents of the other locality through the uncontrolled releasing into the community persons infected with venereal and other communicable diseases so as not to endanger the health of others.

If it appears that the defendant is suffering from a mental illness, he may be instructed to seek the help of a psychiatrist or mental clinic. Indication of his willingness to cooperate in such a plan should first be secured; otherwise, little success can be expected.

Treatment of Alcoholics and Narcotic Addicts

Some courts are prone to place excessive drinkers on probation after admonishing them not to drink or visit places where liquor is sold. Strict compliance to this order would prohibit them from entering innumerable restaurants and eating places, particularly in large cities where liquor is more often than not available to patrons. At any rate, it is unwise to release an alcoholic into the community unless some treatment plan is inaugurated, for without it he is most apt to violate his probation in a relatively short time.

Under the act establishing the narcotic hospitals, federal courts are empowered to commit narcotics offenders as probation patients with the condition that they remain in the hospital until pronounced cured of their addiction. This sentencing practice can best be applied to those whose history indicates relative freedom from prior criminality.

Spending Part of Probation in Jail

While it is believed advisable to commit probationers to hospitals in certain instances, it does not follow that it is good procedure to commit probationers to county jails or other correctional institutions for the first sixty days of their period of probation as permitted by some state statutes. The imposition of such a sentence tends to defeat the very principles and advantages of probation treatment by subjecting the probationer to the degrading influences found in institutions and by causing dislocation in his employment and family life, not to mention the resultant stigma that is attached to one who "has done time."

Denying Privilege to Drive a Car

Another condition not infrequently designated is the restriction that the probationer may not drive an automobile. This seems to stem from a punitive desire on the part of the court; and in many cases it results in hardship, especially where a car is needed for transportation to and from work. Cars are no longer a luxury but, on the contrary, are indeed a necessity in most localities; therefore, the imposition of this restraint tends to decrease the likelihood of a satisfactory adjustment. Unless the probationer has clearly demonstrated that he is an unsafe driver and a hazard to the public, the privilege of operating a motor vehicle should not be denied him.

Requiring Marriage

Occasionally courts grant probation with the special provision that the probationer enter into marriage. This requirement is generally made in order to provide a paternal name for the unborn child or for one born to the couple out of wedlock. The intent of the court is admirable, but it is unlikely that the marriage will prove a harmonious one under those circumstances.

Conditions Should Be Realistic and Purposeful

In conclusion, it can be stated that the imposition of purposeful and realistic conditions of probation is essential to successful treatment; that they can best be selected after the submission of an adequate presentence report; that these should be presented in written form to the defendant in court for his acceptance or rejection, for unless his wholehearted approval is obtained, rehabilitative efforts will be met with only superficial response without appreciable benefit to the United States or to the probationer.

PROBATION REVOCATION*

Just as disparities in sentence have been of concern to judges and probation officers, so are the disparities in the revocation of probation. The criteria for revoking probation are not uniform in district courts throughout the country and, at times, not even among judges in the same district court.

Some judges and probation officers insist that convictions for new offenses should be the only basis for revocation. Others believe that infractions of the conditions of probation other than the commitment of a new offense should also be justification for revocation, particularly where such violations are committed by an indifferent probationer who is unwilling to cooperate with the probation office and the court. Other judges contend that the circumstances of the violation, the general attitude and outlook of the probationer—his adjustment with his family, in the community, and on the job; and his efforts to comply with the conditions—should also be considered by the probation officer before recommending revocation and by the court before revoking probation.

It is the purpose of this section to focus attention on the question of when and when not to revoke probation and to offer some guide lines which will help the probation officer in making recommendations to the court where there are alleged violations.

---

* Reprinted by permission of *Federal Probation.* Eugene C. DiCerbo: When should probation be revoked? *Federal Probation, 30*(No. 2): 11-17, June 1966.

I have long been of the opinion that it should not be necessary for the probation officer to bring each probation violator to court. The court should have sufficient confidence in his probation staff to allow it to decide when any single infraction or series of infractions should be brought to the court's attention.

What, then, are some of the criteria for determining whether to bring a case to court on a revocation hearing and to recommend for or against revocation?

Minor Violations

Let us begin with a discussion of the more or less minor infractions of the conditions of probation. Suppose a probationer, who otherwise has been cooperative, does not keep an appointment or two. Is this sufficient grounds to bring him to the court as a violator? Hardly.

Consider the probationer who on two or three occasions overlooks sending or bringing in his monthly supervision report. Should he be brought to court as a violator? Hardly.

If a young probationer persists in staying out late hours despite the admonition of his parents, does this constitute a valid reason for reporting him as a violator considering the fact that he does not get into trouble? I have had but few cases where a compromise could not be reached—where the parents, the probationer, and probation officer could not arrive at an understanding as to what hours the probationer should maintain.

What is to be done with a probationer who, now and then, receives a traffic ticket for illegal parking, for driving five or ten miles over the speed limit, for failing to come to a complete stop at a stop sign? It is my contention that these infractions seldom fall within the criteria for revoking probation.

What should be done with a probationer who purchases an automobile or motorcycle contrary to the instructions of the probation officer? The probation officer may be concerned about serious consequences that may result if the probationer has a car or motorcycle. Instead of bringing the probationer to court, would it not be better to ask the probationer to sell the vehicle? Should he not comply, then revocation proceedings might be instituted. If liability insurance is the concern, he should be asked either to obtain the insurance or to sell the vehicle.

Should a probationer be brought to court when he, contrary to the instructions of the probation officer, marries? It is doubtful whether any court would revoke probation in such a case. Some courts would even regard this as an unreasonable and unwarranted restriction.

Is a probationer who quits his job without first clearing with his probation officer in violation of probation? Should not the probation officer determine the circumstances for his leaving the job, especially if it was on short notice? Were there interpersonal relationships and problems on the job which made it unpleasant or even unbearable?

What if the probationer refuses to take a job suggested by the probation officer? Should the officer not first learn the probationer's reasons for not doing so? They may be quite valid and understandable.

What if a probationer refuses to attend group counseling sessions? Is this to be considered in violation of his probation? He may have good reasons for not participating in group meetings.

Felonies and Misdemeanors

We now come to violations which involve convictions for a new felony or misdemeanor.

A probationer is convicted of a minor offense such as *disorderly conduct* or *assault and battery* in a fist fight with no serious injury resulting. Is his probation to be revoked? It is my feeling that the matter should be brought to the court's attention. But in his report the probation officer may recommend that probation not be revoked if the probationer's probation adjustment has been satisfactory.

Take the case of a probationer with no prior criminal record and an excellent probation adjustment who was convicted and committed for a minor offense for which he served a thirty-day jail sentence. The offense and the jail sentence did not come to light until sometime after his release from jail. Meanwhile the probationer returned to his place of employment and continued to work regularly. The officer is faced with the decision whether to institute revocation proceedings or to notify the court of the offense and recommend that probation continue. True, the welfare of the community takes precedence over the welfare of the individual. But this man posed no threat to society and, moreover, was highly respected by the members of his community. Would society benefit more from additional punishment or more from his rehabilitation which was interrupted by the short period of incarceration?

Let us assume that the same person was committed on a felony conviction and for a longer period. What consideration, if any, should be given to the absence of a prior criminal record and an excellent adjustment up to the time of the new offense? At first glance, this might appear to be a clear-cut violation of probation. A closer examination into the facts might reveal a more complex situation because of the presence of mitigating factors and extenuating circumstances. Perhaps the probationer should receive the benefit of the doubt if he manifests redeeming characteristics, if the details of the offense indicate nothing heinous, if he became involved unwittingly, or if the period of incarceration is of such length that there would be little gained by additional confinement.

There is the question whether a conviction is necessary before any court action can be taken in a revocation proceeding. The following case illustrates the question in point.

Amassing a record of nine arrests, all for illicit liquor and all pending in local court during active supervision, a bootlegger was referred to the court for violation of probation because there was continuation of a pattern disclosed in the presentence report. He had no visible means of support and was, in effect, making a mockery of probation. At a hearing before the court, he maintained he was being harassed by the local police and that he was innocent of all of the charges. In deferring action, the judge elected to wait for a conviction on the alleged offenses. The probation officer fulfilled his obligation by calling the alleged violation to the court's attention.

Cases pending in local and even in federal courts present a problem when the five-year maximum probation period is soon to terminate. Should the probationer be brought before the court despite the fact that disposition has not been made of the pending case? In view of the possibility of an acquittal, it would seem unfair to declare a probationer a violator. Perhaps the wisest course would be to permit probation to terminate on the assumption that if convicted the probationer will be punished adequately for the new offense. Another possibility is to have a warrant issued and execution deferred until the outcome of the pending case.

Realistic Conditions of Probation

The degree to which probation conditions are violated is directly related to the extent to which the conditions are realistic. Unrealistic conditions invite violations. Whether sanctions are to be imposed for violating a condition of probation would depend to a large extent on whether they are reasonable and enforceable. A comprehensive presentence investigation report will assist the court in deciding what special conditions of probation should be imposed in a given case. If the court, for example, contemplates assessing a fine, the presentence report will inform the judge of the financial status of the defendant. Too often a fine or restitution places a burden on the defendant, adding to the financial problems that got him into difficulty in the first instance. Nothing is gained by imposing a fine or restitution that he obviously cannot live up to and which actually cannot be enforced.

Other unrealistic conditions of probation which may be difficult to enforce are regular attendance at church, abstaining completely from alcoholic beverages, association with persons with arrest records, leaving the boundaries proscribed by the court or the probation officer. When such conditions are established, the probationer who does not comply may believe he is getting by with something; or he may have a sense of guilt for circumventing the conditions without disclosing the violation to his probation officer. Neither reaction is good.

Conditions of probation should be established by the court primarily to assist the probationer to become a law-abiding, self-respecting person. Conditions of probation should not be imposed as a punitive device. Nor should rigid compliance be expected in every instance. There should be flexibility in the application of the conditions, depending on the merits of the individual case.

What will be the position of the probation officer when the court imposes conditions that are unrealistic and almost impossible to enforce? The probation officer is charged with the responsibility of seeing to it that the probationer complies with all conditions. When he finds the conditions are unreasonable and he is losing control of the situation, he should notify the court that the conditions are difficult to enforce and also offer suggestions for modification of the conditions.

It is important that the probation officer make certain that the probationer fully comprehends each condition of probation and what is expected of him. It is not sufficient merely to have him indicate by his signature on the "Conditions of Probation" form that he understands each condition.

Fines and Restitution

Where the court orders payment of a fine or restitution at a fixed rate within a prescribed time, should the court be notified when an otherwise cooperative probationer falls behind a payment or two? It would seem that this condition is akin to the requirement that monthly supervision reports be submitted by a certain date each month. The probation office should have the responsibility for determining whether it is necessary to bring a probationer to court when a specified amount is not paid by a certain date.

In evaluating the financial situation of a probationer, the probation officer is confronted with two considerations: Was the probationer in a position to make payment of even nominal amounts, manifesting good faith; or was he unable to make payments because of inadequate earnings, illness, or other valid reason? Deliberate failure to make payments, on the other hand, is tantamount to flouting the order of the court.

Recently, two brothers on probation were brought before the court for failure to make regular payments on a sizable fine. One was delinquent in the amount of several hundred dollars; the other had failed to meet a deadline date but later paid the fine in full. Expressing the opinion that these men had deliberately defied his order and that there were no mitigating circumstances, the court revoked probation and imposed a prison sentence. In an appeal, the decision of the district court was upheld by the circuit court of appeals.

By no means academic, these questions are based on actual cases. When they arise, they require the careful examination of every probation officer. They also vividly portray the need for a common denominator for determining what type of action the officer should take when a probationer jeopardizes his status. Careful consideration is especially required where a balance remains as the 5-year maximum period of supervision draws to a close. Although I do not generally subscribe to the policy that a jail sentence be imposed for nonpayment of fine or restitution, I do believe that the attitude of the probationer and his reasons for failure to comply demand careful scrutiny. The following court decision covers this very point:

> Where one convicted of tax offenses was granted probation on condition that he pay fines within a specified time, bare nonpayment of fines was not conclusive of disobedience of probation terms and did not subject him to imprisonment as of course; his probation was not beyond redemption if in reality he was too poor to pay, not to blame for it, and sincere in his try. . . . Even though accused accepted probation when sentenced, two years later when he defaulted in payment of his fines and his probation was revoked he could deny commensurate fairness of fines. [*U.S. v. Taylor* (4th Cir. 1963) 321 F. 2d 339]

Judges often have remarked that they do not deem it wise to have their orders ignored or to leave defendants with the impression that the court does not always mean what it says. Therefore, where a balance remains on a fine or restitution, the court should be so apprised. If a justification exists, probation may be allowed to terminate with restitution remaining as a moral obligation and the fine either remitted or left as a money judgment to be confessed at some future date if circumstances so warrant.

Where conditions of probation are unfulfilled as the expiration date of probation approaches, the action taken by probation officers may vary. In some districts the court allows the probation officer to determine whether probation should be allowed to terminate without fulfillment of the conditions imposed. In our court, when it appears a condition of probation will not be met, the matter is brought to the court in advance of the expiration date, often with a plan or suggestion for a course of action—for example, extension of the period of probation. In this respect, it would be helpful if each court would let its probation officers know what types of unfulfilled condition should be brought to its attention.

Is the Violation Deliberate?

When a probationer violates the conditions of his probation, the probation officer must determine whether the violation is deliberate, whether the violation is the result of an unrealistic condition, whether the probationer is the victim of a generally poor social adjustment. We are dealing with persons who are "socially wrong" or "socially sick." We are dealing with patterns of behavior that have been firmly established over many years. Some of these patterns are acceptable to the cultural group of which the probationer is a part but are not necessarily acceptable to the larger society. For many of our probationers, general adjustment to school is not good, school truancy is high, trade training and industrial skills are lacking, there are marital breakdowns, there are poor adjustments to military service, and social and moral values are in conflict with society in general. Life, for such probationers is filled with maladjustments of one kind or another. In many instances, violations of probation may be symptoms of a poor social adjustment, but a poor social adjustment should not necessarily be regarded as a violation of probation.

In determining whether to recommend revocation, the probation officer must keep in mind the attitude and outlook of the probationer. Certainly a person who is penitent and who has done his best to live up to the conditions of his probation should be placed in a different category than one who is indifferent, or even arrogant, and whose only regret is that he was caught. And it is especially important at this time for the probation officer to help the probationer appreciate the advantages that will accrue when he meets his financial and moral obligations and measures up to the trust the court has placed in him.

The probation officer should avoid setting limits for his probationers based on his own standards of living and moral and social values. The standards of conduct he establishes must not only be realistic but also meaningful and acceptable to the probationer.

Revocation Should Serve a Constructive Purpose

When it becomes necessary to revoke probation, a constructive purpose should be served. A plan should be formulated that is in the best interests of the probationer, his family, and the community. Little is gained where the court disposition is for the sake of punishment only.

It may be that the probationer has demonstrated that he is not a law-abiding, responsible person, and even poses a threat to society. He may need the kind of discipline and training he will get in an institution. If employment has been his problem, he may obtain in the institution the kind of training needed to find a job.

Assuming the probationer is not in need of discipline or training and does not impose a threat to the free community, should probation be revoked? This would depend upon a number of factors, including his attitude, his home, and community adjustment; his adjustment on the job; and the nature of his probation violation. Imprisonment should be imposed only as a last resort.

The argument that commitment for violation of probation serves as a deterrent is not without merit. Several years ago, an epidemic of theft and forgery of government checks in the form of income tax refunds spread through a section of our district. Despite that fact that these checks had been issued in rather small amounts, the practice became more than a nuisance because restitution was not made in a majority of the cases. As more and more jail terms were imposed for violation of probation, not only did restitution payments increase in the active probation cases but thefts also diminished to the point that they were no longer widespread.

Thus far our discussion has centered for the most part around the probationer and the officer. In restitution cases that eventually result in violation of probation, what consideration should be given to the aggrieved party? When a probationer is sentenced to imprisonment for failure to make restitution, the victim suffers the entire loss. If the probationer is not a menace to the community, perhaps a recommendation can be made that probation be allowed to continue if for no other reason than to satisfy the losses suffered by the victim. This problem will be resolved, in part, when we have legislation providing compensation to victims of crime.

There is also the possibility that the probationer believes he is getting away with something and that the court does not mean what it says. What has to be resolved, then, is the question, do rigid compliance and swift justice make for better probation or a fuller appreciation of probation on the part of the public?

Violation Hearing and Report

It is the general practice of courts to require a violation report in connection with a revocation hearing. In it are presented the facts surrounding the alleged violation. Included in the report should be a summary of the probationer's conduct while on probation, and his general attitude and outlook. The report should indicate whether the violation is incidental or a part of a general pattern. The probationer is required by law to be present at the revocation hearing. 18 U.S.C. 3653. See also *Escoe v. Zerbst,* 295 U.S. 490.

It is not necessary that the violation hearing be conducted as a trial. With respect to specification of charges or a trial upon charges, it is not formal. *Manning v. U.S.* (5th Cir. 1947) 161 F.2d 827, *cert. denied,* 322 U.S. 792; 68 S.Ct. 102. *Bernal-Zaguetta v. U.S.* (9th Cir. 1955) 225 F.2d 64; *U.S. v. Hollien* (D.C. Mich. 1952) 105 F. Supp. 987.

The law further stipulates that "As speedily as possible after arrest the probationer shall be taken before the court for the district having jurisdiction over him." 18 U.S.C. 3653.

With the recent decisions of the Supreme Court that a defendant be represented by counsel at every step of due process, it would seem that the probationer's attorney should be present at the hearing. The United States attorney should also be part of the proceeding to make whatever comments or recommendations are indicated.

If, after listening to all parties concerned, the court decides to revoke probation, it might be limited with respect to the sentence it can impose. In the event that imposition of sentence was suspended originally, the court is empowered to impose any sentence within the limits prescribed by the penalty provisions of the statute involved. *Scalis v. U.S.* (1st Cir. 1932) 62 F.2d 220; *Gillespie v. Hunter* (10th Cir. 1948) 170 F.2d 546; *Roberts v. U.S.*, 320 U.S. 264; 64 S.Ct. 113.

If a definite sentence was imposed originally and the execution of the sentence was suspended, the court may not exceed the original sentence. *Roberts v. U.S.*, 320 U.S. 264; 64 S.Ct. 113.

There are occasions when a probationer is serving a state or local sentence which continues beyond the expiration date of the period of probation imposed by the United States district court. To allow the probation to terminate or to seek a warrant for violation of probation is a question that, at times, is difficult to decide.

If returning the probationer to court in the distant future will not serve a constructive purpose, perhaps the ends of justice can be met by permitting probation to expire or, better yet, by the court entering an order terminating probation. To impose additional imprisonment after a lengthy period of incarceration is tantamount to adding salt to the wound.

In such cases, careful scrutiny of the presentence report and an evaluation of the probationer's conduct while under supervision can help determine the proper course of action. If a person poses a threat to society, a warrant is in order. The court will then have, at the time of the probationer's release, a report of his attitude toward authority, his adjustment in prison, and also the presentence report.

What shall be done about the probationer who absconds? After all possible efforts have been made to locate the probationer, a warrant should be requested. In fugitive status a probationer may possibly become involved in other infractions of the law in order to avoid apprehension.

Some years ago, we supervised a thirty-five-year-old unmarried male whose background was favorable and whose adjustment was most satisfactory. Suddenly he moved and quit his job to accept another without notifying the probation officer. Members of his family were asked where he lived and where he was employed. They did not know. The family saw him occasionally, reporting that he was well and was working regularly. Each time the probation officer's message was relayed to him, asking that he get in touch with his officer.

Convinced that he had not absconded, the probation officer continued to make inquiries until there came to his attention the name and address of an acquaintance of the probationer who might know his address. In writing to the acquaintance, it was explained that unless the probationer was heard from within ten days, there would be no alternative but to refer the matter to the court for appropriate action. It had been nine months since the last monthly supervision report had been received. Within a few days, all nine reports, properly executed, were received in the mail. When the probationer was interviewed later, he explained that he was frightened when he entered into a clandestine relationship with a woman who was separated from her husband. At our insistence the affair was terminated and the probationer successfully completed the balance of his period of supervision.

No doubt this was an extreme case, and nine months was an unreasonably long time. Nevertheless, it illustrates the need for exercising patience and understanding lest the officer fall victim to a hasty and faulty decision.

In general, it is my belief that after all possible leads to locate an absconder have been exhausted, the probation officer has valid reason for petitioning the court for a warrant.

Summary of Guide Lines for Revocation

1. Conditions of probation should be realistic and purposive and geared to help the probationer develop into a law-abiding, self-respecting person. They must be flexible in their application. Each case should be judged on its own merits—on the basis of the problems, needs, and capacity of the individual offender. Unrealistic conditions which cannot be enforced invite violations.

2. The probation officer should make certain that the proba-

tioner fully understands the limitations placed upon him in the general and special conditions imposed by the court. Merely signing the "Conditions of Probation" form does not mean he has correctly interpreted each condition.

3. Violations of the conditions of probation do not necessarily reflect a poor probation adjustment. The conditions imposed may have been unrealistic. Perhaps too much was expected in requiring some probationers to live up to certain conditions. The customs, feelings, attitudes, habit patterns, and moral and social values of the cultural group of which a probationer is a part should be considered in assessing his noncompliance with the conditions. Probationers differ in their ability to comply or conform. It is entirely possible that we are imposing a standard of conduct which is realistic for us but not for the probationer.

4. In offenses where a fine, restitution, or both are being considered by the court, the probation officer should explain in detail the defendant's financial obligations and resources in order that the fine or restitution imposed will be commensurate with the defendant's ability to pay. In too many instances, an automatic fine or restitution is imposed without knowledge of the financial burden it places on the probationer and his family.

5. While I do not advocate revocation of probation merely for failure to keep appointments, to submit monthly reports, to observe a curfew, to remain within the district, I do believe that a generally unfavorable attitude and deliberate noncompliance with the conditions of probation and the instructions of the probation officer are grounds for revocation.

6. Although I believe that all convictions for new offenses should be brought to the court's attention, it does not follow that probation should be automatically revoked. No violation should result in automatic revocation. It may be more beneficial to society, and also to the probationer and his family, to have him continue on probation than to sentence him to imprisonment.

7. If a probationer is arrested on a new charge and is held in jail, I do not believe he should be regarded as a violator until he has been convicted. There is always the possibility of an acquittal. And we must keep in mind that, in some local jurisdictions, considerable time elapses between arrest and trial.

8. Lest the probation officer be guilty of usurping the power of the court, all unfulfilled conditions of probation—for example, not paying a fine or restitution in full by the terminal date—should be brought to the court's attention in advance of the termination date. Recommendations for a course of action should be included in the report.

9. To assist the court at the revocation hearing, the probation officer should prepare a formal report containing details of the alleged violation, factors underlying the violation, the probationer's attitude toward the violation, a summary of his conduct during supervision, and his general attitude and outlook.

10. The probationer should be present at the revocation hearing. It would seem that the United States attorney and also counsel for the probationer should be present. But it must be remembered that the revocation hearing is not a new trial.

11. If it is necessary to revoke probation, imprisonment should serve a constructive purpose and not be used merely for punishment's sake. In certain cases, particularly where an indifferent probationer deliberately fails to comply with the conditions of probation, it may be necessary to revoke probation so that the public—and other probationers, too—will have a fuller appreciation for probation and will realize that the primary purpose of probation is the protection of the public, that the court means what it says, and that the conditions of probation are not to be flouted.

It is hoped that this presentation has achieved its purpose, namely, to stimulate thinking about criteria for determining when and when not to revoke, and to assist the probation officer in making recommendations to the court when a probationer has violated his trust.

Chapter Six

Juvenile Probation and Aftercare

JUVENILE probation, which permits a child to remain in the community under the supervision and guidance of a probation officer, is a legal status created by a court of juvenile jurisdiction. It usually involves (1) a judicial finding that the behavior of the child has been such as to bring him within the purview of the court, (2) the imposition of conditions upon his continued freedom, and (3) the provision of means for helping him to meet these conditions and for determining the degree to which he meets them. Probation thus implies much more than indiscriminately giving the child "another chance." Its central thrust is to give him positive assistance in adjusting in the free community.

JUVENILE PROBATION*

Historical Development

Though juvenile probation has had its major development in the present century, its roots run back through a rather considerable history. In England, specialized procedures for dealing with youthful offenders emerged as early as 1820, when the magistrates of the Warwickshire Quarter Sessions adopted the practice of sentencing the youthful criminal to a term of imprisonment of one day, followed by his conditional release under the supervision of his parents or master. This practice was soon thereafter further developed in Middlesex, Birmingham, and London, where probation supervision was first supplied by police officers, then by volunteer and philanthropic organizations, and finally by public departments.

In the United States, juvenile probation developed as a part of the wave of social reform characterizing the latter half of the

---

* Reprinted in part from *Correction in the United States* (A Survey for the President's Commission on Law Enforcement and the Administration of Justice). National Council on Crime and Delinquency, 1966, pp. 41-53. Footnotes are omitted.

nineteenth century. The new and enlarged definition of the state's responsibilities to its children produced such precursors of the future of child welfare practice as (1) laws directed against cruelty to children, (2) philanthropic associations for the protection and aid of the dependent and neglected child, and (3) specialized institutions segregating the child offender from adult criminals. Probation emerged as another of the new era's means of mitigating the harshness of the criminal law and of employing the developing knowledge of the behavioral sciences on behalf of the child. Massachusetts took the first major step toward the development of a juvenile probation service. Under the act passed in 1869, an agent of the state board of charities was authorized to appear in criminal trials involving juveniles, to find them suitable homes, and to visit them periodically. These services were soon broadened and strengthened so that by 1890 probation had become a mandatory part of the court structure throughout the state.

The emerging social institution, with its individualized, parental approach to the erring child, made a central contribution to the development of the concept of the juvenile court. In fact, in some states the early supporters of the juvenile court movement accepted probation legislation as its first step toward achieving the benefits which the new court was intended to provide. In turn, the rapid spread of the juvenile court during the first decades of the present century seems often to have brought about the development and enrichment of probation. The two closely related and, to a large degree, interdependent institutions sprang from the same dedicated conviction of the educability of the young and the same positive affirmation of public responsibility for the protection of the child.

At the mid-1960's, juvenile probation became a large, major, complex social institution touching the lives of an enormous number of our children and young people. In 1964, about 686,000 delinquency, 150,000 dependency and neglect, and 442,000 traffic cases were referred to the country's juvenile courts. According to rough estimates, about 11 per cent of all children will be referred to the juvenile court on delinquency charges during their adolescent years, and as much as 18 per cent of all boys will be so referred. Juvenile probation has the main responsibility for processing and servicing most of these cases. As a service, it represents investments in future citizens. It cannot be cheaply purchased. At present, it costs an estimated $74,750,727 a year.

Goals

The dominant purpose of the total correctional process is promotion of the welfare and security of the community. Within this overall goal, juvenile probation's specific assignment includes (1) preventing a repetition of the child's delinquent behavior, (2) preventing long-time deviate or criminal careers, and (3) assisting the child—through measures feasible to the probation service—to achieve his potential as a productive citizen.

Thus, the central services of probation are directed to the child found delinquent by the court and, often, to his family. However, in some jurisdictions, probation departments are also assigned responsibilities in broader, delinquency-prevention programs. Though the proper boundaries of probation's services in this role are not clear and may vary from one jurisdiction to another, it seems clear that a probation department should at least assume the responsibility for assembling and reporting its special knowledge about delinquent children, their needs, and the community conditions that produce delinquency. It is also vitally necessary for the department to be an active partner in the process of community planning for meeting the needs of young people.

Functions

The modern probation department performs three central—and sometimes several auxiliary—functions. Its central services are (1) juvenile court, probation department, and detention *intake and screening,* (2) *social study and diagnosis,* and (3) *supervision and treatment.*

Intake and Screening

The juvenile court and the probation department are highly specialized sociolegal agencies. The scope of their jurisdiction and services is defined and limited by law, but their limitations are not understood by everyone in the community, and their intervention is not effective in all types of cases. Further, many of the agencies referring cases to them do not have the time or the staff with trained diagnostic skill to determine whether a specific case can best be served by the probation department. As a result, a probation staff member must engage in preliminary exploration with the child, the family, and the referring source to determine with them whether there is a legal basis for court intervention or whether the problem can be resolved better by use of the services of some other community resource.

Frequently the probation department must also decide, or participate in deciding, whether the child should be admitted to, continued in, or released from detention—pending disposition of his case by the court. Removing the child from his home and family and holding him in a detention facility, even for a temporary period, constitute a major intervention in his life and his family's. For some children, this may be necessary and helpful; for others, it may be deeply damaging and may contribute powerfully to alienation from conforming society and its institutions. The problem is rendered even more tragically complex by the fact that, in many jurisdictions in the United States in the 1960's, juvenile detention is provided in facilities that degrade and brutalize rather than rehabilitate.

Social Study and Diagnosis

Characteristically, the juvenile court exercises tremendous power to make authoritative decisions concerning vital aspects of the lives of children and families found to be within its jurisdiction. The delinquent child may be returned to his home and family without further intervention, he may be placed under probation supervision, or he may be removed from his family's control for a period ranging from a few weeks to several years. Such decisions, therefore, which may powerfully shape for good or evil the total future of the individuals involved, must be made only on the basis of the most careful and competent diagnostic study.

Such a study involves the awesome task of predicting human behavior. The focal concern is the probable nature of the child's response to the necessary demands of society. Will he or will he not be able to refrain from offending again if permitted to continue residing in the free community? An even more complicated question is, what will be his adjustment under the various possible conditions of treatment—that is, if he is returned home without further intervention, or if he is provided differing sorts of community supervision and service, or if he is confined in an institution? Only by illuminating such questions can the social study be of value to the court's dispositional decision.

If the diagnostic study is to accomplish its purpose, it must include skilled analysis of the child's perceptions of and feelings about his violations, his problems, and his life situation. It must shed light on the value systems that influence his behavior. It must consider the degree of his motivation to solve the problems productive of deviate behavior, as well as his physical, intellectual, and emotional capacities to do so. It must examine the influence of members of his family and other significant persons in his life in producing and possibly solving his problems. Neighborhood and peer group determinants of his attitudes and behavior must be analyzed.

All of this information must be brought together into a meaningful picture of a complex whole composed of the personality, the problem, and the environmental situation which must be dealt with. This configuration must be considered in relation to the various possible alternative dispositions available to the court. Out of this, a constructive treatment plan must be developed.

Accomplishment of this enormously complicated task by the probation staff requires dedication, intelligence, professional understanding of the forces shaping human behavior, and highly developed skills in interviewing and in making use of the potential contributions of medicine, psychiatry, education, religion, and numerous other professional disciplines.

Supervision and Treatment

Probation involves far more than giving the child "another chance." This last phrase often describes a course of action in which the child is returned unchanged to a family and community situation that produced delinquency in the first place and can be relied on to do it again. Consequently, probation has been assigned the task of contributing to the process of change, through supervision and treatment, in the situation and behavior of the offending child.

The three major elements of effective supervision and treatment are *surveillance, service,* and *counseling.* Usually, no one of these elements is effective by itself; each is a part of an interrelated whole.

SURVEILLANCE. The officer must keep in touch with the child, his parents, his school, and other persons involved in and concerned about his adjustment. He must keep generally informed of the extent to which the probation plan is being carried out. Is the family providing adequate care and supervision? Is the child responding to parental supervision? Is he attending school, or working, or in other ways conforming to the general probation plan? Properly used, surveillance constitutes much more than a threat. It is a method of helping the child become aware of his responsibilities and the demands that life makes upon him as a member of the society. It is a resource for the individualization of such demands as they apply to his particular life situation. It constitutes a confrontation with reality, and it may be a source of support by contributing a precise understanding of that reality and the consequences of his failure to respond to it. It provides assurance that society, represented by the court and a court officer, is aware of and interested in him, is concerned that he not engage in future violative and self-defeating behavior, and is determined to assist him in avoiding such behavior.

SERVICE. The officer must determine the extent to which the problems confronting the child and the family may be alleviated by use of available community services. He must then muster such services in an organized way and help the child and family make use of them effectively—often an extremely complicated task when he is dealing with a family that has long been at odds with, and suspicious of, any agency it regards as representing the authority of society.

COUNSELING. Counseling, the third aspect of the officer's task, makes it possible to perform the other two effectively. The child and family and other persons concerned must be helped to understand and face the existence of the personal or environmental problems productive of the child's delinquency. Frequently they must be helped to gain some degree of understanding of their roles in the production—and thus in the solution—of such problems. They must be encouraged and stimulated to mobilize their strengths and energies and to invest them in the problem-solving process. The performance of this function depends upon the officer's professional ability to offer these persons understanding, his obvious dedication to helping them find satisfaction in a socially acceptable manner, his skillful presentation to them of society's demands that they conform to its minimal expectations, and his determination to help them do so.

Auxiliary Functions

In addition to the three central functions noted above—intake and screening, social study and diagnosis, and supervision and treatment—probation departments frequently perform significant auxiliary tasks. Large departments often operate mental health clinics providing diagnostic and, sometimes, treatment services for children referred to the court. Some administer a variety of other treatment services, which may include foster-home programs, forestry camps, group homes, and other residental or nonresidential treatment facilities. Others vigorously engage in community planning and community organization efforts on behalf of children and youth. Some operate delinquency-prevention services for endangered youth.

Direct operation of many of the treatment and delinquency-prevention programs noted above is considered by most authorities to be a proper responsibility of community agencies other than the court and the probation department. Some experienced practitioners disagree with this position, however, and they point out that, in many instances, courts organize and operate these programs through community default—that is, because no other resource has shown willingness or capacity to do it.

Standards for Evaluating Practice

Universally accepted standards proved by research methods to correlate with movement toward specified goals have not been developed for the field of juvenile probation. The same statement can be made of all other aspects of correction, as well as of education, public administration, political science, and most other fields concerned with human behavior. This does not mean that the quality of a probation system cannot be assessed. However, the criteria by which such assessment is made must be recognized as a sort of distillate of current "practice wisdom" rather than the product of definitive inquiry. This process has resulted in standards generally accepted among experienced practitioners and eminently applicable to today's practice. Among the most useful compilations of such standards are (1) the one prepared by the Special Task Force on Standards (President's Commission on Law Enforcement and Administration of Justice), (2) NCCD's *Standards and Guides for Juvenile Probation,* and (3) the Children's Bureau's *Standards for Juvenile and Family Courts.*

As noted above, juvenile probation is charged with the loftiest of goals. Like any other major social institution, its worth, in the long run, must be judged not only by its goals but also by its performance.

The assumption that probation contributes to the achievement of its defined goals depends on the validity of two prior assumptions: first, that probation actually does have the theoretical and knowledge base that would enable it to predict and influence behavior; and, second, that the manpower, the money, and the other resources necessary to its effective performance actually are or can be made available.

The survey permits only very general consideration of the degree to which probation's theoretical and knowledge base are adequate to the task at hand. However, it does make possible some fairly specific assessments of the availability of necessary manpower and other resources.

The theoretical and knowledge base upon which probation operates is still in the process of formation; it is by no means universally agreed upon and is nowhere clearly stated.

Traditionally, the theory embodied in the law and its allied functions has been that behavioral change can be coerced by deterrent punishment. Probation cannot perform so as to undermine the deterrent power of the law; however, few persons are unaware of the peril of too-easy reliance on the ancient but never tested assumption that our deterrents do, in fact, usually deter. The correctional agency's clientele seems to consist largely of persons repeatedly subjected to—and unaffected by—many of society's sanctions. We can produce fear in the offender. But in so doing we also produce hate and the determination to strike back. Further, the client appears generally not capable of weighing the pleasure of immediate gratification against future (and uncertain) punishment; and he is subject to peer group and other pressures stronger than those we are able to engender.

Thus, modern probation is generally dedicated to other theories of behavioral change. These depend largely on the combination of (1) confronting the offender with the behavioral alternatives available to him and the probable consequences of each and (2) helping him solve the problems of social functioning that impede his securing necessary and normal human satisfactions in socially acceptable ways. Thus, it is hoped, he will internalize conventional value systems and will come to perceive such values as inherently appealing and productive of satisfaction.

In their efforts toward these ends, some practitioners seem to operate on the basis of little or no organized theoretical framework. Others are committed to any one of a variety of theoretical positions, some of which stress the dominance of one variable or another—intrapersonal, intrafamilial, subcultural, or sociocultural—in the production of deviant behavior. Many of these positions stress only the origins of such behavior and provide few action guides for influencing behavioral change.

Nonetheless, a practice wisdom and a practice theory seem to be gradually emerging; these stress the work of the officer in (1) seeking out, stimulating, and drawing into the problem-solving process the offender's motivations and his capacities to solve his problems of social functioning and (2) working with the offender and other persons and social institutions in his environment toward expansion of the opportunity structure available to him.

One of the major challenges facing scholars and practitioners is to formulate the assumptions upon which present practice is based and then to test and further refine them.

SURVEY FINDINGS

Probation Coverage

Juvenile probation service is authorized by statute in each of the fifty states and the Commonwealth of Puerto Rico. The study conducted in conjunction with the preparation of this report shows that in one recent year some 192,000 written social studies were made on behalf of children referred to our courts and that some 189,000 children were placed under probation supervision. At the time of the survey, approximately 223,800 children were under such supervision. Supervision usually extends over significant periods of the child's life. Among the agencies included in the sample, the average period of supervision ranged from three months to 3 years, with a median of thirteen months. In the sample of 250 counties, 233 had probation services.

Fundamental to any definition of desirable probation practice is the availability of paid, full-time probation service to all courts and all children needing such service.

The survey reveals that, though every state makes statutory provision for juvenile probation, in many states probation service is not uniformly available in all counties and localities. The data on this point may be summarized as follows:

1. In thirty-one states, all counties have probation staff service.
2. A total of 2,306 counties (74% of all counties in the United States) theoretically have such service. In some of these the service may be only a token.
3. In 16 states that do not have probation staff coverage in every county, at least some services are available to courts in some counties from persons other than paid, full-time probation officers. The sources of such services include volunteers (in 6 states), child welfare departments (in 5 states), and a combination of child welfare, sheriff, and other departments (in 5 states).
4. In 165 counties in four states, no juvenile probation services at all are available.

Generally, the country's more populous jurisdictions are included among the counties served by probation staff. However, in the smaller counties, service may be expected to be spotty. Comments such as the following occur in the observations of the experienced practitioners gathering the survey data:

> The . . . State Department of Public Welfare does provide, upon request, probation and aftercare services to the courts and to institutions. These services are part of the Child Welfare Program, and no differentiation is made as to specific caseloads. A *general impression is that . . . there is not an acceptance of this service, and it is not used in many counties.*

Many of the state agencies that are theoretically responsible for providing services are not prepared to be so. However, some child welfare departments acknowledge the provision of probation services as a major responsibility, assign capable staff to the function, and provide services of good caliber. *However, the development of practitioners in the court setting who have specialized knowledge of the diagnosis and treatment of acting-out, behavior-problem children remains a challenge to probation practice. This task is doubly difficult when the staff is not oriented specifically to these problems.* It is particularly inappropriate to expect specialists in law enforcement (sheriffs, police, etc.) to become skilled in probation diagnosis and treatment as well as in their own specialized functions. And rare is the volunteer who has the time, energy, and resources to so equip himself (though the volunteer often plays a valuable role when working upon carefully defined problems in cooperation with a trained and experienced member of the probation staff).

Whether a child who is subjected to the truly awesome powers of the juvenile court will be dealt with on the basis of knowledge and understanding, usually the product of a good probation social study, is determined by chance—the accident of his place of residence. The same accident determines whether the community treatment resource of probation as an alternative to incarceration will be available to him. The following observation about one state was made by a member of the survey team:

> In the entire state, only two counties have probation services. The other counties have *no* service. A child placed on probation in these counties is presumed to be adjusting satisfactorily until he is

brought back to the court with a new charge. . . . The Department of Welfare will not accept referrals of delinquent children from the courts.

Organization of Services

Juvenile probation services are organized in a state in one of the following ways:

1. A centralized, statewide system.
2. A centralized county or city system, the services of which are strengthened and supported by state supervision, consultation, standard setting, recruitment, assistance with in-service training and staff development, and partial state subsidy of the local department.
3. A combination of the above systems, with the more populous and prosperous jurisdictions operating their own departments and with service being provided by the state in the other areas.

Which of the three organizational plans is to be preferred is a question that has to be resolved by such factors as prevalent state administrative structures, political patterns and traditions, and population distribution. However, for many states a well-coordinated state plan appears preferable. Such a pattern (1) has greater potential for assuring uniformity of standards and practice, including provision of service to rural areas; (2) makes certain research, statistical and fiscal control, and similar operations more feasible; (3) best enables recruitment of qualified staff and provision of centralized or regional in-service training and staff development programs; (4) permits staff assignment to regional areas in response to changing conditions; and (5) facilitates relationships to other aspects of the state correctional program.

In some states, it may be that local agencies are in a better position to respond to changing local conditions and to assure investment of local resources in the solution of essentially local problems. These benefits usually occur in a city or county relatively high in tax potential and progressive leadership; corresponding progress does not take place in adjoining jurisdictions. To assure at least acceptable performance throughout a state where probation is a local responsibility, state supervision, standard-setting, consultation, assistance in staff recruitment and in-service training, and similar services are required. The problems all too often resulting from the absence of either a centralized state probation service or adequate standard-setting for local services are illustrated by another comment emerging from one of the state studies:

> In [the small state of . . .] juvenile probation . . . offers eleven different programs, with widely differing philosophies of institutional use, much variation in procedures, and no possibility of influencing the quality of probation work through any centralized training effort. Political appointment of officers is standard practice and there is no merit system offering the possibility of a career in probation.

Intrastate uniformity in achieving acceptable standards often requires that local probation be subsidized by the state. State expenditure for this purpose is an excellent investment, for it mitigates against the ever-present danger of indiscriminate commitment to the state correctional program. This and similar benefits seem to have been obtained by such a program recently introduced in one state, where the conference with correctional officials held in connection with the survey produced the following observation:

> Juvenile probation has . . . seen substantial improvement in the past few years with the help of a state subsidy that provides that in order to participate the local county must *add* to its existing staff. A number of small counties which had never had probation services prior to this study have now created departments. Larger counties have been able to expand their services. . . . The general effect of the subsidy has been to generate considerable interest on the part of some judges where little or no interest previously existed.

Court Administration v. Administrative Agency

County and city systems are organized mainly according to two patterns. In the prevalent one, probation services are administered by the court itself or by a combination of courts; in the other, the services are provided to the court by an administrative agency such as a probation department established as a separate arm of local government.

The survey reveals that juvenile probation is administered as follows:

By courts in 32 states
By state correctional agencies in 5 states
By state departments of public welfare in 7 states
By other state agencies in 4 states
By other agencies or combination of agencies in 3 states

Some authorities arguing in behalf of the first pattern, in use in most jurisdictions, hold that administration by the court is necessary and desirable since the court is responsible for determining which delinquents are to remain in the community and under what circumstances they are to be permitted to do so. Proper discharge of this responsibility, they say, means that the judge must have the authority to select and control the probation officer, who functions as an extension of the court.

Other authorities argue that the more widespread use of the first pattern may well be the result of historical accident rather than careful analysis of the advantages and disadvantages of the two plans. They point out that conditions have changed since the administration-by-the-court pattern was first established and that now many probation departments are large, complex organizations. Their administration requires a background of training and experience in, as well as an inclination toward, administration—qualifications that do not necessarily accompany judicial function. The judge should be an impartial arbiter between contending forces. His administration of an agency often party to the issues brought before him in the courtroom may thus impair, or may seem (to one or the other of the parties) to impair, performance of his judicial function. Further, if the court is composed of many judges, it is likely that the juvenile court judgeship assignment will rotate frequently, so that true assumption of administrative leadership may never take place.

In any event, the major administrative leadership role in the operation of probation services must be clearly recognized. The total juvenile court function is rendered almost impossible without good probation service, which cannot develop without good administration. It may be that some judges can perform both the judicial and the administrative function effectively. But, as Keve points out:

> It seems that at this point in its history, the juvenile court must face its growing administrative task and decide whether it is to relinquish its administrative duties to a separate administrative body, or accept the administrative character of the juvenile court and deliberately develop the structure and capacities of the court to a greater extent than is usually true now.

CITIZENS ADVISORY COMMITTEES. Whether administered at the state or the local level, the juvenile probation department often finds that a carefully selected citizens advisory committee or board is enormously helpful. The functions of such a committee should include (1) participation in the department's policy-making processes so that the thinking of major forces in the community and major sources of pertinent expertise are represented and (2) constant interpretation to the community of the functions, problems, and needs of the department.

The committee should include representation from business and industry, organized labor, the bar, medicine (including psychiatry), the social services, education, religion, and other pertinent community forces.

PROBATION TREATMENT IN DELINQUENCY*

Regardless of the nature of the delinquency, the major contribution in direct treatment by a probation officer will consist of forming a strong, friendly bond to the delinquent—a relationship that will let the delinquent know the probation officer is on his side, and that the probation officer believes the child is behaving in the only way he knows how. The probation officer must believe this deeply, or the delinquent will have little use for him since, at best, it is difficult to get the aggressive delinquent to accept an adult as an ally. He has thought of the adult for too many years as an enemy who cannot be trusted. Many delinquents have been disillusioned repeatedly by adults and, though the individual delinquent senses the probation officer as his friend, he prefers to withhold significant information for a long time. If, as is occasionally the case, the probation officer is so conditioned by his own

---

* Reprinted by permission of *Federal Probation*. Hyman S. Lippman, M.D.: The role of the probation officer in the treatment of delinquency in children. *Federal Probation, 12*(No. 2): 36-39, June 1948.

early experiences and training that he has a condemning attitude toward the delinquent and his behavior, this will soon be sensed. He will not depend on what the probation officer says any more than the probation officer will rely on his remarks. As a delinquent, he has had to learn to spot his friends quickly; he will detect by a frown or sudden quietness or tenseness that the probation officer cannot accept him deeply. A sensitive probation officer may have difficulty in retaining a feeling of warmth for a boy who struck his mother who has just returned from the hospital; for an adolescent girl who got in after midnight after repeated promises and assurances this would never happen again, for an aggressive boy who tells in a convincing manner that his school work is satisfactory though the probation officer knows he has not been to school since the last interview. In this connection, the probation officer probably never will reach the stage when one of these clever delinquents will not be able to really convince him of his sincerity while he is telling a succession of lies.

To complicate matters, there are delinquents who will have no respect for the probation officer if they can outwit him. To some extent, this may be due to their need to be punished and to have their aggression checked. More often, however, it is an expression of their narcissism; they form their relationships on a narcissistic basis and can only develop a tie to someone who can outsmart them. Fortunately, this group is in the minority, because underlying this behavior mechanism is considerable emotional conflict that is resistive to treatment in the hands of the most experienced therapist.

The probation officer may be discouraged if his success seems to end without having formed this bond of friendship with the delinquent. The officer is aware, through talks with the foster parents, school personnel, and others, that a given delinquent suffered greatly as a young child; was subjected to scenes of cruelty by an alcoholic mother, and knows he was illegitimate—and yet he tells the probation officer nothing of these facts. He becomes defensive when his family is referred to and prefers to stay on a superficial level. At the same time, he looks forward to coming in, and he has been more pleasant in the home and school

—there has been a lessening of the delinquent behavior. The probation officer, acquainted with psychiatric literature, knows the part played by early emotional experiences in the development of delinquent behavior, is anxious to do something of "real value," and wants to discuss the early life experiences with the delinquent. The delinquent will give the kind of material the probation officer wants only when he is ready to do so (and he never may be ready)—when he is sure of him, when he is convinced the probation officer will not be critical of him or think less of him or can be relied upon not to repeat to the foster parents or the judge what he tells the probation officer. It is routine to assure the delinquent early in the treatment that what he tells the probation officer is in confidence, but it may be months before this is accepted.

In some instances the delinquent talks freely from the outset. Usually, however, if this is the case, he will tell the probation officer what he has told others, and the telling will add little to the treatment. In some instances, there will be a great deal of talking, much of which is intended to leave the probation officer with the feeling of trust in him but which actually is a defense against revealing significant material.

There will be many delinquents who never will disclose traumatic experiences even after long periods of casework with them. They may continue with their delinquency, and admit this to the probation officer, but want to maintain contact with him; and so the probation officer is not justified in concluding he has not helped a delinquent because his delinquency persists. He may have checked a career in crime by his casework but may never know this.

The interview is the chief tool of the probation officer in his treatment work. The capacity to be relaxed and get the delinquent to relax develops only after experience. It will not develop quickly if the probation officer is working under the pressure of a big caseload or is on a staff that demands quick results. One cannot speed up casework on order without affecting the result. The delinquent, it must be recalled, has been sent to the agency; he has not come for help. He would have preferred to go on in his own way of delinquency, to have his pleasures without meeting reality. He has little interest in our taking this only adjustment he knows away from him. He has enjoyed the behavior which has furnished him an outlet for his hostility to a society that has rejected him and that he in turn has rejected. He must be wooed for a long time, in many instances, to keep the resentment down, if he is to continue trying to behave acceptably. There will be more temptations that will pull him back to delinquency than will keep him working with a social agency. Any pressure may start him off on a delinquent career if it stirs up the resentment that made him delinquent in the first place. The task of keeping him close to the probation officer is easier if there is something tangible in the treatment that allows the delinquent to feel that the probation officer is doing something for him. In the larger cities, membership in a YMCA, a part-time job, tutoring help, and removal from sources of unhappiness are useful.

Effecting Changes After Confidence Has Been Established

After the probation officer has gained the confidence of the delinquent, he will be in a position to make those changes in the delinquent's surroundings which he believes are important. The statement is made in this manner purposely because of our interest in the individual delinquent at this point in the discussion. One can make many changes in the environment that will not touch the delinquent, unless he is interested in seeing these changes made. The probation officer will be much further ahead in getting him to see the value of living in a foster home, before moving him. Many of our failures in foster-home placement of the older child result from the fact that everyone wants him in a foster home except the boy himself. He wants to be with his own neighborhood group and prefers his companions in school and the home that he may be able to dominate. To give him a choice early between a delinquency institution and a foster home does not help matters much, because then the foster home represents to him a method of punishment. It is a different matter if he is told later in the treatment, when the probation officer's counsel means something to him, that he will be smart to get away from a neighborhood that is largely responsible for his delinquency and give foster-home placement a trial, especially if he is told that the probation officer's interest in him will continue and the probation officer expects to see him often while he is trying to make the new adjustment.

Probation Officers Must Expect Failures Too

It may be well also to realize before beginning to deal with delinquents that probation officers, through no fault of their own, will fail with at least half of their cases. We often make the mistake of wanting to cure all or most of the delinquents we see. If half of them are helped, we still will have done a great service to society. The reaction to the delinquent will be different if we keep this fact in mind. We will be gratified then by the number who improve, rather than being disillusioned by the number who fail.

In the group of those delinquents who are most likely not to respond to treatment are the mentally retarded, those with organic disease of the central nervous system, and those who are deeply conflicted emotionally. An adolescent who belongs in these groups needs special care that the probation officer alone cannot provide. This does not mean, however, that advantages of casework should not be supplied the delinquent just because the possibility of curing him is remote. Actually, intensive casework may provide the best means of diagnosis—of obtaining the information that will help decide on the need for institutionalization.

This leads to the subject of the neurotic delinquent, who has been one of the chief interests of the psychiatrists dealing in problems of social psychiatry. I purposely shall avoid discussing the treatment of the underlying emotional conflicts of the neurotic delinquent because there is little in the intensive treatment of such an individual that will be a part of casework, without the help of a psychiatrist. Such conflicts are of an unconscious nature, are deeply imbedded, and can only be brought to light by the psychiatrist trained in psychoanalytic techniques.

There are certain phases of the treatment of the neurotic delinquent, however, that can be carried on by the caseworker. First, and foremost, is again the development of a relationship that will lessen the need to vent his hostility on others and to attack himself. Psychoanalytic observations have demonstrated the presence of an excessive amount of cruelty in the neurotic delinquent who reacts to these deep drives with a feeling of guilt and a need for punishment. Most agencies have had experience with adolescents bright enough to know better, who have managed their delinquencies—without being aware of it—in such a way that they were apprehended easily and punished. What happens in the everyday life of the delinquent is that small frustrations in the home and in the school stir up the more serious underlying frustration that has always been with him. To be denied the lesser things means again that he is not loved, that he is rejected, and that his efforts to change the *status quo* will never get him anywhere. The probation officer must keep in mind the facts that the neurotic delinquent almost invariably comes from a family where other members, particularly the parents, are neurotic and that there are, therefore, numberless opportunities for stilling up the feelings of hopelessness and revolt. The probation officer may be an all-important person in breaking up this vicious circle. A positive tie may make it possible for the delinquent to find the kind, accepting parent in the probation officer unless the delinquent is too overwhelmed with guilt. To the delinquent, it may mean that all adults are not cruel and rejecting, but it will not mean this during the first few weeks. He will have to be convinced of the probation officer's good intentions and his being consistent, over and over again. If, and when, he can give up his need to change his own parent and accept the probation officer as a substitute, in some instances the delinquency will stop—there will be no more need for its existence.

At the same time, it may be possible for the probation officer to work with the neurotic parents, at least to see that something is done for them. Sometimes it is inadvisable for the same probation officer to work with the delinquent and the parent because of jealousies that arise and the possible needs of each to interfere with the satisfaction of the other. There are many things that can be said about the casework treatment with the family of the delinquent, but I am omitting them at this time. It is sufficient to say that, unless this casework is done, the work with the individual delinquent in most instances will suffer.

To get back to the problem of direct treatment with the delinquent—the probation officer must keep in mind the fact that in most instances the delinquent is suffering from feelings of inferiority. These grow out of his school failure and his rejection in the home and community. The school failure has resulted from a lack of motivation and the development of poor work habits since school work is hard work and the child does not work unless he is making somebody happy through it. This feeling of loyalty is usually lacking in these delinquents. Sometimes the feeling of inferiority comes from a feeling of guilt related to masturbation and other sexual practices. The delinquent may be sensitive about an alcoholic father or a psychotic parent.

Anything that will strengthen the ego of the delinquent will lessen his feeling of inferiority and will in turn make him feel more secure. The biggest ego boost will come from the realization that he is good enough, and worthy enough, to be accepted by the probation officer. If the probation officer can get the delinquent's permission to go to his school, talk to his principal and teachers, the probation officer may be able to arrange the delinquent's schedule in a way that will make it possible for him to enjoy school. Perhaps he can change his school or be allowed to drop one of his subjects. The probation officer may even motivate him to study for the first time in his life. He may be able to get the school to help him in his attempts to change the delinquent's attitude toward school and life.

Checking Emotional Disturbances: One of the Main Functions of the Probation Officer

To sum up, one of the probation officer's main functions will be to check anything that emotionally disturbs the delinquent. He will have to search carefully among the various situations to which the delinquent is exposed and reduce friction wherever possible. In the home, he may locate favoritism for another child, an overly critical father, a nagging rejecting aunt. These influences will have to be controlled, or the irritation will continue daily—hourly—and keep the boy in a state of turmoil with a need to fight back, either in an attempt to punish or to reduce the tension. In the school, he may be trying to do seventh grade work though only able to do fifth grade work; or he may be able to do seventh grade work well but may be totally deficient in reading. The failures to compete successfully with his fellow students can cause more or less continual unrest. Or the delinquent may be picked on by several older boys, or under the influence of an older sexual pervert whom he fears and thus may feel guilty and ashamed of this behavior. These and many more precipitating factors may keep him in a state of conflict or rebellion which invites the many forms of behavior assumed by neurotic delinquency. This does not mean that there is a lesser need to get at the underlying unconscious factors also, but this is not the function of the probation officer.

Perhaps the probation officer will be fortunate enough to get the youngster to discuss spontaneously his preoccupation with sexual problems and his anxiety about what will happen because of his masturbation. The probation officer's assurance that masturbation does not cause insanity, and his continued acceptance of the delinquent in spite of his behavior, may go a long way toward relieving him of tension and worry. The prevailing attitude in all officer's contacts with the delinquent must be one of optimism, and this must persist when the probation officer fails and the boy is sent to an institution. The probation officer's interest in his welfare must continue so that the relationship can be reestablished after the boy leaves the institution.

Demands for quick decisions present themselves more often in dealing with cases of young delinquents than with other child welfare problems. Pressure is applied to get immediate action because the community wants to be rid of the delinquent's hostility and aggression. It would be unfortunate if the probation officer yielded to this pressure and formulated a plan before he knew all the important contributing factors. One learns by experience that there are few real emergent situations that cannot wait long enough to permit thorough study—without which needless errors are made. To deal intelligently with each child so that a diagnosis of the child, and of the total situation in which the child finds himself, can be established, requires a limitation of cases assigned to the individual worker. There are few probation officers who can handle successfully a caseload of more than thirty or forty young delinquents, and when one hears that a probation officer is dealing with 100 to 150 juvenile delinquents, the conclusion must be reached that most of the cases are inactive, or the work is of a superficial nature.

I purposely have emphasized what a probation officer can do with young delinquents, independent of the help he can receive from a child-guidance clinic or an outpatient psychiatric department in a hospital, because so many probation officers are not in a position to take advantage of these services.

GROUP REPORTING IN JUVENILE PROBATION*

Although the current interest in group therapy extends to almost all kinds of social agencies, there seems to have been little use of it in juvenile probation offices. At least, few reports of such activity can be found in the literature.

This section will present one probation department's experiences with group reporting sessions for three groups of juvenile probationers. All three groups were conducted experimentally by probation officers who came from different backgrounds, had no special training, and used different techniques. All the probationers and officers involved agreed completely that the group method had many advantages over individual interviews, and few disadvantages.

Group composition and processes and problems encountered will be described in some detail, followed by a discussion of some of the ideas and principles which evolved from the experiment.

Group Composition

After some investigation of group literature, the probation officers concluded that such writing could be of little help with the unique problems of the juvenile probation setting. The officers then decided to experiment and improvise freely; they were par-

---

* Reprinted by permission of *Crime and Delinquency*. Olive T. Irwin: Group reporting in juvenile probation. *Crime and Delinquency, 11*(No. 4): 341-348, Oct. 1965.

ticularly determined not to be limited by the cautions of group therapists in other settings.

At the start, two caseloads were combined to form three groups: (1)seven adolescent boys, (2) six adolescent girls, and (3) five preadolescent boys. Each group contained some children who were under the supervision of the probation officer leading the group and some who were not.

The criteria for choosing group members were simple: intelligence should not be lower than dull normal; the age span within each group should not be greater than four years.

The meetings, to be held once a week, would take the place of regular individual reporting.

At first, participation was not voluntary. (At a later time, members became willing to make concessions to be allowed to remain.) There was little open objection, even though the idea of group reporting was new to all but one. As soon as the boys saw what it would be like, they all appeared to welcome it. Their attendance generally improved, except for some in the younger group who sometimes seemed unable to remember to come when school was not in session.

Some of the girls missed sessions because they repeatedly ran away or otherwise continued their previous impulsive behavior. As nearly as could be determined in this small sample, there was no higher percentage of this than in the department as a whole, but we had no way of being sure. A more serious problem seemed to be the mixing of middle-class white girls with lower-class Negro girls. The latter were absent much of the time and, when they were present, there was little interaction between the two racial groups. The Negro girls, passive and deeply deprived socially (much more so than the white girls), confronted a combined aggressiveness among the white girls with which they could not cope. Everyone, including the leader, contributed to the conspiracy of silence about the racial feelings in the group; the leader, by not bringing the problem out in the open, let it persist. Finally, she released the obviously uncomfortable Negro girls. Later, she learned a simple and effective technique for dealing with racial tension: confront the group repeatedly with the problem and force them to deal openly with it.

The Groups

Older Boys' Group

Five of the six adolescent boys (aged 13 to 17) were fairly healthy emotionally; the exception was unable to relate to the others. All but one were newcomers on probation, and all except the isolate were discharged within eight months of the group's formation. The group leader, a young woman with no graduate education, was vigorous, intelligent, quick, and resilient. In her hands the group process became a friendly but tough-minded challenge. The boys gave her at first grudging, then frank, admiration. Deep feelings were not analyzed; problems were not probed; discussion was usually superficial and sometimes intellectualized. Yet it was obvious that this was a therapeutic experience.

Possibly the most noticeable change was the relaxation of the group's racial prejudices after a Negro boy—from a home of deprivation and resentment, even open hatred, of white people—was chosen as the group's leader.

The probation officer who led this group broke possibly every orthodox rule on group treatment. Nevertheless, the force of her personality and her determination to be forthright and honest helped her to deal effectively with the boys.

Preadolescent Boys' Group

The preadolescent boys' group was formed of children nine to twelve years old. Of the three groups, these boys expressed the widest range of behavior differences. One boy was garrulous; another said not four sentences the entire year. One was relentlessly hyperactive; another was quiet and self-disciplined throughout. Their probation officers had found it difficult to communicate with any of them individually.

For these boys, a long table was set up with a few simple and adaptable play materials: paper, crayons, water paints, modeling clay, scissors, a hand printing set, a weaving frame and materials, and a blackboard. For a half hour, the boys were free to use the materials or not. The probation officer made no suggestions or comments. Rules were simple and quickly enforced: reasonable quiet and no running, no throwing, no fighting.

The probation officer sat with them, working with one of the materials, talking or silent, responding to a boy's statement or possibly bringing up a subject. She might tell of a problem of a hypothetical probationer, or mention a news item and relate it to the boys' own lives, needs, or probation rules. Sometimes there would be lively response, sometimes none. Often the conversation was nothing but chatter. She fostered an atmosphere of firmness, reliability, and warmth, and made no attempt to discuss problems deeply or extensively. If the lack of structure led to noise and playful or angry scuffling, she restored order immediately. The group had no discipline problem; the boys accepted the rules with surprising readiness.

Older Girls' Group

The adolescent girls were the most difficult to handle, partly because of the greater depth of their problems. It was immediately evident that this was the most troubled of the three groups, and that the greater disorder in the girls' homes contributed considerably to the problems of maintaining the group.

Group composition was not stable. There were frequent interruptions for temporary detention of some members and eventual commitment of a few to institutions. When a girl left permanently, she was replaced by a new girl. The character of the group altered almost completely three times during the eighteen months of the program. At one time, two groups were being conducted; later they were consolidated into one.

Free discussion was promoted by the leader and accepted by the group. The leader tried, frequently without success, to focus discussions on problems of one kind or another. The girls were flighty; their attention span was short. They did not really become a cohesive group during the first year, when the leader's efforts lacked a consistent philosophy. Yet even with this group, there were obvious advantages over individual interviews, which will be discussed below.

Concurrent Individual Interviews

It has been suggested that group meetings should be supplemented by individual interviews when a child shows special needs. This technique was tried with a small boy who appeared to be asking for more of the probation officer's time than could be given in the group. It was quickly seen, however, that the boy himself found the individual interview unsatisfactory after having been in the group; he seemed bewildered by differences in the quality of the relationship. With relief, he returned to the group as his primary contact with the probation officer.

When the same thing was tried with some of the older girls, the group's vitality was drained. The girls who saw the probation officer individually began to take little part in the group. When the probation officer became aware of this, she refused to see the girls individually, thus forcing the important problems back to the group. She found that the problems which had been thought to need individual treatment were in fact resolved adequately or even better in the group.

Confidentiality

The question of confidentiality of material brought out in the discussion was seldom mentioned. It seemed evident to all the group members that the responsibility for keeping quiet was theirs. In my experience, however, juvenile probationers do not often seem concerned about confidentiality. They share personal information about one another freely with all their peers as a legitimate part of the social game. The leader can make therapeutic use of this subject, helping them see their responsibilities in the light of their experiences as betrayers of confidences.

Consultation with a Specialist

After one year, when the girls' group was the only one remaining, consultation began with an experienced group therapist. At this point, the group was excitable and uncontrolled; some members were openly hostile to the probation officer. There was little group cohesion and little effort among the girls to make therapeutic use of the sessions. The taped group sessions were discussed in detail every week with the consultant. As the probation officer developed a more consistent philosphy and thus modified her technique, behavior of the group members changed significantly. In seven months, it seemed like an entirely different group of girls, all of whom could be considered for discharge from probation.

Possibility of Damaging a Probationer

It is quite unlikely that a group member could be hurt by the leader's mistakes. To a great extent, we deal in probation with behavior disorders which are already heavily defended against determined intervention, of long duration and intensity, from other sources. The strength of probationers who have resisted, year after year, the benign influences of teachers, clergy, group leaders, and often their parents, is impressive. By the time these children become probationers, they have become accomplished at self-protection; they deny problems, reject responsibility, and resist relationships skillfully and consistently. Whatever mistakes the leader might make could have damaging effect only on a deeply emotionally ill child whose defenses are much weaker than those of most probationers. This type of child is unlikely to be on probation if any kind of social-psychological diagnosis is made at intake; if he is on probation, he can be recognized easily and not included in a group. Any inadvertently harmful act by the probation officer is more likely to be damaging in a one-to-one relationship, where the child does not have the protection from emotional involvement which he has in the group. In such circumstances the dilution of relationship in the group is an additional advantage.

Unusually Unacceptable Offenses

Some persons hold that certain offenses are too serious to be discussed in a group and that therefore a probationer who has committed any of these should not be a group member. I do not believe that this has to be considered. For example, one girl in my group had engaged in several forms of deviant sex behavior. She never alluded to this in the group and was not pressed when she parried inquiries about her offense. Her problems of relating to peers and adults (which underlay the sexual acting-out symptoms) were evident in the group interaction and could be treated without any reference to the symptoms.

However, probation officers who do not feel secure enough with these problems to risk exposing them to the group should probably exclude such offenders. There is no magic in mixing all kinds of characters and problems indiscriminately and none in special combinations. For the beginning leader embarking on a first group experience, I would suggest a fairly emotionally healthy group until he finds that the job is not as difficult as he thought it would be.

Results of Group Reporting

One development which immediately became evident was that almost all the probationers were more willing to report. Absences, whether excused or not, became almost nonexistent—with exceptions among excessively impulsive girls, one or two deeply hostile girls, and preadolescent boys during periods when school was not in session.

The preadolescent boys who continually failed to report lived in homes with histories of lax observance of time schedules. Their parents also showed a marked lack of cooperation with the probation department, which could be expected to continue. Since these boys obviously enjoyed the sessions when they did come, apparently they genuinely did forget, as they claimed, when there was nothing (i.e. attendance at school) in their day's activities to remind them.

Excessively impulsive girls who could not control their urges to run away provided another exception, as did some deeply hostile girls who expressed defiance by irregular reporting. In time, however, to reduce the problem of absences, a reliable technique was developed that was based on the probationers' obvious preference for group reporting over individual interviews. To be allowed to continue in the group, the members must agree to be present most of the time. If they are not, they have to go back to individual reporting. Once the benefits of the group have been experienced, no probationers have been found willing to be expelled. Only in rare circumstances, when the probationer is not experiencing the benefits of the group, is he willing to be expelled.

A second outgrowth of group sessions was the increase in verbalization. Probationers who in individual interviews were mostly silent and indifferent, withdrawn or sullen, talked freely in the group and began to discuss matters of considerable importance and emotional investment. In the entire list, only one, a nine-year-old boy, remained nonverbal, and he communicated in many other ways—something he had never done more than minimally in the two years he had been known to the department.

It is not necessary to recapitulate here the many reasons why young people cannot talk freely with an adult alone but can if flanked by a group of peers. Group work has amply demonstrated the value of group interaction and protection. Even young people well-disposed toward an adult find interaction alone with him difficult, particularly on a verbal level; we forget that many probationers, with their hostility, fear of relationship, and inaptitude at speech undoubtedly find the weekly individual report hard to face. Too often it degenerates into a meaningless routine of question and answer, or superficial chatter, with no real therapy resulting. In these circumstances the probation officer has as his only measure of improvement the absence of recidivism. In a group, there is ample opportunity to share experiences which are meaningful; the members bring the subjects up themselves or the leader can use his own observations of the group's behavior as subjects for discussion. Primarily the perception of reduced threat to the individual makes each one better able to risk himself in the group. This increase in meaningful communication also provides the probation officer with rich material for evaluating the individual's progress.

The use of activity materials was found to be without value in the older groups. The boys did not need it. The girls were almost completely without manual skills and were afraid to try to learn any. Because of the apparent difficulty in verbalizing, an attempt with one girls' group was made to introduce crafts early in the period, but this plan was abandoned shortly afterward because it evidently produced increased anxiety. Subsequently, discussion itself proved possible with all the girls and was felt to be more valuable as a therapeutic tool. This is not to say that activities should not be a part of the group treatment, but that they should not become the only tool used.

A third advantage was a patent one: the saving of time for the busy probation officers. They could telescope five or six interviews into one.

Group Recidivism

A cherished belief of many who deal with delinquents is that allowing them to associate with one another will encourage them to engage in more delinquent acts together. In our program, this was not true. Of the total of twenty-five probationers in group treatment, one of the older boys and four of the girls got into further trouble serious enough to require action. One girl, after four months in the group, was committed to a correctional school because she continued to run away. One girl was committed after six weeks of group treatment on a second charge of theft (along with a girl who was not in the group). Two, after longer group experience, committed separate thefts, quite apart from any other group members. None of the boys in the preadolescent group got into more trouble.

The girls' group, after almost dissolving through release of its members, was augmented by four girls who had committed extensive vandalism together. In spite of the initial protests of all their parents, they were seen as a group by the probation officer during their entire year on probation and continued to be friends. After a year of probation, one, the oldest by three years, stole something from a store in the company of a boy unknown to the other three, who are now ready for discharge.

These experiences, in face of the fact that the groups were not chosen with any attempt at eliminating those with tendencies to recidivism, support the idea that group association of probationers does not promote recidivism. On the contrary, further study may show that there is less recidivism among group members.

Suggestions for Beginning a Group

Following are a few suggestions for probation officers who would like to start group work without having had special training.

1. *Either all the members of a group should be the probationers of the leader, or none of them should.* The group often brings up problems of probationary authority and supervision and demands statements from the leader on fine points which might be handled differently by another probation officer. Instruction and information are a part of the group leader's function and have a valid place, but opinions and practices of one probation officer can conflict with those of another without those of either being wrong. If different probation officers are represented in the group, interpretation can be difficult for the leader, and members can become confused. In addition, it is known that probationers are skillful at catching their probation officers, as well as other adults, in inconsistencies, and will use them as a proof of either corruption or foolishness. Having the authority vested in the same individual for all members of one group makes consistency easier and eliminates the need for conferences between probation officers.

If none of the members belongs to the leader, he is freed of all authority problems and can simply refer them to their probation officers. With this arrangement, however, an opportunity is missed for an important area of group therapy—the constant grappling with authoritative limits. Traditional convictions to the contrary, these groups have demonstrated that therapy can be achieved with an authority acting as therapist and that progress may be the more rapid because of the leader's double role.

2. *A high degree of nondirection is possible only for the preadolescent boys.* They need to be able to respond spontaneously in an absence of direction or questioning and to be free to experience an atmosphere of unhurried, undemanding, yet interested attention from an adult in authority. For some of them, this is possibly a unique experience. Even if this atmosphere cannot be established, the group is still the best means of reporting for all preadolescents except those so disturbed that they are disruptive.

3. *With the older members, nondirection leads only to confusion and uncontrolled excitement.* The leader must intercede actively in whatever way is appropriate for him. One might be easily able to start lively interaction with just a provocative manner. Another might need to introduce subjects and raise questions. A third

might pick up and make meaningful whatever the group started talking about. The subject matter is the whole adolescent world. The discussions can be at once educational and self-realizing experiences.

4. *Do not hesitate to form a group with the probationers at hand (but avoid extremely disturbed juveniles, excessively hostile ones, or ready victims for an aggressor).* The very differences in a group promote interaction. A beginner would do well to start with a fairly emotionally healthy group that will not raise problems of procedure before he gets enough confidence to handle them. He need not fear that some inadvertent act or unskilled omission will hurt any of the members. They are all experienced in fending off adults with all kinds of intentions—hostile or benevolent—and they can protect themselves likewise from the mistakes of the probation officer.

5. *The sessions should be taped if possible.* The leader can learn and develop ideas from listening later to these tapes, preferably with a more objective colleague. Tapes can be therapeutic for the group as well. All of the groups described here have been interested in the taping and have listened intently to selected passages. On one occasion, a preadolescent boy, usually timid, insisted that a part of the tape be played where he had firmly reproved an aggressive boy. Both listened carefully, one with elation, the other impassively. This experience marked the beginning of improved behavior in both boys.

6. *Seek consultation from an experienced group therapist.* While this is not necessary, it can greatly enhance the possibilities of therapeutic results.

Beginning group leaders sometimes feel that group counseling is far too complex to try without special training. This need not be true in juvenile probation. If one is content with the fairly limited but important goals of increased verbal communication, more faithful reporting, a chance to exchange thoughts and possibly feelings, a more agreeable attitude toward probation, greater opportunity to give the probationer miscellaneous information that might help him, and a saving of time for the probation officer, then group work can be done on a fairly easy level. What more is accomplished in the time-consuming and often unsatisfying individual interview?

FOSTER CARE AS A CORRECTIONAL RESOURCE*

The use of substitute home care for children in difficulty with the law is not new to the American correctional scene. In some communities, foster care has been used as a positive corrective experience for the delinquent while he is allowed to remain in the community. More often than not, however, use of foster care has been negatively oriented. That is to say, if the child must be removed from his own home, then the focus has been to place him anywhere except in an institution, perpetuating the myth that the last place on earth you send a child is to an institution. In similar fashion, when institutional administrators have made use of foster care as an alternative to sending the child back to his own home, it has been because of certain disabilities which exist in that home.

Why is the community important to the success of foster-home care? Foster-home care can only be successful when it is carried through in its entirety. It can, in fact, be undesirable if it is not based on a complete program which involves the family, the school, and full community resources.

Treatment of delinquent children is not just the responsibility of the professionals. The community must take a real part in treatment, not just be a medium in which treatment takes place. The adolescent delinquent is a product of the community, not just another "baby" of juvenile court. He comes from the community; he will be placed within the community; he will return to the community.

The mobilization of community responsibility requires education and reorientation of those working with community resources: *knowledge* of what the child needs from the community; *knowledge* of limitations of community service facilities; *awareness* of archaic attitudes toward treatment of delinquency.

---

* Reprinted from *The Quarterly*. Charles L. Newman: Foster care in the treatment of juvenile delinquency. *The Quarterly, 20*(No. 1):8-14, March 1963.

The delinquent child needs more than a foster home which is an island to itself within the community. He needs to develop relationships with adults other than the caseworker and the foster parent. He needs to know the kinds of things other children do and enjoy in the community. He needs an ongoing program within his school, including an educated school administration and teacher-worker plan.

More important, he needs the full mobilization of community resources educated to the current realities of the changing social scene . . . the changing patterns of social life which limit the range of placement homes available—the limited employment opportunities for youngsters ready for independence.

Courts, too, present a major reality because they can determine whether a child is kept in his own home or placed elsewhere. Concern for leadership, dignity, and operating caliber of the court is a major community responsibility.

Because the strength of the foster-family home may be weakened by the shortcomings of agency staff, the community must keep abreast of the needs of its agencies: the problems of coordinating services and keeping personnel at a high level. A community council can serve an important function in this field, helping to coordinate resources such as church groups, character-building activities, educational facilities, and so forth, as well as helping solve jurisdictional problems between several agencies.

To answer these needs, the community must be aware of the limitations of their agencies and placement facilities, as well as the basic structure of their courts. The community should constantly examine the conditions which contribute to delinquency within that community.

Foster-home care for whom? For how long? For what purpose other than housing? The ideal foster home would be one in which sufficient latitude is present for the child—dependent or delinquent—to work out his relationships with parental figures and find room for his own personality development. Even for the older child who is seeking parental emancipation, individual home care can be meaningful if foster parents can provide the necessary milieu. Ideally, foster-home care should be part of "treatment" of juvenile delinquents as well as placement for dependents.

Shortage of aware foster parents, limited trained workers to help them become aware, the changing social scene which provides fewer middle-class foster homes, the older child's reluctance to make new family ties—all are problems needing consideration in the usefulness of the foster home as a placement facility.

Although the older child can make a satisfactory adjustment in a foster family, he usually prefers a youth boarding home. Also, foster parents are normally reluctant to take older children; when they do accept such a placement, the family's increased dependency needs must be considered.

The following are not placeable in a foster home: the hyperaggressive type and the extremely passive. Both make difficult adjustments.

If the child is to benefit from the foster family, he must know how he is to define the "parents" . . . what to call them . . . the nature of his relationship with them. The problem of authority is important to this relationship: who sets the limits on hours, friends, and activities? Whether it be the parents or the agency, the youngster will thoroughly test these limits.

Why are resources for foster care shrinking? The foster care scene is complicated by the neighborhood movement in our changing social scene. As more middle-class white families move from the city to the suburbs, they are replaced by lower-class whites and Negroes, many of whom will be the parents of youngsters needing foster care.

Because our traditional middle-class foster-parent family is moving away and because many youngsters coming from problem families are unable to adjust in a home of higher culture, our resources for foster care are shrinking. Too, there is less opportunity to use upper-lower-class families because of crowded apartment buildings, *de facto* racial segregation, and increased employment of both parents.

When we do find the families, we still find problems: foster parents do not always take the same interest in schooling the ward as they take in their own children. The natural parents often tend to interfere in their youngster's adjustment, and the foster parents often overinvest emotionally in the ward, complicating his release.

Ironically, a number of foster-family homes are working successfully in providing treatment and care for the adolescent delinquent, but the homes do not meet the minimum standards for licensing.

Recognizing the value of foster home in the treatment of juvenile delinquency, how do we develop them? Frequently community and professional concepts are hindrances in developing resources for adolescent delinquents: such concepts that say a foster family must consist of both a father and a mother figure; that low income rules out a home; that foster parents interested in the financial profit should be suspect. Even in the cases where the professionals have taken a fresh look at these concepts, they have still not sufficiently acquainted the community with changing patterns in the field of placement.

What are some special placement problems? Foster parents are not equipped to be therapists, nor would the realities of such a living situation be possible. This makes it difficult for them to accept disturbed children. These children often have unresolved guilt inhibiting their development of new and meaningful relationships.

Adolescent placement is always difficult because of normal emancipation needs. Frequently the delinquent adolescent is working out aggressive feelings of distrust and anger, not only toward his own parents but toward any adult in an authority position. Also, some adolescents are not suited for either normal foster-home placement or for traditional institutional placement. Some, in fact, have had extended placement and still have not found roots by the time they reach fifteen years of age. A *specialized group setting* seems to be the best answer for such youngsters. Younger adolescents usually are ready and anxious to associate with others of their own age and receive therapeutic benefits from the group interaction. Often these group settings are in apartment units which help, particularly for the *city* delinquent. Even the more aggressive youngsters have been able to move into these group activities—with some assistance—due in part to the reduction in the demands on them for personal relationships with adults.

The Adolescent

Among delinquents, adolescents stand out as the largest group with special characteristic needs. The adolescent may know that he wants to change his behavior but still resists because he feels that he is "marked" and "so why bother?" The adolescent is typically hostile. He needs means—including physical—of venting this hostility. To meet these needs, the adolescent uses withdrawal and passiveness as often as he uses a social behavior; this pattern must be understood.

The delinquent adolescent is no different than any others of his age in seeking identification with his peers; but because of his experience and background, this peer group identification drive can be a problem unless properly directed.

Those youngsters in the middle and upper teens—fourteen years and beyond—usually have trouble accepting substitute parents. This older adolescent, on the other hand, is also ready to take his first steps into the adult world and cannot accept the personal limitations of institutional living along with the other restrictions.

Delinquent girls have special problems peculiar to their sex: they tend to reinforce each other's delinquent behavior when placed in large numbers. Also, there is limited placement potential for their needs to identify with the roles of the opposite sex.

There are children of all ages who cannot take foster-home treatment, although they might seem to need it. At the same time, they do not need institutional living. Such youngsters may have a strong relationship with one parent and yet feel rejected by the other. They tend toward run-away behavior and present a special problem.

The Parents' Roles

The parental view of the child is critical in the dynamics of good placement. *The foster parents* must be prepared for the eventual release of the youngster. *The natural parents* must be prepared to hold down interference—particularly those immature parents who tend to compete with the foster parents. Too restrictive a policy regarding parental visitation, however, can be damaging in the long run to the new relationship between the child and the foster parent.

The Community's Role

Usually the extreme adolescent delinquent is only *one* of many, but he is the one the public sees as the typical delinquent. Care must be taken to plan for the majority—not the extreme—when utilizing community resources for the treatment of delinquents.

The community must come to appreciate the implications of social change upon delinquent and other children: the impact of the suburban movement, young marriage, lack of employment opportunities. All available knowledge on the problem should be placed before the public to provide understanding of delinquent needs.

Special Dynamics of Placement

Adhering to the principle that resources should be selected in terms of the child's needs, some facilities which might fit in particular cases are briefly described.

The Group Foster Home

This setting is particularly for the adolescent who has reached the threshold of emancipation from parental control. Through group activity, the adolescent feels freer to express his emotions. The group process also helps him "see" and "recall" the details of supportive casework discussions.

Part-time Foster Care

This provides for children who need temporary removal from the pressures of their own community. Often such placement for two or three days a week—with counseling and structured group activity—will help them adjust to their own community.

Forestry Camps

Such a setting yields a particularly therapeutic effect on young boys, who need masculine productivity in a situation with noninstitutional controls. Camps also give the adolescent boy a chance to identify with a father figure. This is better for him than the institutional cottage mother if he comes from a home where there has been a dominating mother figure. Most children need both a father and mother figure, but some boys adjust better in a facility staffed by a father figure; some girls require a facility with just a mother figure.

Camps should be used selectively, however, because they are remote from the child's community and offer activity unrelated to city life. The distance hinders strengthening of parental ties, and the lack of opportunity for visits can outweigh other therapeutic effects.

Planning for Change

Where the child has spent a period of time in an institution, prerelease planning is of the highest importance; but work in this area is weak because plans typically do not start until weeks ahead of the child's release. In one of the more recent techniques attempted, group counseling was arranged to include both foster parents and real parents in a discussion of their feelings about the release.

A youngster who succeeds in school or on the job often makes a good adjustment in the community. For this reason, every effort must be made to coordinate his school program to his needs. Agencies must let the school know the needs of their special groups of children in the school in order to aid in curriculum planning. Summer workshops for teachers and summer welfare jobs for school personnel might help to establish the mutuality of agency-school problems.

License laws, mentioned earlier, must be liberalized if we are going to explore further the trend toward group foster homes. Children need the protection of acceptable safety, health, and accommodation standards, but the laws should be broadened to provide the flexibility of a noninstitutional setting. Generally, state standards are unrealistic and seldom adaptable to the specialized type of facility—such as the small-group home for the adolescent and the one-parent home for the child whose emotional needs require it.

The trend toward group homes for the older delinquent is a significant one. Structured group activity is the best tool for his treatment: he feels freer and more willing to express his feelings in the dynamics of group process.

Operational research of pragmatic use to agencies is still limited and will remain so unless agencies state their hypotheses in a testable fashion, encourage finances for research, and take advantage of available findings and resources. Agencies should perform, write up, and disseminate their findings and plunge more boldly into research endeavors.

New Approaches—The Patterns of Change

The placement field needs to smash stereotypes relating to criteria for selecting a good foster parent. What constitutes treatment? What are the physical requirements for a foster home that can provide satisfactory placement and treatment?

We must look at what we are doing and ask if we are thinking in stereotypes or planning dynamically. Do we know if younger foster parents might work well with some delinquent types? Should we continue to match all female delinquents with female workers or male delinquents with male workers? Do we look too closely at the chronological age, at the expense of the emotional age of the child? Do we always need a two-parent home? Are we still thinking that forestry camps create an end in themselves?

One of the reasons for failure in foster-home placement is the lack of thorough evaluation of both the child and the home. To allow for the range of crises which will probably develop with older delinquents, we must recognize that our intellectual preparation of the foster parents does not necessarily prepare him emotionally. "Preparing the parent" may be one of our stereotypes; bringing the foster parent into the program as part of the working team for a child is a dynamic approach to "preparation."

Conclusion

To match the needs of the child with the appropriate facility, there is an urgent need for a diversified range of "substitute facilities." All children do not do well in the same or similar placement. Some need room for acting-out behavior. Some need highly structured situations. The younger child often does well in the traditional foster family; the older delinquent does well in small-group foster homes. Some children adjust better in a one-parent home. Needs differ by age and by sex. Finally, in long-term treatment, needs change and sometimes call for placement changes. There is a great need for foster group care for the delinquent, but the development of the group-home concept has been slow.

To establish a diversified range of substitute facilities, state license laws need updating. Licensing which is too rigid is unrealistic and rules out a number of potential homes which would provide service to children in need. Historically, placement workers have tried to provide homes with physical opportunities the child has missed in his own home. This concept should be examined to provide a "situation" in which the child can develop, based on realistic expectation of how the child will function socially. Work with the natural parents while substitute care is going on to create a healthier "real" home for his return is far better than trying to "create" a home meeting needs he has missed.

Foster-home care is not a panacea. There is a growing need for placement situations known as halfway houses, transition houses, intermediate type homes, or group homes. To hold down detention time and still provide an adequate period for evaluation geared toward appropriate placement, we need more of the transition-type facilities. Treatment is the object, but we are more willing to pay $3,500 a year to punish a child in an institution rather than treat him by proper placement. Time is of the essence in proper placement—we need as complete an evaluation for placing a delinquent youngster in foster care as we do in placing children for adoption.

We must educate the public regarding attitudes toward the delinquent child if we are to find noninstitutional resources for him. The lay public wishes to get delinquents from sight, not rehabilitate them. The concept of foster care developed around the needs of the dependent, neglected child; therefore, the community has more tolerance for this group. Actually, children who are declared delinquent match nondelinquent children in personality types and behavior disorders.

All children do not benefit from foster-type care; some require a period of institutionalization—but, for most children, the appropriate substitute placement can serve as treatment in itself.

JUVENILE AFTERCARE*

Juvenile aftercare is defined as the release of a child from an institution at the time when he can best benefit from release and from life in the community under the supervision of a counselor. Use of the term *aftercare* rather than *parole,* though not yet fully accepted even within the field of juvenile correction, has been encouraged by persons interested in social service in order to separate juvenile programs from the legalistic language and concepts of adult parole. The concept of aftercare has wider acceptance than the term, but the survey of aftercare programs in the United States today reveals wide variations in structure and program content.

Introduction

Aftercare service for juveniles first appeared in the United States in the early nineteenth century, but it has become an integral part of correctional rehabilitation for the young offender only in the past decade. In most states, aftercare is the least-developed aspect of correction; in the opinion of many observers, it is less adequate than its counterpart, adult parole.

Aftercare originated in New York and Pennsylvania, where houses of refuge identured child inmates to work in private homes for several years. The child's daily regimen rarely included anything but work. Total responsibility for the child was vested in the family that undertook to feed and clothe him, and it was the family that determined when he had earned his freedom. This form of postinstitutional treatment persisted for over half a century.

The Rationale of Aftercare

When the behavior of a juvenile becomes sufficiently antisocial to warrant confining him in an institution, a complex array

---

* Reprinted from *Correction in the United States* (A Survey for the President's Commission on Law Enforcement and the Administration of Justice). National Council on Crime and Delinquency, 1966, pp. 99-112.

of correctional services is set in motion. Part of it deals with the planning and operation of a program that will help him when he leaves the institution.

In the United States, children and youths from eight to twenty-one years of age are committed to juvenile training schools. On any one day, the total population of these schools is about 42,000. Because of the wide range of age and experience, differing placement plans are essential. Preadolescent children need programs different in content and philosophy from those needed by young adults, who may have been in the labor force before confinement. To meet such varied needs, aftercare programs must be flexible and creative, rather than routine and superficial as they are in parts of this country today.

The rationale for aftercare is simple. Each juvenile must have a carefully planned, expertly executed, and highly individualized program if he is to return to life outside the institution and play a constructive role there. Successful reentry into society is often made difficult both by the effects of institutional life on a juvenile and by the attitudes of the community to which he returns. The aftercare plan for him must take both these factors into account.

Institutionalization does different things to different children. Some become more antisocial and more sophisticated in delinquency than they were when they entered the training school. Others become dependent on the institution and must learn how to break the ties gradually.

Community settings also differ widely. Some juveniles go back to the very conditions in which their previous delinquency was rooted. Most must face the possibility of the stigma attached to confinement in a correctional institution.

Aftercare is traditionally described as the last point on the juvenile correctional continuum. Yet, because it is in some respects the last opportunity to achieve the correctional objective, planning for aftercare must be an integral part of institutional programs. Indeed, it should begin immediately after commitment to an institution.

A good aftercare plan uses many resources inside and outside the institution. Since implementation of the plan takes place within the community, the aftercare counselor should use a variety of community resources to make the juvenile's reentry meaningful and productive. He should be working with all details of the case related to the ward's community even during the period of confinement in the state institution, forestry camp, or other setting attached to the training school.

It has taken this nation a long time to recognize the importance of aftercare services for young people leaving correctional institutions, forestry camps, or halfway houses. Few well-developed aftercare programs were in existence fifteen years ago. Some states have not yet initiated organizationally sound programs. On the other hand, a few have developed programs which stand out as models for those emerging elsewhere.

Survey Findings

An Overview of Aftercare Today

The major items in this survey include data from the forty state-operated special aftercare programs,* but not from programs administered by city and county correctional systems, private institutions, and noncorrectional services of child and public welfare departments, since full information could not be obtained from them.

The forty states reported a total of about 48,000 youths under aftercare supervision. Estimates for the other states, based on a projection of that figure, indicate that about 59,000 are under aftercare supervision in the United States. The number of juveniles in state programs ranges from 110 to 13,000.

Any study of aftercare today at the national level is plagued by inadequate statistics coming from the fifty states and Puerto Rico. As long as this situation persists, attempting a thorough study of juvenile aftercare can be described only as an exercise in futility. The gaps in vital information are so great that the reliability and validity of the few national statistics which can be gathered must be viewed with extreme caution. Efforts are being made to change

* States which do not operate centralized juvenile aftercare programs are Alabama, Arkansas, Kansas, Maryland, Mississippi, New Mexico, North Carolina, North Dakota, Pennsylvania, and Virginia.

this condition, but extensive organizational programing for statewide data collection is needed.

State operating costs range from $7,000 to over $4,000,000 a year. Together the states are spending about $18,000,000 a year. Average per capita cost is $320 a year.

This expenditure is small in comparison with the cost of state-operated juvenile institutions, which spend over $144 million a year to care for an average daily population of slightly over 42,000 at an average per capita cost of about $3,400 a year.

The fact that aftercare costs less than one-tenth as much as institutional care is nothing to be proud of. As reported by the forty states, its relative cheapness reflects the inadequacy of the programs at least as much as it demonstrates inherent economy. It is not uncommon for 250 adolescents to be assigned to a program staffed by only two or three aftercare counselors located at the state capital or training school which may be hundreds of miles from the communities where the juveniles are supposedly under supervision. Aside from the excessiveness of the supervisors' caseloads, sheer distance reduces the effectiveness of the program.

Thus, aftercare programs should not be judged solely by their relative economy of operation. Rather, the question should be asked, How much should be spent to make aftercare truly effective? For it should be remembered that effective aftercare is one of the best methods of preventing recidivism.

Organizational Arrangements

According to the standard, responsibility for aftercare should be vested in a state agency which is administratively responsible for institutional related services for delinquent children.

As shown in Table 6-I, the organizational arrangements through which juvenile aftercare services are administered vary widely among the states. In contrast to other programs for juveniles such as public education, which is always administered by a state educational agency, juvenile aftercare has no clear organizational pattern. Administration may be the responsibility of, for example, a lay board, an adult correction program, a public welfare agency, a youth authority, or the training school itself.

TABLE 6-I

ORGANIZATIONAL ARRANGEMENT FOR ADMINISTRATION OF AFTERCARE

Type of Structure	*Number of States*
State Department of Public Welfare	13
State Youth Correction Agency	12
State Department of Correction	10
Institution Board	6
State Training School Board	4
State Department of Health	1
Other	5
	51

The issue of administration is further complicated by the survey finding that in only thirty-four states does the state department which administers the state juvenile institutions also provide aftercare services for juveniles released from these institutions. For example, in five states, local probation departments are given responsibility for aftercare even though they have no official relationship to the agency administering the training schools. Patterns of local jurisdiction have developed for various reasons. In some states, there was no state agency which could provide supervision at the local level, and therefore a local social service agency was asked to perform this function. In other states, state officials preferred to give jurisdiction to local agencies because they believed the youths would receive better care from local agencies than from centralized, state-operated programs. In their opinion, local programs helped avoid duplication of services at the state level.

According to the standard, the law under which a juvenile enters a state training school should provide that the agency which is granted legal custody should have the right to determine when he shall leave the institution.

The opportunity for legal and jurisdictional disputes is always present. In nine states, the problem is complicated by the fact that the committing judge becomes involved in the decision to release a juvenile for aftercare services. If he is thus involved in the release decision, he must be thoroughly aware of the child's behavior and growth at the training school as well as of the factors in his home community; actually, in the nine states where this procedure is followed, the judge rarely has this information. In five of the nine states, the committing judge must approve all releases; in the others, he must approve only certain ones. A training school staff that has worked daily with a ward may find its aftercare plan disapproved by a judge unfamiliar with all the circumstances of his case. Where the state provides aftercare services, it should be unnecessary for the committing judge to approve aftercare plans for children released from state institutions.

Length of Commitment

According to the standard, the law under which a juvenile enters a state training school should provide that the child remain there for an indefinite period of not more than three years and of no specified minimum before being released on aftercare.

The survey found that specific minimums are authorized by law in three states: In one, the specified minimum is twelve months; in another, it is eighteen months; in the third, it varies. And in many other states, the survey found, specific minimum length of stay in the training school has been established *informally*—without legal authorization of any kind but firmly established nonetheless—by superintendents, classification committees, and other groups or individuals.

Statewide Reporting

According to the standard, an adequate statistical reporting system should be maintained, with data on parole and aftercare uniformly and automatically reported to a central correctional statistical agency in the state.

The survey found that more than two-fifths of the states fail to meet this standard. A few states have excellent reporting systems, but the great majority have no reliable procedure, not even for simple data. A little more than half the states have a central statistical unit responsible for statistical information on the state juvenile aftercare operation. Table 6-II shows the auspices under which these units function.

TABLE 6-II

STATE CENTRAL STATISTICAL REPORTING UNITS FOR JUVENILE AFTERCARE

Location	*Number of States*
Correctional Agency	17
Department of Public Welfare	6
Board of Control	1
Department of Health	1
Not specified in the report	4
	29

Juvenile Paroling Authorities

According to the standard, the authority to approve placement should be vested in the parent state agency. The decision on the readiness of the youngster for placement should be based on the considered opinion of the appropriate training school staff committee.

According to the data gathered in the survey, the authority to release juveniles from state training schools rests with a wide variety of persons, groups, or agencies. Table 6-III shows the patterns of organizational structure of central paroling authorities. (Releasing mechanisms operated by individual training schools are not included in this table because they are not central paroling authorities.)

In most cases, these authorities are composed of members appointed by the governor. Only seven states in the nation have

TABLE 6-III

CENTRAL PAROLING AUTHORITIES FOR RELEASE OF JUVENILES

	Number of States
Youth Authority	4
State Training School Board	3
State Institutions Board	2
Department of Correction	2
Department of Public Welfare	2
Parole Board	2
Board of Control	1
Ex officio Board (Members: governor, secretary of state, state treasurer, state auditor, state superintendent of public instruction)	1
	17

aftercare boards on which the members serve full time. Over half the states that have aftercare boards do not pay the members —state officials or lay citizens—for this service. In eight states, aftercare board chairmen are paid, and in seven the board members receive salaries ranging from $6,000 to $18,000 a year, most frequently at the lower figure. Most board members are unpaid, are not trained for the board's special responsibilities, and are politically appointed.

Use of a central board, a relatively new event in juvenile correction, has been debated extensively. Those favoring it say the board can make sounder decisions than any other kind of releasing authority. Those questioning its usefulness say that board members are, in effect, assuming staff functions and cannot possibly know the details of the cases well enough from reading reports or hearing short presentations to make proper decisions. They believe further that competent staff members in the training school or other facilities within the parent agency are better equipped than any outside group to make realistic decisions based on a thorough awareness of the details of a case.

The trend in the mid-1950's was toward the establishment of juvenile aftercare boards. This trend has ended. A large group of juvenile correctional administrators is now urging establishment of a pattern in which the training school (or other facility such as a forestry camp or halfway house) would make release recommendations to the parent agency which, in turn, would authorize release.

Length of Aftercare Period

The survey found that approximately 59,000 young people—about 47,000 boys and 12,000 girls—received aftercare services during the most recently reported annual period, 1964 to 1965. The boy-girl ratio, slightly less than four to one, is the same as other findings in most other statistical reports on delinquency comparisons by sex.

The average length of stay under aftercare supervision varies.* Of the states reporting, twelve keep their juveniles in active after-

* Thirteen states did not report average length of stay on aftercare.

care supervision programs for an average of less than one year; twenty-five give aftercare supervision for an average of one year or more.

The state reports show a trend toward keeping girls under aftercare supervision longer than boys. The explanation may lie in our society's attitude that the young female requires protection for a longer period than the young male. Girls are kept longer in institutional settings than boys are, and staff members working with the delinquent girl feel she needs more intense and prolonged services than the delinguent boy does. Of fourteen states reporting on length of aftercare supervision, ten show an average substantially longer for girls than for boys; four report an average period longer for boys.

Personnel

Standards have been developed for appointment of juvenile aftercare staff, educational requirements, and salaries.

The standard on the first of these matters states that all aftercare personnel, as well as supporting personnel, should be appointed through a civil service or merit system from a register established through rating of examinations opened to qualified candidates without consideration as to residence. Much of the correctional field has been plagued by its close association with politics at the state and local levels. The courts, institutions, and parole programs in a number of states have been affected by political considerations that have influenced staffing and program operations.

Of the forty states reporting personnel data for the survey,* twenty-three have civil service or merit system coverage for the director of juvenile aftercare services, twenty-six have such coverage for the district supervisor, and twenty-nine have it for the aftercare worker.

The standard for minimum educational requirements states that the juvenile aftercare worker should have a bachelor's degree with a major in the social or behavioral sciences, plus one

* No data on personnel were reported by Alabama, Arkansas, Illinois, Kansas, Maryland, New Mexico, North Carolina, North Dakota, Pennsylvania, and Virginia.

year of graduate study in social work or a related field or one year of paid full-time casework experience in correction.

Of the forty states, thirty-four report that they have such a requirement. The survey found, however, that not all juvenile aftercare directors actually enforce this requirement when they hire aftercare workers. The fact of the matter is that many aftercare workers have less than a college education. The minimum standard is approved in principle but not observed in practice.

Another standard calls for payment of adequate salaries commensurate with the qualifications, high trust, and responsibility required for aftercare work.

That this standard is seldom met is shown by Table 6-IV. The reported annual salary ranges of $4,000 to $18,000 have little meaning. The median is $8,000 to $9,000 for a director; $7,000 to $8,000 for a district supervisor; and $5,000 to $6,000 for an aftercare counselor. The opportunity for a counselor to earn more than $6,000 a year is extremely limited in most states. One state reports that it pays male counselors more than female counselors for presumably the same work. Even if the counselor does advance to a supervisory level, he can rarely earn more than $9,000 a year.

TABLE 6-IV

BEGINNING SALARIES OF JUVENILE AFTERCARE PERSONNEL, BY NUMBER OF AGENCIES

	Director	*Supervisor*	*Counselor*
$ 4,001- 5,000	0	0	10
5,001- 6,000	0	4	17
6,001- 7,000	1	7	10
7,001- 8,000	7	11	0
8,001- 9,000	11	6	1
9,001-10,000	4	0	2
10,001-11,000	8	0	0
11,001-12,000	3	1	0
12,001-13,000	2	0	0
13,001-14,000	0	2	0
14,001-15,000	0	0	0
15,001-16,000	0	0	0
16,001-17,000	0	0	0
17,001-18,000	0	0	0
Over 18,000	1	0	0
	37	31	40

Caseload and Work Assignments

The standard calls for the juvenile aftercare counselor to have a maximum workload of fifty active supervision cases, with one pre-release investigation being considered as equal to three cases under active supervision. (Although no standard has been formulated on the matter, good practice calls for assignment of every child in a training school, or in some other facility of the parent agency, to an aftercare counselor who should work with the parents and others in the interest of planning for the child's release.)

Table 6-V presents the variation in caseload size, the number of children under supervision, and each caseload category's percentage of the total number of children under supervision throughout the forty states where special aftercare staffs are employed. Average caseloads range from 30 to 125 *supervision cases,* with the median in the 61 to 70 range. Since these caseloads are not weighted for the number of investigations made or for the number of children worked with by the aftercare counselors in the institutions, the actual caseload size is substantially larger than is indicated in the supervision caseload.

Caseload geography complicates the operation of a statewide juvenile aftercare service for wards released from a state training school or some other facility within the parent agency. In many

TABLE 6-V

AFTERCARE CASELOADS IN STATES HAVING SPECIAL AFTERCARE STAFF

*Size of Caseload**	*No. of States*	*No. of Children under Supervision*	*Category's Total Number under Supervision (%)*
Under 30 cases	3	536	1.12
30-40 cases	10	8,612	17.98
41-50 cases	5	4,339	9.06
51-60 cases	5	2,244	4.68
61-70 cases	6	23,382	48.81
71-90 cases	9	4,875	10.18
Over 91 cases	2	3,914	8.17
	40	47,902	100.00

* Number of children under aftercare supervision. Does not include children in institutions.

states a vast distance must be covered by each member of the small aftercare staff. Thus his contacts are usually crisis-oriented; that is, the counselor sees the child only when an emergency arises. In many states, supervision generally consists of a monthly report, written by the juvenile himself and mailed to the state office. Wards released to rural areas rarely, sometimes never, see the aftercare worker. Youths from urban areas are likely to receive more active supervision than those from small towns. Unless several regional offices are set up in the state, released wards whose homes are distant from the central office are neglected. Courtesy supervision is occasionally requested of local welfare, court, or voluntary personnel, but these services are spotty and irregular. In short: supportive, sustained, and positive implementation of an aftercare plan is, more often than not, rare.

The total staff complement in the reporting states is as follows: district supervisors, 133; district assistant supervisors, 76; aftercare counselors, 1,033.

The range in number of state juvenile aftercare workers is from 2 to 273 per state, and the number of counselors for the entire country is exceedingly small. Isolation of the training school, vast distances to travel, diversified and excessive caseloads, and low salaries serve to complicate the work and frequently frustrate the aftercare staff.

As previously indicated, caution must be used in stating personnel totals. In many states the juvenile aftercare counselor works for a probation or welfare or similar agency and carries a caseload for that agency in addition to his aftercare assignment.

Staff Development

According to the standard, a staff development program should be provided, with staff assigned specifically to the training function.

The findings in this survey reveal a great lack of in-service training programs. Aside from the eleven states that have no statewide aftercare services at all, eight of the forty that do have such services have no in-service training program. Table 6-VI points to the failure of many states to train their staffs properly. No information is available on the type, format, instructional quality, faculty, curriculum, or other important details of the training programs—information necessary for evaluating their quality. The table shows only availability and frequency; quality is another matter.

TABLE 6-VI

IN-SERVICE TRAINING PROGRAMS IN JUVENILE AFTERCARE AGENCIES

Frequency	*Number of States*
Weekly	4
Monthly	14
Quarterly	9
Annually	3
Irregularly	2
Never	8
	40

According to the standard, an agency training program should include educational leaves with pay for graduate training.

Table 6-VII shows the number of stipends with educational leave reported as available for personnel in juvenile aftercare services. The figures further reflect the little attention paid to staff development through graduate stipends with educational leave for personnel assigned to correctional programs having exclusive responsibility for juvenile aftercare cases. Stipends are provided in not more than thirteen states; the other twenty-eight states with special state-operated aftercare programs have no educational enrichment programs outside the agency for their staff personnel.

TABLE 6-VII

EDUCATIONAL STIPENDS FOR AFTERCARE PERSONNEL

Number of States	*Number of Stipends*
1	22
1	18
1	17
1	7
1	5
1	4
3	3
1	2
3	1
28	0
10	Does not apply
51	79

Diversified Aftercare Services

The standards call for the provision of diversified aftercare services and facilities for children returning to the community from the institution or another correctional facility.

The survey found that services to released juveniles range from superficial supervision, consisting of nothing more than the juvenile's written monthly reports, to highly sophisticated aftercare innovations that meet the standards of good practice.

The survey asked the question, "Does the aftercare program also operate foster homes, group homes, and halfway houses?" Of the forty states with statewide programs, twelve answered *yes,* including two which reported they did not pay for foster care but did use free home placements and three which qualified their positive reply by stating that local child welfare departments found and supervised foster homes for aftercare placements. Individual foster homes are used more frequently than group foster homes. Four state-operated programs reported the use of halfway houses for aftercare.

Three types of imaginative or unusual rehabilitation programs were reported more frequently than others. They are best described as efforts at the use of groups in treatment, family-centered services, and youth employment programs specifically designed for the released ward. Some of these programs were described as experimental and new. They occur only where the state-operated program is well established and has an adequate budget.

Implications

The survey findings presented above are the harsh realities of the nation's failure to come to grips with the juvenile aftercare problem. For years the response by many states to the needs of a large group of young people has been made with little boldness and no imagination. As it stands today in many states, juvenile aftercare is a monument to neglect. Each year about 59,000 youngsters leave a correctional setting after having spent a substantial amount of time there. They leave with the hope of restoring themselves to meaningful lives in our society. Their greatest need is assistance through a sound aftercare program. Most of them receive only minimal help during this critical period in their lives.

Many of the delinquents released from training schools cannot return to their own homes, and many others should not. For some, extensive restructuring of their social environment is essential. An entirely new social fabric is in order—especially, as the case records illustrate, for girls. Many neglected, dependent, and antisocial girls return to small towns to face hostility or indifference. Their past sex delinquency or incorrigible behavior is not the kind of thing small communities tolerate. Effective aftercare for them must encompass a variety of placement plans. Those who cannot or should not return to their home towns need placement plans based on proved alternatives.

The following discussion notes some important trends noticeable in the findings of this national survey.

Organization and Management of Aftercare Programs

The trend is toward the development of state-operated aftercare programs. Adequately financed and soundly planned state aftercare agencies have merged as an efficient pattern of organization. The trend is away from program direction by staff at the training school.

The state aftercare agency needs clear lines of responsibility and authority. The working relationship with the training school appears to be most effective when both agencies, the training school and the aftercare program, are in the same administrative structure. Separate administration creates friction between the two on questions of release, overcrowding, responsibility for the ward, and initiation of aftercare planning.

Release Procedures

The authority to release a juvenile on aftercare is not vested in the same kind of structure in every state. Use of a juvenile aftercare board similar to the adult parole board, established in several states, entails certain difficulties and is viewed as undesirable by many training school superintendents. In those states where a parent agency has responsibility for both the institution and the aftercare service, the institution should be responsible for aftercare recommendation, with the parent agency responsible for final concurrence or disapproval.

A Reporting System

A statewide reporting system is essential to competent programing. Several states have no statistics on the number of youths under aftercare supervision. Data should be collected at the state level. Research staff is essential to the state agency for planning, program development, and effectiveness in agency activities. At present, a reliable national study of aftercare is impossible because of this deficiency in reporting and statistics. The trend is toward the establishment of statewide reporting systems. It should be encouraged in every possible way.

Staffing and Staff Development

The trend is toward employment of trained, qualified, resourceful counselors with skills in group treatment as well as casework. From top management to beginning aftercare counselor, the staff must be included in a civil service or merit system. The state agency must be able to draw upon a budget to purchase services it does not have, whenever necessary, to insure the successful implementation of an aftercare plan.

An effective staff is one in tune with the rapid changes produced by new knowledge in the behavioral sciences. Thus it needs a sustained and enlightened staff development program. Yesterday's answers may lead to today's mistakes. In short, the aftercare staff must be surrounded by an educationally sound and financially rewarding program. Salaries and working conditions need improvement at all levels. Staff development should include orientation, in-service training, and stipends with educational leaves for qualified personnel. The trend is just beginning in these areas. A great deal of stimulation is needed, with assistance in technical and financial matters, at all governmental levels. Without these rewarding elements, the staffs of most aftercare agencies are likely to experience low morale, high turnover, and routinization of programs. One of the most successful recruitment devices is the assurance to prospective or new staff members that they are entering an effective, productive agency with high professional standards.

Programing Aftercare Services

An important development in the trend toward positive aftercare services is the initiation of aftercare planning immediately after commitment. This practice enables the institution and the aftercare staff to collaborate in formulating an aftercare plan and to cooperate in implementing it.

The staff needs many alternative resources in its planning. The trend is toward the use of substitute homes such as foster homes, group care, and community-centered homes. A staff having these alternative resources has the opportunity to make the placement plan realistic and responsive to the needs of the young ward.

In addition to alternative home placements, the trend is toward extensive use of community resources in planning and operating aftercare services. Youth employment services, vocational rehabilitation counseling, special vocational and public school programs, and medical and psychiatric services are all part of the community complex from which depth can be added to the state agency. The aftercare staff must be aware of these services and be able to purchase them when necessary.

Conclusion

Both the findings of this survey of aftercare and the implications drawn from them show clearly that aftercare must be an integral part of a comprehensive correctional structure. Many gaps in the rehabilitation process are a direct result of its separation into three uncoordinated areas—probation, institutions, and aftercare. The question, therefore, is not how to relate aftercare to correction but how to make it contribute to the objective of the whole correctional system—rehabilitation of the offender.

Chapter Seven

Treatment Strategies in Probation and Parole (Part I)

THERE are two methods, broadly speaking, by which probation and parole endeavor to protect society.

The first is legalistic. It imposes discipline through various restraints and restrictions which are placed upon the conduct of the offender. While a willingness to agree to the conditions is precursor to granting of probation or parole, the ability of an individual to abide by those rules and regulations will determine his success in that status. Thus, as a means of social control, the legalistic method has a value which cannot be ignored.

Restraint and restriction have certain coercive value, but force without counseling services is unlikely to incur a true change in the character of the individual. The second method then, one of reeducation and redirection, is far more subtle. Influencing and changing human behavior is a very delicate and difficult task. In the treatment process, the corrections officer attempts to have the offender see himself as he actually is—as a person who has not been playing the game according to the rules of society—and to modify that self-picture through actual change of personality so that the offender can become a law-abiding, contributing member of the community.

Obviously, there is no one way of treatment with the law violator. While there are some generic similarities to be found among all people, and the offender is no exception, each personality is made up of a number of elements which are blended together in proportions and relationships which are unique to the individual. Thus, direction and education must follow a pattern dictated by the needs of an individual.

External changes can be effected through an alteration of his social environment and associates, but internal changes must accompany such social alterations in order to assure that the offender will not recidivate. It is through a fusion of these external (social) and internal (psychological) therapies that the probation officer directs his energies.

The establishment of a relationship (rapport) between the agent and client is a first step, but not the only one. Treatment involves a plan which is workable and practical with regard to the offender's background and capacities. Moreover, it demands continuity, for therapy invoked at the whim and fancy of the officer without regard to the needs of the client is apt to do more harm than good.

From time to time, the officer is faced with the situation in which a community agency is better equipped with specialized personnel to render the services needed by the offender. Such services should be utilized whenever possible, and the corrections officer should make it a part of this duty to know what his community has to offer by way of auxiliary services. This is especially true when the needs of the offender are manifested in some special behavioral disorder.

In dealing with the individual in the community, there is frequently a proneness to treat with him "as if" he were in a vacuum. Behavioral problems have their genesis in a number of sources. The corrections officer must be alert to the family situation of his client, particularly where the wife or other family member seems to be the subtle instigator of the offender's antisocial conduct. Where it is not feasible to remove the offender from such an environment, the officer might well consider the use of private social agencies to assist in the social readjustment of family members not under supervision.

Social adjustment is the goal in probation and parole. The techniques employed in obtaining this end result can be the product of many disciplines. What matters is the end result and not the academic label attached to the method used. The aptitude and skill of the probation officer and his participant associates define the degree of success which will be obtained.

The success or failure of parole as a practice can be decided to no small extent by the effectiveness of the prison program which precedes it. Parole, it is worth repeating, is a part of the total correctional experience rather than a segmented, isolated entity.

The classification unit of the prison, the vocational, social, and psychological education and training which the inmate receives as part of the retraining program, *as well as the benefits which undoubtedly accrue from the custodial aspects of a controlled living environment,* contribute to the remaking of the citizen.

The parole board, through its careful selection of parole candidates, attempts to discover which inmates are most ready to serve the balance of their sentences in the community setting. It must be recognized, however, that the vast majority of inmates are ultimately released, and that, in spite of the desirableness of selecting only the best parole risks, the practical reality of the situation is that, *with* or *without* parole, most inmates return to the community. Hence, supervision and treatment following institutionalization become a necessity for all. While this idea has gained some acceptance from the professional community in parole, it is questionable whether the larger community, which frequently continues to regard parole as nothing more than an *act of clemency,* would accept the idea of parole supervision for *all* inmates. Where commitments are made on the basis of indeterminate sentence, however, there would not be any particular problem involved since, on failure, the parole could be revoked and the inmate returned to prison until such time as a true change in his behavior could be detected. Thereafter a new parole period could be initiated.

As in probation work, the task of parole supervision and treatment is to fulfill a dual goal: the protection of society from repeated transgressions by the offender, and the culmination of the treatment and reorientation of the inmate in the community setting.

In some instances, neither of these goals is achieved, nor will they ever be so long as we continue in our thinking that custody *per se,* alters character, and that, in the community, only strict surveillance will eliminate recidivism. Certainly as long as prisons continue to go "through the motions" of rehabilitation with "window dressing" programs, it cannot be hoped that the less-secure community environment will effect the necessary changes when the counselor contacts are, at best, periodic.

The elements of good supervision in parole are the same as

those in probation. The issue of whether probationers and parolees should be supervised by the same officer is an academic one since, with practical reality, there are sufficient cases in most jurisdictions to allow an officer to supervise either one group or the other. Admittedly, there may be differences in the experiences of the probationer and the parolee, but it does not necessarily mean that the probationer has not had institutional experience, perhaps as a juvenile or on a previous conviction.

As in public assistance, there is a tendency to group caseloads with one of the various forms of categorical assistance (such as Aid to Dependent Children, Old Age Assistance) for administrative convenience. So it may be argued that probation and parole caseloads should be separated. In those states where probation and parole services are not amalgamated into a single administrative unit, the question of joint supervision does not occur. (Probation has developed as a court function within the separate jurisdictions of a state, while the history of parole, in the United States at least, has been marked by initiation on a statewide level.)

The purposes and objectives of parole supervision and treatment can be simply stated: to provide the individual with the setting and guidance he needs in working out his problems subsequent to institutional release. Certain conditions, rules, and restrictions are placed upon his behavior to assure that he will not become exposed to the situations which are presumed to be causative in etiology of criminal behavior. The function of the parole officer is twofold: to assist the individual with his problems and to protect the parolee against himself and the community through surveillance. The former involves the use of counseling and casework skills to diagnose and *treat* the underlying social and emotional problems. The latter, surveillance, involves the skillful use of authority, ascertaining the parolees' conduct, activities, and whereabouts to control the parolees' behavior in such a manner so as not to impede the treatment process. It is important to remember that the prognosis in every case is not equal, and thus, we must expect a certain number of parole failures. The essential element is to discover those failures before they do the maximum of harm to themselves and the community.

CONCEPTS OF TREATMENT IN PROBATION AND PAROLE SUPERVISION*

The word *treatment* is probably one of the most overworked words in the correctional lexicon. Whatever its semantic meaning, *treatment* and the *treatment approach* have several connotations: that "it" replaces an "old system" of dealing with offenders; that trained people can do "it" better than untrained ones; that "it" is more effective than other systems of dealing with offenders; that "it" considers the person, his needs, strengths and limitations as they differ from other individuals around him. Increasingly within the correctional field, we have come to accept the idea that the treatment approach to the offender is better than any other method. Hopefully we can eventually demonstrate the greater effectiveness of this method over any other "nontreatment"-oriented approach.

These are values to which we must subscribe, even though the research to date does not substantially support our position. Part of the difficulty rests with the fact that the treatment approach requires of the field not only an ideological acceptance of the philosophy, but also the preparation and existence of a corps of suitably trained persons with the technical know-how, and the actual implementation of treatment practices. Even when so-called intensive treatment programs have been tried, it has frequently been with the use of personnel with limited professional training, in an atmosphere which is suspicious of, or even hostile to, new approaches.

Within the correctional field, we are probably further ahead in an acceptance of the philosophy involving treatment of the offender than we are with adequate staffing, but this would be hard to support in the face of punitive and coercive restriction which is so much a part of the entire correctional cycle: police, courts, probation, institutions, and parole.

Redirection and reeducation of persons who have demonstrated

---

* Reprinted from *Federal Probation*. Charles L. Newman: Concepts of treatment in probation and parole supervision. *Federal Probation, 24*(No. 1):11-19, March 1961.

antisocial and illegal behavior are complex matters requiring both time and skill. Involved is the discovery of strengths within the individual offender which can be mobilized for constructive social behavior. Not infrequently, it will involve modifying the social situation in which he finds himself. But so long as we continue to assume, as we seem to do in so many jurisdictions, that probation, parole, and institutional treatment services can be provided by anyone with the proper political affiliation, one head, a good heart, and a meager appetite for the luxuries of life, then it will be a long time before we can truly implement the philosophy and goals of the correctional field.

Most correctional institutions make no claim to the provision of more than a custodial program for their inmates. But continuously, in both probation and parole, we claim to provide community treatment. Query: Can we, or do we, under the circumstances?

We recognize that the basic purpose of probation and parole is the protection of the community. Any system which runs contrary to that precept cannot be acceptable to society. When an offender has been institutionalized, we are reasonably assured that, for a while at least, he will not be involved in further depredations against the community. But in our wisdom, we have learned to recognize that not all offenders need the physical control which an institution provides. This decision-making process must involve more than sentimentality, sympathy, charity, or a count of prior violations. Rather it demands a meaningful diagnosis and a prognosis that the individual does have sufficient internal strength to return to the community where essentially the same physical, social, and psychological forces are present as were at the time of commission of his criminal act, and to make an adequate adjustment in spite of those factors.

Treatment as an Interrelated Three-stage Process

In order to assist the individual to adjust to the community, the field correctional worker implements a three-stage treatment process: investigation, diagnosis, and treatment supervision. Contrary to the popular misconception that a given set of preliminaries is necessary before the treatment stage can be implemented, it should be clearly recognized that interaction (and consequently, treatment) occurs from the very first moment of contact. Obviously, if we are to work successfully with a person, we must be able to understand his inner-working.

In the investigation stage, we attempt to find out what is, and was, within him and outside him that made him the person with whom we are dealing. With skillful questioning, he will find himself looking at aspects of his life, a process so very necessary if he is to gain insight into the nature of his behavior. From this frame of reference, it is not too difficult to see the investigation as a very vital part of the treatment process.

In our culture, we place a great deal of emphasis on putting labels on all sorts of things, including behavior. The words *neurotic, psychopath, psychotic, behavior disorder,* and many others are used with such ease that we sometimes think we know what they mean. In the diagnostic process, the goal is not to attach a label to the person. Rather, the diagnosis is the codification of all that has been learned about the individual, organized in such a way as to provide a means for the establishment of future treatment goals. It becomes immediately obvious that, as we learn more about the individual through future contact, the diagnosis will be modified and the treatment goals raised or lowered as the case may be.

The treatment supervision process, as it will be discussed here, entails the elaboration of knowledge about the individual through the process of communication, so that the individual will gain a more realistic appraisal of his own behavior, thereby enhancing his own ability to function more acceptably in the community. The provision of certain material services may also be involved in the treatment process.

Investigation for Treatment

In the finding-out process, the most important source to help the officer is the offender himself. He frequently is also a most difficult source. The offender may consider it to his interest and advantage to give a misleading picture. Here is the real test of the correctional officer's skill—the art of understanding and dealing with human nature. The extent to which a person reveals himself is in direct proportion to the degree of confidence (rapport) which the worker has succeeded in developing. Other sources of information lie outside the offender himself and require tact in approach and intelligence in selection. A problem which every worker faces is to obtain, within the limits of time, as many illuminating facts as possible without causing discrimination against the offender. The investigation should give a comprehensive picture of the offender's own world, his personality, his relationship to others, and his immediate environment as seen in relation to himself. We should know something about his likes and dislikes, his hopes and desires, his values and disappointments, his ambitions and plans (or lack of them), his assets and qualities, as well as shortcomings. However, we should not let our own cultural biases and values seduce us into giving "feeling content" to that material which the probationer or parolee may not have. But truly knowing what are his feelings in regard to past and present experiences is central to dealing effectively with him in a treatment relationship.

Listing a series of isolated physical and social facts about a person provides only a bare skeletal diagram of that person. So frequently, for example, presentence, classification, or preparole reports will be limited to a cursory statement about the family composition, designating the names, ages, and occupations of family members. What do these facts mean? Without elaboration or interpretation, such facts are of limited value in arriving at a recommendation or in providing meaningful supervision. What we really need to find out is the type of relationship which has existed between the person and other significant people in his life: natural family, family by marriage, friends, neighbors, co-workers.

We have no hesitation about discouraging continued contact with previous associates. But what about family? Are these relationships always worth maintaining? With knowledge about those interrelationships, it may be most desirable to encourage the person to stay far away from his family as well as previous associates. Even though our culture strongly supports the notion of enduring marriage, we cannot assume, *a priori,* that a positive family relationship exists solely because a man and woman are living together in marriage. Nor can we assume that a person has necessarily been damaged emotionally by the fact of growing up in a broken home. These are things we must find out.

Basically, the point is this: in the treatment relationship, the generalizations about human behavior (to which most of us subscribe) have applied value only to the degree that they fit the circumstances and the personality of the individual situation. We must know the individual first in order to understand him and to counsel with him.

An interview is a conversation with a purpose. In his role, the correctional worker is not interested in persons in the aggregate, but in the specific individual. Our goal, through the interview process, is to be able to know the offender's personality in action. We are interested in his immediate environment, the way he reacts to frustrations and opportunities. We want to know his attitudes toward others and himself. From that point, we can assist him to gain a better self-understanding, thereby affecting his ability to function constructively in the community around him.

Whether the interview occurs during the presentence investigation or during the period of supervision, it is important to recognize that both the worker and the offender bring prior life experiences into the interview situation. If the worker has been able to develop insight and self-awareness about his own behavior, there is a likelihood that he will be more tolerant and effective with the persons with whom he is working. This is particularly necessary in the implementation of authority. The mature worker will recognize that it is the situation and not his own need for power, which calls for the use of authority.

Treatment Begins With the First Contact

While it can be true of every session, the first contact between the worker and the offender is of extreme importance. In all probability the person will be experiencing a certain amount of anxiety which, with skillful handling, can be mobilized from the very beginning to achieve the treatment goals. The person should be given the feeling that there is no need to hurry in exploring the many avenues which may develop in the initial interview. If the worker takes time to listen, the probability is that he will hear more than if he devotes the time to talking himself. At the beginning, the offender is making a number of observations about the officer, the office, and comparing his current impressions with his own preconceptions. At the same time, the worker should be making his own observations, such as the person's appearance, the way he enters the office, the way he conducts himself, how he sits down, how he talks, the tone of his speech, and other nonverbal communicative aspects. Whether we are capable of observing it or not, in many instances a transference occurs from the individual to the officer from the very beginning. The mature worker will recognize that fact and will interact accordingly.

The content of the first interview, as with all subsequent contacts, will vary with the individual. Part of the time is spent in gathering factual information. However, unless there is a reason to believe that information already on file is erroneous, generally there is no need to repeat the operation. Being asked the same questions over and over again can easily give the impression that it does not matter too much what you say since no one pays any attention to the answers. Accurate recording (even though it takes time) is a vital necessity if we hope to do a respectable job of treatment. By recording basic information as well as progress contacts, we are in a better position to see the progress which has been made in the case and alter treatment goals accordingly. Without such information, a shift in caseload requires the new worker to start from the beginning, which we would agree is a great waste of time and effort.

After the initial interview, the officer is faced with the monumental task of making a fast appraisal, on the basis of a single interview, of the person's ability to reside in the community with only limited external controls. One of the better means of appraisal comes from an understanding of the degree of discomfort which the individual feels in relation to his social or emotional problem. Further, the officer will have to determine what part others may have in the problem and the extent to which they are affected.

The timing of subsequent interviews must, in large measure, be determined by a variety of factors, including the type and immediacy of the problem, the size of caseload, and the need of the person for support and control. Unfortunately, too much of probation and parole supervision is little more than routine monthly reporting. Admittedly, in some cases, this minimal type of control may be quite adequate. But generally speaking, where problems of adjustment to the home and community exist, it is questionable whether any value is derived from infrequent contact. In too many probation and parole offices, moreover, a person is seen only after he has demonstrated some emergent problem situation. To insure the protection of the community, as well as to assist the person in adjustment, probation and parole supervision must provide preventive as well as remedial treatment services.

Surveillance Versus Counseling

Within the context of the need for sound correctional treatment programs, several elements emerge. First, we must recognize that the community continues to be concerned about the activities of the probationer and the parolee. Whether or not he is involved in further illegal activity, the law violator has demonstrated his capacity to disregard society's rules and regulations. By virtue of his prior behavior, the community is justifiably concerned.

Secondly, we must recognize that it is neither feasible nor desirable to maintain continuous surveillance of the offender's activities. At best, we can sample his behavior at various moments and hope that we are able to detect certain indicators which suggest that the person is more of a presumptive risk to himself and to the community. Greater protection than this to the community through surveillance is not possible in a democracy. Moreover, surveillance, as opposed to treatment supervision, is essentially a police responsibility. It involves techniques which the therapy-oriented and trained practitioner in corrections is unprepared to handle with maximum effectiveness. This does not obviate the need for surveillance, but rather places its implementation in the hands of the police, whose responsibility it is in the first place.

It becomes obvious, then, that the correctional worker (whether in the institution or field services) should be in a position to recognize, understand, and deal effectively with subtle as well as obvious shifts in the behavior and personality of the offender. Not infrequently, these shifts can be indicative of problems which the individual is experiencing and for which he is unable to find a solution. I do not mean to suggest that to find a person in a particularly irritable mood during a field visit is cause for revocation. On the other hand, such irritability, persistently detected, may be a clue which directs our attention to the movement of the person into behavior which ultimately may get him into difficulty.

Rules and Treatment

Recalling our intention to protect the community through probation and parole services, we impose a number of controls upon the offender and his behavior. Not uncommonly, the person is instructed to abide by a series of rules and regulations which is universally applied to all offenders within the particular jurisdiction. Many times, a specific rule may not have any particular relationship to the offender and his prior conduct. The imposition of rules and conditions can have a therapeutic value. However, to do so, the rules must have a relationship to the prior behavior pattern of the individual upon whom they are imposed. Moreover, the officer must see these rules as a part of his treatment plan rather than external controls imposed by someone other than himself, and which, reluctantly, he must enforce.

Limit-setting involves specifying what behavior the officer, as the community's representative, will or will not accept from the person under supervision. First, however, the limits must be clear in the officer's mind. Reluctance or vacillation in the enforcement of rules can easily lead to a situation where the officer will be manipulated by the person under supervision. If limits and rules are consistently applied, the spurious argument that one concession calls for another is easily overcome.

The point should be quite clear: if the boundary limitations or prohibitions are specified for an individual because it is known that he will endanger himself or others if he violates, then the officer has a clear course of action. Failure to be consistent adds only to confusion on the part of the person under supervision. If the violation of a rule does not result in the offender doing harm to himself or others, then the rule is not necessary in his case and should not be invoked.

The Therapeutic Relationship

One of the first major accomplishments of treatment comes about when the offender becomes aware both intellectually and emotionally that the officer represents not only authority with the power to enforce certain restraints and restrictions, but that he is also able to offer material, social, and psychological adjustmental aids.

Hardly a day passes that the correctional worker does not come upon a situation where a statement made has fallen somewhat short of the truth. Sometimes these statements may be the consequence of faulty recollection, or they may involve outright misrepresentation. The "natural" reaction is to feel irritated. From a treatment focus, however, one would have to ask the question, Since the account seems unreasonable, what defenses are being used that prevent a more truthful representation? Then, What purpose do these defenses serve for the individual? Do they contribute to his sense of well-being, or do they provide him with the needed sense of discomfort? The next step in counseling emerges from this knowledge.

I do not mean to suggest that probation and parole officers should attempt to practice psychiatry or to otherwise involve themselves in depth analysis with their caseloads. In correctional work, we should be dealing primarily with conscious-level material. Thus we do not get into dreams or use narcotherapy. But there is a wide range of difference between depth therapy and a "go forth and sin no more" approach. Few correctional workers have the skill or training to approach depth therapy with competence, and the moralistic approach does not work too well in the long run.

In the therapeutic clinical management of the probationer and parolee, crime prevention is incorporated in the treatment process. As was pointed out earlier, probation and parole supervision must go beyond mere surveillance, for recognition of possible future antisocial behavior through an awareness of the individual's deteriorating personal and social relationships is more effective for community protection than periodic barroom visitation.

The officer's awareness of the fact that the person is having a problem in adjustment is seriously handicapped when interviews are held across a counter in a crowded office, and limited to a two- to five-minute examination of the previous month's activity report. The "how are things going" probe is more suited when sufficient time, interest, and understanding are provided than when the response of *okay* or *so-so* is expected.

The correctional worker will lose one of his most important tools if he defines very carefully and structures very rigidly the interrelationship which he will allow between the offender and himself. If the probationer or parolee is not permitted to express anxiety, hostility, or other feelings toward the officer, employer, wife, or even the next-door neighbor, then the interview is forcing a response pattern which does not give an accurate picture of the person's feelings. Nor does it allow for the implementation of counseling techniques which interpret and assist in the resolution of the problem with the person. This is not to suggest that the probation or parole supervision interview should be devoted solely to ventilation. Rather, the officer must be in a position to recognize that, as a social therapist in an authoritative setting, certain types of interrelationships are desirable and necessary. The interaction must be geared to the dynamics of the offender's personality, and not to the exclusive satisfaction of the worker's own ego.

Beyond this, the officer must go into the field, into the family home, the neighborhood, and the job setting. No offender exists in a vacuum, and it is not improbable that adjustmental problems will be related to external as well as internal, intrapsychic factors. Discretion, of course, is both desirable and necessary because we do not want to jeopardize what acceptance the offender may have been able to reestablish for himself in the community. It is essential, however, that we constantly remember that the offender must do his adjusting in the community and not in the probation office exclusively. Adjustment is a great deal more than showing the necessary and expected deference to the wishes of the correctional officer.

A not un-common type of client found in probation or parole offices is one who appears to be unable to function effectively in the working world. Our middle-class morality suggests that work is desirable and that "good" people want to work. Hence, failure and unemployment are often considered to be related to lack of motivation, laziness, or a configuration of morally related values. Frequently, we find that these same individuals express a feeling of paralysis in what appears to them to be a hostile world. We can write off these complaints as characteristic of the convict culture, or we can seek more definitive answers for the individual case. In evaluating the situation, there are a number of questions which the officer can explore. When attempting to find out how long a problem has existed, the officer should also evaluate the degree of discomfort which the person feels about it. Are his feelings appropriate to the situation, and are his actions consonant with his stated feelings? Looking to the employment situation, for example, the officer can ask, Is what has been demanded of this person really compatible with his true potentialities? What has been the relationship between the offender and his employer, and to what extent do these external factors impinge upon the stability of the family relationship? Obviously, this is not the sort of information which can be obtained when the only knowledge about employment is taken from the monthly income report.

A person's previous employment record can be a very valuable diagnostic tool if it is evaluated in depth. And from that evaluation, certain treatment goals come to the fore. It is wise to look at the direction of change in position of employment, as well as the frequency. Did the person move from job to job with no appreciable improvement in position or salary? Has he been on the skids? Or, has the direction of change been in terms of upward mobility? Have external factors put demands upon him to move upward socially? If so, why? We can see then that a variety of reasons may account for vocational instability. It is vital that the officer does not try to implant his own moral values on the facts, but rather that he derives their values from those who are directly affected by them.

In a reported situation, George A. was constantly in and out of work before he got into difficulty with the law. His references were poor in that they showed him to be quick-tempered, with a "holier than thou" attitude. George had married in his second year of college, and with great struggle managed to graduate shortly before his wife bore them a second child. The wife appeared to be a very passive, yet demanding person. Her demands were always in terms of an improved living situation, which in her own eyes, at least, were realistic demands. George's change of jobs in part reflected her demands. But the job changes also reflected his inability to present himself in a desirable perspective so that he might get a much wanted promotion and increment in salary. Writing checks in nonexistent accounts finally led to his downfall.

Placed on probation, George was able to adjust quite readily in the counseling relationship. A job was found, and the position lasted for almost a year. Then, one day, George came in to report that he had just had an argument with the office manager of the firm where he was employed and that he had quit. The officer asked about the circumstances, but George was sullen and uncommunicative, somewhat daring the officer "to do something about it." Referring to his record, the officer then reviewed some of the glowing comments that George had made about the employer: how kind and considerate he had been, etc., etc. Yes, those things were true, but not that blankety-blank office manager. For the next five minutes, George ventilated about the office manager and covered most of the transgressions of man and nature. Finally, in a very tired voice, he told the officer that his wife was pregnant again and that she was putting the pressure on him to get a better job. Had the worker responded with authority at the beginning, he would have lost what eventually developed into a situation where effective counseling could be accomplished.

Only as a person is able to gain insight into the nature of his behavior will he be able to make a satisfactory adjustment within himself. If the behavior seems unreasonable, then the counselor must seek to find what defenses are preventing a more accurate perception of reality. Importantly, though, the officer must know how vital it is to the probationer's or parolee's sense of equilibrium that he maintain a self-defeating defense pattern. Creation of anxiety in the counseling situation is an important factor in precipitating change, but such a technique must be handled with a great deal of dexterity, and with the knowledge that it will not push the person into undesirable behavior, which may have been his pattern of reaction under earlier circumstances.

The correctional officer must be aware continuously of the concept that man's behavior and thinking are the outgrowths of his life's experiences. But man is not the blind product of social and physical forces around him. From the moment of birth, a relationship is established between the outside world and himself, and for which a reciprocal interrelationship evolves. Mother influences child, and child affects "mother-husband-other child" relationships. The whole confluence on the individual is extremely difficult to evaluate, particularly in the face of the large number of interactions we experience during the course of a lifetime.

The Need for Security

Although human needs can be stated in an almost endless variety of ways, survival is a deep-rooted impulse of the organism. In order to survive, it is necessary to be safe; any threat to security causes a person to feel either anger or fear. Anxiety is the response to an internal feeling of threat. Whether that threat is directed from physical survival or from psychological and social concomitants, excessive anxiety interferes with physical and mental well-being. Further, when anxiety exists, a person strives to resolve it or defend himself against it. There are specific psychological mechanisms which he may employ as a defense against anxiety-producing situations, and the consequences may take either adjustive or socially disapproved forms.

The Need to Express New Feeling

A person's feelings are mixed when he experiences a mutual incompatible combination of feelings. When feelings are mixed, anxiety arises; the greater the anxiety, the more the feelings are mixed, and so on. Conflict is almost inevitable when feelings are mixed. Some of the kinds of behavior rooted in conflict are inconsistency, procrastination, hostility, unreasonableness, seclusiveness, inability to make up one's mind, rigidity. Chiding the person, or shaming him for these and related behaviors serves only to alienate him and does not get beyond the symptom of the disturbance. When the correctional therapist understands the motivating forces behind such behavior, he is then able to provide the needed help.

One way is to help the person bring true feelings into the open for an airing, and to help him grasp the idea that double feelings are universal and there is nothing wrong in having them. This is not to suggest that we condone destructive behavior, either inner-directed or vented against the external world. But we do accept the person as an individual and help him to cope with the mixed feelings. In the matter of criminality, offenders probably experience every conceivable degree and every possible combination of positive and negative feelings: from joy of not being institutionalized (as on probation or parole) to bitter resignation and resentment at being tricked by fate.

The correctional worker can sometimes provide a desired treatment effect by listening and feeding back (nondirectively) what has been said with patience and acceptance. At other times, particularly with individuals whose response patterns reflect a primitive level of development, the officer may find it necessary to teach how to behave less disturbingly in confronting life situations. Some instances call for support; other situations call for the creation of anxiety to accomplish given treatment ends.

Conclusion

Treatment is a sophisticated process involving both time and skill. It is not something which starts after a given set of preliminaries, but rather gets underway, desirably, with the very first contact. Obviously, there is no one method of treatment with all law violators, or any other group of individuals who manifest unacceptable behavior. There are certain generic similarities to be found among all people, and the offender is no exception to this rule. But each personality is made up of a number of elements which are blended together in proportions and relationships which are unique to the individual. External changes can be accomplished through a change in the social environment of the individual; but without the vital internal changes in personality, we cannot expect more than a repetition of the previous unsuccessful and unsatisfying behavior. The objective, regardless of the approach, is to create in a person a self-acceptance which did not exist before.

A THERAPEUTIC APPROACH TO PROBATION AND PAROLE*

There are two major approaches to the treatment of criminal behavior. One approach assumes that criminal behavior is learned in the same way as any other kind of behavior. According to this approach, the presence of criminal behavior does not indicate the presence of neurotic, maladjusted, or antisocial personality traits. The other approach sees criminal behavior as a manifestation of such neurotic tendencies as inferiority feelings, irrational hostility, and self-hatred. This section is directed toward those cases of criminal behavior where there are observable manifestations of personality maladjustment and where some form of psychotherapy is indicated. Although what follows is related to the probation officer, the same approach is also applicable to the work of parole officers in particular and counselors in general.

An individual placed in the role of a counselor, has, generally speaking, three major problems confronting him. First of all, there is the problem of how to relate to his client. If he errs in relating himself properly, he finds that his own behavior is more inclined to reinforce the defenses of his client, thereby reinforcing his general maladjustment. To avoid the danger of making the client worse, the counselor is usually advised to be respectful of the patient's individuality, to accept him as a person, to treat him honestly and fairly at all times, to be consistent in his approach. The beginner, generally, has no difficulty in finding suffi-

---

* Printed by permission of the author, Albert E. Quade, Ph.D. From an original unpublished manuscript, Florida State University, 1957.

cient books and articles to advise him as to how to approach his client.

The next problem is that of diagnosis. The counselor must develop his ability to take the content materials presented to him by the client and organize them into some kind of a consistent structure. Those trained in the traditional schools are most likely to organize the material according to the theories presented by such pioneers as Freud, Jung, and Adler. An academic psychologist is more likely to organize the material along the lines of learning theory. The sociologist will organize the same material according to development of the self-concept within a group structure. *So far as effective counseling is concerned, the question is not which of these theoretical orientations is most important, realistic, or popular, but rather that the counselor be firmly rooted in one or another of them.* Generally speaking, skilled counselors from one discipline have about as much success as skilled counselors from other disciplines. A strong theoretical background is of great importance in assisting the counselor in defining the nature of the problem and assessing its most probable causes.

The third major problem is that of therapy. There are many aspiring counselors who can orient themselves well to the treatment of the client and who can develop excellent rapport with their clients. They move onto the stage of diagnosis and do a very creditable job, but they are often surprised to see that after extensive hours of diagnosis there are no apparent changes in either the client's attitudes or his behavior. It is unfortunate that, from the therapeutic viewpoint, an excellent diagnosis sometimes functions only to increase the client's negative conception of himself. The mother, for example, who has been taken into custody for abandoning her children, may plead that she is fearful that her children might die. This might be properly diagnosed as a rationalization of an unconscious death wish. Unfortunately, for the client, this only serves to destroy her defense mechanisms and leaves her more vulnerable to her own negative attitudes toward herself as a person.

We are concerned here with both the problem of diagnosis and the problem of therapy, giving special attention to those techniques which are therapeutically effective.

The primary consideration in any form of therapy is the extent to which the client manifests self-acceptance. Various schools of psychological thought have assigned different terminology to this concept, but basically they all treat it similarly. The analytic schools refer to self-acceptance as ego strength. The sociological and psychosociological refer to this as *self-concept*. This concept easily distinguishes between the well-adjusted individual who adjusts the satisfaction of his needs to the culture in which he lives, and the maladjusted individual who is unable to adjust himself to society. There is usually a definite and predictable relationship between how an individual sees himself and how he adjusts that self to his cultural milieu. The individual who is basically satisfied with himself as a person assumes, unconsciously, that other people, once they come to know him, will find him as likeable as he finds himself. His general behavior pattern, therefore, in the presence of other persons, is to express himself so that others come to see him as he is and develop a basis for liking him.

A person with a negative self-concept, or low ego strength, dislikes himself, with varying degrees of intensity, for possessing feelings and attitudes that run counter to his moral and ethical standards. Not liking himself, he is never able to find concrete reasons why other persons would find him likeable. Horney believes that there are three general adjustments the individual makes to negative self-concept. First of all, the individual is strongly inclined to reject his own convictions as a guide for life and to use instead the approval of others. Counselors of sexual delinquents are often surprised to find that the actions of the sexual delinquent run counter to her own moral convictions. Seeing herself as an unlikeable individual, the sexual delinquent is left only with sex to use as an attraction to the male. Since, in this case, the need for approval is an overcompensation for the feelings of self-disapproval, such individuals will be found engaging in behavior which violently contradicts their own moral codes but which they feel will bring them some measure of approval from others. The same principle is at work in delinquent gangs. There are many adolescents who are not proud of the behavior patterns in which they engage, nonetheless, they continue these patterns seeking the approval of their peers.

A second adjustment to self-rejection is hostility. The hostile client, like the compliant individual discussed above, is almost completely organized personality-wise to believe that the rewards of life are attainable only by submission to the whims, desires, and caprices of others. Whereas the compliant individual sees no alternative and prefers to maintain the existing pattern, the hostile person rebels at the belief that he will not be accepted as an individual. The overexpression of hostility does not really differentiate the hostile client from the compliant individual. There is about as much hostility in the compliant individual, but since expression of hostility would run counter to attempts to win approval, the compliant person inevitably represses the hostility. The primary motive in both personality types is overcompensation for feelings of self-rejection.

A third adjustment to a negative self-concept is withdrawal. This individual can see no reasons why other individuals will accept him as a person. Whereas the hostile client becomes angry with others because they refuse to accept him, the withdrawn person sees no reason for acceptance. His only alternative is to retire from people. If he enters into crime, he is likely to be a "lone wolf" operator. One should not assume that his client will fall clearly into one or another of these categories. Some clients will at times be compliant and will alternate this with periods of withdrawal. Some clients may vacillate between stages of withdrawal and hostility. A number of combinations are possible. This need not be confusing to the counselor, however, since he may safely assume that in each case, or in any combination of cases, the basic problem remains that of a negative self-concept.

The primary function of diagnosis is to probe behind this superficial veneer of compliancy, hostility, or withdrawal and to show the client that his basic motive is an attempt to win affection from others, even though he sees nothing about himself that merits approval, acceptance, or affection.

The primary objective of therapy, then, is to increase the client's self-acceptance to the point where his behavior is no longer governed by the approval or disapproval of those about him. It should be apparent to the reader that a brilliant diagnosis may leave the client with only a more painful feeling of how unlikeable he is and may give him no clues as to what factors produced such negative feelings and what behaviors might assist the client in overcoming them.

Another objective of therapy is to get the individual to a point where his behavior is self-determining, is consistent with his own moral and ethical codes, and his convictions about life in general. These two objectives are not at all inconsistent since the individual, once he realizes the nature of the factors which made him dislike himself and comes to see himself as a likeable person, builds self-respect by sticking to his convictions and defending them even though this might bring disapproval or hostility from those about him. This does not mean that we attempt to assist the client in reaching a position where he is no longer interested in the approval of others. What he should come to realize is that approval is wholesome, but that it is unhealthy for him to go to the point where he violates his own convictions to win that approval. The better adjusted person is very aware of approval from others, but he will not yield his individuality to violate his convictions in order to win more approval. The very fact that he defends his convictions and often thereby wins greater approval gives him the feeling of pride and self-respect that he did not have previously. Attempts to compensate for self-rejection by winning the approval of others appear to be disturbingly common. Unfortunately, the practice is almost always self-defeating. The individual usually starts out submitting to others in order to gain certain goals. As the process continues, however, the goals become sacrificed to win approval. In the end the client is left without a feeling of identity or individuality. It is erroneous to assume that there are no goals, objectives, or convictions in these clients. What is more likely is that these have been repressed in favor of approval. An understanding of the following behavior patterns will assist the counselor in making a more correct diagnosis of his client and will orient him more directly toward the therapeutic process.

1. *Probation officers are too often deceived by the semantic meaning of the term "compliancy."* They expect to see an individual groveling, apologetic, and retiring. On the contrary, an extremely compliant individual might superficially appear to be

quite friendly, outgoing, and talkative. The clue, therefore, is not so much in the overt behavior of the individual as much as it is in the content of his conversation. If the probation officer listens closely, he will begin to realize that although clients may speak fluently, feelings are never manifested. The client may go into great detail describing experiences which he has had, but he at no time reveals to the probation officer the nature of his emotional reactions in those experiences. He has a good reason for not doing so. He is afraid that, not liking these feelings in himself, he will provoke similar negative reactions in his counselor. For example, he may describe a situation in which the average person would become angry. At no time in his discussion does the client indicate he was angry, nor does he indicate any angry feelings as he recounts the situation. He fears that this anger will be punished by the counselor. If the tendency in the client to conceal feelings is especially strong, the counselor will note a "flatness" in the client's tone of voice. Other clients, somewhat more sophisticated, will attempt to conceal their feelings, attitudes, and opinions behind a veneer of popular cliches. The absence of feeling should always be reflected back to the client so that he becomes aware of the fact that in his social interactions with others he represses those feelings which constitute the essence of his being. A well-adjusted person is quite free in expressing his feelings on all subjects. Such a person is easy to relate to because others know where he stands. In the maladjusted person, there are usually feelings of inadequacy or fear of failure where human interrelationships are concerned.

2. *The second important characteristic which may also appear in disguised form is the feeling of worthlessness.* The only manifestation of this in the initial counseling situation may be an apology for wasting the counselor's time. Most clients in a marriage counseling situation are baffled by the question, "Do you feel that you are a loveable person?" The juvenile delinquent and the adult criminal are also equally baffled by the question, "Do you feel that you are a likeable person?" Often such individuals will respond glibly that they are. When the counselor follows up with a question such as, "What is it about you that is likeable?"

the client is again baffled and usually incapable of offering a single trait of his personality that he sees as likeable. At this point the untutored counselor almost inevitably hastens to reassure the client that he is indeed likeable, and almost inevitably the client interprets the reassurance as a selfishly motivated attempt on the part of the counselor to appear kind, polite, and interested. Experienced counselors realize that assurance rarely accomplishes more than a temporary good feeling in the client. There is a high correlation between the ability to accept one's self as one is and the ability to accept others as they are. The well-adjusted counselor, therefore, who basically accepts himself, will also be inclined to accept his client. It may surprise him that this apparently likeable person suffers with such intense feelings of self-hatred.

3. *Another clue to self-rejection is overemphasis by the client of the importance of achievement.* Finding nothing in himself likeable to other persons, the client often takes the second alternative of achieving goals which will bring acceptance and respect. Such individuals are characterized by compulsive achievement drives. In some cases, they actually reach high levels of attainment. Unfortunately, this does not solve their basic problem since they feel that the acceptance they have gained is still not on the basis of themselves as individuals, but rather on the basis of achievement. Such individuals are inclined to be dissatisfied with their own achievements and continually strive toward more acceptable and socially approved achievements. Our culture places great emphasis upon personal improvement and achievement. If he is not wary, the counselor may be deluded into accepting this aspect of his client's behavior as a normal trait in this culture. Consequently, he may overlook the fact that an attempt to better one's self is based psychologically on the premise that one is not good to begin with. Juvenile delinquents are often inclined to define delinquent acts as forms of achievement. The "stoolie" is often a useful adjunct to law enforcement because some criminals are so inclined to boast about their criminal achievements. In law violations, were this not an essential part of the dynamics of self-rejection, many criminals would go unappre-

hended. The law violator is often averse to going straight because the achievements of a more mundane life are not sufficient to compensate for his feelings of worthlessness. He abhors the more quiet and inconspicuous life of the law abider. The drive toward achievement does not always motivate the individual toward criminal behavior. In fact, an identical drive may lead the individual to achieve eminence in a profession. It is noteworthy that, even though the professional achievement may command respect, many such individuals are incompetent to carry on wholesome relationships with their family, friends, and colleagues. The criminal achiever often finds himself in the same predicament.

The notion that achievement can be a matter for therapeutic concern may be obscured by the fact that we live in a culture which puts great emphasis upon individual achievement. There are two factors which the probation officer should be cognizant of at all times. First, he should remember that the individual may be using achievement to mask feelings of personal unworthiness; and secondly, that the avenues toward achievement may take antisocial tendencies and appear as criminal actions. Because the feelings of unworthiness and inferiority are so great, the normal daily rewards and achievements of the law-abiding citizen may be insufficient compensations for the maladjusted individual. Achievement is meaningless to him unless it supersedes the achievements of the average person. Furthermore, the achievements of the maladjusted individual serve only temporarily to overcompensate for the feelings of inferiority. Consequently, achievements must come frequently and must be outstanding.

The feelings of inferiority which usually underlie strong achievement motives may, on occasion, be temporarily masked by the fact that a recent achievement sufficiently overcompensates for the feelings of inferiority. Considering the gang, his peers, and the criminal group as his frame of reference, both arrest and sentence may serve only to reinforce, in the maladjusted individual's mind, the achievement factor. The probation officer attempting to reorient the probationer to an acceptable socially conforming type of life may often overlook the fact that the rewards of this type of life are insufficient to overcompensate for the feelings of rejection. He may struggle with persuasion, cajoling, reassurance, and many other tricks of the trade and still find that he meets with defeat. His real problem is that he is not properly oriented to the basic emotional impulses arising from within the client.

So far as therapy is concerned, it is important that the individual be brought to realize that the basic motive force behind his tendency to engage in criminal behavior is his strong sense of self-rejection. The first attempts on the part of the probation officer to relate this information to his client may result in a considerable amount of defensiveness on the part of the probationer. Accusing the probationer of being defensive or resisting usually serves only to increase the intensity of the defensiveness. There is another vital element which underlies the major problem. In order to preserve some measure of self-respect, the individual is strongly inclined to rationalize his perception of life and to project this rationalization into his understanding of the world of people in which he lives. Each individual develops his self-concept out of the reflections he receives from the treatment accorded him by others. If the treatment he receives is essentially negative in the nature, the materials he must use to build his self-concept are essentially negative. In his developmental period, most of these negative reflections initiated from those close to him: parent figures, relatives, peers. The individual "generalizes" from his own particular experiences and expects similar treatment from all those with whom he comes in contact. He is able to build a quite logically consistent conception of the world of people in which he lives, which is highly consistent with his own developmental experiences but which might be quite contradictory to the attitudes and outlooks of the probation officer, whose background was probably more favorable and more accepting of him as an individual. When the probation officer attempts to persuade his charge to accept the idea that he is a likeable person and that he would be even more likeable if he conformed to social norms, his comments sound essentially strange and unrealistic. The first resistance of the probationer, therefore, should not be immediately interpreted as an unwillingness to accept what the probation officer offers. The counselor should understand that, although his own comments are true, they do not strike his client as being either true or logical. The client might wish with all his heart that what the probation worker says is true. His own experiences assure him that, although this would be a desirable state of affairs, it is not a realistic approach to life. The probation worker and the parole worker are often accused by their clients of having a ridiculously unrealistic attitude toward the real world in which life must be carried on.

Secondly, the attempts on the part of the probation officer to inform the client of his feelings of inferiority might meet with defensive measures because, although true, these interpretations conflict with the client's image of the kind of a person he wants to be. A male struggling to manifest, at all times, red-blooded masculine behavior might be inclined to be strongly resistive to interpretations which reveal him to himself as being less than what he wishes to be. A straightforward presentation of this type of diagnosis often leads to resistance. The probation officer must take another approach to the problem. He should remember that this individual strongly wants approval from others, in fact, this is his *raison d'être* for living. Because he is so desperate for the approval of others, he often attempts to do what will please others. If the counselor approaches this as a self-sacrificing attitude, the individual is much more likely to respond favorably since implicitly there is a sense of injustice to the client. Instead of seeing the probation officer as an antagonist, the client comes to see the officer as someone who is sympathetic with the client's own position. Unfortunately a probation agent is often deceived by the antagonistic and hostile attitude he receives. It does not seem logical to him that there lies behind surface behavior strong self-sacrificing feelings. If he can accept the assumption that self-rejection lies behind compliancy, hostility and, withdrawal, he will not be so inclined to be thrown off the track by the more aggressive responses.

Once the compliant or self-sacrificing aspect has been accepted by the client, the next task of the probation agent is to reinforce the conception. Although the client may have been aware of feelings of inferiority, he either has not gained insight into their influence on his interactions with others, or they seem so right that it has never occurred to him to question them. One approach to this type of reinforcement is to encourage a client to pay close attention to the manner in which he responds to those with whom he must interact. He should be encouraged to note how many times he feels free to assert himself, and how many times, comparatively, he tries to go along with those with whom he interacts. The client will often return to the probation officer overwhelmed by the degree of submissiveness in his own behavior. On the other hand, it is surprising how often the client is able to persuade the probation officer that these interpretations are basically incorrect. The client often attempts to prove his own self-assertion by citing incidents in which he spoke sharply to those with whom he interacted. If the probation officer looks closely, he will notice that those to whom the probationer speaks sharply are people who "don't count." They are underlings whose approval is not particularly important. The picture immediately changes when the concept of "persons whose approval is important" is discussed. It is important at this point to realize that no effective therapy can be expected until the client has accepted his diagnosis of his behavior and its motive.

If the client accepts this diagnosis, and if the diagnosis is reinforced by measuring the diagnosis against actual behavior, the next step is to encourage the client to test the hypothesis of self-assertion. First attempts at self-assertion on the part of the individual will be essentially reflections of the maladjusted personality with which he is already troubled, and the assertions are likely to be both unrealistic and antisocial. The first impulse of the probation officer is usually to react against these attempts of self-assertion since they are both unrealistic and antisocial. This impulse on the part of the probation officer usually counteracts the first healthy tendencies. Unfortunately, the role of the probation officer is often so defined that he is given no freedom whatsoever to respond to these first maladjusted self-assertions in an accepting fashion.

Suffice it to say that a considerable amount of analysis and reorganization of the probation officer's role is necessary if he is to become an effective therapist attempting to reorganize the attitude, impulses, and feelings of the client toward a more conforming attitude regarding society's expectations. Although the probation agent accepts these negative assertions on the part of his charge, this does not mean that he agrees with these self-assertions. The assertions may be essentially emotional in nature, and may be attitudes of resentment or hostility toward the probation officer. The fact that the probation officer, an individual of some importance in the client's life, is willing to accept these feelings manifested toward him is sometimes the first experience the client has had in asserting himself to an individual in authority and having assertion accepted. The acceptance by the counselor often forces the client to reconsider the intent of his hostile gesture.

As the individual learns to assert himself as an individual, a number of his outstanding symptoms begin to diminish. Second, as he asserts his opinions and feelings, he finds that they are at least respected by others. His own esteem in his ability to affect people is enhanced. As he moves into the stage of asserting himself, he often becomes confused. He is attempting to reach a better-adjusted orientation toward the world in which he lives, but he is required to do so with a maladjusted personality. The confusion arises over the fact that some of his self-assertion involves hostility developed by his maladjusted attitude.

He sometimes finds severe defeat in attempts at self-assertion because, instead of being defensive of his rights and expressions of himself as a person, these self-assertions are often expressions of his negative attitudes. This point should be clarified with the client. If the attempts at self-assertion are successful, the client begins to experience a sense of freedom he has never known before. He feels better since he is defending his convictions; he feels better that individuals outside himself respect those convictions, and he sees a world of freedom to himself opening before him.

Again, he is somewhat inclined to be defeated by the maladjusted personality with which he is operating. Very often, although he senses and realizes the great implications of freedom, he has not yet given up his conception that other individuals are domineering, exploitative, selfish, greedy, and so forth. He now begins to build defenses to protect the measure of freedom he has attained.

Usually, his first defense is that of complete emotional and economic independence from others. He may begin to manifest to his probation officer an apparently healthy interest in preparing himself for some occupation. The counselor should look closely at the motives of the client at this point. Very often the client believes that, although his freedom is a wonderful experience, it will be taken away from him. He continues to believe, at this point, that others still expect him to comply before they will give him personal and social rewards. The individual now believes that this is not possible and begins to build a world of total independence. His inclination in this direction should be again brought to his attention. When he reaches a state of sound personal and social adjustment, he will have come to realize that his early attempts to generalize and assume negative response from everyone are erroneous. On the contrary, he should not be persuaded to believe the opposite is true (i.e. that all individuals are kind and generous and faithful). Instead, he should arrive at a point where he is able to differentiate between those who are accepting and trustworthy and those who are not.

This transitional stage between the client's old maladjusted conception and the development of newer more realistic conceptions will be a stage of confusion, disorientation, and sometimes crisis. The old conception, although erroneous, was a conception which gave him a feeling of security. As he moves into the newer conception, he feels insecure in the transitional stage. He has no definite convictions one way or another to orient himself. He is caught between seeing the error of earlier conceptions and yet not being sufficiently persuaded to accept the realities of the newer conceptions. To terminate the counseling at this time presents dangers to the client, because he has less to orient himself to than he had before the diagnostic and therapeutic periods began.

During the entire period of time in which the probation worker has been attempting to show the client the nature of adjustment to life, there should be attempts to show the probationer how his feelings of self-rejection developed in his early developmental era. From the causative analysis of those factors in early developmental years which created his self-rejecting attitudes, the client often infers that given other circumstances he would have developed differently. The counselor should watch closely to see whether the client draws this inference. If he does not, the counselor should make it his responsibility to specify this implication clearly.

Implied in this corrective approach is the educational function of the counselor. Too often the client is beset with the idea that his behavior is inherited. So long as he believes that his tendencies toward crime are congenital, he cannot believe that anything can be done about them. The counselor's attempts to emphasize the causative relationship between background factors and personality development show the client that there were alternative modes of development.

The counselor's effectiveness is often counteracted by the age of the client. This approach will be much less effective with a client fifty years of age than with one closer to twenty. The older client will have fifty years of reinforcement of his erroneous concept toward life. The probability that this can be altered in the amount of time available to the counselor is minimal. On the other hand, this approach will be highly effective with the youthful offender who has not as many years of experience which serve to reinforce his negative and antisocial conceptions of life. Another important factor which affects this approach to correction is the degree to which the client believes he can trust his probation agent. The very fact that he is on probation may lend the client to conceal from the probation agent those very experiences which necessitate thorough analysis. The probation worker is therefore beset by handicaps which do not ordinarily confront the counselor whose clients come to him on a voluntary basis. In ordinary circumstances, the material related to a counselor by the client will be held in the strictest confidence at all times. For the probation officer, this is not usually the case. He is required, often by law, to place in the probation file an accurate record of what transpires as his knowledge of the client increases. Those agencies whose organizational structure prevents the probation officer from holding in confidence material presented to him by the client can expect to have a higher rate of recidivism.

If the client responds to this form of treatment with a greater acceptance of himself as a person, he inevitably develops a greater acceptance of, and respect for, those about him. He discards his old notions of compliancy, or hostile resistance against compliancy, and develops pride in his own new-found ability to accept and respect others for what they are. It should be noted that an implicit assumption underlying this approach is the faith in the client to develop a more socially conforming attitude—given the freedom to do so. The counselor who does not have faith in the clients who come to him will find the approach discussed here entirely unsuitable to his own personality.

THE PROBATION OFFICER AND SPECIAL PROBLEM CASES*

A great heart specialist, addressing a body of general practitioners, told them that they, the general practitioners, were the real heart specialists for they saw the early development of heart disease, they saw the beginnings of the trouble, they could take measures to heal and to cure, to prevent and to advise, long before the patient came to the so-called specialist who saw too much of the end product of a series of events when it was too late to be of much service.

In the correctional field, the probation officers are the real specialists. Final answers to many of our most perplexing problems of human behavior await the result of their observations, their wisdom, and their knowledge to tell us how a normal baby—with all potentialities for good—grows into an individual whose lax moral standards, thoughtless hedonism, callous conscience, and rebel-

* Reprinted by permission of *Federal Probation.* Manly B. Root, M.D.: What the probation officer can do for special types of offenders. *Federal Probation, 13* (No. 4):36-46, Dec. 1949.

lious aggressiveness necessitate that he be locked up by society for its own protection.

Alcoholics

Drinking in general is certainly to be discouraged in your clients. The reasons for this are many. It is, at best, an expensive luxury which any man struggling to make his way in the world can ill afford. How often do you and I listen to the woes of a client who tells of the hard financial struggle he has had—but has to admit that he has found money for drinks. Alcohol, a most remarkable drug, has as one of its many effects the lessening of inhibition—that control which, like the governor of an engine, keeps the mind from following up impetuous desires, keeping the human spirit from running away with itself. With the loss of this governor, moral standards evaporate until "anything goes." Alert intelligence, the ability to tap the reservoir of past experience and judgment, is relaxed. Of all men, our clients need acute judgment and self-watching perhaps the most; and yet they so often tempt fate by taking into their bodies that drug which is specific in its ability to put the censor to sleep.

Social Drinking

Again, drinking usually takes place, at least for most of our clients, in what we call bad company and in a mentally and morally unhealthy environment: where ideals are low and moral standards are lower; where profanity and vulgarity are the rule; where it is smart to flout ethical ideals; where criminal exploits are often planned; and where a man can put away his timidities and reserve and become great by being especially daring in the company of those who are ready to exploit him. Such a man becomes a ready tool, and we all know that a great number of violators would not have resorted to folly except for their drinking.

The time of drinking is also important. Most "moderate drinkers" do their drinking in the evening; the time passes quickly and soon it is morning. The client, with an overpowering need for prompt appearance at work in the morning, has a hard time getting there if he has been drinking until a few hours before he is due at work. To avoid this, many clients resort to Saturday night drinking—a well-established custom among us. This is better than weekday drinking, but it is hard to hold to this; and even so, it does not encourage church attendance where a man may at least hear a weekly lecture, concentrate for a brief hour on good ideals, and live in an atmosphere of high aspiration—at most find a philosophy and a faith in a way of life led by the Greatest of Counselors.

As in all categories, let us not be dogmatic. Let us not forget that a great many of us drink, that the drinking of millions of persons does not get them in trouble. If a client's drinking is done wisely and socially, it is best to point out the dangers, to advise abstinence for reasons discussed above, and then not to worry too much about it. We have no right to expect our clients to maintain standards higher than the average; we are foolish and insincere if we expect them to maintain standards higher than our own.

Drinking by Neurotics

Drinking by neurotics takes place when they turn to the "sure but dangerous and only temporary" relief from the tensions and conflicts which torture them. Clients whom you know or believe to be neurotic should be helped to understand this. Get all the psychiatric help and advice you can, but *much* (sometimes *most*) of the assistance the neurotic needs must come from you, from the parole advisor, and from friends and the family. What seems a blessing to a neurotic individual in his ever-increasing search for peace of mind—namely, alcoholic escape from the harsh cruelties of reality—becomes, because of its effects, only another cause for tension. So the neurotic must learn that the alcoholic "treatment" only adds other symptoms to be treated. In other words, the neurotic can never safely drink. In this connection, an allied group of patients—the psychotic (insane)—often drink heavily as a manifestation of early symptoms of mental disease. Drinking then becomes a part, not a cause, of the mental disorder. We must be on the lookout for this, especially in persons who have not been heavy drinkers previously. Much time can be lost and much harm done by the failure to recognize this type of symptom-drinking.

The Alcoholic Defined

The true or "real" alcoholic belongs in a different category. He is not primarily neurotic or psychotic, though he may become so as indeed any person with one disorder of personality, character, or mind may develop another disorder.

For our purposes and for our discussions and explanations with our alcoholic clients, an alcoholic may be defined as an individual who is unusually sensitive to alcohol, in whom alcohol produces character and personality changes so that he does things he would never do while sober—often with amnesia of incomplete memory for the acts. It is realized that this definition of an alcoholic stresses only one factor, namely, alcoholic sensitivity. Complicated physical and emotional factors, together with social and cultural diatheses, unite to produce an individual—driven by forces which he does not understand and which he cannot control—to seek happiness in the very cup which makes such a fool of him and jeopardizes his chances for happiness and success. Unconscious conflicts, particularly in the field of psychosexual pathology, inferiority broodings, and aggression-submission battles within the personality are frequently at work. The various combinations of these factors produce acute and chronic states of mind characterized by emotional tensions which certain individuals cannot stand. These tensions can be dissolved in alcohol, which seems almost specific in its ability to lessen the tyranny of the superego—which is the psychoanalytic name for conscience, or a sort of emotional governor which provides the civilized restraint necessary to keep us from yielding freely to our emotions and instinctive drives. Alcoholics, as well as neurotic and psychotic individuals, cannot handle all this conflict and retreat into their varied forms of escape and fantasy. An alcoholic, then, is a person who has developed the particular alcoholic method of achieving peace of mind—effective for the time being but disastrous for his integrity, his character, and his future success. However, in initial talks with alcoholics, all this cannot be discussed. They eagerly grasp at the sensitivity idea, which relieves them for the time being of moral guilt feelings and which at the same time makes very clear the important point that they cannot ever safely drink. Later, less superficial analysis of deeper mechanisms is necessary.

A "pure" alcoholic is quite normal and socialized when not drinking; he shows varying degrees of irresponsibility and character faults when drinking. Less liquor is usually necessary to make him intoxicated than is the case with the average man. The Alcoholics Anonymous organization teaches its members that they have "an allergy of the body and an obsession of the mind."

For the initial contact, I have found it effective to talk to the alcoholic somewhat as follows: "You are sensitive to alcohol in much the same way as other persons are sensitive to ragweed or strawberries. When we have allergies, it means that we react to certain substances differently from the average man. These reactions may be physical as shown by hay fever or the hives; they may be mental as in insomnia after coffee; they may be in the field of character as shown by your behavior after a few drinks. So the stuff (alcohol) is pure poison to you. Others are able to drink without doing themselves any harm. They would probably be better off if they did not drink; they would certainly save money, but they can get by with it—at least for a time. You are different, it is not your fault; but, because you are different, it is literally a matter of life and death to you, a matter of success and happiness or failure and disgrace. This is not due to any moral weakness or character fault; it is a matter of this allergy of yours. You can never 'handle' liquor, but it can and has put you in jail."

Contrary to common opinion, the alcoholic does not have a "craving" for drink between his bouts. His backsliding, or his return to drinking after leaving prison, does not occur because of any craving. In the great majority of cases, it happens under one of two circumstances: (1) the man takes his first drink after a time of abstinence in company with other drinkers, just to be sociable, or because of trouble, sorrow, happiness, despair, or celebration or (2) the man drinks under the mistaken impression that he is not really an alcoholic, that he merely drank too much before, that he can be a "normal" or "social" drinker. Once an alcoholic does take a drink, there is truly craving of a malignant sort, and all the king's horses and all the king's men cannot stop the drinking until the bout has run its course. We must use all our persuasiveness and all our ingenuity and all our influence to convince the alcoholic that he cannot ever become a social drinker. He must never take a single glass of beer or liquor; his only hope of safety and success and happiness lies in understanding that *once an alcoholic, always an alcoholic.* He may get away with it at times, but he cannot afford to take a chance.

Alcoholics Anonymous

Alcoholics Anonymous appears to be one of the most successful organizations ever developed by victims of any disorder for their own improvement. One of the strongest reasons for its success is probably the fact that it *is* a victim-sponsored and managed organization. It is easier to be helped by persons like yourself, by people who have gone through the same struggles you have and have won out, than to be treated or preached at by others who have no way of knowing how you really feel about things. AA, as the members call it, has helped drinkers to stop their drinking where parents, wives, clergymen, doctors, and psychiatrists have failed. The organization has rescued men from the skids by thousands. There have been backsliders, of course, but there are many, many successful men whom it has rescued from the alcoholic's seemingly inevitable end. If an alcoholic can be induced by you to meet with and join an AA unit, you have performed one of the most helpful services to your client. In my opinion, you should have AA literature in your offices and give or loan it to your alcoholics to read and study.

Not all alcoholics can be interested in AA. No one joins until he is convinced that he cannot refrain from drinking by his own efforts; he must seek some help from without his own personality. By confession and discussion of his alcoholic troubles before other alcoholics, by helping others to stop drinking, by open-meeting consideration of the whole problem, by association with fellow victims, the AA member becomes fired with the enthusiasm and faith and confidence which keep him dry from day to day and from year to year.

The members practically date their lives from the day they took their last drink, realizing the life and death nature of the problem.

By all means, get the help of AA for your alcoholics if at all possible.

Drug Addicts

In most cases, users of narcotics are criminals only incidentally in their need to supply their habits. To them, all other needs are subordinate.

An addict who is getting all the drugs his system requires is apparently quite a normal individual. This is in striking contrast to the alcoholic problem, for the alcoholic is quite normal when not drinking. The stories of "drug crazed" criminals are fantasy. The drug addict is "crazed" when he craves the drug and turns to criminal activity to get it. All drug addicts must, if they are not wealthy, turn to some kind of criminal activity because they cannot earn enough to buy their drugs; and as many have told me, "I don't have time to work."

It is practically impossible to control, except under close supervision (under guard), an addict who has an active habit. He must get his daily dosage or suffer severe pains, terrible anxiety, and mental agony. Such a man is in need, of course, of hospitalization or imprisonment under medical supervision.

A former addict, just released from hospital or prison, presents serious problems for his supervisor. Some drug users, deprived of drugs while in prison or hospital, wish to live without drugs; others look forward to getting drugs at the earliest possible moment. Certainly some of them do go for days, weeks and months without drugs; some who have used drugs stop their use. If the addict wants to get along without drugs, there is at least some hope for him. Remember that he is a sort of lost soul, longing for the drug which alone can make him feel normal. If he is trying to do the right thing, he leans heavily for support and encouragement on you, on friends, and on his family. The best advice you can give him is that he stay away from people and places which have been associated with his habit in the past. Many an addict has gone for a long time without drugs, courageously carrying on the good fight, only to backslide after meeting an old addicted friend or visiting a place which fostered his habit in the past.

Many addicts in their honest search for respectability try to choose a lesser evil. They must find some surcease from the agonizing tension of their drug-longings. They want to stay free from narcotics, so they try drinking as a substitute. This shows their dependence; it brings new troubles of its own, it does not help at all, and it usually leads back to drugs.

There is a difference of opinion as to whether everyone can become addicted. In studies of addicts, certain types of personalities are found, but I believe (with many others) that anyone who uses drugs for a long time will eventually be "hooked." The man of character and good sense will not try drugs initially for the thrill which unstable personalities seek, but I believe that certain addicts correctly trace their addiction to long-continued use of drugs during painful illnesses. This is a danger which all physicians realize and try to avoid.

As a final word regarding addiction, let me urge you to try to understand the terrible hold it has on the human personality. You may be unable to see an addict without disgust and revulsion, but remember that his need of drugs is partly physiological. The longing for drugs in an addict, deprived temporarily of his accustomed dosage, is probably comparable only to the longing a man lost in the desert feels for water. I have tried to understand, in talking to addicts, how strong their craving is. I have told many of them that one of the strongest longings of a human being is for sexual satisfaction and have asked them to compare that with the desire for drugs. Without exception, they have told me that there is no comparison—that the craving for narcotics is far greater. We can talk to the addict about willpower, but the willpower necessary to combat narcotic craving is a hundredfold stronger than any we nonusers have ever been called upon to muster.

Marihuana

The general belief at present is that the dangers in the use of marihuana have been greatly exaggerated. We read formerly of its terrible effects, and some of these seem to have been fairy tales. Its use is to be discouraged, but it is nonaddicting, it probably causes little or no trouble, and it certainly is not an important contributor to criminal activity. When a prisoner tells me he committed a crime when intoxicated or because of his need for narcotic drugs, I frequently believe him; when he says he was under the influence of marihuana, I do not believe him. Marihuana seems to alter the sense of time, to exhilarate the individual; but that it influences him to perform acts outside his usual moral code is probably not true. It is against the law to have it or sell it, and this law is probably a good thing.

Psychopathic Personality

It is an old idea that certain people, not insane, feebleminded, epileptic, or neurotic showed such variation from the usual standards of their cultural level that a special name was needed to describe them. They have been called moral imbeciles and psychopaths and many names between these designations, and still we do not know how or why they are as they are. The conception is a very useful one—and yet a very dangerous one—for we are likely to fall back on it when we do not understand a man. By calling him a psychopath, we are somehow unconsciously relieved of the necessity of trying to understand and help him. And if we fail to supervise him successfully, how delightful to tell ourselves that he was a psychopath whom no one could have helped.

Psychopathic Personality Defined

Fifty psychiatrists will give you as many definitions; and notice how they squirm as they give them! There is none of the assurance which we have when we tell you about dementia praecox or general paresis. The definition is usually one of exclusion. If a person does not conduct his affairs with ordinary judgment, he acts impulsively; if he does not profit by experience and mistakes, lacks the capacity to plan wisely, goes through life sinning, blundering, stumbling as though trying to get himself into as much trouble as possible and trying to get himself hated or killed —and if we cannot prove that he is feebleminded or insane—then we say he is a *psychopath* if he is not neurotic. Most of us are sure that there is such a person, but the danger lies in making a diagnosis by recounting all the troubles into which the man has plunged, and then calling him a psychopath because of this history. You probation officers in the field must help us understand these people. It may be that here is a special type of personality; it may be that such irresponsible persons represent a type of real mental disease as Dr. Hervey Cleckley and Dr. Ben Karpman believe. It may be that they are "rebels without a cause" in the words of the title of Robert Lindner's book. Or it may be that they do as they do because of mental conflicts, or as a result of experiences in early life which would have made anyone a psychopath. We simply do not know.

The great medicolegal dilemma presented by these psychopaths is this: Are they sane or insane; responsible or not responsible? Legal procedure at present considers them sane and responsible, and unless and until we are more sure of the belief of some of us that they are irresponsible, the present legal attitude would seem to be the most practical. For we must remember that they often are persistent evil-doers and if we ever excuse them from punishment as we do the insane and feebleminded, we must have an appropriate disposition, for they cannot be allowed to mess up themselves and the world without restraint. The only possible disposition would be similar to that of the insane, namely, commitment to some sort of hospital, not for a definite term but for an indefinite period—till cured. The psychopaths and their lawyers would hardly appreciate this. The present common cycle of court to mental hospital and back to freedom and on to delinquency and court again would be many times extended. The probation and parole officer has little to do with this dilemma. At present, he must consider the man sane and try to guide and influence him as best he can.

Characteristics of the Psychopath

Outstanding among the tragic characteristics of the psychopath is his inability, or at any rate his failure, to develop loyalties. The probation officer, in his management of ordinary clients, relies to a large extent on this loyalty which he tries to develop toward himself, his friends, and his family. The psychopath must not be expected to develop this loyalty, so we who deal with him lack a very useful tool. We must steel ourselves against being shocked when these strange people act so penitent and ashamed and friendly and loyal and loving, and then within days or even minutes act in a way which shows that these emotions have no meaning whatever for them.

It is easy to recount the peculiarities and sins and weaknesses of the psychopath. It is harder to give advice as to how to help him. My advice will not be very helpful, as I am one of those who regards the problem of the psychopath as well nigh hopeless, as far as our influencing his thought, idealism, and behavior. I repeat my theme song, "do your best." The only hopes I know of lie in three main categories.

Many psychopaths become more normal as time goes on. I can attribute this only to a gradual maturity. So much of the behavior of a psychopath seems explainable on a basis of delayed or stunted emotional maturity, particularly in the field of appreciation of the rights of others and in the concept of their personalities, characteristics, and desires in relation to the same desires of others and of the state. The professional criminal has, we believe, normal appreciation of these things but chooses to ignore them. The psychopath does not seem to have such an appreciation. Many psychopaths mellow and seem to develop this socialization, and in this maturity lies our greatest hope. I have asked many of them who seem to have matured—at least to the extent of finally learning to restrain themselves enough to build up a good record in prison—what, in their opinion, could have been done earlier to have helped them to adjust at home, at school, in correctional schools, in prisons. Their answer invariably is to the effect that nothing could have been done: "I just had to learn my lesson the hard way."

By trying to rid yourself of the hopelessness of no longer trying to help a psychopath, you can always say to yourself, "maybe this kid is not a psychopath after all." You will experience many heartaches and cruel disappointments, but you may also rid yourself and your client of the feeling of utter frustration and may find ways to help him to a better way of life. So try it, and if you fail, don't feel too bad; if you succeed, yell for joy!

I do not believe it irreverent or far-fetched to say that it is a miracle of a sort when one of these irresponsible, blundering persons suddenly or gradually settles down and begins to act like a normal human being. This happens in prison and happens to your clients. After the change is the time to try, as we do, to find out what caused the change; and then to try similar techniques on similar clients when they come along.

Extra supervision and guidance obviously are needed, far more than are required for other types of offenders. The psychopath of course resents the very supervision of which he is in such crying need. In a way, he will hate it and yet I am sure that he knows he needs it. He likes to talk about his troubles. He likes to exaggerate his good points and accomplishments and likes to tell of the sins and unwise behavior of others. He loves to ask for favors and wants your good opinion. While he is offering excuses and fancied or rationalized evidence in mitigation of his misdeeds, there is a chance for us in the prison system and you in the field to discuss, advise, and offer guidance and leadership. Some of the words of wisdom you offer for his benefit may not be wasted. And remember that, for some strange reason, most of the psychopaths who become criminalistic are of average intelligence or better. Others in close contact with the man—employer, friends, family—should be taught to encourage conversation, to praise when possible, to warn wisely, to help form a solid rock of stability which this type of person needs as a refuge. It is, of course, an art to advise and counsel without being too "preachy." Our counseling efforts must be highly developed to be at all effective in helping these people. Concentration as much as possible in conversation on "neutral" subjects, matters of interest to the client which carry no emotional charge and which have nothing to do with right and wrong, is advisable here. In "passing the time of day" with our clients, much can be done in building up friendship or at least friendly feeling which is the most important factor in establishing rapport which is so necessary if we are to influence successfully another person, psychopathic or not.

It is better to have psychopaths live with others and work with others than to have them lead more solitary lives. There are exceptions, but the constant brake of other people's needs and rights and emotional drives must be on hand to be used by the psychopath if his maturity begins to develop. This is in line with his need for special supervision and guidance. Employers, friends, and family need not know that the client is considered to be a psychopath. They usually should not know this, but they should be told that the client is unusual, that he is "nervous," that he needs extra help, that he frequently needs to be left alone, that he can be talked to sometimes and not at other times, that he is often disappointing and disloyal, but that you are trying to help bring out the best in him. Get his associates interested in the fascinating, though difficult, problem of helping and influencing for the better a peculiar individual who "needs just the help that you can give him. That is why I am asking you to take a special interest in him."

Sexual Deviates

The attempts to understand sexual deviation are hampered by our lack of knowledge of what constitutes a normal or average sexual life. Kinsey's recent book and the multiple of reports and publications concerning it have confused rather than enlightened us. Honest attempts at understanding this important part of life are to be encouraged, of course, but the complicated physical and emotional factors involved are far beyond the scope of this text. Here we must be a little dogmatic and call sexual life "normal" when the individual turns for sexual expression to those of the opposite sex and manages his sexual life with discretion and self-control to the extent of receiving and giving happiness from the relationship and avoiding the flouting of laws and customs of society. The highest ideal, of course, is the happy marriage with the formation of family life.

Most Common Sexual Deviations

There are several common sexual deviations with which this section is concerned.

Uncontrolled Heterosexuality. Persons who offend in this manner belong in general in one of two groups: (1) Individuals whose sexual aim is union with one of the opposite sex, but whose relationships never develop to the point of enduring satisfaction.

Such are the so-called Don Juans among men and the so-called nymphomaniacs among women. A neurosis of a severe type is usually the basis for these conditions. (2) Psychopaths whose sexual life follows the same pattern of irresponsibility as the rest of their life activities. They seduce and rape in their restless hedonistic search for the satisfaction which they never really find except for the passing moment.

Active Homosexuality. These persons have as their sexual object a person of the same sex; as their sexual aim, sexual union with the other person. They desire the masculine role, acting toward their homosexual lover as a normal person would toward a lover of the opposite sex.

Passive Homosexuality. These persons have as their sexual object a person of the same sex; as their sexual aim, sexual union with the other person. They desire the feminine role, acting toward their lovers as normal persons would toward lovers of the opposite sex.

Remember these distinctions: the active homosexual (when a man) treats a male lover as though he were a female. The passive homosexual (when a man) treats the male lover as though the lover were a male, and he (the passive homosexual) a female. All three of these types may be aggressive or not; that is, they may seek the lover or may respond to the lover's seeking. All three may be constantly true to their abnormal type, or may be what we call facultative, that is, sometimes "normal" and sometimes "abnormal." In the field of personality distortions, hardly anyone is the same sort of person all of the time.

Polymorphous Perverse Sexual State. There are individuals who seem never to crystallize their sexual aims or desires. They are essentially children or, at most, adolescents in their psychosexual behavior and attitudes; they are ready to try any kind of sexual expression, particularly if it seems smart to them or if they have never tried it before. Some of these are probably psychopaths, others are probably definite victims of neuroses.

I realize that the foregoing is such a brief discussion that it may only have led to confusion in your minds. There is no way of really making the matters simple. These conditions all lie in the field of sexual pathology. Those of you who are really interested in this complicated and involved field of study may read psychoanalytic works. They, again, may only further confuse you. The very best introduction to a serious attempt to understand the sex deviate is to read Freud's *Three Contributions to the Theory of Sex.* As an antidote to all this, and to restore your sense of humor and to keep you from worrying too much about it, I suggest that you read Thurber and White's *Is Sex Necessary?* Best of all, in most cases, study the individual you are trying to understand, to help, and to guide, and get all the psychiatric advice you can. And to revert to my theme song, "do the best you can."

One more word about helping your client with his sex problems: Advise and discuss, but do not be "preachy." Almost everyone has some peculiarities and worries and guilt feelings and conflicts about his or her sex life. Commonsensical discussion is of tremendous help if you can become genuinely interested and avoid being, or at least acting, shocked. The sexual difficulties of most people, serious as they are, tend to fade away as they mature. It may or may not be "normal," but think of the many people you know as good people and yet who have transgressed our sexual code.

How Tensions May Be Relieved

Remember that you cannot control another person's sex life. You can only give guidance and leadership.

Many clients will appreciate talking over their sex lives and problems with you; others will not. Clients of the latter sort are worried and ill at ease no matter how much they may deny their anxiety. If they will talk these important matters over with you, the mere talking may do much good, especially if you can keep your own emotions under control and hidden if your clients shock you. Much of the good done by doctors, by friends, and by priests at the confessional, comes from what psychoanalysts call catharsis—letting off steam and relieving tension by talking to a sympathetic listener. Another point to remember is that the tension caused by a person tortured by psychosexual pathology can be relieved in only four ways, as follows:

1. *Frank acceptance of the abnormal sexual desires and frank yielding to them.* This results in the individual becoming an overt participant in his particular kind of sexual pathological activity. He is then no longer ashamed of his longings and activities, enjoys them, and considers the people we call normal as narrow-minded. Tension leaves him, for he has avoided conflict about the matter.

2. *Frank acceptance of the abnormal sexual desires but refusal to yield to them.* This results in some tension because of the constant restraint, but the acceptance of the abnormal desires does away with the more serious conflict which always occurs when an individual refuses to admit his personality or character peculiarities, sexual or otherwise. His mental state is then to be compared on a heterosexual level to the normally sexed man or woman who for some reason remains unmarried and continent. He is consciously exercising self-control, not fighting an inward conflict.

3. *Relief of tension by sublimation.* This word, which is taken from physics, refers to the purification of an impulse, tendency, or desire into a socially acceptable form of activity. This is not done consciously like the solution just discussed under 2, but is an unconsciously developed mechanism. Its explanation lies in the field of psychoanalytic theory, not at all universally accepted. It is generally believed, however, that many people find happiness by satisfying their antisocial tendencies in a way which does good instead of harm. To give specific examples of this sublimation in a text prepared for nonmedical readers might cause some embarrassment. Suffice it to say here that any overpowering interest or vocation or avocation which your clients show may lead the way to a possible sublimation of antisocial or abnormal sexual tendencies.

4. *Repression of the sexual conflict.* Another and always tragic solution of an individual's conflict about his sexual peculiarities involves repression. According to psychoanalytic theory, at least, such a person is actually able to repress his conflict. Thus a homosexual, for instance, comes to believe that he is not a homosexual at all. If this were all, it would be a happy solution. Unfortunately for such a patient—for such persons then become psychotic

—the repressed desires remain active and seek repression in some way. These ways take place through delusions and hallucinations in which homosexual threats seem to come from other persons. Depending upon the subject's personality makeup, varied symptoms may develop and the individual becomes the victim, as he sees it, of a hostile world which is trying to force him into homosexuality, and of hallucinations and voices which accuse him of the very perversions he has repressed. Thus a person cannot safely repress his desires without becoming psychotic or without exhibiting some sexual deviation.

For the sexual deviant, the only safe way of keeping his mental health would be through the first three alternatives just described. It is probable that we can do little to help the probationer as to the way in which he solves the conflict, but we should try to lead and advise him to accept the second or third alternative rather than the first or last.

In talking over these sexual peculiarities and conflicts with a probationer, the strongest talking point is somewhat as follows: "You are for some reason unusual in your psychosexual life. You cannot help this, but you can and must accept it if you are to remain mentally healthy. The desires which you have and which society calls abnormal cannot be allowed free sway. You must exercise self-control, and it may be no more difficult than the control which you use in other fields of personality."

I tell a homosexual man that he cannot help being what he is, but that he can control it, just as a more normal man controls his heterosexual impulses. This conscious control is a far different matter from repression, for the latter involves splitting of the personality—pretending that he is what he really is not. He is never as effective an individual as is the man who accepts his peculiarities and succeeds in controlling them.

Aggressive Sexual Psychopath

Another type of sexual abnormality, the victims of which are really in danger, is represented by the so-called aggressive sexual psychopaths. These persons are of different personality patterns but are similar in their aggressiveness. The case history and medical and psychiatric opinions usually have spotted most of them. Share your knowledge and opinions with your professional co-workers and get what help you can from doctors and clinics. Many states have put into effect laws which provide for indefinite commitment of sexual psychopaths. Become familiar with these laws if your state has them. If you suspect, believe, or know that a client—or anyone for that matter—has or is likely to attack others, particularly children, you must not take the responsibility of keeping it to yourself. State authorities or city police should have the benefit of your knowledge in order that they may get medical advice and act as seems best. Remember that these unfortunate but dangerous individuals cannot or have not developed the normal or controlled adult status of heterosexual love as a force to be sublimated or refined toward marriage and family ideals. They long for sex expression and, not being able to make love in the usual way, turn in desperation to rape or sex intimacies with young children. The fear of being caught and the intense feeling of guilt may then lead to the killing of the victim. Try to inspire these clients with higher ideals; help them with common-sense sex discussion. But do not keep your knowledge to yourself; otherwise you may have plenty of reason for guilt feeling yourself if your client is involved in one of the sex crimes.

Neurotics

It is beyond the scope of this text to go into the classification and description of the sorts of nervous disorders to which the human mind is susceptible; the same applies to psychotic (insane) people, discussed below. You are not expected to be a psychiatrist, but you do have to deal with neurotic (nervous) clients. Get all the help you can from psychiatrists and other doctors; learn some of the danger signs which may point to the presence of a neurosis; learn common-sense methods of advice and management. Try to learn how far you may safely go before the client *must* seek medical help. And remember that the doctor will probably need and request help from you, friends, and the family.

Neurotic persons frequently are nondelinquent for the probable reason that neurotics are persons who succumb to their conflicts submissively, while delinquents, on the other hand, aggressively try to fight their way out of their dilemma. But we do have nervous clients. Many of these "nervous" clients, however, may be frustrated psychopaths, and we need a great skill to distinguish them from the true neurotics. Again, much "nervousness" is an early expression of physical disease which makes early medical examination and diagnosis necessary.

Common Danger Signs

Anxiety, brooding, undue worrying, insomnia are all possible symptoms of neurosis. Moodiness, inability to think clearly or to concentrate, inattention to family and employment responsibilities—these may all be evidence of neurosis rather than merely character faults. Frequent physical complaints and the so-called hypochondria may become as serious and crippling as actual heart or stomach disorders. A whole new field of medicine, as most of you know, is concerned with what we call psychosomatic disorders, that is, mental conflicts converted into physical complaints and illnesses in a rather mysterious way, probably through the complicated connections between emotions, ductless glands, and the sympathetic nervous system. We must learn that much actual physical pathology begins in emotional conflict, and that after a time the process may become irreversible. When this happens the physical disorder is the important thing. Certain disorders are believed to always begin in mental conflict, for instance, toxic goiter, gastric ulcer, and migraine. You may be out of your depth when you try to do the best you can for these patients, but most of their treatment and management will fall upon you.

How the Neurotic Can Be Helped

Naturally you will have to fall back on the help of doctors wherever you can, but the necessity of doing much of the actual advising yourself makes it imperative that you become as informed as possible about these symptoms. You can help in several ways.

Common-sense advice may or may not help. Try it. Not all neuroses are so very serious, and a good interested friend is sometimes all that is needed. Very important as a measure of your ability to help a nervous client is your ability to enter into his feelings, to understand the things he is worrying about, to be able to put yourself in his place and find out what you would do. You will really be a partner of your client in his struggle and you will attain a chastening sense of humility in your probable realization that he is grappling with problems which would have stumped, thwarted, and de-energized you as much or more than they have tortured him.

Time spent in letting all clients, and particularly nervous clients, talk it out is usually well-spent time. There is a limit to your time, of course, and you have to use common sense in budgeting it. But the turning point in the improvement of many a neurotic patient has been the privilege of talking himself out to a sympathetic listener.

A few words of advice concerning the tone of our remarks when talking to neurotic people may be helpful. We must remember that neurotic symptoms, though not based on physical pathology, are very real to the patient. A general air of encouragement is in order, but the breezy "cheer up" usually does more harm than good. It is not in order to belittle the patient's symptoms. Many neurotic patients are driven to despair by our constant inability to understand their condition as they see it. Above all, do not refer to the complaints and symptoms as imaginary, for indeed they are not. They frequently are beyond our understanding, and they lie outside the realm of ordinary physical disease. Nevertheless, a neurotic suffers from exceedingly crippling and embarrassing disorders. A true neurotic is not a malingerer but usually is considered one. He probably should be regarded as an "unconscious malingerer," no more responsible for his mental tensions, worries, and phobias than is a diabetic responsible for his faulty pancreas.

Neurotic symptoms and neurotic patients are susceptible to two kinds of treatment. The underlying cause, usually unsolved emotional conflict, can be helped by analytic psychotherapy; this lies within the province of the psychiatrist and should not be attempted by others. Replacement and suggestive therapy, however, is given by doctors and lay alike, often better by the latter. Sympathetic understanding, cheerful attitudes toward getting well, and suggestions and advice regarding everyday living can be attempted by all. It is probably in the field of helping the patient to develop healthy vocational, avocational, and recreational interests that you and the patient's family and friends can be of most help. A neurotic person does not have time to worry and fret if he becomes busy and interested in outside interests; often, but by no means always, this is true. The danger in this kind of treatment lies in the fact that even if the patient feels and acts normal, his unsolved emotional problems still remain. They sometimes evaporate, but often they do not; and if they do not, they are likely to break out anew at any time.

Psychotics

Many of the points discussed in regard to neurotics also apply to the psychotic (insane person). Psychoses, however, are much more serious, much more dangerous, far less likely to be affected by anything you can do. Out of any group of persons, certain ones are going to be psychotic.

Danger Signals

You must be familiar with certain danger signals which may point to a possible mental disease. Among these are the following:

1. Any change in character or personality. Any indication that the person seems to be a different person from his usual self.
2. Unwanted withdrawal from the society of others and from activity formerly enjoyed.
3. Undue exhilaration or depression.
4. Fear of going insane. Neurotics frequently say this, and need to be encouraged that they are not. It is all right to similarly encourage psychotics, or potential psychotics as well, but reassure the patient and not yourself. Do not try to diagnose mental disease, or a neurosis either.
5. Fear of being controlled, of having the mind read, of not being one's self, all are common early symptoms.
6. Presence of paranoid ideas (ideas of persecution). In our

work where our clients so often are already antisocial and interpret prosecution as persecution, it is frequently difficult to differentiate between truly paranoid ideas and surly hatred of the world which is, indeed, often "against them." The psychotic paranoid ideas tend to be fantastic and impossible but are not always so. All ideas of this sort place the client under suspicion.

7. Fantastic delusions (false ideas) are characteristic of psychoses, but here again it is often hard to tell.
8. Hallucinations (false sensory impressions) are certainly evidence of mental disorder.

A doctor, preferably a psychiatrist, must be called to examine a man you suspect of mental disease. Unfortunately we are not always sure at first, so you may have to worry your way through early symptoms.

How the Psychotic Can Be Helped

States have different laws regarding emergency, observation, and regular commitments to state psychiatric hospitals. You must be familiar with these. A doctor and also courts are needed to obtain commitments. Emergency commitment often may save the patient's life; accordingly, you should know the quickest way to obtain a commitment in your community.

Common-sense advice is needed here, of course, but such advice is usually for the family rather than for the patient when there is actual mental disease. Do not depend upon your knowledge of mental disease, good though it may be. The responsibility for the commitment, care, and treatment of mentally diseased patients rests with the state, its courts, and its doctors.

It is well to remember a few points about psychotic persons.

Paranoid patients frequently believe they are in danger and have to defend themselves. They are thus potentially dangerous. Anyone who knows of the possibility of a paranoid condition must share that knowledge and get the best advice possible, or bear a good share of the responsibility if disaster occurs.

Depressed patients are always potentially suicidal and must be guarded every *second* till proved not suicidal.

As is the case with any disease or abnormal condition, the

earlier diagnosis and treatment can be secured, the earlier may improvement result. It frequently may become one of your responsibilities to counsel with families of clients when commitment to a mental hospital has been advised. The strongest talking point is that the danger of stigmatizing the patient by residence in a state hospital is far less than the danger of putting off treatment and commitment till it is too late for the most effective treatment.

Any nervous or mental disease in a person who has had syphilis should be considered possibly due to syphilis of the brain and spinal cord unless examination of the the spinal fluid shows that this is not so.

Our old friends of several pages back cause us a lot of trouble in our consideration of possible psychoses. I refer to the psychopaths, those who are sort of "half crazy" all the time and who develop both real psychoses at times and strange behavior which may not be actually psychotic at other times. In this connection, your judgment probably will be as good as the doctor's, possibly better; and you both often will be unsure of your ground. Use the best combined judgment you and the doctors can summon, and even then prepare to be often outwitted by the psychopath.

PROMISCUOUS GIRLS ON PROBATION*

In response to the civilian and military pressure during World War II, numerous social agencies attempted to offer an effective rehabilitation service to the prostitute. Baltimore's answer was the Protective Service for Girls, a service that works with girls who are arrested for prostitution and placed on probation to us by the courts—and girls who come to us of their own accord, seeking help with their promiscuity. Most agencies have approached the prostitute and her problems with a need to examine the causes for the girl's behavior. They have gone into the past to find reasons for the present. The unique focus of the Protective Service for Girls is that it works with the girl and her present problem. This has proved to be a vital dynamic in helping her to change.

We know that the promiscuous girl, like the rest of us, has her

---

* Reprinted in part by permission of the National Probation and Parole Association. Evelyn C. Hyman: Holding the promiscuous girl accountable for her own behavior. *NPPA Yearbook, Bulwarks Against Crime*, pp. 190-201, 1948.

weaknesses. We see her greatest weakness in her projection of blame onto others for her plight. But we see no value in making her relive her past. We attempt to help her to live more positively in the present. Our focus is on helping her reorganize her strengths. Maybe you think a prostitute does not have strength. It is only natural to believe that the girl who has always said *yes* is a "weak sister." From our experience, we know that many promiscuous girls have real strength but that most of them are using it negatively. Their very coming to us is a sign of strength, for it is very hard to take help from another person. Have you ever lost your way while driving along a strange road? How often have you, instead of asking directions, just fumbled along alone hoping to come out all right? Just as such independence is a common trait among all of us, so it is typical of the prostitute, but additionally, when she seeks help, she must fight her embarrassment and feelings of guilt. And so, if she gets to the point where she can come to us for help, she is already one step on the way toward being different. As we relate to this inherent strength, we make it possible for the girl to begin affirming herself as a person.

The Protective Service for Girls has carved out an authoritative casework method in which we hold the girl responsible for some demonstration of an attempt to change. Just her saying she wants to do differently is not enough. Whether the girl comes to us voluntarily or on probation, we hold her to our requirements. One of the most important of these requirements is keeping regular appointments with her worker. This is a big order for the prostitute. A girl who has been sleeping all day and living at night must rearrange her entire mode of living to get to our office during business hours. More than this, she will find it hard sharing with another adult the problems she has created for herself as a result of her own promiscuous behavior.

Another requirement is that the girl live in a neighborhood where she feels she can stay out of trouble. Invariably this means moving to an entirely new neighborhood and living differently. But we cannot merely require her to move without helping her to get located. If she has no place to go and no funds, we will pay her room and board at the Salvation Army Women's and Children's Residence until she can take over for herself. If having her own room or apartment seems right, we will refer her to accredited room registries or discuss neighborhoods with her.

In addition, we require that all girls have an examination at the health department. This can be a very fearful experience, as it involves the possibility of having to face the fact that they may have contracted a venereal disease. Very often it is in discussion of this requirement with her worker that for the first time the girl begins to trust as she shares her former behavior and present apprehension.

Finally the girl must secure dignified employment. And that means she cannot go back being a waitress or barmaid in cheap restaurants or taverns where advances of the men customers are part of the job. This is, for many girls, the most difficult of requirements. Before this, she has not applied through an employment service but has picked up jobs with the same casualness as she has picked up men. She has little to give her confidence in making application for a totally different kind of job. But at the state employment office, she will be met as a person claiming a right and will be respected as a person capable of making the best choice for herself. All of this is new and fearful, of course, but another important experience for her.

These requirements provide a structure against which she can test her strength and against which we both may evaluate her desire and efforts toward change. We believe they give her the opportunity to know that she can live within authority and not be destroyed by it.

A Trusting Relationship

At the start, in order that she will feel supported in her smallest efforts, she will have frequent appointments with her caseworker. This is one of the most important factors in helping her change, for it gives her an opportunity to have a meaningful relationship. While her caseworker is always expecting of her and holding her to some evidence of change, she is at the same time always there for the girl, showing that she cares. We believe that only through such an experience in relationship can the girl begin to trust and be capable of trusting relationships outside.

During these interviews with the girl, we will not take over the making of any decisions for her but will help her with the process of making considered choices. For instance, many times, girls will ask during their first interviews, "But I can't go to a bar, can I?" or "Don't I have to be home by ten o'clock?" To these we answer, "Can you go to a bar and keep out of trouble?" and "*You* feel you'll get into trouble if you're on the streets at night." And so in our discussion we put more and more responsibility for decisions on her. It is up to her to ignore the wolfish whistles of the boys. She must use her own strength to refuse the first drink, and each time she demonstrates to herself that she can do these things and not be destroyed by the decision or the doing, her sense of pride and respect for herself increases. As she takes on this stature, she expects more and more of herself and requires less holding up by the caseworker. It is certain that she has begun to think of herself not only as a person with obligations but also as one who has rights, and she can begin to make some demands of her own. Very often the meek little wife will tell her alcoholic husband that his drinking must stop. The heretofore patient woman will serve notice on her nonsupporting male that he must be a more responsible father. In putting out such expectations for a better life for herself, she is demonstrating that she has begun to internalize the authority needed to live more affirmatively.

Just as we make use of expectation and requirement in working with the promiscuous woman, so we make dynamic use of time. Since she had no purpose and had felt no achievement, living seemed endless. We know this to be unrealistic, for all experience is limited—broadly by birth and death, and more partially by the completion of each endeavor. In order to help the promiscuous girl get hold of some wish to achieve, she must feel some awareness of time. To this end, we consciously put time limits on all our expectations of her. For instance, the girl who is on probation for a year may feel that this is forever and therefore much too long for her to remain out of trouble. She can feel beaten before she starts. We therefore discuss with her how she can manage today, whether between a Friday and a Monday appointment she can keep out of trouble, and then since she was able to do so for a week, is there not reason to think she can continue for another week? We know that movement is slow and growth never straight ahead. The girl must be free to fail and to know this will mean rejection. With the same consideration of its dynamic value, we set a time limit in which we will expect the girl to secure employment, report to the health department, and come to a decision about her living arrangements. And so the girl begins to succeed in different phases of her living. She is then made aware of her growth by being given fewer appointments and more responsibility.

This process of engaging the prostitute in being accountable for what she does begins in the very first interview. This interview is most often in places to which her antisocial behavior has brought her—the prison, the jail, the health department, the police station, or the court. Here her characteristic of projecting blame is most outstanding. We hold her to deciding whether she wants to remain in such a static state or whether she desires to move ahead.

It is often very difficult to hold the promiscuous girl accountable for her behavior in these first interviews. That it can be done is illustrated in the following piece of case material.

Interview in a Lockup

Miss Henson is a tall, slim, fair and rather attractive young woman of twenty-three, who was extremely negative, frightened and quite tightly put together. She quite obviously trusted no one and yet was somehow pleading for someone to care about her.

I began the interview by telling her my name and that the judge had sent for me because she was found guilty of prostitution. Although her lower lip trembled and in a few seconds she cried, she at once retorted with great belligerence. "I know it, but I am not guilty of anything. I didn't do it. I didn't do nothing to be arrested for." I thought that if she felt she was being held and sentenced unfairly, she had better say so to the judge. With the same bitterness she jeered at this idea. She knew and she thought I too should know that "those vice squad men" who had arrested her, and the judge, all stick together. I said I didn't know that, but if she felt that way even though she had done nothing, I supposed she would have to serve her time in prison. Miss Henson said she didn't want to go to prison! There was no reason why she should. All she had done, she said, was to go to get something to eat with this fellow who stopped and talked with her as she came out from the midnight movie. Then as they were in the restaurant, he had given her some money. She didn't take it "to have intercourse with him as they said in court." All she had done was take the money. Did I see anything wrong in that? I wondered why she thought a friend of such a few moments would be giving her money. She said she didn't know— and I said I didn't believe that. She asked me if someone wanted to give me some money, wouldn't I take it? I said we were talking about her. She had taken the money and was in real trouble because of it. I believed that she had been around enough to know what she was doing and to know it was against the law. But Miss Henson said she absolutely did not go with this man and didn't intend to. I held that she knew what she was doing, and why she had accepted the money, and had had previous experiences of this kind. I couldn't believe she too didn't consider it strange to accept money from strangers. Showing her first yielding, Miss Henson said that was right, she knew it was wrong and against the law to do what she was doing, but she said, "I'm so confused I don't know what I'm doing."

I said it could feel like confusion—I thought she was afraid and worried about herself. She had been pretty much on the loose for a few weeks now, on her own, away from her family. I supposed she and her family were having trouble and she didn't seem to be caring what she did. Miss Henson very rapidly and defensively told how she had first gone away to Pennsylvania for a short time. Although since her return to Baltimore a few weeks ago she had not gone home to live, she stoutly attempted to impress me with the fact that she is a girl who had a "good mother and stepfather." They would be disgraced if she went to prison. I wondered if they knew of the trouble she was in. Miss Henson said her mother did, but she was not in court today. Miss Henson then began anew to fight for herself. She said even though she had accepted this money, which was wrong, she had never gotten into trouble before. I asked if it were not true that a few years ago she had to go to the health department. Miss Henson quietly but quickly agreed. I said it sounded then as if she had been running around for quite a while. She started again to cry, saying she didn't want to go to prison and didn't feel she should. I said maybe that was the only thing for her. I had come over with the intention of taking up the possibility of her being on probation, but I realized now she wasn't really ready for that. Real angry, Miss Henson said she could be on probation. She didn't *want* to go to prison, but that wasn't reason enough for me to be willing to tell the judge we would give her a try on probation. We then had quite a struggle. Miss Henson said, "The trouble with you all is you never want to give anybody a chance. All you want to do, when a girl gets in trouble, is to send her away to prison." I let her know this was how she looked at it. For my part I believed in giving everyone who seemed able to use it, not only a chance to do differently, but help in doing that also. Miss Henson said she wanted a chance. She didn't want to go to prison. She knew some girls who had been to prison, and when they came out they did lots worse things than when they had gone in: "They swore a lot and did a lot of things." I said she seemed to like being a part of this group. And I didn't think swearing was new to her. I did not think she could behave differently because she was so tied up with this group; hence considering probation seemed futile. Miss Henson, with real determination and at the same time a desperate tone, said she could drop her friends. They hung around, and she did too, at the Bijoux and the Overland Bus Station. She didn't think much of it now, it seemed, and wanted quickly to separate herself. I could agree this could have a lot to do with her getting into trouble, but I doubted she could make a break, and there would be just no point in being on probation if she weren't going to be able to do differently. She said she knew and she could. After all, "I have a mother and father—and parents help a girl, don't they?" I thought it was good she felt hers would—that was real important—but it would be she who would be on probation, not they. Miss Henson said that was all right. She could still do it. She could be different. I said I wasn't sure—she hadn't said much to convince me yet that she thought she was doing anything that needed to be changed. Miss Henson put the blame on everybody else. She said, "I know I have to change, but I'm not all bad like"—and as she stopped, I said, "people think you are." She agreed. She then said, "I know I have some good in me—everybody does—and I could be different." I agreed everyone did have some good, but it seemed to me as if she really didn't care. Miss Henson said, "I do care. I don't know why I've been doing all these things. I'm all confused." She said, with a lot of feeling, that being in the jail for these few days had been enough. It was the first time and "awful."

I wondered what she saw that could be different—why did she think she had been prostituting? Miss Henson said very frankly, "Because I don't have enough responsibility." She explained that she had gone out just about every night. She said that she had to give up her job because of this situation. Then, added, she also takes care of a sailor's baby. She denied this was her child, but that she and the sailor want to be married as soon as he can obtain a divorce. While I could understand her feeling of boredom with this situation, I told her I had no idea how these things could be changed so she could feel more "responsible." Miss Henson said, "I do. I could get a job." She felt that different plans would have to be made for her mother who was ill. Anyway, she said, she is better now, and more able to care for herself. I felt she was too quickly trying to make everything plausible and easy. I knew it would be harder than that, and I doubted she could get hold of herself so simply.

Miss Henson said she knew she could. She said, "If I ever get out of this, I know I could be on probation. I'd go to Pennsylvania where I don't go with this kind of a crowd. After all, you know a girl's environment is what makes her get into trouble. I know I could be different someplace else." I said I did think environment was mighty important, but I knew it wasn't everything. What a person really wants for herself has a lot to do with it, and if she were on probation the hard part would be that she would have to remain right here in Baltimore and still change—stop prostituting. Miss Henson was startled that she would have to remain in Baltimore but, quickly recovering, said if she had to stay she could and still be different. She sounded so sure. How could she? Miss Henson said, "Because I have a will. And if I say a thing and make up my mind to do it, I can. I know I can. You can't know unless you give me a chance to show you." I thought she had something there. However, I said neither the judge nor we were anxious to try someone on probation if she wasn't going to be able to make use of it. And she should be the least anxious, for if she did violate, it would mean serving her time anyway. Miss Henson realized this, but said she knew she could do it. She knew she'd try as hard as possible and "that's the most a girl can do, isn't it?" I thought it was. Miss Henson was much quieter now. As I stood up I said I'd be talking with the judge now. I felt her attitude was somewhat different from what it was when we started. She was seeing that she had a part in getting herself into this trouble—and while I still had my doubts, maybe she could do something to get herself out of it. I would tell this to the judge and then it would be up to him to decide if he wanted to send her over to our office where we could talk more specifically about probation and decide if she still wanted it and could use it. Miss Henson sat with her head lowered and said nothing as I left.

In this one brief contact, her first with the agency, Miss Henson met someone as strong as she who was not judgmental but who continually held her to a recognition of her part in her arrest. When she could begin to accept this, she was then held to deciding whether she could and wanted to do anything differently. The fact that she felt she could was the basis for my recommendation to the judge that she be given an opportunity for probation. From then on, she began taking over responsibility for herself. She came from the courthouse to our office alone, she has kept all appointments, and recently, after evading all attempts on the part of the health department for over a year to get her to report for treatment, she has gone to the Rapid Treatment Center and been cured of syphilis. While Miss Henson, who is still on probation, is experiencing many difficulties in meeting our requirements and saying *no* to the boys, she is able to continue because she knows we believe in her ability to change. By relating to the girls' strengths and showing them that we care and have respect for them, we are able to help most of them through to successful endings. And it is because of this firm warm belief in them at the beginning that many of them come back to say, as one recently did, "What means most to me are those first hard times I had with you."

This is a broad picture of how we hold the promiscuous girl accountable for her own behavior. It is a strong, direct, authoritative method of helping people come to something for themselves. It is carried by our conviction that people who are not in harmony with society cannot be in harmony with themselves. And its real authority is in our belief in people, their right and capacity to live with that most precious gift of all, human dignity. Not only for the sex delinquent but for all of us, this dignity comes in part at least from being accountable for and able to live with our own behavior.

GROUP SUPERVISION OF PROBATIONERS AND PAROLEES*

Classical probation and parole supervision have been based upon the notion that the most effective therapeutic process is the one-to-one relationship between the supervising officer and his client. Now, after more than a half century of always working with offenders on an individual basis, correctional practitioners are beginning to utilize alternative techniques, the most significant of which is the group method of supervision.

---

* Printed by permission of the author, William H. Parsonage. From an original unpublished manuscript, The Pennsylvania State University, 1968.

The increasing use of the group method for supervising probationers and parolees can be traced to accumulating evidence that it is more effective than the one-to-one approach for the community reintegration of many offenders. There is little doubt that many probation and parole officers, who are not presently working with offenders in groups, will be doing so in the future. A key factor in insuring a successful group experience for the worker and in insuring that services derived by clients will be of high quality is the extent to which realistic planning precedes the actual conduct of the program. Our purpose is to identify and discuss factors connected with the planning and operation of group supervision projects.

There is a variety of reasons favoring the supervision of offenders in groups. Among these are (1) improvement of the quality and quantity of supervisory services to offenders to a level otherwise impossible under the pressure of overwhelming caseloads; (2) reduction of barriers which exist between agent and client in the traditional one-to-one relationship that serve to block the development of a helping process; (3) involvement of parolees and probationers in a mutual commitment to the restorative process by affording them visible decision-making responsibility and an opportunity to determine their own destiny; (4) conversion of questionable associations among offenders to constructive purposes by legitimizing their contact and orienting it to the task of mutual assistance; (5) provision of a nonthreatening opportunity for the supervising officer and his clients to explore and clarify each other's legitimate roles in the supervisory process and to develop a more genuine understanding of each other as people; and (6) provision of an equalitarian setting wherein issue and concerns can be freely and fully discussed. All of these goals are obtainable to a significant degree when sound program organization facilitates a high level of interaction among group members and the development of a group identity.

Designing the Group Project

In the establishment of group supervision projects (or for that matter, any correctional program), the first and most critical step is the development of a project design. The function of the design is to identify what the project is intended to do (purpose), how it is to be accomplished (method), and the techniques that will be used to measure its effectiveness (evaluation). Additionally, the preparation of a design serves to identify needed resources and the types of agency commitments of policy and support necessary for the optimal operation of the project.

Although different styles may be used establishing the project design, there are some basic content requirements which should not be overlooked. The statement of purpose should describe what is intended to be done, why, and whether there is existing evidence to support the approach. The section on purpose should also identify the population to be served, and, if there are any hypotheses, they should be clearly stated.

Another component of the design is the description of methods which have been selected to implement or carry out the purposes of the project and to test any hypotheses which may have been identified. Formulating questions regarding the conduct of the project is a meaningful way by which to identify methodological requirements. For example, how will group participants be selected? When, where, and how often will the group meet? What ground rules will be necessary to govern the conduct of meetings? What records should be kept and how will they be used? What techniques will be used to orient group members? How should the group leader function and to what extent will he exert his official authority over the conduct of group activity? How will associations among group participants be controlled away from the meeting place and what strategies will be employed to resolve any agency suspicions? What should be the limits of group authority over its members in terms of making official decisions regarding revocation, discharge, permission to marry, changing employment, going into debt, traveling out of state, and so forth? What attendance requirements should be imposed upon group members and how will they be enforced? Will the content of meetings be confidential and, if so, how will confidentiality be maintained?

No correctional program should be operated without a meaningful evaluation of its effectiveness. If the intent of a group supervision project is to provide more efficient and effective supervision for offenders than is possible in using the individual approach, evaluative methods must be employed to test objectively the extent to which such purposes are realized in practice. How will the progress of group participants be measured? What means will be used to determine the effect of the group on their progress (or lack of it)? What types of offenders respond most favorably to the group supervisory technique? Evaluative methods and the manner in which they are to be used should be stated in the project design.

There are some very obvious reasons for initiating a discussion of the development and operation of group supervision programs in the framework of a project design. First, the design format stresses the critical import for systematic planning in the creation of programs which are intended to produce changes in the behavior and status of offenders. Mere desire to try new approaches to help clients is laudable but not enough; there must be reasonable assurance that the capability to administer the program is commensurate with the desire to do so. The logical and systematic procedures of establishing a project design dramatically reduce the possibility of overlooking critical dimensions which could affect the operation of the program. Second, by developing project plans and procedures within the limits of acceptable methodology, it becomes possible to identify and report results which may contribute to the knowledge of the correctional field and facilitate replication by others interested in testing the process.

Selecting Participants

When selecting clients to participate in group supervision projects, one must take into account a variety of factors. For example, should the group be homogeneous or heterogeneous in composition? Most probation and parole caseloads are heterogeneous in composition and include a wide range of personal and social characteristics. If the group project is directed toward the solution of problems confronting offenders in community reintegration, a heterogeneous composition poses no special problems. Indeed, group discussion can be enhanced by bringing to bear on the problems the differential experiences and perspectives of a diverse group.

Selection of group participants must also take into account their availability to attend meetings. One issue of availability is the offender's willingness to attend meetings or to become involved in the group process. In an "Experiment in Adult Group Parole Supervision" conducted in Minnesota and reported in *Crime and Delinquency* (October 1965), parolees were required to attend group meetings as a condition of their parole. In evaluating the group project, participants identified the mandatory attendance feature as desirable and necessary. It was their view that offenders regard all correctional programs with suspicion. Requiring attendance initially, they thought, was necessary to provide offenders with an exposure to the group process and thereby facilitate constructive involvement.

Another consideration in the selection of group participants concerns the spatial distribution of offenders and the time and location of meetings. Conflicts with work schedules or school are the most common problems which must be overcome. Generally, scheduling group meetings for weekday evenings is the most satisfactory.

When the intent is to compare effectiveness between group supervisory techniques and the traditional mode of supervision, special care must be taken in the selection of group members. The makeup of groups must be comparable. One of the most effective ways of insuring valid comparisons is to make assignments to the experimental and control groups on a "group-frequency matching" basis using such variables as race, marital status, education completed, intelligence estimate, highest occupational class on admission to probation or parole, offense classification, number of previous felony convictions, and number of previous placements on probation or parole. When the distribution of these characteristics is the same for the groups being compared, it is possible to make valid statements about the relative effectiveness of techniques.

Another decision one must make in the development of a group supervision project is the size of the group, and whether it should be closed or open-ended. In establishing a group supervision project for probationers or parolees, a membership of from eight to ten is optimal. This size allows sufficient time for thorough discussion of problems which confront members while at the same time insuring that there will be enough happening to keep meetings lively and vital. It is preferable that the group be open-ended, that is, structured so as to maintain the size of the group by recruiting new members to replace those either returned to the institution or discharged from probation or parole for reason of good adjustment.

Selecting the Meeting Place

The selection of a site for group meetings has important implications for the success of a project, apart from considerations of geographical convenience. For example, it is preferable to conduct meetings in a "neutral" setting such as a community center. Meeting at the correctional agency simply adds some negative features which outweigh any convenience afforded the supervising officer. In addition, agency facilities are often unavailable at the desired times and seldom offer the comfort and/or other accouterments which can enhance the conduct of meetings.

Association Among Offenders

In structuring a group supervision project, the question of association among offenders is inevitably raised. Most jurisdictions, for example, have agency regulations which prohibit association among probationers and parolees. In spite of such restriction, offenders continue to see each other. Perhaps a principal cause of negative outcomes of such contact is the regulations which have the effect of causing their associations to be consummated in a devious manner. In the Minnesota experiment referred to above, it was found that association among offenders under controlled circumstances yielded positive results rather than negative results. The best way to control the impact of associations among offenders is to constructively facilitate them. Indeed, this is one of the strengths and purposes of group supervision projects.

Structuring Meetings

In structuring the conduct of group meetings, it is very important to develop basic ground rules which will facilitate the process without inhibiting it. Useful ground rules may include the following:

1. Members are not required to participate verbally, although they are encouraged to discuss any topic, using language with which they feel comfortable
2. Although the sessions will be taped and other records kept, all discussion will be kept confidential
3. When a member speaks, he should be permitted to finish his statement without interruption
4. The group leader (agent) may suggest topics for discussion, but the group may choose not to discuss them
5. Disputes cannot be physically acted out in any way harmful or threatening to self, others, or property
6. Group recommendations for official action will be considered in arriving at decisions, although the group leader may not always be able to endorse them
7. The group leader may make collateral contacts relating to group members; however, members will not be contacted personally outside group meetings except in cases of immediate emergency.

The basic element in the development of ground rules for group supervision projects is that such rules should provide participants with a structure which enables them to interact with reasonable assurance that what takes place will be purposive.

Visitation of Group Meetings

It is useful at the outset to develop a policy concerning visitation of group meetings. In many cases, group meetings have been hindered, even deterred from their basic purpose, by allowing persons to observe group activities. When the purpose of a group is to discuss thoroughly those problems confronting offenders in their interpersonal and social adjustment, members must be assured that visitors will not be allowed without their express permission, and then, only when the presence of nonmember holds some value for the group in its deliberations.

Frequency and Duration of Meetings

Under the traditional mode of supervision, offenders' contacts with their agent have often been sporadic, infrequent, and dominated by hurried grapplings with crisis situations. The frequency and duration of group supervision meetings should avoid this and be calculated to provide the qualities of regularity, continuity, and afford offenders an opportunity to plan for their participation. This can be done by scheduling meetings on at least a biweekly basis for a duration of approximately ninety minutes. Meetings should not be so frequent as to become a crutch and deny group members the responsibility of dealing with day-to-day problems as they arise during the process of community living.

The Leader's Role

There are several things that should be given primary attention in the conduct of group meetings. Of these, the most critical consideration is the role of the group leader. The group leader's function is to mobilize the experience and judgment of the group members. To mobilize group resources effectively, the leader must clearly focus responsibility for the discussion and resolution of problems confronting its members on the group itself. The leader must demonstrate by his actions that he has confidence in the group process by taking a part in group discussion without dominating it. He must encourage honesty in group discussion by treating group members with complete honesty and openness. The leader should always acknowledge the value of constructive criticism by accepting it when it is directed toward him. Finally, the group leader should avoid denying the group the opportunity to arrive at its own decisions and insights. The propensity to provide the group with "answers" is probably the greatest failing of novice group leaders. Another failing of many new group leaders is to attempt to restrict the development of indigenous leadership within the group. Such leadership will emerge in a vital group supervision project, and the group leader should be sensitive to his role in making such efforts valuable and productive.

Just as the group leader has the responsibility of facilitating the group process, so he has the obligation to consider group decisions which have application to the official decisions he must make as the probation or parole officer. This does not mean that his decisions regarding revocation, discharge, and so forth should be dictated by the group. Rather, the group's advice should be seriously considered by him as a decision-making resource. It is important that this differentiation be made clear to group members from the outset. Once official decisions have been made, however, the group should have the opportunity to discuss them fully.

Confidentiality

Another factor to be considered in the conduct of group meetings is the matter of confidentiality. Creating a setting wherein clients are willing to discuss their problems openly requires some assurance that what they say will be kept confidential. Group members must come to honor one another's confidence, and the group as a whole should have assurance that it will have reasonable control over the agent's use of meeting content. There is no easy way to establish confidence in a group; confidence must be built. The group leader can, however, accelerate the process of group trust by clarifying the manner in which group records will be protected. Again, in the Minnesota experiment, one of the ways this was done was asking the group's permission to develop a demonstration tape to be played at a department training institute. After the tape was developed, it was played first for the group and their approval was secured before using it in the training of new agents. The group leader should look for opportunities to demonstrate to the group that the confidence of the group will be preserved.

Content of Group Sessions

When conditions of group identity and mutual confidence prevail, the content of group discussion can be expected to range from the routine parole or probation problems to extremely delicate personal problems of social and family adjustment. For example, in the Minnesota experiment, content of group discussion included the following topics:

1. Orientation to the group parole program.
2. Rules of probation and parole.
3. Association and correspondence with other parolees, probationers, and prison inmates.

4. Responsibility of members to report parole violations of other members to the group.
5. Function and performance of the parole board.
6. Adjustment on parole: continuance, violation, revocation, and discharge.
7. Minor law infractions related to parole status.
8. Permission to own and drive an automobile.
9. Driver's license and auto insurance.
10. Parolee's relationship with employer.
11. Permission to travel out of town.
12. Permission to marry.
13. Role of the parole agent.
14. Tardiness and absences from meetings.
15. Intragroup relationships.
16. Group censure and its effect on controlling members' behavior.
17. Evaluation of the group parole program.
18. Drunkenness.
19. Alcoholism as related to social adjustment.
20. Alcoholics Anonymous as a resource.
21. Finding a job and telling employer about parole status.
22. Job retention.
23. Unemployment and unemployment compensation.
24. Civil Service employment of parolee.
25. Problems of obtaining and maintaining financial credit.
26. Heterosexual relationships.
27. "Girl" trouble.
28. Community acceptance of parolee.
29. Parolee status related to law enforcement's tendency to "accuse" parolees too readily of current crimes.
30. Family problems.
31. Death of family members.
32. House purchase and mortgage.
33. Health problems and resources.
34. Schooling and vocational training.
35. Death of group member.
36. Responsibility of members for one another's welfare.

37. Importance of using good judgment.
38. Establishing goals.

In addition to the value of the group process in opening up a broad range of pertinent topics for discussion, the quality of judgments made on these issues is enhanced by the contributions of several persons derived from their unique experiences in confronting similar problems.

Evaluating Group Progress

Finally, there must be ongoing evaluation of group supervision projects to determine their effectiveness and to identify ways in which performance might be improved. Among the several thrusts that can be used in such evaluation are (1) adjustment of offenders as determined by satisfactory progress on probation or parole as compared to violations of probation or parole; (2) assessment of the content and participation level of group meetings; (3) measurements of attitudinal changes of group members; and (4) evaluation of the effectiveness of the group method by the participants themselves.

Tape recorded sessions provide useful data on group activity for subsequent analysis and evaluation. Only as we are able to review our accomplishments as well as our failures in the calm of past experience can we hope to improve the quality of correctional service in the future.

Chapter Eight

Treatment Strategies in Probation and Parole (Part II)

IT is generally agreed by authorities in the correctional field that preparation for parole begins the day that the inmate enters the institution. This means that the prisoner has to be prepared physically, emotionally, and socially for the day when ultimately he will return to the community as a free man. And, for between 95 to 98 per cent of all persons who are committed to prison, that day of release will sooner or later become a reality.

One of the first steps in the institutional process is that of classification. Initially, classification serves to compile, organize, and evaluate the social history of the inmate. Some of this information may be obtained from the presentence investigation conducted by the probation department. Where such material is not provided by the court, the classification unit obtains the material to compile an admission study, the basis of which is to determine the institutional assignment of the prisoner. Moreover, the classification program makes provision for the periodic reevaluation of the prisoner's progress and planning, so that changes in his assignments can be made, always with the view to preparation for release.

It can be assumed that by the time an individual is ready for favorable parole consideration, he will have progressed to a minimum custody status. As he is drawn closer to the outside world, the prerelease program will provide access to outside persons who will brief the inmate on employment and other conditions on the outside.

Some states have experimented with parole camps as a means of bridging the gap between institution and community. Other jurisdictions have provided special units within the confines of the prison to quarter impending parolees. Community-based halfway houses provide another alternative to assist the offender in bridging into the community. Very little progress has been made in the direction of preparole furloughs to allow the inmate to find employment in the community prior to his absolute release, although, from a realistic standpoint, such a procedure might ultimately improve the adjustment of the parolee in the community once he makes his final departure through the prison gates.

Just as commitment to an institution is undoubtedly a traumatic situation in the life of the inmate, so it can be assumed that return to the community after a prolonged absence will be an anxiety-producing experience. To the individual who has made the desired behavioral changes while in prison confines, there are always the questions of how the community will accept him, whether or not he will be able to go "straight," whether he will be exploited in his employment because of his previous status, or whether anything beyond the most menial tasks will be open to him.

The task of preparation for separation is not unique to prison environments. Hospitals for long-term patients have found it desirable to initiate such programs. The armed services, since World War II, at least, have found it desirable to send men to separation centers prior to their release from service, recognizing the transitional problems which are involved. How much more so, then, the necessity to prepare the inmate for return to community life? In this chapter, we consider some of the treatment strategies in community-based correctional programs.

RELEASE PREPARATION OF THE PRISONER*

In recent years, studies of parole failures indicate that the largest percentage of failures occur within a period of sixty to ninety days after release. This would indicate something lacking in both the institutional preparation of the offender for release and the community's acceptance of the release. Recognition of these facts has resulted in widespread efforts to improve release planning.

Obstacles to Effective Release Preparation

One of the chief obstacles to effective preparation of men and women for return to the community is the traditional custodial

---

* Reprinted in part by permission of *Federal Probation.* Reed Cozart: Release preparation of the prisoner. *Federal Probation, 16*(No. 1):13-16, March 1952.

concept of prison administration. Admittedly a prison administrator has his first obligation to the public for the safekeeping of the prisoner committed to his institution. The second obligation is to attempt to provide a program that will assist the prisoner to improve his chances for adjustment while he is serving his sentence. In many of our prisons, these two obligations are conflicting. Where the emphasis is placed exclusively upon custody, it is necessary that the men be regimented to the point where it is difficult to employ effectively any rehabilitative devices. Much of the training and orientation the average prisoner receives, particularly during the beginning of his sentence, is directed toward fitting him into institutional routines and toward readjusting his life to a pattern where he is thoroughly regimented. Consequently, when the time for release comes, the prisoner must make an about-face when he enters the free world which is relatively free from regimentation.

Two examples of men with whom I am acquainted will serve to illustrate the problem.

Case "A"

"A" was a military prisoner, a Negro from a southern state who was convicted by a general court martial in France shortly after World War I and received a life sentence for taking part in a riot and mutiny. He was suddenly released from a federal penitentiary during World War II after receiving clemency from the Army. During this long period of time, he had lived behind walls without any contact with the world outside except through employees of the institution; he had not worn civilian clothing, handled any money, eaten in a restaurant or private dining room, had never had a social conversation with a woman or child, had never ridden on a bus, streetcar, train or automobile, was entirely unfamiliar with traffic regulations, and had no knowledge of how to even make a purchase in a store. No wonder he was bewildered when the news was given him that he would be permitted to return home immediately!

Case "B"

"B" had a life sentence for murder on an Indian reservation and was paroled at the age of sixty-seven after serving eighteen years. Twelve years had been spent in a penitentiary and six years in an open institution where he had an opportunity to see more of the outside world. The data of his release were known several months in advance, and the institution officials attempted to help him orientate himself toward problems of the outside community by permitting him to take rides to town on the truck. He was taken out on two or three occasions for dinner, either in a restaurant or an employee's home, and had an opportunity to attend prerelease meetings. Even so, he had been out of the community so long that he was totally unprepared to cope with the problems he faced and shortly after released asked to be returned because the free world was traveling at a pace too fast for him.

Release Preparation Should Begin on Admittance

Preparation really should begin when the man is admitted to the institution, particularly if he is serving a substantial sentence. Preparation at this stage can take the form of encouraging him to maintain close ties with his family, friends, and former employers or business associates and, at the same time, encouraging them to keep in contact with him. This can be done through liberal correspondence and visiting policies. Also, it would be ideal if the work assignment received by the man would be in keeping with the type of employment he would have upon release, in order that he may keep his hand in the trade, so to speak. Naturally, he should be kept aware of the importance of his trying to keep up with what is going on outside through reading, movies, and the radio so that he will not be completely out of step.

One of the most essential requisites of a release plan is legitimate, self-sustaining, and acceptable employment. Too often a man, in order to secure a release, accepts a job which provides nothing more than a stopgap arrangement and which does not challenge him in any way. A prisoner's employment should be of the type that he is looking forward to with enthusiasm and hope—the type that he would like to retain and make a go of upon release. Whenever it is necessary to secure temporary employment, the man is likely to go out with very little confidence in his future opportunities. He is very likely to be discouraged unless he can very quickly arrange for suitable employment.

Another very important factor in preparing a man for release is developing the proper attitude on his part and on the part of the community toward his release. In other words, if it is his intention to just try to get by when he is released and to make no serious effort to adjust, all release planning will be to no avail. Many prisoners go out of our institutions with a defeatist attitude, and many times prison employees let the men know they expect them to return. It would be well to concentrate on trying to encourage the men to make a sincere effort to adjust and to build the proper attitudes toward release, helping the men restore their own confidence in themselves and develop a feeling in them that they really will be given a genuine opportunity to make good so far as the public is concerned.

The Prerelease Program

Recognizing the importance of developing the proper attitudes of the men, many institutions have instituted prerelease programs from sixty to ninety days prior to the release date. These programs take on different forms, but a typical one involves some five or six discussion meetings, led by representatives of the outside community.

ROLE OF THE PROBATION OFFICER. One meeting is usually conducted by representatives of the parole authorities who supervise the men upon release. In the federal system, this means the probation officers. The probation officer carefully goes over the parole conditions with the men, explaining and interpreting what parole means and informing the men what will be expected of them. Then an opportunity is given for questions concerning many problems they will face while under supervision. Not only do they receive a firsthand impression of what is expected of them by their probation officers, but they also have an opportunity to size up a probation officer, so to speak, and resolve some of their doubts concerning the sincerity and genuineness of the interest which probation officers may be expected to display.

MEETING WITH REPRESENTATIVES OF EMPLOYMENT SERVICES. Another meeting is conducted by representatives of the public employment services. Here the men have an opportunity to meet with representatives of the agencies which obtain employment for a large percentage of the workers in our country today. The men learn the steps followed in applying for jobs, how much of their record to reveal, and to whom and under what circumstances. They are also encouraged and discouraged, as the occasion warrants, to enter certain fields of employment. For example, the public employment agencies usually discourage men from going to clerical and white-collar jobs and try to encourage them to enter other fields.

MEETING WITH REPRESENTATIVES OF LARGE COMPANIES. The third meeting is conducted by the personnel director or other responsible representative of a large company or corporation. Here the men have an opportunity to receive firsthand information as to what businessmen expect of their employees in the way of performance, loyalty, production. The employers often inform the men that they have more to fear from their fellow workers than from the employers themselves because competition is likely to cause resentment on the part of the employees if they know a fellow worker is an ex-prisoner. Consequently, the men are encouraged not to talk about their prison record, nor should they allow fellow employees to learn about their background.

MEETING WITH REPRESENTATIVES OF ORGANIZED LABOR. Representatives of organized labor meet and furnish the men information on how to secure membership cards or permits, particularly in the skilled trades, how they go about paying off their initiation fees on installments, and just how to make contacts with local unions.

MEETING WITH BUSINESSMEN. Finally, a professional person or businessman conducts a meeting which concerns itself with problems of human relations—how to budget time and money, how to meet civic responsibilities and obligations in the community, and many other things.

After attendance at five or six meetings of this type, the men have had an opportunity to rub elbows with successful business and professional men and to obtain information which gives them encouragement. They gain confidence in these representatives of the community and they feel they can rely upon their advice.

This does much toward building a proper attitude on the part of the men regarding problems they will face on release.

Special Problems of the Alcoholic

A number of men who come to prison are known alcoholics. As a matter of fact, some of them are delinquent as a result of alcoholism. Certainly we should not overlook the contribution to release preparation of the organization known as Alcoholics Anonymous. Many of our prisons in this country have chapters of AA meeting regularly. It may be, however, that in some instances the restrictions placed upon these meetings prevent them from functioning efficiently. I believe that restrictions upon the activities of AA should be held at a minimum. In other words, there should be no screening of inmates who attend the meetings. The discussions should be open to all prisoners who are properly identified as alcoholics. Beyond that, staff members should not be present at the meetings. It certainly is stimulating to have frequent and regular visits from members of outside AA organizations to give inspiration, counsel, and advice to members of the prison chapter. In some instances, even selected inmates are permitted to accompany one of the institutional personnel who is an AA member to meetings of chapters in the community.

The prisoner who participates in a program of this character feels that he is getting the same type of break or consideration that any other alcoholic receives. After all, these meetings are concerned primarily with problems of alcohol. One of the most noticeable results from these meetings is that many men, after accepting the principles of the Alcoholic Anonymous organization, stop rationalizing with respect to their offenses and begin to look objectively at themselves and accept sole responsibility for their own predicament. This certainly puts them in a good position to seek self-improvement. The effectiveness of this organization in this regard is felt within the institution when there is a lessening of disciplinary problems, frustrations, and evidence of neurotic behavior.

The most important result of the program, however, is its carry-over value on the outside. Members of outside groups are willing to meet the prisoners when they are discharged, accompany them to their busses and trains, staying with them and helping them to overcome that great urge to drink as soon as they get out. Also, arrangements are made to have them met at their destinations, where they will again be accompanied and befriended by sympathetic members, helping them to get established in their respective communities. Too much cannot be said about the great value of this organization.

Informing the Public

Perhaps one of the big weaknesses in our program is the failure to inform the public and secure its assistance in the way of preparing men for release. It is very difficult to say how this important problem can best be solved. Prison officials can only reach a very small percentage of people living in the community at large. This is similarly true of the probation officer. Prison officials and probation officers give talks to service clubs, church groups, and so forth, interpreting their work and their problems and asking for assistance from representatives of these organizations. These groups usually are cooperative, and it is not as important to meet them as it is the average citizen residing in the small town or the neighborhood where the prisoner is to be released. To date, there has not been enough effort to acquaint the law-enforcement officials with the importance of assisting men upon release. Consequently, the average prisoner is released perhaps with feelings of hostility toward law-enforcement agencies in general. While there are some exceptions, many law-enforcement officers are equally suspicious of ex-prisoners. There are only rare occasions when there is a real understanding between the law-enforcement officer and the ex-prisoner. It would appear advisable to invite police officers and other agents of law-enforcement organizations to visit prisons and see for themselves what is being done toward helping prepare men for release in order that they may have a more sympathetic understanding.

A word should be said also about the approach the institutional staff should take toward preparing the men generally for release. Undoubtedly too often, prison officials are not realistic enough.

There is often a tendency to overencourage prisoners, to give them a false sense of optimism about their future adjustment. A conscientious attempt should be made to be very realistic and point out to the men the many pitfalls, the roadblocks, the disappointments and letdowns they are likely to face. Most prisoners, when they leave institutions, are concerned about how they will be accepted by an employer and how they will be treated by the police. Actually, however, they have the most to fear from their fellow workers and fellow residents in the community, the public with whom they are in daily contact. The average employer these days would be sympathetic toward a man with a prison record, but the average fellow employee who must compete with him on the job will not be so sympathetic. Particularly is this true where social contacts are made with fellow employees and the wife of a fellow employee hears about the prison record and gossips in the community about the ex-prisoner's wife. This leads to the point that the prisoner should be encouraged not to discuss his prison background with anyone except his personnel director, his employer, or someone who has a legitimate right to any information concerning that part of his background.

One of the main obstacles to a proper information program for the public, so far as prison administrators and probation officers are concerned, is that there are so few prisons in the country and there are so many communities from which the prisoners come and to which they are released. A fairly good job can be done in the localities where the prisons are situated and where the probation officers maintain their offices. It is extremely difficult, however, to reach thousands upon thousands of people throughout our country who have no contacts with a prison, no knowledge of prison life, and no conception of what a prisoner faces upon release. Perhaps the only way these countless thousands could be reached would be through dramatizations on the radio, television, and in movies. Even here the people who really understand the problems would not be the persons in charge of the dramatizations, and there would be the danger of only a superficial job being done—with perhaps more to be lost than gained.

It is my view that the institution personnel and supervising probation officers will have to bear the brunt of release preparations since it is not practicable to really prepare society as a whole for the reception of released prisoners. In other words, those working in the field of corrections will have to intensify their efforts toward preparing the prisoners in every way for reentering the community life, particularly emphasizing to them the realistic situation they are likely to face. It is encouraging to observe, however, that increasingly more thought and attention are being given to the prerelease preparation of prisoners to enable them to meet the varied problems and situations which will confront them when they return to their respective homes and communities, and that a progressively greater effort also is being made to really acquaint society with these problems and needs and its responsibility to aid the prisoner in making the difficult adjustment from the rigid and unnatural environment of prison life to normal living in the community which is to receive him.

THE CORRECTIONS WORKER AND COMMUNITY RESOURCES*

A vital part of the social worker's equipment is a knowledge of, and an ability to use skillfully, the resources of his community in helping the client to reach the most satisfactory solution of his difficulty. No matter how dedicated the individual caseworker, no matter how well he relates to his client or uses the professional skills at his command, he is of necessity limited not only by the boundaries of his capacities, but also by the policies, function, and material resources of his agency.

This generic statement is nowhere more applicable than to the function of the probation and parole worker. For example, during the course of a presentence investigation, the probation worker may become aware of a number of contacts that the individual awaiting sentence has had with a variety of community agencies. The probation worker will then need to communicate with these agencies in order to obtain a rounded picture of the individual under investigation, which in turn will provide part of the basis of his description and interpretation of the offender's situation to the judge. The judge will then be able to arrive, within the limita-

* Printed by permission of the author, Howard W. Borsuk. From an original unpublished manuscript, University of Louisvile, 1967.

tions of the law, at a decision which, hopefully, will be of simultaneous benefit to society and the offender. This will presuppose not only a knowledge of the existence of these agencies but the scope of their services and how they work. In the pursuit of helping the offender abide by the conditions set by the court under probation and helping him deal with the constellation of problems that influenced the commission of the offense, the probation worker may become aware of certain contributing situations, the effective handling of which is beyond his personal resources and the scope of the agency he represents. Similarly, the parole worker, in helping the paroled offender adjust to his social environment in a way that is both satisfactory to himself and society, notes the existence of situations barring the attainment of this goal. In both instances the worker will need at his fingertips a knowledge of those agencies in his community which will be of help not only in supplementing his efforts but sometimes in dealing with a crucial life problem of the client.

The process of referral is far from perfunctory and calls for the mobilization of skills and understanding which are not in the least obvious. The offender must be physically available to his probation or parole worker, perhaps at stated intervals according to conditions set down. Certain aspects of the offender's life are open to investigation on the part of the worker. His relationship with the worker must then, of necessity, carry elements of authority. In this, the offender has no choice. He does, however, have a very significant choice: whether or not to use the worker as a source of help in regard to his situation. The same element of authority is not present in his relationship with voluntary community agencies. He is free to choose whether he wants to contact the agency to which he is referred. The voluntary agency may pose any number of emotional threats to him. The nature of the connection between the voluntary agency and the court may be unknown to him and constitute an additional threat. To deal with these problems, the worker must bring to bear all the skill available to him.

Unfortunately, a detailed analysis of this process is not possible within the limitations of this chapter. The reader, of necessity, is referred to the pertinent literature: Walter A. Friedlander's *Introduction to Social Welfare* (1955); Arthur E. Fink; Everett E. Wilson, and Merrill B. Conover's *The Field of Social Work*, (1955); and Herbert Stroup's *Social Work: An Introduction to the Field* (1948), for a more complete consideration.

Another word of caution. This study presents an array of agencies which are commonly available to residents of large metropolitan areas. Smaller aggregates may have only a portion of these agencies existent in the community or may have a smaller number of agencies which combine several functions. Rural and semi-rural communities are, of course, generally the most poorly serviced of all, and the worker in this case may sorely tax his frustration threshold in finding appropriate resources for his client.

The Family Agency

The Family Agency in many ways represents the core agency of private social work. It has been in the past entrusted with providing financial assistance for the "worthy poor" and is still identified by a large section of the public as essentially in the business of offering tangible assistance to the indigent. Although family agencies are continually engaged in defining their functions, certain trends may be discerned. The advent of the Great Depression overwhelmed these agencies in an avalanche of financial need. It became increasingly clear that the alleviation of financial distress, because of its magnitude and its permeation of the entire economic system, was a public responsibility to be discharged through publicly controlled agencies, in most instances, local departments of welfare. While most family agencies still make provisions for financial assistance, it is given generally on an emergency basis only, when, for instance, the local department of welfare must impose some kind of a waiting period before actual monetary help can be given or when for some reason the client in actual need is not eligible for the department of welfare's services. The emphasis is at all times on the constructive use of this assistance and maintenance. Financial aid is not given except in the above last circumstance.

The function of the family agency can be currently defined as involving the preservation and restoration of harmonious family relationships and the prevention of those conditions which would lead to a disruption of this kind of relationship. In the pursuit of this objective, emphasis is placed on healthy personality development as well as the satisfactory social functioning of individual members of the family. The various services of the family agency are utilized toward this end. They may involve solely a counseling service in respect to a marital difficulty, difficulties in the parent-child relationship, problems involving the adjustment of the aged to current living, or premarital difficulties centering on relationships with the opposite sex. In addition, problems concerning severe mental illness are dealt with, in which the objective is not direct treatment of the individual who is mentally ill but rather the many problems that accompany this condition—such as referral to psychiatric resource, the effects on the family—perhaps necessitating a reorganization of attitudes, feelings, and living arrangements. In short, the family agency deals with the entire gamut of social and psychological problems that the family may become heir to in our complex civilization. Although this definition of function reflects the shift from the administration of tangible services to a more intangible stress, various other services within the agency, if available, may be called upon as part of the process of help. One such service might be *homemaking service* to temporarily relieve a situation in a family whereby the physical presence of a substitute mother is called for, for instance, in the absence or incapacitation of the wife or mother because of illness, psychiatric or other consultation. Another growing development which may be mentioned is *fee charging,* commensurate with the client's ability to pay, still another reflection of the shift from dealing only with indigent clients to servicing every segment of the community. Help is given within the structure of the client-worker relationship involving office interviews, customarily on a weekly basis. This primary method is that of social casework, and the fundamental service is administered through the person of the caseworker as representative of the agency. It is obvious that the probation or parole worker in his contact with the offender will come upon difficulties of this nature in his client. He may want to consider referral to a family agency, which would have at its call greater resources for dealing with the difficulty and which would provide a different focus more helpful than his own. Sometimes the family agency in smaller communities may combine its function in one administrative setting with that of a child-care agency.

Child-care or Welfare Agencies

Under this heading would come those agencies which deal with the placement of children, either on a permanent or temporary basis. This may involve placement of temporary care in foster homes or institutions or placement with a selected family interested in adopting the child. In some communities, these agencies combine both functions in one administrative setting; in others, these functions are administered by two distinct agencies: the foster-care agency and the adoption agency. The services of all child-care agencies have at their base the philosophy that, for healthy physical and emotional development, children need to have the experience of family living. The best possible setting for this is within the natural family. When circumstances do not permit this—for example, when severe neglect on the part of natural parents which defies efforts at alleviation, or other for the moment insoluble physical and emotional problems—foster-family placement is indicated. Although institutions are generally felt to be poor substitutes, they may be considered as more helpful to the child when his emotional damage is such that a successful adjustment to family living is not for the time being possible for him or when placement is for a temporary a period so as to make the stress and strain of adjusting to foster parents not worthwhile. In the case of temporary care the effort is on helping the natural parents reassume their parental responsibilities in a way most helpful to their child and themselves. In the case of children placed for adoption, the stress is on finding adoptive parents who feel the lack of children keenly in the completion of their otherwise successful family life, and who will be able to give the adopted child all the love, warmth, and acceptance that will make for his emergence as a socially and emotionally competent adult.

One of the essential elements in this process, except in the eventuality of a court order, is the exploration with the natural parents of alternative solutions to placement; if placement seems the only feasible alternative, it should be arrived at through mutual agreement and acceptance.

In relation to the utilization of these agencies, it may be that the offender's children manifest some type of problem behavior, the resolution of which would assist the probationer's adjustment.

Again, the primary method is that of social casework. In small communities, private agencies with these functions may not be available. In this case, the child welfare unit of the local department of welfare may assume some or all of these services. The typical large urban private child-care agency will have psychiatric consultation, testing facilities, perhaps medical services and shelter facilities as well.

The Child-guidance Clinic

A more specialized child-care service is that of the child-guidance clinic, whose principal function is to offer help in relation to severe emotional disturbance in the child. Here the primary service is a psychiatric one focused on the child's disturbance. This does not mean that the interrelatedness of the family as providing the setting for the problem is ignored. The family's involvement is seen as a vital part of the helping process. Perhaps the delineation of the clinical team characteristic of the child-guidance agency will provide a clearer concept as to its function.

We have mentioned that the fundamental service is a psychiatric one. Operationally this implies that the psychiatrist has both the responsibility for direct treatment of the child and general supervision of the team which cooperatively deals with the total problem. The psychiatric social worker typically deals with the parents, the focus of help being directed to the parent's part in the problem, planning for both a shifting of attitudes and restructuring of the family's relations with the child.

The psychologist has the responsibility for the administration and interpretation of any number of psychological tests which will be used as an aid to complete the diagnostic picture.

Of late, both social workers and psychologists in many child-guidance clinics have been entrusted with direct responsibility for the treatment of the child, usually under psychiatric supervision. Thus, there has been some blurring of the lines of demarcation between the various disciplines. However, the function remains the same, therapy for children with emotional disturbance.

Characteristically, the child-guidance clinic is a private agency, usually confined to large urban aggregates. It may exist, however, as a division of service in the larger mental hygiene clinic or within a university setting, the principal goal of the latter being the provision of training for future practitioners. Some of the smaller child-guidance agencies may be staffed solely by psychiatric social workers and psychologists, principally because of the unavailability of psychiatrists. However, there is usually provision for psychiatric consultation. Fees may or may not be charged, depending on the setting.

The Mental Hygiene or Mental Health Clinic

Here, too, the principal service is usually a psychiatric one. In structure the mental hygiene clinic duplicates that of the child-guidance clinic, treatment being provided for the adult with severe emotional problems who is still able to function outside of a mental hospital. Family members may be seen by the psychiatric social worker, depending on the situation, for purposes of making a social study which will be integrated into a coherent diagnostic framework, and which will aid in the evolvement of the treatment plan. Again, family members may also be seen by the psychiatric social worker in order to deal with their part in influencing the disturbance and to effect subsequent changes in the family atmosphere. The social worker will commonly have the additional responsibility of utilizing various community resources that will aid in the patient's social adjustment. Again, as in the case of the child-guidance clinics, treatment responsibility has been increasingly assumed by social workers and psychologists, and some of these agencies in small communities will be staffed solely by members of these disciplines.

The mental hygiene clinic may operate as an outpatient clinic of the psychiatric divisions of large metropolitan hospitals or as self-contained clinics without a hospital affiliation. In some communities, they may be private agencies supported by fees and voluntary contributions; in others, they may be public, tax-supported institutions; in still others, they may be a mixture of both.

Vocational-guidance Agencies

Specialized agencies providing vocational guidance are usually confined to large urban centers. The best of them provide testing services to determine vocational aptitudes and interests, and help focused on problems—emotional and otherwise—blocking a successful vocational adjustment. They may or may not include a placement service. Many of these agencies charge fees, sometimes based on ability to pay. The services are administered by trained vocational counselors who will also make use of other community resources, when indicated.

Social Group-work Agencies

Under this category, we might list any number of agencies, such as settlement houses, neighborhood centers, and YM or YWCA's. Their primary purpose is to provide a constructive group experience for their clients. These group experiences may take the form of activity in special interest groups such as arts and crafts, little theater, social clubs, or in guiding activity for various segments of the community such as the aged. Although the emphasis has been traditionally on youth, an increasing interest is displayed in the problems of the older groups of the population. Although, again, these agencies typically exist in large urban centers, group-work activities may be found in small communities under the aegis of the "Y" or Salvation Army. Some of these agencies will have professionally trained group workers in supervisory capacities.

We might also mention, in considering group-work resources, camping facilities which often operate as a service of various group-work agencies. Although the use of adult camps is not as yet widespread, there is an increasing trend in this direction.

There are many more specialized categories of agencies in the arsenal of social welfare. However, the probation and parole worker will, in his work with the offender, rarely have to call on the services of agencies other than those mentioned. Throughout the above, there has been an emphasis on private agencies. It might be worthwhile to note that public agencies, often combined with their material assistance function, offer highly skilled counseling help. As was pointed out in the foregoing, the publicly supported Department of Welfare has the responsibility for administering maintenance financial assistance. However, local practices vary greatly, not only as to amounts and budgets but as to policies concerning eligibility for emergency assistance.

A HALFWAY HOUSE FOR PAROLEES*

The concept of a place of residence for persons recently released from a penal institution, in order to help them bridge the gap between the confining atmosphere of the institution and the relative freedom of life in society, is not new; however, it is still relatively young. Such places of residence, standing halfway between the institution and society have, with increasing frequency, been referred to as "halfway houses." The concept of halfway houses is by no means restricted to residences for parolees. Probably everyone has heard of Synanon, the halfway house for drug addicts. There also are halfway houses for alcoholics. Still another area in which the halfway house concept has been employed is in the rehabilitation of the mentally ill.

In the field of parole, perhaps the best known halfway house is Dismas House, established in 1959 in St. Louis by the late Reverend Charles Dismas Clark, a pioneer in this field. Dismas House has been the subject of at least one article in a national magazine, and Father Clark's role as the "Hoodlum Priest" was the subject of a motion picture of the same name. Another halfway house for parolees which has received national publicity is St. Leonard's House, established in Chicago by the Reverend James G. Jones. There are, of course, other halfway houses for parolees which, although not as famous, are nevertheless striving

---

* Reprinted from *Federal Probation.* Robert G. Meiners: A halfway house for parolees. *Federal Probation,* 29(No. 2):47-52, June 1965. Footnotes are omitted.

to fill a vital need. It shall be the purpose of this section to describe one of them—St. Joseph's House of Hospitality in Pittsburgh, Pennsylvania.

St. Joseph's House

The operation of a halfway house in Pittsburgh dates back to June of 1961. It owes its existence primarily to the efforts of Frank J. Pohl who, together with other Pittsburgh attorneys, started this program for a reason which may be somewhat atypical as far as halfway houses in general are concerned. The men were, of course, aware of the need for a place which would help parolees adjust to their new freedom and bridge the gap between prison and society. However, their basic motivation stemmed more from their being appalled by the number of deserving men who were eligible for parole but who, because of their lack of friends or family, were languishing in prison because they could not produce the required parole plan. In Pennsylvania, a parole plan consists of a sponsor, a place of residence, and a job. Thus, in the absence of any one of these requirements, a prisoner would continue to serve beyond his minimum sentence even though the expiration of his minimum sentence made him eligible for parole. Having resolved that it was time for someone to do something about this, Mr. Pohl and his associates decided that, as a first step, they would each act as a sponsor for a person in prison. Their primary source of information about deserving cases came from prison chaplains.

Having thus satisfied one of the three criteria required for a parole plan, there remained the problems of supplying a place of residence and a job. For a place of residence, they turned to an already established structure. Since Depression days, the St. Vincent de Paul Society of Pittsburgh has operated St. Joseph's House of Hospitality. It is located in an old, three-story building in Pittsburgh's "Hill District." For the past twenty-five years or so, it has served as a temporary shelter for destitute men who have nowhere else to go. There are sleeping accommodations for approximately 150 men, a dozen or so to a room. Two free meals are served each day to the residents, and there is a noon bread line for anyone who cares to drop by. Beds are on a space-available first-come-first-served basis, and men are accepted without regard to race or religion. The group of attorneys secured the permission of the St. Vincent de Paul Society to devote part of the premises to parolees, as a halfway house. They then organized as the Penal Committee of the St. Vincent de Paul Society. Thus began the halfway house at St. Joseph's House of Hospitality.

Once established in an organized form and satisfying two of the three criteria for a parole plan, there remained the third requirement—the job. This proved to be one of the most difficult aspects of the project. Although Pittsburgh is referred to as the "Steel Capital of the World," it is also an area of high and chronic unemployment. The supply of available labor exceeds the demand for it by a considerable margin. Then, too, even when members of the committee were able to track down job leads, they found that prospective employers, although perhaps willing to hire a parolee, nevertheless were not willing to do so sight unseen. At the very least, prospective employers wanted an interview with the parolee.

Faced with this twofold problem, the committee members despaired of ever getting their program into operation. Fortunately, however, the job requirement was not an insurmountable obstacle. The Pennsylvania Parole Board has the discretionary authority to approve a "partial" parole plan. A partial plan is one in which the job requirement is waived. Before approving a partial plan, however, the parole board requires a showing that (1) the inmate has attempted, for a period of three to six months, to secure a regular parole plan but has been unable to do so; (2) the inmate has a sponsor and a place to live; (3) the inmate has a bona fide promise of support. The committee met with success in having the parole board grant a partial plan in cases where an individual committee member acts as sponsor and the parolee is assured of a place in St. Joseph's House. So began the Pittsburgh operation.

The Penal Committee Today

The Penal Committee has been expanded until its members now number twenty-eight. They meet at St. Joseph's House on the first Friday of each month for a formal session, at which current operations are discussed and future plans made. Pending applications from men in prison who are requesting the committee's help in securing a parole plan are discussed. Individual committee members continue to act as sponsors, the chairman assigning them to various cases as they come up. Individual preferences are also possible, in the event that a committee member has an interest in sponsoring a particular applicant. A rule of thumb has been to try to keep the operation in such a state of balance that no individual committee member is acting as sponsor for more than two parolees at one time. The sponsor and his parolee meet on a face-to-face basis at least once each month, although more frequent contacts are encouraged and frequently occur. Care must be taken, however, that the sponsor does not give the impression of being a quasi-parole officer, breathing down the parolee's neck. Flexibility, as to the number of meetings and where they take place, is essential.

Although attorneys still predominate, the committee has broadened its membership to include men from other walks of life. As in the case of the parolees whom they serve, the members of the committee are of various races, religions, and creeds. Of the twenty-eight members of the present committee, eleven are attorneys. Not all of them are active full-time practitioners, one being a judge, one a member of the state legislature, one a judge's clerk, and one a law professor.

The next largest group within the committee would be those members who are engaged in correctional and parole work. One is a guard at the county workhouse, five are in parole and probation work, and one is the educational director at the local state prison. Next largest in number are the clergymen members of the committee. Four members are clergymen, one of whom is the Diocesan Director of the St. Vincent de Paul Society and two of whom are chaplains at the state prison and county workshop, respectively. Two members of the committee are psychiatrists, one of whom provides psychiatric treatment for parolees who were sentenced under Pennsylvania's Barr-Walker Act as sex offenders.

Rounding out the committee membership are an architect, a

personnel manager, and the committee's greatest success story to date. The latter was one of the committee's first parolees, three years ago. He has now finished his parole and has become a committee member and administrative director, job-information coordinator, and jack-of-all-trades. He receives a small salary and lives in the house with the other residents. Because of his prison background (he served 22 months for forgery), the other residents can more easily identify with him and seek his advice. He seldom mentions to them the fact that he holds degrees from Harvard and the University of Pennsylvania.

Parolee Residents

What have the residents of this halfway house been like? In the three years of operation, there have been sixty-two of them. The average stay has been between six and eight weeks. The men are encouraged to go out into the community on their own as soon as they feel able. However, there is no compulsion to leave, and a man may stay as long as he wishes. Three men have been at the house since the program began. However, they could be classified as being special cases. One is blind and two have serious heart conditions.

The average age of the residents has been thirty-six. On the average, they have served between three and five years in prison. Most of them have come from Western State Penitentiary, a maximum-security prison located in Pittsburgh. Others have come from various Pennsylvania state prisons, county workhouses, and county jails. Three have come from state prisons in Ohio, Maryland, and Michigan. No federal parolees have participated in the program as yet.

As has been mentioned, there is no restriction as to race, creed, or religion. Nor is there any restriction as to type of offense. In this respect, St. Joseph's would differ from other halfway houses. It is said, for example, that Father Jones has established a policy at St. Leonard's not to accept psychotics, alcoholics, drug addicts, or professional confidence men. At St. Joseph's in Pittsburgh the residents have included murderers, sex offenders, and persons with a history of drug addiction. Experience has shown that a majority of the residents have a history of alcoholism or problem drinking. These men are encouraged to participate in an Alcoholics Anonymous chapter which meets in the neighborhood. Unlike some other halfway houses, there are no organized meetings in the house at which attendance is required, although there are religious services conducted on a purely voluntary basis. It was thought by the committee that any type of coerced attendance at organized meetings—whether they be religious, group therapy, or Alcoholics Anonymous—was to be avoided since it might tend to give the house an institutional atmosphere not unlike the prisons in which the men so recently resided.

At any given time, there are between fifteen and twenty parolees residing at St. Joseph's. They are not segregated into one group but by design are distributed among the general population of the house.

As far as personal finances are concerned, most of them arrive with little or no money. On this matter, one writer has posed the question, "How would any one of us like to face the world leaving a strange city, not necessarily a prison, with perhaps $10 or $15 in our pocket and a shirt and a tie, a suit of underwear, and a pair of socks?" Yet, that is precisely how many of the parolees arrive at St. Joseph's, especially those coming from city and county jails. However, even those coming from state prisons may be in some financial difficulty. Pennsylvania, for example, does not give a parolee "release money." The most he can get is a $10 gratuity if he lives fifty miles or more from the prison or $5 if he lives closer than fifty miles.

Whatever small amount of money a man may have when he enters St. Joseph's, he is encouraged to save. He is not charged for his room, food, or any clothing that may be given to him as long as he is unemployed. He is, of course, encouraged to find a job as soon as possible. Unlike some halfway houses, unemployed residents are not required to perform any particular duties in the house. They are, of course, expected to keep their beds made. Once a man has a job, he is charged $12 per month for his room and $12 per month for food. This does not cover the actual cost involved.

Operating funds for St. Joseph's came, at first, from two

sources: the St. Vincent de Paul Society and individual contributions to St. Joseph's House of Hospitality. However, a recent grant of $5,000 has been made to the parolee program by the Pittsburgh Foundation, a charitable society.

Success of the Program

It would be gratifying to state that none of the sixty-two guests has returned to prison, but it would not be true. As of this writing, three men have returned to prison and four are currently under arrest, charged with offenses which, if they are convicted, will result in their being returned to prison. Even assuming the worst —if these men are convicted and thus seven out of sixty-two are returned to prison in the three years of operation—this is still lower than the state average. A ten-year study conducted by the Pennsylvania Board of Parole reveals that approximately 30 per cent of those released on parole return to prison either for parole violation or for the commission of new crimes.

It is submitted that the success or failure of the Pittsburgh halfway house or, for that matter, any halfway house, cannot be measured by counting the number of men who have returned to prison as compared with the number who have "gone straight." In evaluating any such program, due regard should be taken of the number of men who have had an opportunity which would otherwise have been denied, of leaving prison under the aegis of such a program. These men make application to groups such as the Penal Committee mentioned herein only because they have no friends or family interested in helping them to obtain parole. Statistically, it is at least arguable that they would represent the group most likely to return to prison. And yet, their return rate is no higher than the state average; in fact, it is lower.

Problem of Employment

In the field of employment, mention has already been made of the high rate of unemployment in Pittsburgh. In a few instances, parolees residing at St. Joseph's have been able to find employment on their own. In most cases, however, the residents have been forced to rely on the committee. In addition to their other duties, all twenty-eight members of the committee seek job possibilities for the men in the program. Any leads are channeled directly to the administrative director who then tries to match the proper man with the prospective job. A further complicating factor is the general lack of education and job skills by most of the parolees. In addition to the job leads supplied by the members of the committee, the administrative director relies on his own ingenuity in the quest for jobs. He makes use of want ads, state employment agencies, parole officers, charitable groups, and other sources of possible job information. In a few cases, temporary employment can be given to some of the residents: They may work on the trucks of the St. Vincent de Paul Society picking up used clothing, newspapers, and other donated items. One Christmas, the committee financed the sale of Christmas trees, utilizing various locations throughout the city and staffing them with parolees who were paid for their work. Regardless of the type of job or its temporary nature, the value of providing gainful employment cannot be underestimated.

Most penologists and sociologists agree that the first sixty days after release from prison are the most critical. If a man can get through this period without getting into trouble, his chances for a successful parole are greatly enhanced. In this connection, the committee at one time gave serious thought to the possibility of starting some form of industry at the halfway house to provide jobs for the residents. The benefits of such a program are obvious. Those men who, because of lack of education or job skills, cannot be placed in outside jobs, could, nevertheless, start work immediately. Thus, during the critical initial period of parole, a man would be busy, productive, and earning a few dollars. After careful consideration, the committee felt that the factors which militated against such a program outweighed those in its favor. The initial cost of raw materials and machinery would have seriously depleted the small treasury on hand. No one knew what kind of industry to start, nor was there any qualified instructor or manager. It would have been impossible to foresee with any degree of certainty how many parolees would want, or be able, to participate. The building, St. Joseph's House, is 160 years old and would have required structural improvements which, due to the fact that it is located in an area which is slated for demolition in connection with urban renewal, would have been impractical. But perhaps the most compelling consideration was the thought that the men should be encouraged to go out into society on their own as soon as possible. An industrial program such as this might tend to make them more dependent on the halfway house and retard their departure. Thus, the program was never started.

Women Participants

What is the role of the female parolee in a halfway house? While it is true that women make up a very small percentage of the prison population of this country, it was felt, nevertheless, that some attention should be given to helping female prisoners obtain parole. To date, this has not been possible in the Pittsburgh operation. Obviously the limitations on the physical plan make it impossible to include female participants within the program as it now exists. But some thought has been given to the possibility of making the plan more flexible. This is still in the discussion stage, and any change is in the distant future. However, such a change, if it were to be made, would be along the following lines.

First, women would be needed on the Penal Committee to serve as sponsors and counselors.

Second, additional housing accommodations would be needed. It is believed that suitable quarters in private homes could be rented to satisfy the residence requirement of a parole plan. Obviously, this would be more expensive on a per person basis than is the present cost per person at St. Joseph's House.

Third, the problem of finding jobs for female parolees would have to be evaluated. An educated guess is that this would prove to be no more difficult than is presently encountered with male parolees. But this is strictly a guess. We just do not know.

A Halfway House Program Without a Halfway House

The terms are not mutually exclusive. The second consideration listed above, housing, is one that may possibly deter groups of interested persons from starting a halfway house operation. But it need not be the case. The Pittsburgh group was fortunate in having a made-to-order residence, St. Joseph's House. But without such an existing structure or the finances necessary to build one, could not such an operation be started? It is submitted that it could. Rooming houses, apartment hotels, private residences, all of these could be utilized to house parolees. In fact, some of these accommodations have been utilized by the Pittsburgh group. The obvious dangers inherent in having very young men living in a centralized operation with older parolees has led the Penal Committee to utilize these other housing accommodations for some of its younger clients. The merits and demerits of decentralizing the operation in this manner will be left to penologists, sociologists, and others who are more qualified to express an opinion. Nevertheless, it has been and is being done.

Need for Shared Knowledge

One of the most recent endeavors of the Penal Committee has been an attempt to open the lines of communication with other similar operations. No formalized channel of communication presently exists. Believing that there is a need for the sharing of information on the operations of a halfway house, the Penal Committee has secured a list of addresses of other halfways houses and has begun writing to them. It is hoped that such efforts will expand, thus benefiting all. Perhaps some sort of newsletter will eventually emerge.

Conclusion

It would seem that halfway houses are serving and will continue to serve as valuable tools in the rehabilitation of men on parole. There would also seem to be a clear need for more such programs. To date, this need has been recognized primarily by religious organizations. Perhaps in the not-too-distant future, other community organizations will participate. Father Clark, a pioneer in this field, would urge, however, that this movement be kept in private hands rather than have state participation. Perhaps even Father Clark would not have objected to minimal participation by the state in order to enable a halfway house to begin operations, such as was done at the 308 West House at Wilmington, Delaware. In that instance, the State of Delaware donated the house and the Federal Government made a grant to help pay for the staff, but the house is privately administered rather than operated by either the State or the Federal Government.

It would seem that the best possible operation of a halfway house would include a private dwelling with a permanent resident director, available for consultation at any time. A charge should be made for room and board if for no other reason than to give the individual a feeling of dignity and prevent his feeling like a charity case. This charge could, however, be deferred until the individual is gainfully employed. Active job counseling and placement should also be part of the program.

Every effort should be made to avoid an institutional atmosphere. In this regard, organized meetings at which attendance is mandatory should be avoided entirely or kept to a minimum. Also, rules should be minimal and clearly explained. For example, as a practical matter, alcoholic beverages would probably be banned from the premises as a requirement of the parole board. If it is felt that a lock-out time is desirable (St. Joseph's House, in theory at least, does have one), it should be realistic.

And finally, the community should be made aware that it also has an obligation. Society's obligation should not end when a man is placed behind bars but should continue until he is successfully rehabilitated into a useful member of the community. If for no other reason, economic self-interest would demand this. As a federal judge has stated recently, "Parole . . . is a far cheaper method of custody than physical incarceration." And in Pennsylvania, for example, it costs the taxpayers $1,927 to keep a man in prison for one year. It costs only $234 to supervise him for a year on parole. The investment in human lives, however, would seem to be far more important. As one commentator has said, "Our chief concern, however, is not with dollars and cents but with the prevention of crime and the saving of human lives."

Halfway houses are not panaceas. They have had their failures and will, in all probability, continue to have their failures. It seems to me, however, that their failures are far outshadowed by their successes.

RELEASE PREPARATION: PAROLE CAMP*

A 1952 study of parole violations in Michigan showed, much to no one's surprise, that the majority of men who violated parole did so within the first six months after release. The inference drawn, again to no one's surprise, was that we were releasing on parole many men who had not been made ready for life outside prison walls.

Like most states, we had some sort of prerelease program functioning in the penitentiary. However, we were not particularly proud of what we had, and the survey gave added support—not that any was needed—to our argument that the candidate for parole must be specially prepared for community life and that a parolee stood a pretty good chance of being returned to the institution in a few months unless he received some special attention before release.

We debated the issue of just what kind of "special attention" would best meet the preparolee's needs and ours, and came up with the idea of separating him from the general inmate population and placing him, before his return to the community, in an environment as nearly approximating a normal community setting as possible. To fill the bill, we designed a preparole camp, which went into operation under the administration of the state parole division. It makes no claim to exciting originality (the practice of segregating men about to be released has long been used in the armed services, for example) and it will not lead all of us out of the correction wilderness, but there is no denying that segregation is a new idea as far as parole candidates are concerned. Nor is there any denying that parole departments need new ideas, and old ideas need to be expanded and refined, at least as much as they need better budgets.

Our prison camp division constructed a 125-bed preparole camp, at a cost of $37,500, about a half mile from the main prison building at Jackson. The site, surrounded by a thick growth of tall trees, already had on it an attractive brick cottage, which was remodeled into offices. The construction crew erected a long,

---

* Reprinted by permission of the National Probation and Parole Association. Gus Harrison: The Michigan parole camp. *Focus,* 33(No. 2):37-42, March 1954.

one-story white clapboard barrack to house 108 inmates. The beds are double-deckers, and the windows have curtains. The building includes washrooms, a barber shop, and other small service rooms. One wing of the dormitory contains the classroom; another, the lounge. Close to the dormitory the men put up another long white building containing the dining room and a spacious kitchen. Near the mess hall are quarters for seventeen trusties (for operation and maintenance work) on loan from the Prison Camp Program of the Department of Corrections.

The walls of the lounge are painted, and the windows have drapes. The blond wood furniture is arranged in groups conducive to conversation; there are library tables and a small collection of varied reading material. In the dining room, which is approximately 100 feet long, the men sit at small tables in groups of four, six, or eight. The food is served in cafeteria style, on dishes (not on the conventional institutional trays). The kitchen —large, airy, and equipped with the latest in cooking, refrigeration, and storage equipment—is staffed partly by trusties and partly by preparolees. The food is well prepared, varied, and plentiful.

Undoubtedly there are persons—including some in the corrections field itself—who sneer at the type of environment we have provided as "too good for a bunch of cons," but most of us agree that people are influenced by their surroundings and it was that principle which justified our spending a good deal of time and effort (plus $37,500) toward making the camp buildings and grounds as attractive as possible.

Regulations and Routines

We try to orient the newly arrived inmate as soon as possible after his entry into the camp. We find that giving him a rundown on his prime concerns at the moment—his prospective release date and our regulations about laundry, purchases, mail, and visits—makes him more receptive to instruction in the educational phase of the program.

The men wear regulation prison clothing except on Sundays and holidays and during visits, when they are permitted to wear their "going home" clothing.

Each friend or relative on a man's visiting list can make one four-hour visit or two two-hour visits a month. Prospective employers may visit at any time.

Preparolees spend an average of three and a half weeks in camp before receiving a certificate of parole. The law in Michigan, as in most states, requires that a man eligible for parole must have, before he is released, assurance of gainful employment. Issuance of a parolee certificate is held up if a camp inmate does not have a job by the time his release date rolls around. Prospective parolees who for this reason cannot leave the camp after the customary twenty-five-day "cushioning" period are detailed full-time thereafter to various work crews around the camp grounds. Sometimes this presents a problem. Men who have gone through the preparole school feel that they should be given preferential treatment, not be assigned to just any trivial task that happens to be lying around loose, and they tend to become more and more restless with every day spent on the "overdue" list. We try to allay their fears and anxieties by making special efforts to find employment for them.

The men in the camp never return to the main prison, except in the case of serious misconduct. They are dressed out, cleared medically, and so forth without further contact with the big institution. Their availability in one spot for interviews and counseling on their parole programs is an important advantage of the parole camp.

Custodial personnel assigned to the camp consists of one sergeant and four officers. Sometimes the men chafe at what we consider light restrictions. They feel, for example, that they should be permitted greater freedom about the grounds. There are no fences, and movement within the camp boundaries is not restricted. But we do not want to endanger the program, and we have to be realistic. We know that if we do not take certain precautions, some overdue men, as well as some who are subconsciously fearful of their return to the community, may be impelled to take flight. So far we have had no runaways.

Mornings are taken up with gardening, working in the mess hall, and various other jobs about the grounds. Lunch is followed by a short interlude for rest and relaxation, after which the budding parolee attends the day's lecture and discussion session in the classroom, which lasts most of the afternoon. There is another relaxation period before chow, after which the men may pitch horseshoes or play baseball, softball, or volleyball. The less actively inclined watch television (the set was donated to the camp), listen to the radio, or play cards or checkers.

Preparolee School Program

We are proud of our physical setup, but not dominated by it. Far more important than the trappings—and I am not decrying their value—is our educational program, which is designed to help men make the transition from the regimentation of prison existence to the individuality of life in a free setting.

The men who give the lectures and lead the discussions in this program—college professors, law-enforcement and parole officers, clergymen, psychologists—are experts in their fields. They receive no compensation for their work. Obtaining the service on a voluntary basis was not as difficult as you may suppose. Our appeal for help practically sold itself. The most important part of promoting assistance from the experts consisted of making clear to them just what we wanted to achieve in the educational program. Once they understood this, they were impressed and interested, and proof of their belief in the work lies in the fact that they have stayed with us. So as not to impose too heavily upon any one guest participant, we rotate the assignments; rarely do we call on any individual to lead the program at the camp more often than once every two months.

We do not believe in "programming down" and have found that top-notch lecturers raise the sights and self-esteem of the students. Whatever small fears we may have had originally that speakers of high caliber would prove too tough for the group to handle were pleasantly dissipated by experience.

The lectures, supplemented by carefully chosen films, cover the following subjects:

1. Getting along with people. Relationships with spouse, others in the family, employer, landlord, work associates, law-enforcement officers.
2. Role of the police in the community.

3. Mental and emotional health. How to recognize and control tensions.
4. Religion as a way of life.
5. The necessity of regular and steady employment; how to apply for a job, and the benefits of good work habits. Budgeting.
6. Physical and mental effects of the use of alcohol; control of drinking habits.
7. Use of leisure time.
8. Interpretation of parole; the role of the parole officer; conditions of parole; assistance offered by parole supervision.

Usually the guest speaker for the day talks for about forty-five minutes, trying to put across several points to open the way to general discussion. During the planning stage, we were a little concerned that the men would be reluctant to speak up in groups, but we saw after the program got going that the men participated in an uninhibited manner. Nothing is sacred, and sometimes we parole officials emerge a bit bruised; but we think it's healthy to let the men air everything.

So convinced are we that the active participation of the students is essential to the success of the program that we have set aside a definite part of each school session to encourage the men to "sound off." In informal preliminary group discussions, our parole supervisor "warms up" the men for the speaker of the day.

Aside from the immediate objective, this has the value of giving the supervisor a good opportunity to spot the "problem children" for later individual attention.

The questions most frequently asked during the discussions after the lectures are those that touch on general community resistance to parolees, projected fears of ostracism because of a prison record, police attitudes toward parolees, and projected mistrust of the parole officer.

As in other situations where experiences are shared by a group under the leadership of a capable person, the individual inmate finds that the anxieties which have been looming so large are not unique to him. As he discovers the many ways in which he is similar to his fellows, his problems diminish and fall into proper focus. Many of the apprehensions of the prospective parolee are disposed of in some measure by the constructive comments of those in the group who had been on parole before and now admit their failure and the reasons for it. Moreover, the group experience enables the prospective parolee to seek and accept help more readily than before.

We know that we are violating some of the principles of guided group interaction, but we know why and how our situation forces us to do so and we are not at all dismayed by factors which make ideal group work impossible. For example, we cannot select our students with fine discrimination, although we do screen out medical cases, men with detainers, and a few others whom we feel would not be good camp material for obvious reasons. These inmates, who make up 5 per cent of the total scheduled for parole, are released directly from the penitentiary under the same procedure that was in practice before the parole camp was established. The other 95 per cent of the men who make parole at Jackson are transferred to the parole camp. They are heterogeneous in age, intelligence, and educational level.

Sometimes, when our camp population gets uncomfortably high, our turnover is rapid; nevertheless we are sure that, on the whole, something good is being accomplished by the lecture-discussion sessions. While it may be expected that some men will retain only bits of the instruction, we believe that the overall impact of the preparole program serves to improve the attitudes of the men toward the free community and toward themselves as members of it.

Most of the men are proud of their role in the camp and are cooperative and serious. The impression the camp has made on relatives, friends, and prospective employers is lasting and salutary. These people are convinced that we are interested in our parolees and, consequently, give us their wholehearted cooperation.

Between the end of last April and December 31, some 739 men were released from the parole camp. Not enough time has elapsed for us to arrive at valid success and failure rates for these men, but the signs are promising and we feel we have made a good start on doing a better job of parole preparation. Our field officers state that graduates of the parole camp are much more relaxed, friendly, and informed than were parolees released under the old system. They note a diminishing of some of the tensions classically found among new parolees and consequently a multiplying of the chances for success.

We are convinced that sooner or later all of us will prepare men to "bridge the gap" between prison and home through programs which are similar to ours but which no doubt will go beyond our present limitations in Michigan. And we look forward to the day when such programs, working deep into the recesses of our institutions, will accomplish what we have been inching toward for years—a system under which "individual treatment" and "rehabilitation" will be actually practiced, not merely professed.

REORIENTATION TO EMPLOYMENT*

Satisfying, steady employment is probably the most significant deterrent to delinquency and crime. This being true, it is surprising that more has not been done to incorporate a strong vocational guidance service as part of every prevention and reform program.

Program of the United States Employment Service

Staffs of correctional institutions and probation officers necessarily must do much of their own vocational guidance. They can get assistance in their work from local offices of the employment service. The employment service is the largest public agency next to the schools which touches the problem of job adjustment. Its primary function is job placement—a service to get the right workers for employers and the right job for workers. The USES, through its affiliated state agencies, provides free employment services in nearly 1,800 local offices throughout the country, but the employment service also has several other valuable contributions: employment counseling, selective placement of the handicapped, special service to veterans, and occupational and labor market information.

Since the prime purpose of the employment service is job

---

* Reprinted in part by permission of *Federal Probation.* Charles E. Odell: Job adjustment for probationers and parolees. *Federal Probation, 15*(No. 2):12-15, 1951.

placement, its staff members contact thousands of employers each month to assist them in filling openings in their firms. At the same time, it registers millions of workers, getting a record of their experiences, training, and vocational interests. In the course of its registration, placement, and employer-visiting work, the employment service naturally gathers a wealth of occupational information. Some of this information is developed and published for use in employment counseling and placement. Much additional knowledge of jobs, their conditions, requirements, and rewards is also available, although unrecorded, in the minds of employment service interviewers and counselors.

Among the many publications relating to employment which have been developed by the employment service, the best known is the *Dictionary of Occupational Titles.* It contains definitions of about 22,028 jobs. This is the standard classification tool of the employment service. It also is used by the military and other government agencies, as well as by industry, for selection, occupational filing systems, and as a general reference tool. Other publications of nationwide significance are *National Job Descriptions, The Labor Market,* a monthly publication, *Job Family Series, Selective Placement for the Handicapped, Physical Demands Analysis, Physical Capacities Appraisal, Occupational Guides,* and several on labor market information. In addition, many states and localities develop and distribute material which is prepared locally.

Aptitude Tests Prove Useful

The General Aptitude Test Battery developed by the USES is now used in more than 575 of its local offices. This battery of tests for ten basic vocational aptitudes relates them to nearly 2,000 specific occupations in twenty fields of work. The abilities measured are general learning ability, word discrimination, numerical ability, form perception, finger dexterity, manual dexterity, spatial imagery, clerical aptitude, aiming, and motor speed. This tool has proved of great value in the counseling of those who are confronted with problems of vocational choice.

A careful analysis, through the interview, of a person's work experience, educational record, physical capacities, leisure time activities, interests, and goals can tell the experienced interviewer much about his abilities, but tests often give additional clues as to undeveloped aptitudes. Besides the practical value of discovering these potentialities and their use in making vocational plans, test results have proved a great morale builder. It is a very reassuring experience for a man to know that objective tests indicate abilities which he has never had an opportunity to exploit through actual work experience. These tests could be used with profit for men leaving institutions.

Reorientation to the Job

Psychological preparation of inmates for reentering work—discussion of right attitudes, the variety of jobs open, development of work-mindedness—and giving of information regarding the requirements and differences in circumstances of various jobs all help orient the parolee. Parolees should be prepared, too, for giving considerable time to job hunting. They need to be prepared for some failures. Discussion as to ways of presenting themselves to employers and putting the best foot forward is important. Here again, some of the materials and personnel resources of the employment service should be helpful.

When jobs are scarce, both the employment service and probation officers will have difficulty in getting jobs for men on probation. Special programs of solicitation will be needed. The selling to an employer of one individual parolee at a time, on the basis of his ability to perform, is the best long-term approach. The employment service can be useful in helping overcome some of the employer's resistance and hostility to those with crime records. When competition for jobs is great, the probation officer also may wish to consider counseling with his clients as to the possibilities for self-employment.

Probation officers working on vocational rehabilitation of parolees should insure that all necessary credentials are available as men leave institutions for work. For example, working certificates are necessary in most states for people under eighteen years of age. Boys should have all necessary papers such as proof of age and their school records before they start out from the institution.

Otherwise, there is a delay in their employment. Employers may turn them away unnecessarily. These frustrating experiences may needlessly set them back. Parolees need help in meeting these routine paper requirements.

Easily discouraged people, as many parolees are, need special help in order not to feel they are getting the runaround. In referring parolees to the employment service, probation officers will help their clients most by making all useful information about the man available to the employment service interviewer. The more the counselor or interviewer knows about the man, the more helpful he can be. The man's institutional record, with an evaluation of his success and failure in work assignments, is useful. Recommendations by social workers regarding the best environment for the individual should be taken into account. Also the more the employment counselor knows of the man's life story, the more interest he is likely to take and the more likely he is to place him in suitable work.

The practice of not releasing a man until he has promise of a job seems an unrealistic one. Most employers will not hire a person without a personal interview.

In referring men to the local employment service office, it is usually better to give the name of a specific individual after telephone arrangements have been made for the interview. This is particularly important in large cities where the impersonal atmosphere may be discouraging. It is important that all data about the applicants reach the local office before the man gets there. It is usually considered desirable to tell employers something of the man's background and the circumstances which brought him into legal custody. This saves questions later and gives the man a greater sense of ease and acceptance.

AN EMPLOYER'S VIEWS ABOUT HIRING EX-CONVICTS*

This section contains a verbatim account of a meeting at the United States Penitentiary at McNeil Island, Washington, of a prerelease group of fifty, together with the owner of a drug firm who

---

* Reprinted by permission of *Federal Probation.* An employer's views about hiring a man who has served time. *Federal Probation, 17*(No. 4):43-46, Dec. 1953.

had been invited to discuss the attitude of employers toward hiring persons who had served time. The questions and concerns of the men and the replies of the employer are characteristic of those that come up for discussion at prerelease meetings. (Editor's note.)

Employer: "Fellows, let's get something straight to start with; I came here to talk to you, not to preach. I'm not much of a speaker, so if you'll all relax I think we'll get along.

"A few weeks ago I was asked to talk to you on how an employer feels about hiring a man that has served time, and while you may not believe some of the things I say—they might not represent what a lot of other people would say or believe—I want you to know, here and now, that what I say, I believe.

"I don't particularly feel I am experienced enough in the ways of the world to give advice unasked, but you want to know how an employer feels and I'm going to do my best to tell you how *one* employer feels.

"First, perhaps I should make my position clear. It is that of the operator of a small drug firm. I know all the people who work for me and know how much I depend upon them. If they were to quit, I'd be out of business because I couldn't do all the work myself. Between me and my employees, there is a relationship that grounds on mutual respect and understanding, and this is also true of most of the employers I have met while I've been in the drug business. Regardless of what you may have heard of the hardheartedness and money-grubbing of businessmen, it just isn't so. No, I'm not trying to tell you the average businessman isn't there to make every dollar he can, but the longer you are in your own business, the more you find out that your biggest business asset is satisfied employees. The most important asset is not the store, not the merchandise, not the money I have in the bank, but my personnel. And how I learned it during the last five or six years when merchandise was hard to get, and good employees even harder!

"During those years when a person came in and wanted a job, you looked up and asked the personnel man, 'Can he walk?' If he nodded his head, you hired the person immediately. It's a bit different now. Our employees get a thorough checking before we let them come to work. We're in a position to pick and choose, and naturally we take only the best. Why? Because a good employee makes the most money for you, and to keep a good employee you go to quite some lengths. At present we are encouraging our employees to buy a share in the company and make it easy for them to do it with small monthly deductions. And we do this because we want them to feel more than that they are just coming to work. We want them to feel they own part of every article they sell; the better service they give, the more goods they sell and the more money we'll all make.

"As I said before, we have passed the state where we had to take anyone. We can now pick and choose, and the basis of our selection is that we pick the person we feel is best fitted for the job. When we get that person, the job is done better and we make more money. And how do you get the best person? You hire the best available and then develop him. And if he can't be developed, can't be improved, you fire him!

"When I was asked to talk to you, my first reaction was to say, 'No.' I wondered what I could say that would matter. And then I was handed a list of questions you asked. I'll read it to you now, or perhaps I'd better just take the questions the writers proposed and answer them one by one. Now whether you like it or not, believe it or not, I'm going to answer these questions as I see the answer."

"Should I tell my employer of my record?"

Employer: "Put yourself in my place or any employer's place. What do you want? You want a man who can do the job and you want to know about the man that is going to work for you. You give him an application to fill out. It asks: 'Name and address; and then, previous employment: begin with the last employer first, fill out length of time you worked for employer, work you did, salary and reason for leaving.' If I filled out one for you and I'd worked last in 1944, what is the first question you'd ask me? You're damn right you would! 'Where have you been the last several years?' and I have to tell or you wouldn't give me the job.

"Put this in your mind and keep it there. If your employer

fires you because you have a record, you didn't have a job in the first place!

"There is only one answer to the question. Certainly you should tell him. And if you don't tell him, then every checkup, every bit of criticism, every heavy look you're going to feel is directed right at you, and you'd really get that if you worked for me. But how the devil are you going to do your job right if you're worried every hour of the day that you are going to lose your job? By not telling, you're being unfair to yourself. You just cannot go to an employer with dirty hands and expect his hands to be clean.

"Don't think just going in and telling an employer, 'I've got a record,' is going to get you a job. You've got to have the qualifications the employer is looking for. If you haven't the qualifications, you're not going to get the job and that isn't being discriminated against.

"And you're not always going to get the job you want, even if you have the qualifications. Sure you're going to have to walk up and down the street and take just whatever you can get and, while you're doing it, don't think you're the only one that ever did the same thing. Shortly after the First World War, in 1919 that was, I walked up and down the streets of Vancouver, B.C., looking for a job. There I was, a college graduate, and couldn't get a job of any kind. Sure, I thought I was being discriminated against. Everybody in all the stores was busy and I couldn't even get anywhere near the kind of job I wanted. Yes, I found a job, at $18 per week. Nice salary for a college graduate, but it was a job I could do and that's why I was hired. And that's the only way anyone gets a job. Because the employer is convinced you can do that job and do it better than someone else. I say this in answer to the second question, which asks:

"Will the employer, because of my record, refuse to start me in a position for which I qualify?"

Employer: "Look, fellows, the average employer is damn glad to get a competent employee, and he's going to try to keep this employee as well-satisfied as he can, within reason. So if you're a top-notch salesman you're not going to make the employer any money by sweeping the floor. If you want to work for me, you are not going to start in my job, but if you're good I'm sure going to do everything I can to keep you."

"Will my employer tell the office manager and staff of my record?"

Employer: "You're here for a reason. You got out for a reason. And if you're made of the right stuff, you belong out and you stay out. And it's the way you conduct yourself that will give people your measure. I know that this sounds a bit like 'blarney,' but I don't think people pay much attention to what's happened in the past. So don't worry about what the other person thinks. Most people don't give your record a thought, and feeling they think about you is a condition largely created in your own mind. Your boss isn't going around to tell the staff whom he hires, or why. After all, that is his job, to hire people. If he hires you, you're going to be with the company until he gets ready to fire you. Don't worry about that record."

"What are my chances of advancement if my record is known?"

Employer: "If you want one man's idea—and it may not be worth anything and I may be the only guy in the world that feels that way—you would be advanced as rapidly as it was possible if you worked for me. Actually I'd have more faith and trust and confidence in you simply because you told me about your record. I am naive enough to believe you are a little smarter than the average fellow because of your experience and that you wouldn't let me down. If you did let me down, I'd just say you weren't half as smart as I thought you were. But if you made good, don't you see what a smart man you'd make out of me? People feel good when their judgment is substantiated. I could say, 'I gave him a place of trust and look at him now.' And everytime I pushed you up another notch, my chest would swell out a little. Why shouldn't I advance you? You bet your boots I would, just as long as you warranted it."

"Did he hire me out of pity?"

Employer: "If you had a job someone gave you out of pity, you wouldn't be working for me. Maybe some philanthropic organization might hire you that way, but if I hired you, it would be because you could do the work and make some money for me."

"Will I be under constant supervision?"

Employer: "Yes! That's how you get the most out of people. You keep prodding them. All of my people are under constant supervision. As an employer, that's all I have to do, and if I didn't do it, the people who work for me would feel neglected and hurt. And incidentally, anytime you're working for anyone, make sure they see you. That's the way you get ahead, by someone noticing what you are doing. If you think I'm going to open your hand every time you take it out of the till—no. But I'll be around to know whether you're making money for me or not."

"If something went wrong would I be automatically blamed?"

Employer: "Get away from the persecution complex. The guys who ask these questions sound like they're scared to death something's going to happen to them. But there is no reason in the world to feel that way if you do your job, regardless of what goes wrong. It makes me think the guy feels that he is prone to accident. You know, one man can walk down the street through broken glass barefoot and nothing happens. And this guy comes along in high-top boots and gets cut. If something goes wrong, someone was negligent. Whoever was negligent is going to hear from me.

"How could I run a business under conditions other than that? You're not going to be blamed unless I'm damned sure you were to blame. You'd probably get more leeway than would an ordinary employee because I'd hesitate to accuse you wrongfully. Forget those thoughts. Come to work ready to look the world in the eyes. You're as good as any man on the job or you wouldn't have been hired. No employer has money to waste on worthless employees.

"When people hire people, they try to get as much information as they can possibly get about them. The employer wants to find out everything he can. What they like; what they don't like; where they go to church; and where they spend their spare time. That's what application blanks are for. And this is why they are studied. The personnel manager doesn't just take your blank and toss it in a drawer; he studies it. And after he's talked to you, he has almost as much to fill out as you did. Some of the important factors the personnel manager must consider are appearance, dress and grooming, knowledge of the job, grasp of job principles, and familiarity of job.

"In my business when I hire a man I want him to look neat. He has to meet the public, and scores of people look at him during the day and judge our store by him. We figure, too, if a man looks neat it also indicates character and habits. And knowledge of the job. Sure, some guy shows up and says, 'I have worked in a drug store all my life.' So I ask him, 'If a customer came in and asked for something for a cold, what would you recommend?' "

Answer from members of group: "Castor oil!"

Employer: "You're fired, even before you're hired! In the first place, castor oil isn't worth a damn for a cold, but more than that, we don't make a nickel on it. What kind of an employee are you? You've got to recommend something that will help the customer and at the same time make money for the store. You see, we're in a position to pick and choose. We look for a man with business acumen, with essential knowledge, and with qualities we can develop.

"This pamphlet I'm now reading from is developed to aid men in evaluating new employees or would-be employees. It's developed through the research of thousands of people who looked for jobs, and a lot of employers use it.

"We employers look for self-assurance. Now that doesn't mean cockiness and playfulness. We look for men who look like they can take care of themselves and not be easily upset. We may even needle a would-be employee to get his reaction. I might even make some remark about your record just to see what you would do. I take a jab at you. I try to get you sore, just to see the reaction.

"Cooperation—ability and willingness to work with others. Now a lot of us think we're cooperative, but we aren't. I have seen a whole organization torn to pieces because some guy came in that wouldn't cooperate. He felt that someone wasn't doing quite all he should, so he didn't either. Result: pretty soon no one was doing his work.

"Command of language and handling of ideas are other factors. Naturally in my business, which is primarily selling, command of language is most important. So if you want to be a salesman, you have to know how to use your language.

"Health, stamina, physical drive, and record of previous employment are also important. I'm going to read you part of a letter that came to the institution. It's from the Blank Company. 'We are glad to aid Mr. Inmate in his rehabilitation. We notice he has operated a jumbo-drilling machine and, as part of our project is 4000 feet of tunnel drilling, he can join our tunnel crew.'

"And there you have it. This man had something to offer. Something the Blank Company could use. He had experience with the drilling machine. Blank Company didn't care about the record, they wanted a man to operate a drilling machine. Experience! I have a dozen applications on my desk right now, all of them from people I would like to hire, except they don't have the right experience.

"And here's another letter the institution received. It's from a union in San Francisco and states: 'We cannot aid you in finding this man a job. At the present time, several hundred of our own members are out of work.'

"So you see, sometimes even when you have experience, you can't locate a job. So how much tougher it's going to be for the fellow without experience.

"Now fellows, I have given you the facts as I see them. I'm just one employer but what I've said, I believe. And I believe, too, that if there's a job open where you make your application, and you have the skill to fill that job, no one's going to give that record of yours much thought as long as you do a good job. If I've done you fellows some good, I'm glad and I want you also to know it's done me some good to talk to you."

USE OF VOLUNTEERS IN PAROLE*

The parole adviser is primarily and essentially a volunteer in the field of rehabilitation. As such, he has a long and honorable lineage. John Augustus, that celebrated Boston shoemaker who is often regarded as the father of probation, was of this group. Of course, he was functioning as a volunteer or unpaid probation officer, but essentially he was a nonprofessional counselor, adviser, first friend, and sponsor to the offenders released under his supervision. The fact that they were technically probationers rather than parolees probably did not alter the relationship established or the techniques attempted.

Aid societies, sometimes subsidized by government, typically were interested in parole cases. However, it is generally considered that parole, as now understood, originated at the Elmira (New York) Reformatory in 1876. The parolee was required to report to a sponsor known as a guardian. The guardian apparently combined the functions of adviser and parole officer.

Development of casework and the use of professionally trained workers naturally combined to relegate the untrained, unpaid volunteer to a lesser role. Furthermore, professional and volunteer workers sometimes failed to appreciate each other or to realize that one may be complementary to the other. In many cases the role of the parole adviser has been reduced almost to the vanishing point. One might question whether an adviser belongs in a well-developed parole system. There may also be the suspicion that an overzealous amateur in some cases might actually disturb the adjustment of the parolee. This might logically bring up the question of whether the whole system could not well be scrapped. Objections implied by these considerations do have a certain de-

---

* Reprinted by permission of *Federal Probation*. Edwin B. Cunningham: The role of the parole adviser. *Federal Probation*, *15*(No. 4):43-46, Dec. 1951.

gree of validity. Others could easily be raised. It may be readily conceded that the adviser relationship is frequently not very meaningful to the parolee. What then is the role of adviser?

Opportunities for Interpretation

Much has been said and published on the premise that parole is a failure because so many parolees are arrested. From time to time, editorials in the daily press criticize parole systems for releasing men who commit new crimes. Too frequently, parole may be considered merely as a device for relieving criminals from punishment rather than as a phase of a rehabilitating program. Actually the citizen who criticizes the system may not have considered the alternatives of parole. Would such a critic advise capital punishment for all offenses; would he prefer life terms for all convicted felons; or would he rather see all inmates released without restriction of any kind? The citizen who has had the experience of having served as a parole adviser is more likely to appreciate these considerations.

In a typical case the applicant for parole will try to suggest a rather representative member of his community as his adviser. This suggested adviser may be interested in the inmate. In most cases, he may not have been aware of parole as a system, but he will usually have a number of questions to ask about his duties and his responsibilities. If the relationship with the parolee turns out to be successful, it may be a matter of gratification and inner satisfaction to the citizen who has had a part in this process. Even if the parolee does not respond, the adviser will usually not begrudge the efforts he made. Nearly always his attitude toward parole and rehabilitative efforts in general will be more sympathetic because of his experience.

Prerelease Planning

It has been suggested that the requirement of the parole adviser in parole planning offers a useful device for interpreting parole to the public. This is not to suggest that the adviser should not have a vital position in the rehabilitative program. If his help is to be utilized, the field officer will need to cultivate consciously some kind of working relationship with the adviser. In practice, the most favorable opportunity for doing this will usually be in connection with the normal prerelease investigation. The adviser may be well acquainted with the prospective parolee; he may have known him only slightly; or his interest may have been enlisted by relatives. In any case the fact that he has consented to serve is evidence of some interest and goodwill. It is up to the officer to make the most of these associations. Certainly the adviser is more likely to exert constructive effort if he understands that his offer of assistance is appreciated and recognized by the professional worker. This interview with the adviser under favorable conditions can be productive and helpful throughout the ensuing parole period.

Selection of Adviser

Obviously, the prerelease interview is part of the required parole report. Does the person suggested impress the probation officer as a suitable counselor for the parolee? Presumably he is qualified by reputation, citizenship, and standing in his community. If there is any doubt, further investigation may be indicated. Ideally, an effort might be made to match advisers and parolees on the basis of what is known of their personalities, characters, experience, and interests. In practice this is hardly feasible. Actually it will be found that almost any applicant for parole, as well as his friends and relatives, will avoid suggesting anyone whose reputation would not bear investigation. In the writer's experience the only exceptions have been in cases of inmates probably not eligible for much consideration in any event. There are, of course, exceptions to this rule. Some inmates are unable to secure help from the usual sources and are compelled to appeal to the field officer. A probation officer who has worked in a community for a few years will have accumulated almost automatically a sort of pool of public-spirited citizens available for such cases. These may come from the ranks of former parole advisers, educators, clergymen, and social service agencies, public and private. Nevertheless, it would seem advisable whenever possible for the applicant to suggest his own adviser. The need of doing this for himself may have the effect of placing some responsibility on the applicant. If he realizes that his entire plan will be investigated, he is not likely to suggest anyone objectionable from a moral standpoint. If he selects a sympathetic individual, so much the better. The inmate is made to feel that parole is something more than a routine reward for doing part of his sentence.

Working With the Adviser

Ideally, the field officer and the adviser should function as a team. In actual practice, this may not be realized since frequent contacts are not always possible. However, even a few contacts between the two can be productive. As hinted above, the probation officer will do well to express in some manner his sincere appreciation for the assistance of the volunteer worker. Such an expression may mean to the volunteer a form of recognition.

Most experienced workers would agree that advisers differ widely in their interests in the particular cases in which they are active. One may feel that by a monthly meeting with the parolee and the act of signing report forms he has adequately discharged his obligations. Another may feel constrained to offer a variety of services. Perhaps it is in the area commonly classified as executive casework that a volunteer aide can often function to best advantage. In rare cases an excess of zeal or misguided effort may disturb the adjustment of a parolee, but such situations can usually be controlled with reasonable use of tact and goodwill. One may recall advisers who knew too much, saw too much, and reported more problems than a busy worker might care to have brought to his attention; but such assistance can usually be turned to good advantage. If that is not possible, the parolee can usually be oriented away from the overzealous adviser without undue friction or disturbance. In short, the adviser relationship has a high potential value with negligible risks.

The Adviser in Rural Areas

These observations apply to parole supervision in general. In rural communities at a distance from the office, the role of parole adviser usually assumes a larger significance. Parolees near the field office will normally see their probation officer frequently and can ordinarily look to him for guidance and counsel. Problems that arise can usually be investigated promptly.

In outlying areas, there is greater need for assistance. Some problems demand attention which cannot be immediately given by the probation officer. These considerations make it almost imperative that the adviser have some conception of the case in which he is interested; for the parolee may have to look to him for a certain amount of counsel and advice. These considerations probably justify more attention to the matter of enlisting the services of competent advisers than is true in urban areas. Furthermore, the officer may have to depend on the adviser for reliable information regarding the parolee's conduct, as well as his adjustment. Sometimes it may be advisable to encourage correspondence from the adviser. Here again the volunteer worker is more likely to accept responsibility if he feels that he has the confidence as well as the appreciation of the professional worker.

There is another important consideration in the supervision of parolees living in remote areas. Visits of the probation officer may necessarily be infrequent. This makes it almost imperative to have some kind of a contact on any given visit. In rural communities, even more than in urban neighborhoods, the parolee may be very sensitive about neighborhood gossip. If no one is home when the probation officer calls, an adviser with some understanding of the case can usually supply more accurate information than would be secured from a chance contact; and this information is secured with a minimum of disturbance to the parolee and his family. Incidentally, certain advisers in outlying sections are often of great service as resources of information in investigative assignments aside from the case in which they are directly interested.

Delegating Responsibility

Sometimes considerable responsibility may well be delegated to the adviser. Assuming that the adviser is an individual of intelligence, goodwill, and insight the parolee can be encouraged to look to him for assistance and counsel. Such procedure is time saving to the officer and may be satisfying to the adviser. Such an adviser, because he understands his neighborhood, may also be in position to interpret the parolee's point of view to the probation officer. Intelligent efforts to meet special problems may strengthen the constructive influence of the adviser.

The following cases illustrate the role that the adviser may play in certain situations.

Case No. 1

Clarence was a twenty-six-year-old man of borderline intelligence, unstable work record, and emotional immaturity. The prognosis for his adjustment was necessarily guarded at the time of release. About the only evident favorable factor was an exceptionally devoted wife who enlisted the help of an active and able adviser.

In this case the adviser performed a variety of services beyond what a probation officer could have been expected to attempt. In the face of discouraging failures, he found jobs for the parolee who, incidentally, was not very employable. Furthermore, this parolee had little vocational training or experience, and he was not well motivated. Most of the services performed by the adviser would be in the category of executive casework. The parolee's borderline intelligence and personality defects rendered him virtually inaccessible to counseling of the nondirective type. Furthermore a probation officer with a heavy caseload would probably not have felt justified in spending more than a fraction of the time and effort the volunteer invested in this unpromising subject. Without this assistance, Clarence would almost certainly have been returned as a violator. Probably the net gain to society was small, but at least failure was averted for a season. Whatever gain was made could be credited almost entirely to the adviser.

Case No. 2

Leonard was sentenced as a juvenile. Poor institutional adjustment led to transfer from the training school to a reformatory. The parental home was maintained under submarginal economic circumstances in a rural neighborhood far from the probation office. Leonard was of dull normal intelligence. The parents, who obviously had little to offer, were unable to assist in release planning. Much counseling and close supervision were indicated in this case.

It proved difficult to find anyone in the community who was willing to work with Leonard. The reluctant citizen who was finally induced to assist would hardly qualify as an ideal choice. He was a very religious person, lacking a sense of humor but with keen awareness of the existence of sin and crime and definitely on record as opposed to both. However, he knew Leonard and his family and was aware of their limitations; he probably regarded his sponsorship as a sort of unwelcome Christian duty.

This parole adviser took his responsibilities seriously and somewhat surprisingly acquired a sympathetic insight into some of Leonard's problems. A degree of wholesome restraint was tempered by some exceedingly frank but sympathetic counsel. Some rather amusing conferences involving the parolee, members of his family, the adviser, and the probation officer were held. There was also considerable correspondence between the adviser and the probation officer.

In this case the influence of a zealous adviser was probably a decisive factor. Leonard has had no conflicts with the law in more than four years since his period of conditional release expired. This alone is a remarkable gain in the light of the juvenile record. A more intelligent, sensitive, aggressive youth would probably have rejected the counsel and assistance of this adviser, who by chance proved to be well-fitted for the task at hand. Incidentally, this adviser has been of assistance several times since Leonard's case was closed.

Case No. 3

This was also a case in which the prognosis was dim. The home situation was poor, and there was little prospect for improvement. Apparent personality defects and an unsuccessful marriage were a few of many unfavorable factors. It was hoped the adviser, who seemed unusually well-fitted for this case, might counterbalance some of the unfavorable elements. After a few weeks crowded with many complications and problems, the sympathetic realistic adviser sent in a resignation with the observation, "You can have him. I'm through!" In this case a competent adviser was not enough to tip the scales, but at least more of a program had been attempted than would have been possible without volunteer assistance since this was another case in a remote community.

Case No. 4

Alfred's capable and sympathetic wife had joined a religious sect distinctive in its tenets and, therefore, somewhat clannish and group-conscious. Since the parolee was believed to be interested in the church of his wife's choice, no objection was made to the pastor as parole adviser. However, the parolee actually rejected this form of religion much to the distress of the sincere and zealous pastor. In this case, it was necessary to reinterpret the situation to both the parolee and the religious leader in terms of diverse and personal viewpoints. This was apparently accomplished without serious disturbance to the parolee. Naturally the relationship became a nominal one, but it was not considered necessary to wound the adviser's sensibilities by formal termination.

Advisers for Probationers

The foregoing considerations also apply to some extent to probationers. In most probation cases, however, the presentence investigation will have revealed a potential sponsor or adviser. Often this relationship has developed on an informal basis and can well be left there. Frequently, especially in cases involving youthful probationers, a referral to a social agency or civic group is indicated. In such situations the appointment of a sponsor or adviser, whether on a formal or informal basis, is usually left to the agency or organization to which the referral is made.

In many probation cases the role of the adviser appears less significant because the probation officer has made recent contacts with individuals and organizations interested in the probationer. In some cases, it will seem advisable to attempt to establish a closer relationship between the probation officer and the probationer and to subordinate multiple or conflicting influences.

Frequently I have had occasion to solicit assistance from local probation workers, particularly in rural counties. In some cases, it has seemed advisable to request probationers to visit a local probation office frequently. Of course, the cooperating official should not be expected to do a lot of reporting or investigating. This arrangement so far has seemed to be especially useful in cases where alcoholic tendencies appear to be part of the problem and where referral to an Alcoholic Anonymous group has not been feasible. Naturally the value of such an arrangement is largely dependent on the personality of the cooperating official. In my experience, officers of local juvenile courts and common pleas courts have apparently been very willing to assist. This would appear to be a useful arrangement to be used sparingly when there is evident need of more casework and more personal contacts than can be given by the supervising probation officer without assistance.

With probationers as well as with parolees, an important consideration is the matter of securing assistance from unofficial sources—in other words, drawing on available community resources. There are surprising reservoirs of good will in almost any community that can be drawn on to real advantage. One problem of the probation officer is to try to utilize these potential resources to the advantage of his clients.

Conclusion

1. Parole advisers offer opportunities to interpret parole to the public.
2. Parole advisers often serve as a key to other community resources that may be utilized profitably.
3. Some sort of volunteer aide is almost indispensable in areas remote from the home office; a parole adviser can fill this need. Whatever risk may be encountered in the use of an untrained volunteer in an advisory role can usually be controlled by the probation officer.
4. It is usually easy and profitable to establish a working rapport with the adviser.
5. While the adviser relationship in some cases remains a nominal one with little real influence on the parolee, there is often the possibility that the help of an adviser may prove to be a vital, favorable factor in any given case.

Chapter Nine

Parole: Administrative Aspects

IN an earlier chapter, we considered the historical development of parole. Now, we are proceeding to examine some details in the administrative components of parole practice.

Those charged with the administration of parole policy can be said to have four principal functions. The first of these is to select and place prisoners on parole. The second is to aid, supervise, and provide continuing control of parolees in the community, according to conditions previously established. When the parolee has reached a point in his parole experience that supervision is no longer required, the parole board, as its third function authorizes the discharge of the individual from that status. On the other hand, if the parolee violates the terms of his parole, either through a technical violation or the commission of a new crime, then it is the function of the board to determine whether revocation and return to the institution are necessary.

If the selection of candidates for parole is skillful, there is a favorable possibility that the individual will react satisfactorily to community custody and treatment. Where, at the other extreme, paroles are granted indiscriminately to relieve congestion in prisons, then the abuse will be manifested in a poor success rate and a negative public opinion toward parole.

The parole board is generally the policy-making group with regard to parole. Since parole has the dual goal of *protecting society* and *rehabilitating* the offender, there is always the danger that one or the other direction may be overemphasized by board policy.

If the board is solely interested in community protection (and to some extent it is desirable that the board have such an orientation), the parole agent will be directed to stress rigid surveillance and to allow no flexibility regarding conformity to conditions. At the opposite extreme, when rehabilitation becomes the sole consideration, the parole officer may permit the community to be endangered by excesses of misconduct of the parolee, using revocation of parole as an undesirable "last resort" method.

Obviously a balance is desirable. When an individual is unable to withstand the pressures of the community and unable to conform to prescribed community mores, and when he is unable to utilize the counseling his parole officer is ready to provide in the freedom of the community, then it is the function of the parole board to return the parolee to the closed environment of the institution.

On the other hand—as with probation supervision—restraint and restriction without counseling and other indirect services are unlikely to effect any true change in character of the individual.

Variations exist, of course, between the different jurisdictions insofar as the nature of restrictions placed upon the parolee is concerned. Uniformity of parole conditions is both desirable and necessary. The National Council on Crime and Delinquency, the American Correctional Association, and the Council on State Government have strongly recommended the adoption of standardized rules of parole practice. The National Conference on Parole (1956) recognized the need for uniform practices and attempted through its nationwide representation to develop standards which the states may follow in the revision of their own parole policies and procedures.

There now exists, between the states, an Interstate Compact on Parole, which permits the parolee to seek residence and employment in jurisdictions other than the one which incarcerated him, enlarging the opportunities available which may result from a change of employment. A continuing problem, of course, is that of what to do with the individual who has detainers filed pending his release from prison. Should such individuals be granted parole? Can a uniform practice be developed in the United States?

Only as the parole board functions as an integral part of the whole correctional system can it be expected to serve its maximum usefulness.

ORGANIZATION OF PAROLE AUTHORITIES*

The administrative organization of parole authorities is another factor that aids or impedes decision making. Again, there are wide

---

* Task Force Report: *Corrections.* The President's Commission on Law Enforcement and the Administration of Justice, 1967, pp. 65-67.

variations in practice among jurisdictions and also a historical separation between the juvenile and adult fields that persists to this day.

Existing Patterns of Organization

In the adult field, every state has an identifiable and separate parole authority, although in four states the power of these authorities is limited to recommending a disposition to the governor. A sense of the growth of parole in this country can be obtained by a review of the Wickersham Report of 1931 which indicated that twenty states had no parole boards at all. By 1939, the Attorney General's *Survey of Release Procedures* indicated there were still sixteen states in which the governor was the paroling authority.

In forty-one states today, the parole board is an independent agency; in seven states, it is a unit within a larger department of the state; and in two states, it is the same body that regulates correctional institutions. In no jurisdiction in the adult field is the final power to grant or deny parole given to the staff directly involved in the operation of a correctional institution.

The situation in the juvenile field is quite different. The great majority of releasing decisions directly involve the staffs of training schools. This is the case in thirty-four of the fifty states and Puerto Rico. In the other seventeen jurisdictions, boards and agencies are used which to varying degrees, are independent of the training school itself. Table 9-I illustrates the variety of releasing authorities used in those seventeen states.

TABLE 9-I*

TYPES OF PAROLE AUTHORITIES FOR JUVENILES, OTHER THAN TRAINING SCHOOL STAFFS, SEVENTEEN STATES, 1965

Paroling Authority	*Number of Jurisdictions*
Youth authorities	4
Training school board	3
Institutions board	2
Department of Corrections	2
Department of Public Welfare	2
Parole board	2
Board of control	1
Ex officio board	1

* Source: *National Survey of Corrections.*

Independence and Integration

The two dominant patterns of the juvenile and adult fields—the juvenile which centers parole decision making primarily in the institutions, and the adult which centers it in autonomous groups—symbolize two points of view about parole decision making. The basic argument for placing release decisions in the hands of institutional staff is that these workers are most intimately familar with the offender and are responsible for developing programs for him; thus they are most sensitive to the optimum time for release. It is also argued that autonomous boards tend to be unconcerned or insensitive about the problems of institutional programs and the aims of their staffs, that their tendency to be preoccupied with issues apart from the rehabilitative aspects of an individual's treatment leads them to make inappropriate case decisions. Such autonomous groups are often viewed by institutional personnel as unnecessarily complicating decision making and infringing on the "professional judgment" of competent staff.

Division of labor between institutional staff and autonomous releasing authorities is complicated by the growing use of partial release programs, for work, study, or the like. The result may be anomalous as when, for example, an institution decides that an inmate should be allowed to go into the community on a work-release basis and he does well there, but a parole board subsequently decides that he should not be paroled. This can occur because a parole board usually takes into consideration various factors which are less emphasized by institutional officials, such as the disposition of codefendants' cases or his probable behavior in an environment other than the town adjoining the institution, where leisure time will be much less structured.

A major argument against giving the parole decision power to institutional staffs is that they tend to place undue emphasis upon the adjustment of offenders to institutional life. There is a temptation to set release policies to fit the needs of the institution, to control population size, and even to aid in getting rid of problem cases—regardless of whether longer control may be desirable. The opposite, but equally unfortunate, temptation is to use unwarranted extensions of confinement as penalties for petty rule violations. Finally, decision making by institutional staff lends itself to such informal procedures and is so lacking in visibility as to raise questions concerning its capability to maintain fairness or even the appearance of fairness.

There have been a number of attempts to devise organizational means for promoting closer coordination between the staffs of institutional programs and releasing authorities. At one extreme is the integration of the releasing authority within a centralized correctional agency, with the parole board appointed by that agency. Wisconsin and Michigan have had such a system for some years, and Ohio has recently adopted a variant of it for its adult system.

Another way of promoting integration between releasing authorities and correctional systems can be found in the youth authority structures in Illinois, Massachusetts, Ohio, California, and Minnesota. Here the power of release is given to the board that has general control over the entire correctional system, both in institutions and in the community. No serious efforts in recent years have been made to extend such patterns to the adult area.

A third method, used in Alaska, Tennessee, and Maine, is to have the director of corrections serve as chairman of the paroling authority, with the members appointed by the governor. This system may produce better coordination, but the director of corrections usually has so many other responsibilities that he cannot adequately carry parole board duties. To meet this problem, Minnesota has the parole board chairman appointed by and serving at the pleasure of the director of corrections, with other members appointed by the governor. Other states have used coordinating committees, on which parole board members sit with institutional officials, or they house both agencies in the same state department, giving each a great deal of autonomy.

In juvenile parole, where only a few totally independent parole boards exist and there have been no significant efforts to establish more, the main issue is whether there should be a central correctional authority with release power or whether this decision should rest entirely with the institutions. The view of most leading juvenile authorities is that there should be a decision-making body within a central correctional agency of the state that controls all releases to the community as well as returns to institutions. Institutional recommendations and opinions should, in their view, weigh heavily; however, final decisions should rest with the central body.

The principal advantages cited for this system are that it (1) would meet the need, in large multi-institution programs, for maintenance of consistency in policies among institutions or among field offices which make revocation decisions and (2) would minimize policy conflicts that can arise between releasing authorities and institutions. Properly developed, this system also could provide procedural safeguards against capricious or irresponsible decisions.

Such an independent decision-making group within a parent agency seems to be the most effective solution to the problem of coordination within juvenile agencies. It is the one to which the juvenile field is apparently moving and is the alternative to which the adult field also seems to be heading.

Parole Board Personnel

Sound organizational structure is important, but it cannot substitute for qualified personnel. Increasing the competence of parole decision makers clearly deserves high priority for the development of effective correctional programs.

In the juvenile field, staff responsible for the paroling functions are, in most states, persons drawn from central juvenile agencies or juvenile institutions. Thus, the quality of parole personnel is generally related to the level of training and experience required of staffs in the juvenile programs of specific jurisdictions. Improving personnel quality for juvenile parole decision making can be undertaken generally in a straightforward way.

For boards dealing with adult offenders, the problem is more complicated. For example, the National Survey revealed that in four states, in 1965, membership on the parole board was automatically given to those who held certain public offices. In one of these states, the board consisted of the governor, the secretary of state, the state auditor, the state treasurer, and the superintendent of public instruction. Clearly, such ex officio parole board members have neither the time nor the kind of training needed to participate effectively in correctional decision making. Correctional authorities have uniformly advocated the elimination of ex officio members from parole boards.

A more pervasive problem in the adult field is the part-time parole board. At present, twenty-five states have such part-time boards; twenty-three states have full-time boards; and three jurisdictions have a combination of the two. Part-time parole boards are usually found in smaller states; of the twenty-one jurisdictions with the smallest population, nineteen have part-time parole boards. Among the ten largest states, only Illinois has a part-time parole board.

Usually the part-time member can give only a limited amount of time to the job, and almost inevitably part-time parole board members also have business or professional concerns outside the parole field which demand their attention and energy. Even a relatively small correctional system requires a considerable investment in time and energy if careful study and frequent review are to be given to all parole cases and if prompt and considered action is to be taken in parole revocation. It would appear that a full-time releasing authority should be the objective of every jurisdiction. Even in smaller correctional systems, there is enough work generally to occupy the full-time attention of board members. An alternative to the complete replacement of the part-time parole board members in states with very small populations is to supplement them with parole examiners, a concept discussed in more detail in a subsequent section.

Appointment of Board Members

One of the most critical issues in obtaining qualified parole board members is the method of their appointment. Table 9-II shows the methods by which adult parole board members were appointed in 1965. As indicated there, parole board members in thirty-nine states were appointed by governors.

In many jurisdictions, highly competent individuals have been appointed to parole boards, and some have gained experience

TABLE 9-II*

METHOD OF APPOINTMENT TO ADULT PAROLE BOARDS, 50 STATES AND PUERTO RICO, 1965

Appointment Officer or Agency	*Number of Jurisdictions*
Governor	39
State officials	4
Corrections agency	4
Ex officio	4

* Source: *National Survey of Corrections.*

through service for many years. But in 1965, parole board members in forty-four jurisdictions in the United States were serving terms of six years or less. It is not unusual to have new parole board members appointed whenever there is a change in a state administration. On some occasions, this system has resulted in the appointment of board members largely on the basis of political affiliations without regard to qualification for making parole decisions.

To avoid this situation, Michigan and Wisconsin have adopted a "merit system" for appointment of parole board members. Appointees are required to have a college degree in one of the behavioral sciences and also experience in correctional work. Some have previously held important positions in correctional institutions or in field supervision.

Other steps can be taken to help insure the appointment of parole board members with requisite education and training. Maine, California, and New Jersey outline some qualification requirements in their laws. Florida requires that appointees pass an examination in penology and criminal justice, administered by experts in these fields. The system of making appointments from a list of candidates nominated by committees of qualified persons, as used in the appointment of judges in some jurisdictions, could be adapted to the parole setting.

Qualifications and Training of Members

The nature of the decisions to be made in parole requires persons who have broad academic backgrounds, especially in the behavioral sciences, and who are aware of how parole operates within the context of a total correctional process. It is vital that board members know the kinds of individuals with whom they are dealing and the many institutional and community variables relating to decisions to be made. The rise of statistical aids to decision making and increased responsibilities to meet due process requirements make it even more essential that board members be sufficiently well-trained to make discriminating judgments about such matters.

The number of persons with the requisite skills is presently quite limited. Training programs designed especially for parole board members are badly needed. An effort in this direction was the National Parole Institute's training programs. Supported by a grant from the Office of Juvenile Delinquency between 1962 and 1965, the institutes provided a series of week-long intensive training programs for parole decision makers and developed useful publications and guides. Programs of this type need to be expanded and maintained on a regular basis.

Another device to aid in improving parole decision making is the use of professional parole examiners to conduct hearings and interviews for the parole board, which delegates to them the power to make certain kinds of decisions within the policies fixed by the board. Under this system, a parole board can concern itself with broad policy questions, directly pass on a limited number of specific cases, and act as an appellate body on the decisions of its examiners.

California now has examiners in both its adult and youth authorities. The U.S. Board of Parole has recently appointed an examiner. The decision-making responsibility given to these persons varies according to the system. Experience thus far indicates that the use of such officers could be greatly expanded.

The major argument for this approach is that it permits the development of a corps of professional examiners who have the background and skills necessary to perform the complex tasks involved. At the same time, it frees the parole board to carry out functions that should not be delegated. Another argument for this system is that professional examiners with tenure, training, and experience in the correctional field would be able to bridge more effectively the gap between parole boards and institutions.

The use of examiners would also reduce the need for constantly increasing the size of parole boards to meet increasing work load. One state now has a parole board of ten members; in others, seven-member boards are not uncommon. With examiners a parole board would perhaps need no more than five members. As noted, in those states where part-time boards were still retained, the professional hearing examiner would be particularly useful.

One objection to use of examiners is that inmates wish to confront decision-making authorities directly. However, the limited experience to date indicates that this need not be a serious problem if examiners are given prestige and authority.

For data on parent agencies responsible for administering services in the fifty states and Puerto Rico, see Table 9-III at the end of this chapter.

PAROLE RULES AND REGULATIONS*

One of the origins of parole is the eighteenth century ticket-of-leave, which played an important part in the British administration of Australia as a penal settlement for transported criminals. The ticket-of-leave was a declaration by the Governor of Australia which exempted a convict from further servitude and permitted him to seek private employment within a specified district.

The English Penal Servitude Act of 1853, which gave legal status to the ticket-of-leave system, substituted imprisonment for transportation and specified the length of time that prisoners had to serve before becoming eligible for conditional release on a "license to be at large." The license was granted with the following conditions:

1. The power of revoking or altering the license of a convict will most certainly be exercised in the case of misconduct.
2. If, therefore, he wishes to retain the privilege which by his

---

* Reprinted by permission of the National Probation and Parole Association. Nat R. Arluke: A summary of parole rules. *NPPA Journal*, 2(No. 1):6-14, Jan. 1956. Footnotes are omitted.

good behavior under penal discipline he has obtained, he must prove by his subsequent conduct that he is really worthy of Her Majesty's clemency.

3. To produce a forfeiture of the license, it is by *no* means necessary that the holder should be convicted of any new offense. If he associates with notoriously bad characters, leads an idle or dissolute life, or has no visible means of obtaining an honest livelihood, etc., it will be assumed that he is about to relapse into crime, and he will be at once apprehended and recommitted to prison under his original sentence.

One Hundred Years Ago

Prisoners released under the Act were not supervised, and it did not take long before everyone realized that the only effects of the Act were confusion and disorder. A system of regular supervision and uniform procedure was urged, with prescribed rules and regulations. This was developed in the 1850's in Ireland, where the "license to be at large" was granted to a convict "from the day of his liberation under this order" for the remaining time of his sentence, except that it could be "immediately forfeited by law" if he were to be "convicted of some indictable offense within the United Kingdom" before the expiration of his sentence, or if it should "please Her Majesty sooner to revoke or alter" the license. It was noted also that "This license is given subject to the conditions endorsed upon the same, upon the breach of any of which it will be liable to be revoked, whether such breach is followed by conviction or not."

The conditions referred to were the following:

1. The holder shall preserve this license and produce it when called upon to do so by a magistrate or police officer.
2. He shall abstain from any violations of the law.
3. He shall not habitually associate with notoriously bad characters, such as reported thieves and prostitutes.
4. He shall not lead an idle and dissolute life, without means of obtaining an honest livelihood.
5. If the license is forfeited or revoked in consequence of a conviction of any felony, he will be liable to undergo a term of penal servitude equal to that portion of his term which remained unexpired when his license was granted.

6. Each convict coming to reside in Dublin City or in the County of Dublin will, within three days after his arrival, report himself at the Police Office, . . . where he will receive instructions as to his further reporting himself.

7. Each convict residing in the provinces will report himself to the constabulary station of his locality within three days after his arrival and subsequently on the first of each month.

8. A convict must not change his locality without notifying the change to the locality to which he is about to proceed.

9. Any infringement of these rules by the convict will cause to be assumed that he is leading an idle, irregular life and thereby entail a revocation of his license.

Conditionally released prisoners were expected to inform their employers of their criminal record; if they failed to do so, the head of the police was responsible for transmitting the information.

That was one hundred years ago. Consider, for a moment, advances in the welfare of other groups which, like the parolee group, are made up of the scorned, the rejected, the handicapped —say, the mentally ill, or religious and racial minorities, or the economically backward. Compare changes in attitude toward these with any changes, if any, toward the parolee. Compare parole regulations of one hundred years ago with those of today.

Fundamental Questions

By and large, parole rules have continued pretty much as they were a century ago. Does this mean that they are satisfactorily meeting their purpose and therefore should not be changed? Does it suggest that there may have been changes in emphasis and interpretation, less obvious but perhaps more important than the fact that the letter of parole rules has changed very little?

Some other questions arise from an examination of parole rules: How are parole rules used? As guides? As coercive devices? As casework treatment tools? Do parole rules help in the community adjustment of the parolee, or do they plague him as continuous reminders of his "second class citizen" status? Are they pitched so high that parole adjustment is unattainable in many cases? Can we establish parole rules which give evidence of awareness of community pressures on the released offender—rules and conditions tailored, as close as possible, to the needs of the parolee and his community?

If it is conceded that parole rules and conditions do not have to be immutable, how can they be modified or amended in specific cases? Should individual modifications be made by the parole officer, or by the supervisor, or by the central office, or by the parole board?

You may have read in *Confidential* magazine (Jan. 1955) an article entitled "Parole—Freedom on a String." The subheading was, "What good is a system that censors your job, bars you from women, and puts you back under arrest without cause? Parole can be an engine of torture that succeeds in redoubling hatred of law, cops, and penal 'experts.' " A large part of the public still accepts that kind of statement as gospel truth, and we continually see its imprint when we interview prospective parolees, especially those who have had no prior experience with parole. Does this not suggest the need for an analysis of our public relations programs so that we may erase or at least begin to minimize these erroneous impressions?

Frequency of Parole Rules

The chart on pages 346 and 347 summarizes the policies of forty-eight of the states in regard to parolee behavior. The twenty-four regulations listed include all that refer explicitly to restrictions on behavior. (However, two of them—17 and 19—really indicate parole board action in the event that the parolee violates his parole.)

The number of regulations indicated for a state on the chart does not necessarily coincide with the actual number in the state's official document handed to the parolee upon release from prison. In some states the references to both liquor and narcotics usage, for example, are combined as a single regulation; and in many states the document may include statements which interpret parole board administrative policy as distinct from those which describe what is and what is not allowed in parolee behavior.

It must be borne in mind, too, that a blank in the chart means only that the regulation is not printed in the state's set of rules; it does not mean that the conduct referred to is ignored in practice. This gap is comprehensively covered in many states by the parolee's signifying his agreement to "abide by such special conditions of parole as may be imposed" on him by his parole officer.

In a few states the number of stipulations about parolee behavior and parole board administrative policy exceeds twenty. How many of these the parolee can reasonably be expected to remember is a good question. Because of this, one of these states includes a regulation requiring the parolee to read the regulations periodically during the entire parole period!

Not a single one of the twenty-four parole regulations appears in every one of the documents of the states mentioned.

The regulations listed below, as in the chart, are in order of frequency.

1. *Use of liquor.* Completely prohibited in forty-one states; permitted, but not to excess, in four states—Florida, Idaho, Michigan, and New Jersey. No restrictions in Missouri, Virginia, and West Virginia.

2. *Association or correspondence with persons of poor reputation.* "Persons of poor reputation"are specified generally as other parolees, ex-convicts, inmates of any penal institution, persons having a criminal or police record, and so forth. New Hampshire policy draws a fine line between association with such persons and correspondence with them, prohibiting the former but allowing the latter when permission has first been granted by the parole officer. In thirty-eight states, both forms of conduct are prohibited; in three other states—Colorado, Michigan, and Minnesota—both are allowed after permission is granted. In six states—Iowa, Montana, New Mexico, Virginia, West Virginia, and Wyoming—the regulations ignore the matter entirely.

3. *Change of employment or residence.* In thirty-nine states, permission to make such a change must first be obtained through the parole officer. It need not be obtained in nine states—Alabama, Arizona, California, Montana, New Mexico, Oklahoma, Vermont, West Virginia, and Wyoming.

4. *Monthly reports.* In thirty-eight states the parolee must fill out a monthly report blank and send it to a central agency. He is

	Alabama	Arizona	Arkansas	California	Colorado	Connecticut	Delaware	Florida	Georgia	Idaho	Illinois	Indiana	Iowa	Kansas	Kentucky	Louisiana	Maine
1. Liquor usage	2	2	2	2	2	2	2	4	2	4	2	2	2	2	2	2	2
2. Association or correspondence with "undesirables"	2	2	2	2	1	2	2	2	2	2	2	2		2	2	2	2
3. Change of employment or residence			1		1	1	1	1	1	1	1	1	1	1	1	1	1
4. Filing report blanks		3	3	3		3		3	3	3	3	3	3	3	3	3	3
5. Out-of-state travel	1		1		1		1		1	1	1	1	2		1	1	1
6. Contracting a new marriage	1		1	1	1	1		1		1	1	1	1	1	1		1
7. First arrival report	3		3	3	3	3		3	3	3	3	3	3		3	3	3
8. Operation and ownership of motor vehicles			1	1	1	1		1		1	1	1	1		1		1
9. Narcotic usage	2		2	2	2		2	2	2	2	2			2	2	2	2
10. Support dependents	3			3				3	3	3					3	3	3
11. Possession, sale, or use of weapons; obtaining hunting license			2	2	1	2		1	2	2	2	2	2	1	1		1
12. Travel out of county or community			1	1	1			1	1	1	1	1	1				
13. Agree to waive extradition	3				3			3	3	3					3		3
14. Indebtedness				1						1							
15. Curfew					6						10:30						11:00
16. Civil rights	1			2	2						2						2
17. "Street time" credit if returned as P.V.																	5
18. Gambling		2						2					2				
19. No "street time" credit if convicted of felony					5												
20. Airplane license				1													1
21. Report if arrested					3												3
22. Treatment for venereal disease								3									
23. Church attendance														3			
24. Enlistment in armed forces																	

KEY—1. Allowed, but permission must first be obtained. 2. Prohibited. 3. Compulsory.

Maryland	Massachusetts	Michigan	Minnesota	Mississippi	Missouri	Montana	Nebraska	Nevada	New Hampshire	New Jersey	New Mexico	New York	North Carolina	North Dakota	Ohio	Oklahoma	Oregon	Pennsylvania	Rhode Island	South Carolina	South Dakota	Tennessee	Texas	Utah	Vermont	Virginia	Washington	West Virginia	Wisconsin	Wyoming
2	2	4	2	2		2	2	2	2	4	2	2	2	2	2	2	2	2	2	2	2	2	2	2	2		2		2	2
2	2	1	1	2	2		2	2	2/1	2		2	2	2	2	2	2	2	2	2	2	2	2	2	2		2		2	
1	1	1	1	1	1		1	1	1	1		1	1	1	1		1	1	1	1	1	1	1	1		1	1		1	
	3	3	3	3	3	3	3	3	3		3			3	3	3	3	3		3	3	3	3		3	3	3		3	3
1	1	1	1	1	1	2	1		1	1		1	1		1	1	1	1	1	1		1		1			1	1	1	1
1	1	1	1		1		1	1	1	1		1		1	1	1	1	1	1		1				1		1		1	
3		3	3	3	3		3		3	3	3	3			3	3	3	3	3	3		3	3				3			
1	1	1	1		1		1	1	1	1		1		1	1		1	1	1	1						1		1	1	
	2	2		2					2	2		2			2	2	2	2	2	2		1	2	2			2			
3	3	3		3	3		3		3			3	3		3	3	3	3		3				3	3	3	3		3	
1	1				1				1	1		1				2	2	1	1						2	1	2		1	
		1	1		1		1	1				1	1	1	1	1		1	1	1			1			1	1			
			3		3		3		3			3			3	3		3	3	3						3	3			
		1	1				1	1	1	1				1			1												1	
		6						6	6			6		6																
												2			2															
5										5							5						5			5				
							2														2									
										5		5			5															
																		1												
										3																				
																		3												
							3																							
															1															

4. Allowed but not to excess. 5. May be received. 6. "Reasonable hour."

not required to do so in ten states—Alabama, Colorado, Delaware, Maryland, New Jersey, New York, North Carolina, Rhode Island, Utah, and West Virginia.

5. *Out-of-state travel.* Allowed, after permission is granted, in thirty-four states; prohibited by Iowa and Montana. No restrictions in twelve states.

6. *Permission to marry.* In thirty-three states a parolee desiring to marry must first obtain the consent of the parole officer. No such requirement is specified in fifteen states.

7. *First arrival report.* In thirty-three states the parolee is required to report to his parole officer immediately upon arriving at his destination after release from prison; in fifteen states he is not required to do so.

8. *Operation and ownership of motor vehicles.* Denied in thirty states, unless approval of parole representative is obtained; no restriction in eighteen states.

9. *Use of narcotics.* Prohibited in twenty-eight states; permitted in one state, Tennessee, when approved by a physician. No restriction mentioned in nineteen states.

10. *Support dependents.* In twenty-seven states the parolee must promise to support his family. No regulation of this sort is specified in the printed rules of twenty-one states.

11. *Possession, sale, or use of weapons; obtaining a hunting license.* Prohibited in twelve states; allowed, after permission is granted by parole officer, in fifteen states. No restriction in twenty-one states.

12. *Travel out of the county or community.* Allowed in twenty-five states upon permission of parole officer; no restriction mentioned in twenty-three states.

13. *Agreement to waive extradition.* This is a condition of parole in nineteen states. No mention of it is made in twenty-nine states.

14. *Indebtedness.* In eleven states the parolee is allowed to incur a debt only if he has the permission of the parole officer. There is no such restriction in thirty-seven states.

15. *Curfew.* In six states the parolee is required to be at home for the night at a "reasonable hour." Curfew for parolees is speci-

fied as 10:30 in Illinois and 11:00 in Maine. There is no curfew regulation of any sort in forty states.

16. *Civil rights.* Civil rights, including suffrage and the right to hold office, are lost to the parolee in six states; in one state, Alabama, they may be restored upon application and approval of the request. In forty-one states, no explicit mention is made of the civil right status of the parolee.

17. *"Street time" credit for parole violator.* In six states the parolee who is returned to prison for violation of parole receives credit for all or part of the time he has been on parole. Such credit is not allowed or is not mentioned in the provisions of forty-two states.

18. *Gambling.* Prohibited to the parolee in five states; no restriction mentioned in forty-three states.

19. *Conviction for felony while on parole.* In four states the parolee is warned that if he is returned to prison because of a felony he commits while on parole, he will be deprived of all "street time" credit. No mention of this is made in the regulations of forty-four states.

20. *Airplane license.* In three states—California, Maine, and Pennsylvania—the parolee must obtain his parole officer's permission to apply for a license that would allow him to operate an airplane. Not mentioned in forty-five states.

21. *Report if arrested.* In three states—Colorado, Maine, and New Jersey—the parolee is required, if he is arrested, to report the arrest to his parole officer. Not mentioned in forty-five states.

22. *Treatment for venereal disease.* In two states—Florida and Pennsylvania—a parolee who has a venereal disease is compelled to take treatment for it as a condition of remaining on parole. Not mentioned in forty-six states.

23. *Church attendance.* In two states—Kansas and Nebraska—the parolee must attend church regularly as a condition of remaining on parole. Not mentioned in forty-six states.

24. *Enlistment in armed forces.* In one state, Ohio, the parolee is required by regulation to obtain permission of the parole officer before applying for enlistment in the armed forces. Not mentioned in the regulations of forty-seven states.

Some Conclusions

Excessive Number of Regulations in Some States

As suggested above, many of the documents listing "general conditions of parole" contain so large a number of regulations that the value of the parolee's signature on the parole agreement is questionable.

The documents are further weakened when they include, as many do, quasi-legal interpretations of parole board policy. The distinction between *law* and parole board *rule* should be clearly drawn in parole rule documents.

It hardly seems necessary to impose a regulation on conduct already governed by the criminal code. For example, if a state already has a law imposing penalties for the illegal sale or use of narcotics (and most states do have such a law), why make it, superfluously, a parole regulation?

General Impracticality of Regulations

Many of the regulations are not realistic and do not lend themselves to practical enforcement. The complete prohibition of the use of liquor by parolees in forty-one states forces us into an unrealistic position that breeds violations and contempt for the value of parole supervision. It seems to me that a "Ten Commandments" form of agreement would provide the framework for more intelligent and functional supervision of parolees.

Lack of Uniformity

The lack of uniformity is, of course the most obvious defect of parole regulations. Consider, for example, the regulation which requires the prospective parolee to agree to waive his right to an extradition hearing in the event of his arrest in another state. There is real question about the legality of this regulation. Furthermore, if the regulation were used either universally or not at all, there would not be the confusion and expense that now result from the use of Form A-3, "Agreement of Prisoner When Permitted to Go to Another State," issued by the Interstate Commission on Crime in the twenty-nine states where the extradition waiver is not included in the list of parole rules.

Some uniformity of regulations should exist among *all* states, if for no other reason than that the number of parolees living in states other than the one in which they were sentenced is increasing all the time.

Parole regulations in the fifty states should be carefully reexamined—not separately in each state but in a coordinated fashion. Lack of uniformity, impracticality, and multiplicity of regulations are not the only defects. Others are redundancy, complexity, legal jargon, inconsistency, and irrelevancy. All of them should be eliminated in the interest of better practice.

THE INTERSTATE PAROLE AND PROBATION COMPACT*

Since 1934, when Congress first authorized agreements or compacts among the states "for cooperative effort and mutual assistance in the prevention of crime," each one of our fifty states has become a full-fledged partner in crime control through the adoption of the Interstate Compact for the Supervision of Parolees and Probationers. Not even the United States Constitution—an agreement among all the states, ratified by all the states—can claim more signatories to a formal compactual agreement calling for coordinated effort and cooperative practices.

Prior to the formulation of the compact, so-called sundown paroles were the order of the day in many sections of the country, and theoretic parolees literally roved the land with no supervision, formal or informal. Today, these men by the thousands are under full, legally binding supervision for the protection of our citizens. Cases constantly arise where, due to family relationships in another state, better opportunities for work and a more conducive atmosphere for rehabilitation will be found if the prospective probationer or parolee can be permitted to transfer to another jurisdiction. But the rehabilitative value of such a move would often

---

* Reprinted in part by permission of *Federal Probation*. B. E. Crihfield: The Interstate Parole and Probation Compact. *Federal Probation, 17*(No. 2), June 1954. Footnotes are omitted.

be lost unless there is adequate supervision, advice, and assistance to accompany the released person when he crosses the state line. The function, then, of the compact is twofold: (1) It serves as protection to the community through providing effective supervision and by insuring a means of retaking offenders who have violated the terms of their conditional freedom and (2) it encourages the rehabilitation of parolees and probationers by permitting their transfer to a receptive environment where their chances of success may be greatest.

Statistics gathered by the Council of State Governments indicate that there are in the neighborhood of 12,000 cases handled in the course of a year under the compact, with some five or six times as many parolees being reported under supervision as there are probationers. These figures are admittedly incomplete, especially with respect to probation, and additional unknown numbers of cases do not enter into the available statistics. Turnover by virtue of new cases and terminations, which roughly balance one another, amounts to approximately 25 per cent per year.

How the Compact Works

Procedure under the Interstate Compact for the Supervision of Parolees and Probationers involves the following steps:

1. Any state may permit a parolee or probationer to go to any other state (the so-called receiving state) if "such person is in fact a resident of or has his family residing within the receiving state and can obtain employment there" *or* if "the receiving state consents to such person being sent there" even though the residence qualification cannot be met.

2. The state to which an interstate parolee or probationer is transferred agrees under the compact to exercise the same care and treatment of such a person as its own state standards require for supervising its own probationers and parolees.

3. If a state desires to retake a probationer or parolee who has left its jurisdiction under the terms of the compact, officers of that state may apprehend the person in another state without any formalities other than establishing the authority and proving the identity of the person to be arrested. The states have expressly

waived all legal requirements to obtain extradition of fugitives from justice in returning such persons, and the individual parolee or probationer is also required to sign a waiver of extradition as a condition precedent to his transfer to another state.

4. Rules, regulations, and forms designed to standardize procedures and foster efficient administration have been developed and are in use by the compacting states as they process out-of-state parole and probation under the compact.

Considerable interest has recently been shown in expanding the compact to include the District of Columbia and the territories and possessions of the United States. A bill granting the consent of Congress to such additional joinder was introduced toward the end of the 82nd Congress but could not be acted upon before adjournment. Subsequently, the administrators of the compacting states adopted a resolution unanimously favoring the inclusion of these additional jurisdictions as "a forward and necessary step" in the development of the compact.

Problems Under the Compact

An excellent job has been done by the states in making the compact an effective cooperative instrument. However, it would be less than candid to maintain that problems do not arise. A basic difficulty lies in the fact that parole and probation systems vary to a marked degree among the states. Despite the fact that lines of authority are delineated clearly by the specific language of the compact, there is bound to be some difficulty when two jurisdictions with differing policies both have certain authority and responsibility with respect to the same parolee or probationer.

Another problem arises because of the lack of facilities and personnel in some states. The addition of even a few interstate cases to an already heavy caseload may prove difficult to the administrator who has two few tools and too few workers at his disposal. This, of course, is a problem that needs to be met basically and even if there were no interstate agreement operation. As a matter of fact, it may well be that the underlying obligation implicit in the compact—to do the job adequately in a spirit of co-operation—can serve well in bringing up the standards of all the states. Moreover, the interchange of information that occurs constantly by mail and frequently by means of regional and national meetings will help to iron out administrative difficulties.

Perhaps the major problem under the compact is related to decisions with respect to termination of out-of-state parole or probation. It is not uncommon for a receiving state to notify a sending state that a violation has occurred, only to learn that the sending state either cannot or will not return the violator. The reason may be that the sending state does not consider the violation to be so serious as to warrant a return, or again there simply may not be enough funds available to cover the cost of retaking the violator if the distance involved is great. In either case the result is unfortunate, for the only effective sanction in case of failure of a person to meet the conditions of his parole or probation is withdrawal of the privilege. The receiving state is put in the position of supervising a person who would be placed in jail if he were one of that state's own cases, or of letting the man go about without supervision.

The Compact and Probation

The compact has been less extensively used for probation than it has for parole. Several times as many parolees are under interstate supervision than are probationers. The reason for this is not hard to find. Parole as a governmental function is centralized commonly in some agency of the state. The compact administrator in most states is the person actually responsible for parole operations. Not so with respect to probation, which is administered most frequently on a decentralized basis through the courts. On occasion, some local probation officials have denied the legality of the compact on the grounds that their political subdivision had taken no action to ratify it! The compact obviously applies no matter what particular probation system is followed in any given state.

A partial solution to the weakness of probation supervision under the compact has been found by many states. In some instances, there is an integrated parole and probation agency at the state level. In other states, there is a separate state agency handling probation, and the necessary coordination can be secured through the compact administrator and through the designation of one state official who will receive all out-of-state probation correspondence. Even in the case of virtually complete decentralization, the problem is not insoluble. California, for example, has enacted legislation requiring that all probation matters involving another state be channeled through the compact administrator, and this system has worked reasonably well. In the final analysis, education is the prime necessity if the compact is to work effectively and to serve fully in the field of probation. The appropriate judicial and administrative authorities responsible for probation, though they be numerous and separate in any state, should be thoroughly familiar with the existence of the compact and should know what it can and cannot accomplish. A concerted effort should be made in every state to develop the required methods of intercommunication and the procedures which will properly carry out the provisions of the compact.

Constitutionality of the Compact

The constitutional validity of the compact has withstood many attacks, and it has always been upheld when under court scrutiny. In such states as California, Arkansas, Washington, and New York there have been important decisions handed down by the highest state courts. It is perhaps unfortunate that no definitive ruling has ever been set forth by the United States Supreme Court, principally because no parole or probation violator has ever seen fit to carry his case that far. Because of this, there will undoubtedly continue to be occasional court cases touching on the constitutionality of the compact. There is no reason to fear that they will successfully attack this well-tested interstate agreement.

The Compact Administrators Association

Since 1946, the official administrators of the compact have been formally bound together into a group known as an Association of Administrators of the Interstate Compact for the Supervision of Parolees and Probationers. All members of the association meet together at least once a year to vote upon matters of policy and any proposals for revision in the rules and regulations that may have arisen. The burden of work for, and on behalf of, the association is devolved upon the executive committee and upon a council of five members. The council acts as a standing committee on rules, regulations, and policies under the compact. In order to secure uniformity in procedure and practice, any administrator may request information at any time as to the council's opinion on the compact's provisions, rules, and regulations, or on administrative practice. Upon recommendation of the association's council, measures may be submitted to the full membership during the year for a vote by written ballot.

During recent years, and at the request of the compact administrators, the Council of State Governments has served as secretariat to the association. The secretariat maintains current rosters of state officials responsible for the operation of the compact, publishes reports and documents of interest to the administrators, arranges and services the annual meetings of the association, drafts proposed language for compact amendments and rule changes, and performs such other services as may be requested.

In 1951, at the request of the administrators, the secretariat developed a looseleaf manual for the official use of those who administer the compact. It consists of separate pages indicating the specific arrangements that should be made with each individual state. A section is included which digests the interpretation of policies as determined by the association's council and as laid down at the annual meetings; tables which show state practices in certain areas of operation are presented. Another section contains the text of all changes in, or additions to, the rules, regulations, and forms in use under the compact; amendments to the compact itself are also shown. A special appendix on legal references contains the text of all currently reported opinions of attorneys general and important court decisions. Other appendices are used to insert various miscellaneous materials which may be of interest to the administrators.

Out-of-state Incarceration Amendment

The purpose of the basic parole and probation compact is to supervise persons in another state *outside* prison walls. An amendment to the compact has now been developed which would permit the supervision of violators *within* a prison. The problem of parole and probation violators is especially serious when such persons have been allowed to go out of state under the compact. Usually there are only two alternatives to follow: either leave the violator free of effective control or bring him back to the sending state. The former is of course undesirable, and the latter may be quite expensive.

Because of this situation, a number of administrators asked that provision be made in the compact to permit violators to be incarcerated in the receiving state rather than going to the difficulty and expense of returning them to the sending state. Such an amendment was drafted and is now known as the Out-of-state Incarceration Amendment. It is to be effective only among such of the states as may specifically ratify it. Under its terms, incarceration of a parolee or probationer may be had in the state where he violates the conditions of his parole or probation *if* the sending state wishes. Since states do not enforce the penal laws of other jurisdictions, the amendment appoints the receiving or asylum state to be the agent of the sending state for purposes of such incarceration and provides that the sending state shall retain ultimate jurisdiction over the prisoner.

The Out-of-state Incarceration Amendment was prepared in 1951 and was considered by several legislatures meeting in that year. The states of Connecticut, Idaho, and Utah ratified the amendment during 1951 and, at the present time, it is effective only as between these states. Rules and regulations to implement the operation of the amendment were perfected during 1952, and it is expected that additional states will consider the enactment of legislation to ratify the amendment at their regular 1953 sessions. Since there has been such a limited amount of time elapsed since the development of the admendment, there is no record of experience to report as yet. It is felt, however, that the amendment will provide an additional instrument for the effective supervision of parolees and probationers by states which wish to adopt this approach. It is also felt that the amendment has been so carefully drawn, and the rules so drafted, that there is little danger of its being stricken down by the courts.

Conclusion

The interstate Compact for the Supervision of Parolees and Probationers has now been in operation for some thirty-five years. From an initial nucleus of about twenty cooperating states, it has gradually grown to the point where every state has fully and officially ratified the basic agreement. The state officials responsible for the operation of the compact have developed their own association which goes far toward smoothing out the rough edges that exist in any complex procedure involving intergovernmental cooperation. The administrators are increasingly interested in working out new and supplementary instruments to enhance the effectiveness of the compact, and in addition have done considerable work on related subjects which ramify beyond the strict operations of the compact. A current project has to do with cooperative returns of prisoners by one state on behalf of one or more other states. Efforts are now being made to expand the compact so as to include the District of Columbia and the territories and possessions of the United States. In spite of difficulties and certain gaps in the effectiveness of the compact, such as in the field of probation, the compact has proved its utility beyond question and should become an even more useful device in the coming years.

PAROLE AND THE DETAINER SYSTEM*

A detainer may be defined as a warrant filed against a person already in custody with the purpose of insuring that he will be available to the authority which has placed the detainer. Wardens of institutions holding men who have detainers on them invariably recognize these warrants and notify the authorities placing them of the impending release of the prisoner. Such detainers may be placed by various authorities under varying conditions, for example, when an escaped prisoner or a parolee commits a new crime and is imprisoned in another state; or when a man not previously imprisoned commits a series of crimes in different jurisdictions.

While it would seem proper that authorities in quest of a violator of the law should have every assistance in returning him to their jurisdiction, nevertheless the detainer system now operates to the detriment of society all too often. The difficulties inherent in the existing detainer system affect the judge, the institutional officials, the paroling authorities, and the individual himself.

The prison administrator is thwarted in his efforts toward re-

* Reprinted by permission of the Council of State Governments. From *Suggested State Legislation Program for 1957*, pp. 74-85. Footnotes are omitted.

habilitation. The inmate who has a detainer against him is filled with anxiety and apprehension and frequently does not respond to a training program. He often must be kept in close custody, which bars him from treatment such as trustyships, moderations of custody, and opportunity for transfer to farms and work camps. In many jurisdictions, he is not eligible for parole; there is little hope for his release after an optimum period of training and treatment, when he is ready for return to society with an excellent possibility of other detainers. A rather long sentence may be indicated, but the judge hesitates to give such a sentence if the offender is going to serve subsequent sentences or if he stands to lose the privilege of parole because of a detainer. The incidental first offender may, and sometimes does, serve years in prison because he has violated the law in several jurisdictions, although only a short sentence or probation would accomplish the necessary rehabilitation. It seems obvious that proper sentencing, as well as proper correctional treatment, is not possible until the detainer system is modified. Ironically, society is the real loser in collecting its debt from the offender. Much money is spent in extra periods of imprisonment, and embittered offenders become recidivists, pyramiding the expense of law enforcement.

Recommended Principles

In 1948, the Council of State Governments served as secretariat for a group known as the Joint Committee on Detainers, upon which there was representation from the following organizations: Parole and Probation Compact Administrators Association, National Association of Attorneys General, National Conference of Commissioners on Uniform State Laws, American Prison Association, and the Section on Criminal Law of the American Bar Association. The Joint Committee's report included the following "statement of aims or guiding principles" which should govern the actions of prosecuting authorities, sentencing judges, prison officials, and parole authorities to the end that detainers will not hamper the administration of correction programs and the effective rehabilitation of criminals.

1. *Every effort should be made to accomplish the disposition of detainers as promptly as possible.* This is desirable whether the

detainer has been filed against an individual who has not yet been imprisoned or against an inmate of a penal institution. Prompt disposition of detainers is a proper goal, whether the detainer has been filed by a local prosecutor, a state prison, a parole board, or a federal official. Detainers lodged on suspicion should not be permitted to linger without action.

2. *There should be assurance that any prisoner released to stand trial in another jurisdiction will be returned to the institution from which he was released.* An important cause of long-standing detainers is the presence of unsettled charges pending against a prisoner held by another jurisdiction. If the charges appear to be valid and if the individual is to be brought to trial before completion of his sentence, then it is essential that the institution holding him in custody be assured of his return after the trial. Unless there is such assurance, many jurisdictions will understandably hesitate to cooperate.

3. *Prison and parole authorities should take prompt action to settle detainers which have been filed by them.* Prison officials and parole boards recognize that detainers create serious problems with respect to prisoners under their jurisdictions. Therefore, when such authorities file detainers against prisoners in other jurisdictions, they should cooperate fully to effect a prompt settlement of all detainers. They should promptly give notice as to whether they insist that the prisoner be returned at the end of his present sentence, or whether they will agree to a concurrent parole. Every effort should be made to cooperate in planning effective rehabilitation programs for the prisoner.

4. *No prisoner should be penalized because of a detainer pending against him unless a thorough investigation of the detainer has been made and it has been found valid.* It should be the duty of prison officials, parole authorities, and judges to make such investigations before denying the prisoner privileges, probation, or parole, or before imposing unusually heavy sentences upon the prisoner.

5. *All jurisdictions should observe the principles of interstate comity in the settlement of detainers.* Each jurisdiction should bear its own proper burden of the expenses and effort involved in disposing of charges and settling detainers. There should be full

faith and credit given to the rights of any state or jurisdiction asserting them.

Recent Developments

During 1955 and 1956, the old Joint Committee on Detainers was informally reconstituted under the auspices of the Council of State Governments, and the membership of the committee was augmented by representation from the National Probation and Parole Association and the National Association of County and Prosecuting Attorneys. Operating under the title of "Committee on Detainers and Sentencing and Release of Persons Accused of Multiple Offenses," meetings of the augmented group were held on June 30, 1955; November 25, 1955; and February 10, 1956.

The committee developed and approved three specific proposals dealing with disposition of detainers and noted, for information purposes, an additional proposal with reference to merger of sentence. Then, on April 14, 1956, a larger group was convened to review the draft proposals. The conference was held in New York City and was attended by over sixty persons representing the following areas of interest: state police, prison societies and correctional associations, bar associations, state legislatures, commissions on interstate cooperation, state and local parole and probation boards (including the Interstate Parole and Probation Compact); district attorneys, state corrections and prison officials, state attorneys general, and representatives of the United States Department of Justice also attended the conference.

Several draft proposals were acted upon and approved at the above-mentioned conference. They cover the following subjects:

1. *Disposition of detainers within the state.* This proposal, based substantially on statutes now operative in California and Oregon, makes it possible for a prisoner to initiate disposition of detainers which have been lodged on untried indictments, information, or complaints arising within the state where he is imprisoned.

2. *Agreement on detainers.* This proposal, including an appropriate enabling act, carries into effect the right of the prisoner to initiate disposition of detainers based on untried indictments, information, or complaints arising in other states or from the

Federal Government. It also provides a method whereby prosecuting officials may initiate such action.

3. *Parole to detainer.* This proposed amendment to basic state parole statutes insures that there is adequate authority for parole boards to release prisoners on parole to answer warrants from other jurisdictions.

Disposition of Detainers Within the State

The Intrastate Detainer Statute is designed for use within a single state. Since most state laws already provide methods whereby prosecutors can bring prisoners already under sentence to trial on other outstanding charges, no attempt is made to include such provisions in the suggested act. However, individual states which may not now give sufficient authority to their prosecutors may wish to review their present laws in connection with their study of the present proposal.

The suggested statute is intended to afford a means of permitting the prisoner to clear up detainers which have been lodged against him. It gives him no greater opportunity to escape just convictions, but it does provide a way for him to test the substantiality of detainers placed against him and to secure final judgment on any indictments, informations, or complaints outstanding against him in the state. The result is to permit the prisoner to secure a greater degree of knowledge of his own future and to make it possible for the prison authorities to provide better plans and programs for his treatment.

The proposed statute provides that a prisoner, wishing to clear a detainer based on an outstanding indictment, information, or complaint, may make a request for reasonable time as defined in the statute. The indictment, information, or complaint ceases to be of any further force or effect, and the detainer based thereon is removed. Other provisions of the statute are drafted to make sure that the prisoner does not frustrate the purpose of the law by escape from custody during part of the interval permitted for trial; to make sure that the prisoner has an opportunity to know his rights under the act; and to provide prosecuting officers with information concerning the prisoner's present status before proceeding to press for custody of the prisoner so that trial may be had on the indictment, information, or complaint which forms the basis of the detainer.

Agreement on Detainers

The Agreement on Detainers applies the same principles embodied in the intrastate act to the interstate field. At the present time, there is no means by which a prisoner may initiate proceedings to clear a detainer placed against him from another jurisdiction. This is equally true on an interstate and a federal-state basis. In addition, the only way that a prosecuting official can secure for trial a person already imprisoned in another jurisdiction is by resorting to a cumbersome special contract with the executive authority of the incarcerating state. Because of the difficulty and red tape involved in securing such contracts, they are little used.

The Agreement on Detainers makes the clearing of detainers possible at the instance of the prisoner. In this report, it is the interjurisdictional counterpart of the intrastate statute. It also provides a method whereby prosecuting authorities may secure prisoners incarcerated in other jurisdictions for trial before the expiration of their sentences. At the same time, a governor's right to refuse to make the prisoner available (on public policy grounds) is retained. Since the problems in the detainer field are both intrastate and federal-state, the Agreement on Detainers provides that the United States may become a party thereto. If this is done, the procedures provided in the agreement will be available on both an intrastate and a federal-state level.

Parole to Detainer

Parole contemplates release to the community and hence the term is not properly used for releases on warrants or detainers. However, authority is needed to release prior to expiration of term in the face of detainers. Some parole boards now deny parole when there is an outstanding detainer, sometimes on the ground that they feel they do not have authority to release. The practice should be to dispose of all detainers as early as possible. Using a detainer to deny parole to a prisoner ready for it not only penalizes him unjustly but also delays the pending proceeding and confuses its meaning.

TABLE 9-III

PARENT AGENCY RESPONSIBLE FOR ADMINISTERING SERVICES*
(By States)

States	*Juvenile Detention*	*Juvenile Probation*	*Juvenile Institutions*	*Juvenile Aftercare*
Alabama	local	Dept of Pensions & Security & local	3 separate & indpndnt bds	Dept of Pensions & Security & local
Alaska	Div of Youth & Adult Authority	Div of Youth & Adult Authority	Div of Youth & Adult Authority	Div of Youth & Adult Authority
Arizona	local	local	Bd of Dir of State Insts for Juv	Bd of Dir of State Insts for Juv
Arkansas	local	State DPW & local	4 indpndnt bds	State DPW & local
California	local	local	Youth & Adult Correc Agency	Youth & Adult Correc Agency
Colorado	local	local	Dept of Insts	Dept of Insts
Connecticut	State Juv Ct	State Juv Ct	2 indpndnt bds of trustees	2 indpndnt bds of trustees
Delaware	Youth Serv Comm	local	Youth Serv Comm	Youth Serv Comm
Florida	local	local	Div of Child Trng Schools	Div of Child Trng Schools
Georgia	Dept of Family & Child Serv & local	Dept of Family & Child Serv & local	Dept of Family & Child Serv	Dept of Family & Child Serv
Hawaii	local	local	Dept of Soc Serv	Dept of Soc Serv
Idaho	local	Dept of Health & local	Dept of Educ	Dept of Educ
Illinois	local	local	Youth Comm	Youth Comm
Indiana	local	local	Bd of Correc	Bd of Correc
Iowa	local	local	Bd of Control	Bd of Control
Kansas	local	local	Dept of Soc Wel	Dept of Soc Wel
Kentucky	local	Dept of Child Wel & local	Dept of Child Wel	Dept of Child Wel
Louisiana	local	State DPW & local	Dept of Insts	State DPW

* Some states also have some local services in addition to state services.

PARENT AGENCY RESPONSIBLE FOR ADMINISTERING SERVICES
(By States)

Misdemeanant Probation	*Adult Probation*	*Local Adult Institutions and Jails*	*Adult Institutions*	*Parole*
Bd of Pardons & Paroles & local	Bd of Pardons & Paroles	local	Bd of Correc	Bd of Pardons & Paroles
Div of Youth & Adult Authority	Div of Youth & Adult Authority	Div of Youth & Adult Authority	Div of Youth & Adult Authority	Div of Youth & Adult Authority
none	local	local	Supt of State Prison	Parole Bd
none	Bd of Pardons, Paroles & Prob	local	Penitentiary Comm	Bd of Pardons, Paroles & Prob
local	local	local	Youth & Adult Correc Agency	Youth & Adult Correc Agency
local	Parole Div & local	local	Dept of Insts	Parole Div
Comm on Adult Prob	Comm on Adult Prob	State Jail Administration	3 separate & indpndnt bds	3 separate & indpndnt bds
Dept of Correc	Dept of Correc	(not applicable)	Dept of Correc	Dept of Correc
Prob & Parole Comm	Prob & Parole Comm & local	local	Dept of Correc	Prob & Parole Comm
Bd of Prob & local	Bd of Prob & local	local	Bd of Correc	Parole Bd
local	local	local	Dept of Soc Serv	Dept of Soc Serv
none	Bd of Correc	local	Bd of Correc	Bd of Correc
local	local	local	Dept of Pub Safety	Dept of Pub Safety
local	local	local	Bd of Correc	Bd of Correc
none	Bd of Parole	local	Bd of Control	Bd of Parole
local	Bd of Prob & Parole	local	Office of Dir of Penal Inst	Bd of Prob & Parole
Dept of Correc	Dept of Correc	local	Dept of Correc	Dept of Corr
none	Dept of Insts	local	Dept of Insts	Dept of Insts

TABLE 9-III (continued)

States	*Juvenile Detention*	*Juvenile Probation*	*Juvenile Institutions*	*Juvenile Aftercare*
Maine	local	Dept of Mental Health & Correc & local	Dept of Mental Health & Correc	Dept of Mental Health & Correc
Maryland	State DPW & local	Dept of Parole & Prob & local	DPW	Dept of Parole & Prob & DPW & local
Massachusetts	Youth Serv Bd	Prob Comm & local	Youth Serv Bd	Youth Serv Bd
Michigan	local	local	Dept of Soc Serv	Dept of Soc Serv
Minnesota	local	Dept of Correc & local	Dept of Correc	Dept of Correc
Mississippi	local	local	Bd of Trustees	State DPW & local
Missouri	local	local	Bd of Trng Schools	Bd of Trng Schools
Montana	local	local	Dept of Insts	Dept of Insts
Nebraska	local	local	Dept of Public Insts	Dept of Public Insts
Nevada	local	local	Dept of Health & Wel	Dept of Health & Wel
New Hampshire	Bd of Trustees	Dept of Prob & local	Bd of Trustees	Bd of Trustees
New Jersey	local	local	Dept of Insts & Agencies	Dept of Insts & Agencies
New Mexico	local	local	4 separate bds	local
New York	local	local	Dept of Soc Wel	Dept of Soc Wel
North Carolina	local	local	Bd of Juv Correc	local
North Dakota	local	DPW & local	Bd of Adminis-tration	local
Ohio	local	local	Youth Comm	Youth Comm
Oklahoma	local	local	DPW	DPW
Oregon	local	local	Bd of Control	Bd of Control

Misdemeanant Probation	*Adult Probation*	*Local Adult Institutions and Jails*	*Adult Institutions*	*Parole*
Dept of Mental Health & Correc	Dept of Mental Health & Correc	local	Dept of Mental Health & Correc	Dept of Mental Health & Correc
Dept of Parole & Prob & local	Dept of Parole & Prob & local	local	Dept of Correc	Bd of Parole & Prob
Prob Comm & local	Comm on Prob	local	Dept of Correc	Dept of Correc & local
local	Dept of Correc & local	local	Dept of Correc	Dept of Correc
Dept of Correc & local	Dept of Correc & local	local	Dept of Correc	Dept of Correc
none	Bd of Prob & Parole	local	indpndnt bd	Bd of Prob & Parole
Bd of Prob & Parole & local	Bd of Prob & Parole	local	Dept of Correc	Bd of Prob & Parole
none	Bd of Pardons	local	Dept of Insts	Bd of Pardons
local	District Judges Assn	local	Dept of Public Insts	Bd of Pardons
Dept of Parole & Prob	Dept of Parole & Prob	local	Bd of Prison Commissioners	Dept of Parole & Prob
Dept of Prob & local	Dept of Prob & local	(not applicable)	Bd of Trustees of state prison	Bd of Trustees of state prison
local	local	local	Dept of Insts & Agencies	Dept of Insts & Agencies
Bd of Prob & Parole & local	Bd of Prob & Parole	local	Bd of Dir of state prison	Bd of Prob & Parole
local	local	local	Dept of Correc	Div of Parole
Prob Comm	Prob Comm	local	Prison Dept	Bd of Parole
Dept of Parole & Prob	Dept of Parole & Prob	local	Bd of Administration	Dept of Parole & Prob
local	local	local	Dept of Mental Hyg & Correc	Dept of Mental Hyg & Correc
none	local	local	Bd of Public Affairs	Pardon & Parole Dept
Bd of Parole & Prob & local	Bd of Parole & Prob & local	local	Bd of Control	Bd of Parole & Prob

TABLE 9-III (continued)*

States	*Juvenile Detention*	*Juvenile Probation*	*Juvenile Institutions*	*Juvenile Aftercare*
Pennsylvania	local	local	DPW	local
Rhode Island	Dept of Soc Wel	Dept of Soc Wel	Dept of Soc Wel	Dept of Soc Wel
South Carolina	local	local	Bd of State Indus Schools	Bd of State Indus Schools
South Dakota	local	local	Bd of Charities & Correc	Bd of Pardons & Paroles
Tennessee	local	Dept of Correc & local	Dept of Correc	Dept of Correc
Texas	local	local	Youth Council	Youth Council
Utah	local	State Juv Ct	DPW	DPW
Vermont	Dept of Soc Wel	Dept of Soc Wel	Dept of Insts	Dept of Insts
Virginia	local	local	Dept of Wel & Insts	local
Washington	local	local	Dept of Insts	Dept of Insts
West Virginia	local	Dept of Public Assistance & local	Commissioner of Public Insts	Commissioner of Public Insts
Wisconsin	local	DPW	DPW	DPW
Wyoming	local	local	Bd of Probation & Parole	Dept of Prob & Parole
Puerto Rico	Dept of Health	Adm Office of Courts	Dept of Health	Dept of Health

* From: *Correction in the United States.* A survey for the President's Commission on Law Enforcement and the Administration of Justice. National Council on Crime and Delinquency, 1966, pp. 250-253.

Misdemeanant Probation	*Adult Probation*	*Local Adult Institutions and Jails*	*Adult Institutions*	*Parole*
none	local	local	Dept of Justice	Bd of Parole
Dept of Soc Wel	Dept of Soc Wel	Dept of Soc Wel	Dept of Soc Wel	Dept of Soc Wel
Prob, Parole & Pardon Bd	Prob, Parole & Pardon Bd	local	Dept of Correc	Prob, Parole & Pardon Bd
none	Bd of Pardons & Paroles	local	Bd of Charities & Correc	Bd of Pardons & Paroles
Dept of Correc	Dept of Correc	local	Dept of Correc	Dept of Correc
local	local	local	Dept of Correc	Bd of Pardons & Paroles
Bd of Correc	Bd of Correc	local	Bd of Correc	Bd of Correc
Dept of Insts	Dept of Insts	local	Dept of Insts	Dept of Insts
Dept of Wel & Insts	Dept of Wel & Insts	local	Dept of Wel & Insts	Dept of Wel & Insts
local	Bd of Prison Terms & Paroles	local	Dept of Insts	Bd of Prison Terms & Paroles
DPW	DPW & local	local	Commissioner of Public Insts	Dept of Public Insts
DPW	DPW	local	DPW	DPW
Dept of Prob & Parole	Dept of Prob & Parole	local	Bd of Charities & Reforms	Bd of Charities & Reforms
none	Adm Office of Courts	Dept of Justice	Dept of Justice	Dept of Justice

Chapter Ten

Corrections Research and Prediction

WHAT is the relationship between probation, imprisonment and parole, or between imprisonment and any period of release after incarceration? Due to the extravagant claims of early reformers, a portion of the public has come to believe that prisons are established and equipped to rehabilitate prisoners as well as to keep them in safe custody. As a result, when prisoners are released on parole today the burden of proof is shifted from the correctional authorities to the convict since the latter is presumed to have been rehabilitated in prison. Even parole officials are often inclined to adopt this view and to assume that the parole period is a period of trial to determine whether the criminal has or has not been reformed in prison. Instead of approaching with the attitude that the parole agent is assisting the individual to make good, there is an inclination to watch and see if he fails. The effect is often a boomerang to both the prisons and to parole.

To evaluate the prison in relation to parole, it is essential to understand the functions of parole as well as of prisons. Parole is not, as often assumed, an exercise of executive clemency which permits complete return to normal society; it is a period of servitude under supervision, just as is the time spent in prison. In anticipation of this later period, prisons do not complete the job; they merely prepare for another stage of the correctional process. Safekeeping and isolation from society, diagnosis and observation, and training for the future are the chief functions of the prison; resocialization, the chief function of parole.

In this chapter, we consider information inputs from probation, prisons, and parole. What are the criteria for the selection of prisoners who are to be granted parole status? How effective are the various predictive techniques? How do we match officer and client for maximum effectiveness?

Selection for probation or parole should be based upon the readiness of the individual to be returned to the community. This determination is developed from a thorough examination of all the best information from many sources close to the individual: the institutional classification service; personal history data developed by the probation staff prior to commitment; medical, psychometric, psychological, and psychiatric data; institutional progress reports; as well as recommendations from institutional diagnostic-treatment staff.

Due to the complexity and sometimes inconclusiveness of prediction methods, it is unlikely that many boards will base selections of potential parolees solely on actuarial techniques. This is not to minimize the necessity of continuing research into the factors which make for the success or failure of paroled offenders. It does suggest, though, that the day is still far off when we can feed punched cards into a mechanical sorter and determine the readiness of the individual for parole on the score which he records.

COMMON SENSE AND CORRECTIONAL SCIENCE*

We seem to be getting accustomed to the fact that delinquency and crime are the natural and predictable outgrowths of a carelessly urbanized society. Accelerating crime figures have become commonplace. Now it takes a Watts riot (or perhaps the youngster next door) to remind us of our need to do something about the rising costs of the alienation and ineffective socialization which lead to delinquency and crime.

We also seem to be getting comfortable with our achievements. We can take pride in the modern prison by reflecting on the demise of punitive revenge and the "con boss" system. The educational programs available to many offenders compare favorably with those of our public school systems. In higher education, studies are underway, through assistance from the Ford Foundation, to determine the feasibility of developing a prison college that would operate side-by-side with San Quentin.

Probation-in-lieu-of-imprisonment incentives to counties, com-

---

* Reprinted by permission of the authors. Robert H. Fosen and Jay Campbell, Jr.: Common sense and correctional science. *Journal of Research in Crime and Delinquency*, July 1966, pp. 73-81. Footnotes are omitted.

munity correctional centers, halfway houses, prerelease centers, and reduction of parole caseloads, though not uniformly accepted throughout the country, nevertheless are answers to the demand to "do something now." Recent amendments to criminal law, permitting such innovations as civil commitment for narcotics addicts and work furlough during prison terms, buttress belief in the progressive growth of criminal justice.

Since public protection and restoration of the offender to trouble-free community living represent at least the manifest goals of most correctional systems, there is generally uniform agreement on the objectives implied and the actions taken in producing these changes in correctional programming. Decisions to maintain existing practices or to wrestle with innovation are based on assumptions which require only that present or contemplated policy reflect a common-sense compatibility with these general goals. There can be no argument with the goals. And to challenge the need for innovation would be obviously absurd.

"Common Sense"

The point of challenge must be directed at our assumptions, and specifically at our apparent willingness to live with them interminably. One such assumption is, *Common sense is sufficient as a means of advancing and defending correctional policies and practices.*

Common sense is *not* enough. In medicine, bloodletting was once accepted as a common-sense cure for many ills—ranging from high fever to incorrigibility. In the history of penology, it was at one time common sense to attempt redirection of behavior through the "silent system" and corporal punishment. It is presently common sense to assume that psychiatry has knowledge everyone needs and no one has—including psychiatrists. Is this common sense good sense? It may or it may not be. But we *are* living comfortably with the assumption that it is.

Common sense by itself not only is insufficient but also can be dangerous. Some relatively high-prestige forms of treatment may be detrimental to some offenders. Research carried out through the U.S. Navy Retraining Command at Camp Elliott, California, reveals interesting differences in the postrelease adjustment of military prisoners exposed to intense and professionally directed living-group treatment while confined. Assignment to treatment followed classification of each offender as either "high" or "low" in maturity. One of the most striking (and statistically significant) findings of this study was that psychodynamic, living-group treatment apparently produced decidedly different results with the high-maturity as contrasted to the low-maturity offenders. Follow-up of adjustment six months after release from confinement indicated a restoration-to-duty success rate of 70 per cent for the high-maturity men and 41 per cent for the low-maturity men. A challenging difference—especially when we consider that the average success rate for *all* high- and low-maturity offenders (including those supervised under treatment teams of custody-oriented staff predicted to be least effective) was a remarkable 62 per cent! It may be common sense to assume that if a little psychology is a good thing, more psychology will be better—or that offenders have similar treatment needs. But this study strongly suggests that different offenders have different treatment needs, that some forms of treatment may be detrimental to some offenders, and that to assume otherwise may not be good sense.

A similar result was obtained in Phase I of the PICO (Pilot Intensive Counseling Organization) Project at the Deuel Vocational Institution from 1955 to 1960. In this setting, youthful offenders were judged by clinical staff as either "amenable" or "nonamenable" to a treatment program consisting of individual counseling sessions and periodic group therapy. Random assignment of these two types of offenders to experimental (treatment) and control (no treatment) subgroups permitted observation of post-release behavior over four parolee classifications (amenable-experimental, nonamenable-experimental, amenable-control, and nonamenable-control). One view of community adjustment, calling for comparisons on percentage of postrelease time spent in *return to custody*, presented some unexpected results—especially thirty-three months after release from confinement. At this point the average time spent in reconfinement for the amenable-experimental youths was 2.06 months—the best performance among the four groups. However, the average reconfinement time for the nonamenable experimental subjects was 5.50 months—the poorest performance among the four groups. Again, a significant and provocative outcome—particularly when we discover that the average reconfinement time for all PICO Phase I offenders (including the amenable- and nonamenable-control subjects who received *no* treatment) was only 4.29 months! Parallel to the Camp Elliott research, the PICO study suggests a serious need to plan and devise *kinds* of treatments for *kinds* of offenders. And there is little hope that common-sense assumptions will do this for us.

Common-sense correctional programing has had its day. And quite a day at that! Under its guidance, the so-called new penology abandoned indifferent and self-righteous confinement of the offender, and efforts to restore the offender to crime-free and responsible community life replaced the philosophy of control and punishment. The new penology, or the deepening of humanitarianism, reflected good common sense and produced and carried the prison reforms of the twentieth century. There are now few major prisons which do not offer some opportunity for individual growth and development. Therapies are in abundance. The word therapies (individual and group) of the psychiatrist, psychologist, sociologist, and social worker are pressed forward with increasing determination. The teaching therapies, pursued by academic and vocational education, are backed by an expanding list of still others—work therapies, religious therapies, recreation therapies, occupational therapies, and now inside and outside community therapies.

A preliminary analysis of survey results indicates that only a few correctional agencies in the country are currently attempting serious evaluation of any programing. Of the forty-eight responding agencies (46 states, the Federal Government, and the District of Columbia), nineteen report some kind of research operation. Approximately $1,300,000, or roughly one-third of 1 per cent of the total annual budget in U.S. adult correction (over $400,000,000), is invested in self-study through these organizations. Over one-half of this small research investment is spent in California and New York.

We spend over three hundred times as much on running our business as we do on evaluating our product. Yet, there is some basis for optimism. Three-quarters of the agencies report a definite interest in either initiating or expanding self-study within their jurisdictions.

An Emerging Model for Correctional Science

It is now time to bring correctional science to the aid of common sense. Two critically important and interrelated problems face us. First, we must unravel the right kinds of programs for the right kinds of offenders. This is another way of saying that the new penology never gave us client-specific treatments. It simply said that all offenders ought to have opportunities to make gains across-the-board—in such areas as individual treatment, education, and vocational training. Present evidence indicates little, if any, improvement in recidivism rates when offenders are in this way assumed to be the same and are given the same treatment. We are undoubtedly getting here what might be called masking effects. That is, the gains in treatment by some offenders are concealed by an understandable lack of response by others. As illustrated by the Elliott and PICO studies, lack of response may all too often be coupled with detrimental impact in producing the masking effect we see as "no measurable difference following treatment."

Second, we must address directly the question of who should come to prison in the first place. Progress has not kept pace with the problem beyond the point of agreeing that there are some people in prison who probably should not be. Finding out who these people are, how many of them are currently incarcerated and will be in the future, and what program alternatives to incarceration would be effective is a difficult and unavoidable challenge. We have to get started now. And we can get started with the reasonably safe assumption that the resocialization value of the institution has been overestimated. Also, it may be true that public interests in protection, restoration of the offender, and cost will be best served through management of some offenders in the community.

Pioneering work in this area is under way in the California

Community Treatment Project. Jointly sponsored by the California Department of the Youth Authority and NIMH, this action-research program provides for random assignment of male and female juvenile offenders to experimental and control programing. After brief reception-guidance center confinement, juveniles in the experimental group are returned immediately to the community, while those in the control group are assigned to traditional confinement and management. Treatment in the community is *not* the same for all of the youngsters in the experimental group—and this is the chief significance of the project. Through tailoring relatively standardized treatment techniques (such as supportive counseling, analytic psychotherapy, and guided group interaction) to the widely different and measured maturity levels of the juveniles treated in the community, a major breakthrough is apparently being achieved.

Fifteen months from date of release to this community-based intervention, the experimental group juveniles (combined as 1 group) have produced a recidivism rate of 35 per cent. The control group exposed to essentially similar counseling and therapeutic techniques—but in the traditional institutional setting and undifferentiated with regard to specific maturity level or client type—demonstrated a recidivism rate of 47 per cent after fifteen months.

Again, the significance (statistical and otherwise) of this study lies in the strong implication that treatment is effective *when* treatment is adapted to clients—in this instance, *within* the community as an experimental alternative to incarceration.

The point here and earlier is not that our common sense has failed us; it is rather the absolute necessity of combining the power of good judgment derived from correctional experience with the power of science. Why? Because only science can separate what we *hope* from what *is* the case; what *seemed* helpful from what *was* helpful; and perhaps what *never* can be from what *can* be. The need is for objective facts that lie beyond the sum total of past exerience.

Readiness to build correctional science is more complex than simple fusion of need and money. Like all measuring instruments, science has life and functions independent of the desires of the consumer. The readings do not always tell us what we want to hear—the thermometer tells us we are sick; the stethoscope tells us we are dying. Correctional science, therefore, must be based on a flexibility of mind that permits one to look for the facts.

Science in our field must grow from basic counting and description, but the available narrative records of correctional agencies require serious appraisal. They have consumed enormous amounts of time for preparation, and, as they accumulate, their collective volume alone infringes on needed storage space. More important, the utility of voluminous records is increasingly questioned, even for individual case decisions and casework supervision. These records have been compiled as aids to decision—but experience indicates that they are unwieldy and the retrieval of information from them is excessively time-consuming, even if we could grant their objectivity and completeness.

Nineteenth-century habits of recording experience with clients, efforts to deal with clients, and assumed results must give way to modern methods. As opposed to the interminable chronicles of quasi-relevant historical facts and guesses, the critical focus must be on what we do to whom, and why, and with what consequences.

Contemporary data-processing techniques promise not only to reduce the time of recording this more useful information, but to make the information accessible for management decisions as well as for research. Admittedly, the phasing-in period of automation is time-consuming, initially frustrating, and expensive. Ultimately, however, it will permit access to accumulated experience and will free personnel to plan and develop treatment relationships with their clients.

Modern access to information will facilitate the development of actuarial prediction equations. These prediction devices permit the formulation of baseline estimates of performance, in essence, "the known efficiency" of agency operations. While admittedly crude, such devices have more than held their own when compared with professional clinical judgments. There is little reason to believe that they cannot be improved as more standardized and objective information is made available. As an aid toward the development of release criteria, and as a means of identifying treatment impact, they permit a practical exploratory evolution toward more sophisticated studies in which variables, such as exposure to a specific program, can be manipulated and tested with some scientific precision.

Armed with better access to the correctional experience of clients and some prediction capability, research can make visible the processes and results of progressing correctional activity. Constant measurement of additional delinquency, rearrest, parole violation, or commitment of new felonies is fundamental. Combined with measures of recidivism, answers to what we do, to whom, and why permit attainment of correlational research and progress in scientific management. Eventually, guessing about recidivism and its relationship to programing will become obsolete.

Correlational research is, in effect, clue-hunting among measures of what we do with our clients and the outcomes we observe. More meaningful and useful inquiries will develop into experimental designs in which relationships between kinds of offenders, kinds of staff members, and kinds of treatments are examined. Within this framework, the number of experimental variations possible is unlimited, and the selection of research strategy is dependent on existing information, clues, and creativity. For example, an experimental design could be developed in which offenders of a known recidivism class are randomly assigned to experimental and control treatment programs. The high recidivism rate of the alcoholic bad-check writer is an illustration of the type of offender to be studied by this methodology. Variations between traditional institutional treatment and treatment in the community are long overdue for this and many other identifiable offender groups. Numerous other experimental designs are possible. They represent not only the most precise scientific approach but portend advancement in correctional policy and practice.

Scientific Management: An Evolving Imperative

Democratic social and legal institutions have brought about limited compliance with the law among the majority of our citizens. Has this compliance come about through a positive absorption of these institutions into the society, or has it resulted from punitive sanctions? The fact remains that the overwhelming majority of the population does not test our correctional apparatus. The negative side of the ledger, however, does indicate shortcomings in our traditional methods of social control and corrective treatment. Criminogenic influences become apparent, but unspecified, as we measure increases in crimes reported to police, increases in numbers of convicted offenders, and increases in the incidence of recidivism.

Such problems of correctional systems are frequently eclipsed by the more "worthwhile" and redeemable plights presented by the physically handicapped, the mentally ill, and the needy. The rationale for this, if any is stated, is that the adult prisoner deserves what he gets. Progress made by correctional agencies in the journey from outright barbarism to at least reasonable care and custody usually results from crises—such as riots, brutality, and corruption—rather than from serious study.

To the extent that the law and the courts specify length of confinement—in effect, the kind of intervention—the correctional apparatus is limited in its choice of alternatives. Whatever intervention is attempted *must* be applied within the custodial setting specified by the courts or the code. A nationwide survey indicates that sentencing is stipulated by the law in about 20 per cent of forty-eight reporting jurisdictions, and left to wide judicial discretion in about 66 per cent of the reporting agencies. Mandatory definite sentences for most offenses are delineated by law in over 20 per cent of the jurisdictions. Over one-third report that the institution of confinement is specified by the courts. Correctional systems, therefore, and their developmental needs must be viewed in a broad perspective—preferably in a broad context of social control, but at least within the context of the administration of criminal justice.

In efforts to discern capacities for correctional research, evidence accumulates that precious little choice is left to administrators of adult correctional institutions as to alternate dispositional interventions. In all jurisdictions, it is mainly within the custodial setting that the administrator must attempt to apply those hopeful but rarely tested techniques of rehabilitation.

The control of crime through the manipulation of the known offender, while admittedly only one facet of the solution to the crime problem, is at least tangible and definite action which is susceptible to scientific investigation. Over 215,000 adult felons are confined in the United States. Over one-third of them are incarcerated in California, New York, Texas, and the federal system. The cost of confining them is more than $400 million per year. Over half of the total expenditure is in California, New York, Michigan, and the federal system.

For a nation whose technology promises to place a man on the moon by the 1970's, it seems ludicrous that we have our head in the sand when it comes to applying scientific techniques to the solution of the problems presented by thousands of confined offenders. Current knowledge of correctional effectiveness falls short of accurately estimating the number of these offenders who will commit new crimes. More embarrassing is the void of information on which correctional interventions, if any, have been effective in meeting rehabilitative objectives. Less than half of the reporting jurisdictions indicate even a minimal attempt to determine an overall recidivism rate within their domains. For the most part, comparative statistics are simply unavailable. It is difficult to achieve even a primitive understanding of jurisdictional legal definitions of crime, let alone any evidence for the treatments which may be effective for some offenders. Complexities in the management of massive, confined populations underscore the need to adopt those technical management tools so effectively utilized by private industry. Information from those jurisdictions which report a serious research effort illuminate, for the most part, the fact that we are running blind. Although most of our efforts are expended in compiling voluminous records and making decisions, little is done to systematically relate those activities to the offenders or to evaluate the impact of decisions and programs on their future adjustment.

Both the researcher and the administrator predicate their planning and action on the facts of the past as a clue to the future. The success of the administrator is determined, to a large degree, by how accurately he has been able to study his past experience and apply this understanding to the current decisions which face him. With perhaps more precision, and probably less hurry, the researcher compiles his data, applies the analytic techniques of science, and makes his interpretations or formulates his hypotheses. Both researcher and administrator are increasingly faced with complexities of operation in which, without the tools of science, the problem cannot even be comprehended, to say nothing about making effective decisions to do something about it.

The essential facts needed for effective administration are often the same as those needed by the behavioral scientist to conduct his investigations. The methods the scientists uses to ascertain the reliability and validity of his information can assist the administrator to separate the extraneous from the relevant. The rules governing the growth of science—essentially, clear thinking and rigorous investigation—can guide the administrator toward the general policies needed for scientific management. Wilkins points out that research can give the administrator immediate help with decision problems while at the same time enabling the scientist to evolve the generalized theoretical formulations needed to satisfy the the tenets of science. A workable compatibility is essential in which the manager can be given immediate information for current decisions as the scientist evolves more applicable universalities of human behavior.

The action needs of the correctional administrator and the increasing financial and human costs of his action constitute a mandate for scientific management. Complacency by either manager or researcher contrasts sharply with increasingly serious responsibilities. Human needs overshadow organizational and academic concerns, and the case for more effectiveness is written in human despair.

Blueprint for a Merger

The idea of developing correctional systems to include the functions of social research laboratories may be difficult to sell. Answers to the questions of effective institutional and community programing cannot be expected to simply tumble forth following acceleration of research activity. As evidenced by the studies reviewed previously, significant gains *can* be expected from scientific management—but we must be prepared for the frustrations that will parallel achievement.

First, answers have an irritating tendency to raise new questions. Even if we learn more about effective programing, we find ourselves directly confronted with the following questions:

1. How can we improve staff training to match *more* efficiently the resocialization needs of different clients?
2. How do community forces such as shifting employment patterns, increasing industrial automation, law enforcement practices, and public opinion act upon our attempts to retain the probationer or parolee in the community?
3. What does increased treatment impact in institutional and community programing tell us about causes of delinquency and crime? Are we getting feedback to the etiology of deviance from efforts to correct deviance?
4. What role should modern correctional systems play in public efforts to check the rising incidence of serious nonconformity?

Second, moving into scientific management involves more than friendly cooperation. Correctional researchers and correctional operators have to develop teamwork—a concept easily stated but not easily implemented. Scientific management forces us to ask who has to do what to make it possible.

Operations staff can do the following:

1. Develop program objectives *with* research staff if evaluation is to be carried out. Research cannot assess action in the absence of knowing its intended target.
2. State the operations or models through which the objectives are to be achieved and share the plan with research staff.
3. Work with researchers in stating program and research schedules as a single package. This forms an action partnership.
4. Be realistic about program continuity. With it, research is possible; without it, research must be postponed in favor of different approaches to evaluation.
5. Call on researchers to explain methods and findings and

to assist in implementation of results. Researchers need identity *with* action as much as operations staff need research *for* action.

6. Contribute to the staff time and energy needed to do the job. This is imperative. Institution and community research require that operations staff work "on the other end." For example, until we keep better records of what we are doing, *whatever* it is we are doing will escape evaluation. Operations staff are essential in the task of developing and maintaining relevant records—the raw materials of scientific management.

Research staff can do the following:

1. Join the team whose responsibility it is to run and manage an entire operation, not just a social research laboratory. This means that some questions which research must answer may be uninteresting, but nonetheless necessary, in running the system.
2. Be explicit about what they have to offer and be prepared for such questions as: "It's interesting, but how will it help?" "Why will it take so long?" "What do you want me to do?" "Does this have the support of top administration?" These are legitimate questions. Researchers must be ready with the answers.
3. Acknowledge that the process of stating and clarifying questions for research is a joint venture. These questions range from comparatively straight-forward ones about population numbers and movement to those about group process and response to treatment. Since no one group of us has all the knowledge needed to state these questions, our best bet is to do it together.
4. Keep operations staff (particularly administrators) informed of how it is going and what it means. Resistance and loss of valuable time and action are the products of "surprise" research findings.

Epilogue

It is the evolution of functionally accurate typologies, through the joint efforts of research and operations personnel, that will have the greatest impact on correctional practices and on the field of applied criminology in the next few decades. By delineating specifically the methods and procedures which may be usefully applied to one kind of criminal behavior, while recognizing their limited applicability to others, we will be able to formulate interventional strategies directly related to correctional objectives. More effective treatment of deviance may generate better understanding of the causes of deviance. We expect that the development of behavioral theory and correctional policy will make parallel gains through the behavioral sciences. By encouraging correctional science along the applied continuum, we may expect our growth to be reasonably parallel to the advances made in medicine. This does not contradict the need for theoretical development. It merely indicates that theories must be generated with sufficient clarity and delimitation of scope to permit some kind of empirical reference and test. Theory must be evolved from experience rather than solely through contemplation from a safe distance.

MATCHING PROBATION OFFICER AND DELINQUENT*

Casework procedure in the handling of delinquents on probation generally operates on two assumptions: first, that the youth will be given the benefit of community services made available to him through the activities of the probation officer; and second, that the relationship between the youngster and the probation officer, the interacting of their personalities, will have a positive effect leading to a healthier social adjustment for the youth.

There is considerable evidence that benefit can result from a constructive adult-youth relationship formed for the deliberate purpose of providing the youth with a atmosphere in which he is encouraged to reorient what has previously been antisocial behavior. On a semiprofessional level, such organizations as the Big Brothers operate almost exclusively on this premise.

Maximum success in the first aspect of probation casework pro-

---

* Reprinted by permission from *NPPA Journal.* Gilbert Geis and Fred W. Woodson: Matching probation officer and delinquent. *NPPA Journal, 2*(No. 1): 59-62, Jan. 1956.

cedure—the exploitation of available community resources—occurs when a probation staff is adequately trained and especially cognizant of the various routes along which a delinquent boy may be directed for help. Vigilance must be exercised to see that the probation staff keeps abreast of the developments in community aid programs and stays aware of the various treatment nuances in available facilities; that is, of their likely advantages and disadvantages for given individuals, as well as their special services. Many valuable suggestions along this line pervade the literature on probation.

Less attention, however, has been focused on the second problem, that of deriving the best results possible from the officer-delinquent match. Essentially, the problem springs from the difficulties involved in taking organized account of the seemingly infinite variations of personality types, both of officers and probationers, and then of determining the presumptive outcome of the matching of two of these types, with the added complication of the dynamics of the relationship as it progresses.

Little research appears to have been directed toward resolving the problem of probation matching. One of the most extensive investigations of delinquency control, the well-known Cambridge-Somerville study, made some faltering, intuitive steps along the lines of adequate matching but never really grappled in an empirical way with the basic problem. Called in later to analyze the Cambridge-Somerville results, Helen Witmer attempted to remold the study's original experimental design to produce some answers to the matching dilemma, but these answers were, largely because of the nature of the material, rather unsatisfactory.

In the Cambridge-Somerville study, only a few general matching rules were observed. Women counselors, for example, were usually assigned to younger boys, and men sometimes replaced women if the youths appeared to be particularly difficult. Typical probation work operates on about the same principles. In fact, some statutes require that very young boys be dealt with only by women probation officers. In addition, female probationers are almost invariably assigned to women officers. Such broad rules, of course, fail to take into account the particular needs of clients beyond those which they would seem to share with a stereotyped sex-age group. More important, they fail to utilize to the utmost the special abilities of the probation officers themselves.

Further refinement of the matching process in larger urban areas where such a process would be practicable is obviously desirable. The remainder of this section will not pretend to resolve the problem or to present a complete set of working rules. Rather its purpose is, first, to draw attention to the importance of a matching approach in probation work; and second, to explore some of the avenues leading to a solution of problems involved in matching.

Probation Officers

Professional probation practice is based on recognized casework principles which may be learned from systematic instruction. Leading probation workers stress, however, that academic training must be combined with a personal approach that often seems to border on art. Appointment to probation positions, on the other hand, is essentially based on the applicant's training and knowledge rather than on his personality assets.

The basic assumption must be made that all the members of a probation staff are technically competent and possess, in addition, special, though different, casework attributes. The initial problem then becomes one of determining more precisely the nature of these attributes. We suggest that each member of the staff be classified in a number of seemingly relevant areas, such as (1) identification traits—sex, age; (2) background, experience, and interests; (3) personality traits as determined by a battery of psychological examinations; and (4) expressed interest in various types of clients. Categorized lists of probationers might be drawn up and the worker would choose the ones he believes he would like to work with and could help most.

Probationers

Most probation staffs possess, or will possess, considerable material on the attributes of the clients being handled by them. The problem becomes one of classifying this material in a meaningful way so that handy, workable portraits of delinquent types may be obtained. Probationers can be classified according to the first three categories outlined for officers. Very important also would be the delinquency pattern that the individual is following, though this item might well be subordinated to the type of person the prospective client is.

Family relationship must also be given a great amount of weight in ascertaining the characteristics of the individual to be handled. If we accept the summary finding of the Gluecks, based on careful research, that the family and parents play a "crucial role . . . in the inculcation of socially acceptable, or antisocial, ideals and habits," then the shortcomings of family living in each particular case must be carefully chartered. We must seek to discover in what way the individual's family appears to be inadequate in satisfying his needs. We must find out whether any members of the family are missing and what are the particular deficiencies of those members present. Then, in light of all this information, the critical question may be asked: Which of the probation officers appears to be most likely to stop the delinquency pattern in this youngster's career?

The operation of this process at a beginning level can be illustrated by some recent cases handled at the Tulsa Juvenile Court.

One boy appearing before the court told about his interest in radio. A court caseworker had a similar interest and on this basis, since no other factors appeared which would make the match undesirable, the case was assigned to this worker. Radio became the catalyst which enabled the worker to interact constructively with the boy. A close relationship was quickly formed; it served as a basis for attacking numerous personality problems besetting the youngster.

Another member of the Tulsa staff, it was found, is particularly well-equipped to work with hostile, defiant boys. He is relaxed, patient, and easygoing, and he never "pushes" a case.

On the other hand, bad matches can be made if care is not exercised to check carefully the relevant characteristics of both client and caseworker. In one such instance in another city, a young boy was assigned to a male staff worker who, on the surface, appeared quite capable of handling the situation. Early in the case, however, the detention home report referred to the boy's habit of going about the home licking the feet of other boys while they were in bed. When the caseworker learned this, both the act itself and its sexual implications upset him so badly that he became ill. Actually, he would have been a stronger person had he been able to work through his own problem in relation to this case, but on a short-term basis this was not feasible.

The Factor of Timing

One of the major situations undercutting probation matching schemes in various areas relates to the chronology of handling cases. Probation staffs may be told that a certain boy has been apprehended and that the court desires a prehearing investigation. Not until this investigation is well launched will certain important information—facts that may be essential to assigning the boy correctly—be at hand. Meanwhile, which staff member should conduct the prehearing check? And, secondly, will it not represent a loss in efficiency and rapport to reassign the case later? Solution of this dilemma lies in determining as early as possible the major points of information necessary for matching. As Sutherland and Cressey point out, "ideally, experts would always make the diagnosis before the offender is admitted to probation." If this is done, at least a psychologically suitable portrait of the individual will be available before assignment. Information on the boy and his family, as well as on other aspects of his social environment, will have to be elicited from the boy himself, and on the basis of this collected data a logical probation assignment might be made.

The elements to be considered in the match, therefore, must be the kind that can be obtained early and rather easily. Continual follow-ups should be made to determine the precise importance of the information being used to make the assignment and to weigh the validity of other items which might be substituted or added to enhance the worth of the matching program.

The administrative problem of balancing the caseloads so that the most suitable officer is available when his counterpart in casework comes within the staff's jurisdiction can be troublesome. Assignments should be made with the aim of helping those probationers who can benefit from the probation experience, which means avoiding the waste of spending disproportionate amounts of time and talent in noble tries on cases which have a very low predictable outcome of success.

Another difficulty that should be mentioned concerns the length of service that the court anticipates rendering. If the probation period is to be of short duration, the case should be assigned to a worker with whom the probationer will relate quickly and easily. A boy who has a warm, accepting mother and a domineering, firm father will probably form a fast and positive relationship with a mother-like woman worker. Should there be indications that the case will be of longer duration, however, it would seem advisable, other things being equal, for the same boy to be assigned to a male worker. While rapport will be more difficult to establish, the whole casework process will be more meaningful to the boy if he can be helped to see through the problem that has arisen from the unwholesome "male world" his father represents.

The Process of Evaluation

The value of any matching program and, in fact, of any therapeutic regime, should be established by a systematic evaluation of results. This allows for a constant streamlining of procedure and theory and for an avoidance of error duplication.

Evaluation of matching should proceed along two lines. One approach should be based on an analysis of results obtained in cases completed during a prior period; the other should be based on a study of cases being handled under the matching system.

Past cases should be examined in terms of categories which will be useful in classifying current cases. The analysis should determine which officers had the greatest success with certain types of cases. Then such cases can be funneled to them in the future.

As a last word, it cannot be emphasized too strongly that the matching program should never represent an invidious method of competition among staff members. It is pointless to deny that some officers will succeed better than others with practically any type of case. This differential ability will be found in any type of operation. In probation, each officer has something of his own, something particular, to contribute. The aim of the matching program is to make the most intelligent use of each member's abilities. Staff *esprit de corps,* the abiding interest of each of the staff members in the total success of the office as a unit, is a vital element in achieving maximum results from a matching program.

In the past few pages, an attempt has been made to draw attention to the importance of assigning the most suitable officers to cases, a procedure that goes to the roots of probation work. It is not the least word on the subject, and we hope it will stimulate others to contribute their thinking, to criticize and evaluate what we have said here, and perhaps to describe work along the same lines in their departments.

PAROLE AND THE DRUG OFFENDER*

Monkey on My Back, a film which dramatically describes the physical and psychological bondage to narcotic drugs, has given millions of Americans some understanding of the tragic ravages by drugs on American youth. The untold misery caused by drugs is responsible for a substantial amount of crime and social disorganization in this country. Within the past decade, many attempts have been made to wrench the "monkey" which has been responsible for so much human tragedy. This section will describe one such attempt.

Although the monkey is still clinging to the unfortunate sufferer's back, we believe that the animal has begun to loosen its stranglehold. With increased knowledge, study, and experimentation, it is hoped that the monkey will entirely relinquish his hold.

In 1960 the Special Narcotic Project of the New York State Division of Parole described the results of a three-year study. The investigation revealed that during the period between November 1, 1956, and October 31, 1959, a total of 344 parolees with a history of narcotic addiction had been under supervision to a specially trained group of parole officers in the Narcotic Project. Of this number, 119 offenders, or 35 per cent, had not reverted to delinquency for any reason whatsoever, drugs or otherwise. In

---

* Reprinted from *Federal Probation.* Meyer H. Diskind and George Klonsky: A second look at the New York State Parole Drug Experiment. *Federal Probation,* 28(No. 4):34-41, Dec. 1964. Footnotes are omitted.

addition, there were thirty-six parolees who, although declared delinquent for other reasons—such as technical violation of parole or arrest by the police for new charges—nevertheless had never reverted to drug usage during their period of supervision. If we were to add these thirty-six delinquents to the 119 who made a fully satisfactory adjustment, then 45 per cent abstained from drugs while under supervision.

That study, popularly known as the *Final Report of the Special Narcotic Project,* raised some questions which could not be resolved at the time.

Need for Further Study

Relatively few of the persons under study in the Final Report had been supervised for the full three-year period; many actually had been supervised for less than a year. As a matter of fact, a substantial proportion of the abstainers had been on parole six months or less. There seemed to be no doubt that some of these parolees were bound to relapse. The Final Report clearly indicated that a further study of the 344 subjects would have to be made at a future date to determine if the percentages would be materially affected with the passage of time.

The case of Henry Smith is a typical example. He was sentenced to a five-year reformatory term for burglary, a crime committed to sustain his narcotic habit. After serving two years at the Elmira Reformatory, he was paroled in April 1959. As of October 1959, the final cutoff date for the study described in the Final Report, he had remained drug-free, was gainfully employed, and in general was making a fully satisfactory adjustment. On parole for six months, he appeared as a statistic in the Final Report as one of the 119 persons who did well on parole. Although the vast majority of relapses take place well within six months, it would have been naive to assume that Smith might never again revert to drug usage. What happened to him in the remaining period of supervision?

Frank Jones, an addict-pusher, serving a three- to five-year sentence for selling narcotics, was paroled from Sing Sing Prison in December 1956, after serving two and one half years. He made an exemplary adjustment on parole and was finally discharged in June 1959. Jones was listed in the Final Report as an abstainer, who had successfully completed his parole. What happened to Jones after he completed his parole? Is there a carry-over of acceptable social behavior in the post-parole period? Or did Jones manage to abstain on parole only because he was fearful of the consequences if he were to relapse? The Final Report pinpointed this question and suggested that a future follow-up study be made.

Finally, it was recognized that the 344 parolees included in the Final Report did not constitute a sufficient number of persons upon which definitive conclusions could be made. What would the findings be after another three-year study? With twice the number of persons than was included in the original report, and extending over a full six-year period, 1956 to 1962, the findings might be more meaningful.

With these objectives in mind, the investigators spent close to a year compiling, analyzing, and interpreting data. This section summarizes the findings of the three follow-up studies which now appear in book form. However, before describing the results, an explanation of the Narcotic Unit's philosophy vis-à-vis the authoritative approach is in order.

Need for an Authoritative Approach

While most persons suffering with a physical ailment seek out medical attention, the problem is different with drug addicts. Because of the tremendous adjustive value that drugs have for their users, they are poorly motivated for therapy. Despite the existence of aftercare clinics, relatively few addicts attend them for any extended period.

The problem applies to narcotic hospital treatment as well, since only a small proportion of drug users utilize these institutions; the majority of patients who do seek voluntary admission seldom stay for the full course of treatment but instead sign themselves out against medical advice.

A study showed that 40 per cent of voluntary patients at the U. S. Public Health Hervice Hospital at Lexington, Kentucky, signed themselves out against medical advice within the first fifteen days, and that an additional 15 per cent did so within thirty days. Only 30 per cent managed to remain for the full five-month course of treatment.

Some authorities in the field of addiction treatment have therefore advocated the authoritative or compulsive approach. Addiction, as a public health problem, has epidemiological components since novices to drugs invariably are initiated by experienced addicts, the contagious carriers. In a joint statement by the American Medical Association and the National Research Council, it was indicated that "Historically, society has found it necessary to employ legal controls to prevent the spread of certain types of illness that constitute a hazard to public health. Drug addiction is such a hazard."

There is a popular misconception that the average youthful drug addict is basically a law-abiding individual who was pulled down into the quagmire of addiction and who must then become a criminal to support the narcotic habit. While there is no doubt that there are some such unfortunate victims, studies reveal that the vast majority of addicts have preaddiction criminal records. Dr. Robert H. Felix, recently retired Director of the National Institute of Mental Health, declared that "An overwhelming majority of these youngsters had a delinquency record prior to an addiction record. . . . Most young addicts did not embark upon a delinquency career to support a habit, that the delinquency career preceded the habit and may have helped to support it later, but addiction was not the precipitating factor for the onset of delinquency."

The use of authority and compulsion has long been recognized as a valuable tool in the treatment of certain mental patients. The medical profession has acknowledged the value of authority in the inpatient phase of addiction treatment. Is the authoritative approach equally valid in casework treatment of addicts in the community?

Use of Authoritative Casework with Addicts

For a number of years the social work profession looked askance at the practice of casework in an authoritarian setting. It was argued that the client must seek the service rather than the service being imposed upon him. Kenneth Pray, one of the early advocates of the authoritative casework approach, pointed out that the probation and parole officer is charged with the specific responsibility of upholding society's standards in the lives of individuals who have been held to account by the community for violation of those standards. The offender does not seek the service because of a voluntary desire to conform to community standards, but because the community has compelled him to subject himself to this new relationship in the hope that he will change. "It is the community's will, not the individual's, that initiates and sanctions the service."

It is unnecessary to go into a discussion of the need to accept limits. Only an anarchist will argue that limits are an infringement on a person's freedom. The function of social casework is not to free the individual from all limitations, but rather to get him to understand and accept the realities of the situation. To teach the client to accept restrictions is essential, particularly in dealing with the offender who has indicated an unwillingness or inability to live by society's standards. The use of authority by the caseworker, therefore, is essential to instill in the offender a respect for legal authority. What has been said about offenders in general applies with even more force to drug users who generally have little concept of limits and who are sharply distrustful of authority figures.

The goal of the New York State Parole Narcotic Program is the internalization of "external" controls by the parolee-addict. These controls have been structured by the parole officer, with whom it is hoped the parolee will identify. The external controls merely provide a crutch which is preemptorily removed at the termination of the sentence. Hopefully, the ego strength developed and strengthened during the supervisory period will have been substantially internalized to sustain the addict in the postparole period.

The Special Narcotic Project

As previously indicated, the Special Narcotic Project was originally created in 1956 as a result of the increasing number of parolees with a history of narcotic addiction. Space does not permit a full description of the techniques, skills, and resources developed by the project personnel, which has been published elsewhere. For our purposes, it is sufficient to state that treatment was predicated upon close intensive supervision which was made possible by small caseloads. Parolees were required to report weekly for an extended period of time. Frequent home visits were made in an attempt to effect a modification of parental and family attitudes which frequently were the cause of the parolee's social maladjustment. Great stress was placed upon continued employment, the development of vocational skills, and constructive leisure-time activities. To a large extent, the differences in approach between the Special Narcotic Project and the generalized caseloads were in degree rather than in kind. Because of the small caseloads, the worker was able to offer more intensive supervision and guidance than could a parole officer with a caseload twice or three times as large.

With more experience and developed skills, the project parole officers developed detection techniques to discover relapse. Arms were not examined routinely out of context with the overall situation. If a parolee worked regularly, appeared cheerful and physically sound, and if the family reported that the parolee was adjusting well, we felt there was no need for examination. As a result of a good relationship developed with families, they did not hesitate to report suspicions of relapse. For the same reason, many parolees voluntarily reported reversion.

In some narcotic parole and probation programs in this country, a parolee who relapses is automatically taken into custody as a parole or probation violator. The project was not wedded to any preconceived method except the general casework method which has always been individually based and as flexible as the need to be served. With the approval of the parole board, various dispositions were available. The violator might be returned to the institution, held in temporary custody, hospitalized with or without a prior period of detention in a local jail, referred to an outpatient psychiatric resource, or permitted to remain in the community with more intensified supervision. Some of the factors entering into a particular disposition were the degree of public risk, previous adjustment, availability of treatment resources, degree of cooperation by the family, loss of lucrative employment if detained, and violator's motivation for treatment.

A special fund was created for use by project parole officers in assisting their parolees. Frequently, money was lent to parolees to purchase jobs at private employment agencies, to tide newly released parolees over until they got their first salary, and to provide transportation expenses for relapsed parolees to the hospital at Lexington, Kentucky. A substantial number of loans have been repaid.

The initial experimental three-year period ending in 1959 reveals that a specialized unit for addict-parolees held some promise. As a result, the unit was expanded and has been included in the regular operating budget of the Division of Parole. After the experimental project phase, the unit has been renamed and is now called the Narcotic Offender Treatment Unit.

It should be noted that the unit's philosophy has seeped down to the generalized caseloads. Many of the skills, techniques, and resources originally developed by the narcotic unit's parole officers have been adopted by the workers in other caseloads which, incidentally, also contain a substantial number of parolees with a history of drug usage.

The Original 344 Parolees

We now turn our attention to such cases as Henry Smith, mentioned earlier. Having abstained for six months by October 31, 1959, the cutoff date for the original three-year survey, he was listed as a "success" statistic. Did Smith continue to abstain after 1959 while still under supervision? How many more so-called successful parolees enumerated in the previous report managed to maintain their satisfactory adjustment during their subsequent parole periods? It had been our hypothesis that with the passage of time, there would be a drop in the abstinence percentages because experience has taught that persons with a history of addiction frequently relapse after prolonged periods of abstention. Perhaps the most frustrating experience encountered by addiction-treatment personnel is the reversion of a prolonged abstainer. This phenomenon points up the difficulty in the treatment of addiction and in the establishment of a prognosis. It accounts too for our use of quotation marks around the word "success." No one has as yet developed a cure for addiction. The best that can be said for abstainers is that they have made progress or that their future looks hopeful.

In an endeavor to follow up the eventual adjustment of the original 344 project parolees, a study was made of them to determine their status as of December 31, 1962, three years and 2 months after the original investigation. As expected, the number of successful adjustments dropped from 119 to 83, or from *35 to 24 per cent,* a drop of eleven percentage points. Additionally, there were nine nondrug-using delinquents, so that the total abstentions were *32 per cent as against 45 per cent* of the original three-year study.

Considering the frequently heard bleak and pessimistic predictions about the futility of current addiction treatment methods, the results of this study, which cover a six-year and 2-month period, are indeed encouraging. Further enhancing of the value of the current finding is the fact that the median length of supervision for the 344 parolees was fifteen months, as against the original eight months in 1959. Another favorable aspect was that practically all the "successful" cases had already completed their parole by 1962, while only 40 per cent fell into that category in the original study.

After Parole What?

What happened to Frank Jones after he completed parole? It will be recalled that he had done well on parole for two and one-half years when he completed his sentence in June, 1959.

In the 1960 Final Report covering the three-year period ending October 1959, we indicated that the relative high rate of abstinence was encouraging, but that it would be necessary to determine if this favorable situation existed after the parolees were discharged from supervision. It was pointed out that, to a large extent, the parolee transfers his dependency on drugs to his parole officer who, in effect, serves as a crutch. If the crutch—the parole officer—is removed, does the ex-parolee fall flat on his face?

In the previous section we indicated that 83 of the original

344 parolees had either successfully completed their parole periods or were still under supervision without any new delinquencies as of December 31, 1962. By eliminating those still under supervision and those who had completed their parole without having at least seven months of supervision, the investigators remained with sixty-six parolees whom they followed up in the field.

In 1962, clearances were made with the Division of Criminal Identification in Albany to determine if any of the former parolees who had done well while under supervision were arrested subsequent to their discharge. Thereafter, three investigators proceeded to locate the parolees to determine from them their abstinence status and employment and arrest records since their discharge from parole. Also, whenever possible, families and social agency representatives were interviewed for the desired information. Locating the parolees was quite a herculean task since most of them had moved from their last known residence. It should be noted that they had been off parole a mean average of two years and 9 months. All but nine of them were located, but pertinent data about these missing persons had been received from relatives, arrest records, and social and law-enforcement agencies.

The sixty-six cases consisted of forty-eight males and eighteen females. A disproportionate number of females could not be located. They had been under supervision a mean average of sixteen months.

The study revealed that thirty-six, or 55 per cent, had completely abstained from drug usage since their discharge from parole. In addition, there were seven ex-parolees who had relapsed subsequent to their discharge from parole, but who had been in a voluntary abstention status for at least three months predating the study (range 3 to 36 months). They must be regarded as having attained some degree of emotional maturation to have voluntarily and independently terminated the habit, even temporarily. In some studies, a person who voluntarily refrains from drugs for three months is regarded as an abstainer. If he were to add the seven who terminated the habit to the thirty-six complete abstainers, then forty-three, or 65 per cent, were in an abstention status at the time of the study.

An interesting sidelight of this study revealed that there was a positive relationship between length of parole and degree of abstinence in the postparole period. Those who were under supervision longest had the best abstinence records, while those with less supervision were more prone to relapse. This has led to some speculation about the advisability of extending supervision for drug users. An article discussing the merits of this proposal was published in the March 1965 issue of *Federal Probation.*

How soon after discharge from parole did the relapsees begin using drugs? The study revealed that this took place at approximately six months (range 0 to 24 months). The investigation seems to indicate that there was a considerable carry-over of abstention for a relatively lengthy period and this is all the more significant because these persons were no longer under legal restraint. The parole deterrence value no longer played any role in their abstention, and it is believed that the parole treatment process might have been at least partially responsible for this relatively favorable situation.

Finally, in the area of employment, a commonly accepted norm of successful adjustment, the abstainers did remarkably well in that 93 per cent were fully and regularly employed while only 31 per cent of the readdicted fell into that category. While it was not the purpose of this study to evaluate the casework techniques utilized by the parole officer, it did appear that the ancillary services provided by the worker, such as vocational guidance and placement services, might have had something to do with the satisfactory employment adjustment of the abstainers. The acquisition of new work habits, a new experience for many persons with a history of narcotic addiction, might have instilled new values and goals in the lives of the hitherto treadmill existence of these socially and economically deprived individuals.

Results of Accumulated Experience

The 1960 Narcotic Project Report has been generally regarded as a landmark in the area of authoritative casework supervision of parolee-addicts. The authors, however, recognize some shortcomings in the method and scope of study.

First, some of the statistics referred to parolees who had been in the project a brief period of time, so that a "success" in that survey might very well appear as a "failure" in a subsequent report. The first study presented in this article was initiated in an endeavor to overcome this objection.

Secondly, it was recognized that the original findings were based on a limited number of persons under supervision for a limited period of time. What would be the results if twice the number of persons were included in a study that would cover a six-year period instead of three years?

In 1963 an investigation was begun of 695 persons who had been under supervision at any time between November 1, 1956 and December 31, 1961. The 695 individuals, of course, included the 344 original parolees. In contrast to the previous study, a one-year observation period was built into the research design so that the adjustment of parolees as of December 31, 1962 could be evaluated. In the 1960 study, a parolee released in September of 1959 would have been included, although he had been on parole for only two months by the cutoff date of October 31, 1959. This undesirable feature was eliminated in the current study by the provision of at least a one-year observation period.

The study revealed that of the 695 parolees studied, 185 or 27 per cent either successfully completed their parole or were still under supervision without any violations as of December 31, 1962. Those in good standing as of the latter date had to be on parole for at least one year. Additionally, there were sixty-two parolees who, although guilty of other violations, had never relapsed while under supervision. If we were to add this number to the 185 completely successful parolees, then 247, or 36 per cent, of all parolees supervised in the six-year, 2-month period, were never involved in drugs. The median length of supervision for the successful parolees was sixteen months.

While these figures appear encouraging, we were concerned about those who failed. Where have we failed? Could we have improved our service? Could we have developed additional resources?

The Narcotic unit's program planners had no preconceived notions about the probable success or failure of its program. The primary concern was to ascertain whether the authoritative casework approach could be of some value in the treatment of paroled narcotic offenders. It was fully anticipated that the vast majority of parolees would relapse. What was more important, however, was to determine whether they need to be sent back to the institution for parole violation. In other words, the project founders did not set as the primary objective a determination as to whether a larger degree of abstinence could be achieved but rather to develop skills and community resources to treat the relapsee in the community rather than in a correctional setting.

In line with this thinking, many parolees were given several opportunities on parole, despite numerous relapses. A parolee, for example, might be given an opportunity to remain in the community after the first relapse, sent to a hospital after the second, temporarily detained after the third, and a variety and combination of treatment techniques thereafter without necessarily being returned to the institution. Naturally, if there were any indication that a parolee has resorted to serious criminal activity to sustain his reacquired drug habit, he was generally ordered returned. As one of the agencies responsible for social control, we would be derelict in our duties if we did not take steps to protect the community. As a matter of fact, one-third of all returned violators were sent back after their very first violation because of the criminal connotations. This compares with 50 per cent returned during the Narcotic Project's first three years of existence. The lesser rate of return now is undoubtedly due to the developing skills on the part of the parole officers. Furthermore, with the increase in narcotic treatment facilities in the New York area, more referrals of drug violators were made to them instead of return for further correctional treatment.

Unfortunately, we apparently have not made considerable headway with relapsees. Despite the number of opportunities granted them, they inevitably relapsed again. As a matter of fact, there was a negative correlation between the number of opportunities granted and the rate of relapse; that is, the more chances given the parolee, the more likely he was to revert within a shorter period of time. While we do have a number of prolonged abstainers after initial relapse, they constitute a relatively small percentage.

As a result of this frustrating experience, it has been advocated by some that drug violators be returned after the second or third violation because the probability of successful adjustment decreases with the number of violations. They felt that staff time, effort, and energy might better be devoted to the more hopeful cases. Perhaps, too, the more structured and controlled institutional treatment program might be of some value in inculcating new sets of values.

However, it is the consensus of most staff members that return to the institution does not necessarily solve the parolee's basic problems, particularly when drug usage is not accompanied by reversion to criminal behavior. Perhaps with additional knowledge, experience, and skill, some progress might be achieved. By returning drug violators, we are in effect sweeping the dust under the rug and are depriving ourselves of the opportunity for further study. In short, we are dealing with two variables—the patient and treatment variables. Does the patient fail to make progress because he is unamenable to treatment or because of the inadequacy of our treatment procedures? Until such a time that we have explored all possible treatment methods, it would be premature to attribute an aura of hopelessness to the patient's potential.

It must be emphasized again that experimentation and research must be placed in proper perspective—the degree of public risk. The parole division which, of course, has law-enforcement attributes, must always be mindful of its obligation to protect the community. This obligation is reflected by the Narcotic Unit's activity in the search for absconders. Over the six-year, 2-month period, there were 148 parolees who had absconded from supervision. Of this number, only eight remained unapprehended as of December 31, 1962. All efforts were extended to locate absconders before they had an opportunity to victimize the community. While some were arrested by the police for new charges, most were located by the parole officers. Absconders have been located in an average of four and one half months. Of the eight unapprehended absconders, six were females. On a pro rata basis, females constituted six times as many absconders as males. Their instability and unpredictability as a group is revealed by other data gathered in the cause of this study.

For a number of years, researchers have hypothesized that, as addicts approach middle age, they begin to abstain. Dr. Charles Winick made a systematic study of records maintained by the Federal Bureau of Narcotics and concluded that there is a sharp drop in addiction within this age group. While the bulk of the Narcotic Unit's parolees were in their twenties, there were a total of 137 over the age of thirty. The findings revealed that 43 per cent of those over thirty managed to abstain, as against 25 per cent under that age. The maturing factor has vast implications for addiction-treatment personnel; if this factor could be isolated and identified, then conceivably it might be introduced in the treatment of younger addicts.

Conclusion

It is believed the results of the studies are encouraging. In the light of insufficient knowledge of treatment procedures, it is indeed gratifying that some offenders with a history of narcotic addiction do manage to refrain from drugs, at least temporarily. Admittedly, working with addicts is frequently a frustrating experience, but this must not interfere with the practitioner's treatment plans and goals, because salvage is possible.

Whatever has been said about the value of authority should in no way detract from the truly dedicated service rendered by private agencies. In some respects, private agencies can do a more effective job than public agencies. A private-agency worker is not as likely to arouse suspicion and fear on the part of the addict, who might regard the public-agency worker as a threatening authority figure. Furthermore, private agencies are generally community-based, in the center of the addict subculture. They are more responsive to community needs, and the addict undoubtedly has greater confidence in an agency attuned and oriented to the community grass roots. A private-agency framework, at times, can provide for greater flexibility, an important element in research. But authority is an integral part of private-agency functioning as well, although not quite to the same overt extent as public agencies like parole. Sanctions and limits are imposed by all agencies, and services are frequently withdrawn when a client fails to cooperate.

Both public and private agencies can and do make significant contributions to addiction-treatment research, each of the agencies within its own field of competence. Their services should complement each other .

It must be stressed that parole deals with convicted offenders who serve part of their sentences outside the confines of a correctional institution. The community expects that its safety and rights will be protected by the agency that supervises these offenders. The community also fully expects that the parole agency will utilize its resources and skills to rehabilitate the offender in the belief that rehabilitation is the best form of protection. Consequently, a delicate balance must be maintained in order to promote both goals—two sides of the same coin. The judicious use of authority vis-à-vis addicts must therefore be employed. The abuse of authority negates its value.

Finally, no claims are made that the parole narcotic program is a panacea for the narcotic problem. It is universally agreed that additional research is essential. We have long advocated many areas of experimentation, including ambulatory treatment. We do contend that the parole program holds some promise. The reader is reminded, however, that the experiments described were limited to parolee-addicts and whatever conclusions are arrived at should be considered in that light. Some of the findings may or may not be applicable to the treatment of drug users in other settings.

HISTORY OF PAROLE PREDICTION*

For over twenty-five years, American social scientists have been involved in the effort to measure the prospect that a person will fail or succeed on parole. Their procedure has been very much

---

* Reprinted by permission of the *Journal of Criminal Law, Criminology, and Police Science*. Karl F. Schuessler: Parole prediction; Its history and status. *Journal of Criminal Law, Criminology and Police Science*, 45(No. 4):425-431, Dec. 1954. Footnotes and tables are omitted.

like that of a life insurance statistician who, by tabulating the mortality experience of a given population, estimates the risk of death at different age levels. Analogously, the parole actuary calculates the relative frequency of failure within selected categories and projects these rates into the future. It appears timely to review the published work on the subject of parole prediction and also to evaluate its significance.

The approximately thirty-year period covered by this research has been characterized by three phases: (1) initial efforts, (2) skeptical but constructive reaction, and (3) postwar studies, predominantly methodological. Hornell Hart was among the first, if not the first, to recognize the possibility of constructing an experience table with a view to predicting parole adjustment. In a 1923 paper, he advocated that parole candidates be scored on the basis of items thought to be prognostic of parole success, and that the risk of violation be established for each score, or score interval. Not so long afterward, this idea was applied by Burgess who, in what would now be called a pilot study, analyzed the records of three thousand parolees drawn equally from three Illinois prisons. These cases were first cross-classified according to (1) outcome on parole and (2) twenty-one items of possible significance, such as type of offense, number of associates, nationality. Then, by giving one point to each subclassification that had a violation rate lower than the overall rate, a parole score was computed for each person. Finally, violation rates were determined for selected score intervals. The regular progression of rates according to the magnitude of prediction scores seemed to affirm the feasibility of prediction from an experience table.

As is true of many scientific accomplishments, almost identical work was going on concurrently in other quarters. In the late 1920's the Gluecks of Harvard developed a methodology of predicting postparole adjustment rates for a group of something less than five hundred prisoners discharged from the Massachusetts Reformatory in 1921 and 1922; the methodology was very similar in form and significance to the table prepared by Burgess. Their procedure differed slightly in that persons were scored on six to thirteen items and items were weighted according to their capacity to differentiate outcome groups. Although these differences appear rather trivial, they do nevertheless represent persistent problem areas, as indicated by continuing research on both topics.

Some intimation that these two pioneer efforts were to mark the beginning of a sustained research movement was provided by two studies that followed almost immediately. Vold's study of 1,192 Minnesota cases is significant primarily because of its attention to the problem of sampling variability in violation rates, and to the possible consequences of not weighting items in accordance with their discriminative value. By randomly dividing his entire sample into two approximately equal groups, he was able to illustrate empirically what might have been expected a priori: that score-specific violation rates would differ somewhat between random samples of parolees just as a matter of chance. The major finding in the scoring experiment was that weighted and unweighted scores arranged parole cases from high to low in about the same way ($r = .92$), and Vold concluded that weighting had little influence on actuarial results, a conclusion which recent research has weakened but not repudiated.

Shortly after its appearance, the scoring procedure devised by Burgess was applied by Tibbitts to a sample of three thousand persons released to parole from the Illinois Reformatory. The scoring was altered so as to eliminate from consideration those subclassifications in which the violation rates did not differ by more than five percentage points from the overall rate; and several additional factors were analyzed. His results served mainly to confirm the point that parolees scored and ranked on items closely associated with parole adjustment will exhibit differential violation rates, an inevitable result whenever there is any correlation between prediction items and the criterion.

Middle Period

The initial group of studies, although modest in claim and scope, was followed by a run of somewhat critical studies. Sanders, for example, expressed skepticism as to whether an experience table, after Burgess, would persist relatively unchanged in the short-run future. To throw light on this question, parole outcome and various items were correlated in a sample of 5,683 federal prisoners released; cases were scored in best items and violation rates computed by score intervals to form an experience table. A follow-up sample consisting of 2,838 parolees was scored in the same way, and violation rates computed so as to make possible a check on the constancy of the score-specific violation rates in the two periods. Although the first set of violation rates showed a regular progression, the pattern of rates in the follow-up table was erratic and quite possibly a result of chance factors. This finding, as significant now as at the time of its discovery, highlighted the possibility that items which rank persons reliably as to parole success in one period may be unreliable for that purpose in the almost immediate future.

The pioneer studies were also criticized on the grounds that they made use of whatever information happened to be on hand and that much of it was irrelevant. A corollary was that progress in parole prediction is tied up with the discovery of significant categories of information. This attitude is exemplified in the writing of Laune, who contended that intimate personal knowledge about a man is likely to be, if not a substitute for, at least an important supplement to, the objective data obtained from a prisoner's record. To this end, he solicited the opinions (hunches) of several inmates in regard to the parole prospects of 150 inmates. It was impossible to check on the accuracy of the raters, as the prospects were still in prison. Inmate ratings acquired a semblance of validity, however, by reason of their fair correlation with Burgess scores ($.34 < r < .54$) and because of fair consistency ($.34 < r < .62$) among the several raters. A recent validation study of these inmate appraisals reviewed in a later section revealed that inmate hunches are no better than objective scores.

The critical attitude of psychiatry toward the neglect of psychological data in previous efforts, and perhaps unconsciously toward the actuarial method itself, is reflected in a paper by Jenkins and his coworkers. A group of 221 boys paroled from the New York Training School for Boys were scored on ninety-five items, including twenty-eight personality characteristics. Although these scores yield different violation rates, no demonstration was provided that psychiatric information did improve prediction significantly beyond what would have been achieved had objective items been used exclusively. This study must therefore be considered as principally suggestive in regard to the manner in which psychiatric material might enhance the accuracy of a prediction table.

Not critical in nature, but falling within the middle period, is the work of the sociologist-actuaries in Illinois who scored nine thousand cases on twenty-seven items, and computed violation rates for selected score intervals. These results, usually termed the 1938 Illinois Experience Table, represent not so much an application of the method devised by Burgess but a continuation of his original work. The Gluecks, like Burgess, did not revise their original method in any significant manner during this period, but they did continue to apply it to the unfolding experience of their now-famous five hundred reformatory cases. They acknowledged that in the absence of validation samples their results were important primarily because of their suggestiveness.

The Postwar Period

It seems fair to say that recent research has concentrated almost exclusively on methodological matters rather than on conditions, personal or situational, which affect behavior on parole. These studies have concerned themselves with the relative efficiency of experience tables, the validity of the 1938 Illinois Experience Table, the validity of the inmate "hunch" method, the optimum number of items in a prediction battery, and the problem of weighting items.

It is almost axiomatic that an experience table, in order to justify itself as a prediction instrument, should make fewer errors than a blanket prediction based on the overall rate (i.e. the modal frequency). To evaluate an experience table from this point of view, Ohlin and Duncan have proposed an *Index of Predictive Efficiency,* defined as the percentage change in prediction error resulting from the use of an experience table instead of the overall rate. The application of this index to twenty-two published tables indicated that these tables were not particularly efficient, the average reduction in error being only 16 per cent. This result, perhaps disappointing to prediction enthusiasts, is immediately due to the heavy concentration of parole candidates in score intervals in which the violation rates are very close to the average—in short, because relatively few candidates were characterized by actuarial risks close to one or zero. This feature of the score distribution is basically due to the inability of available prediction items to discriminate sharply between violators and nonviolators.

As a check on the validity of the 1938 Illinois Experience Table, Hakeem computed score-specific violation rates for 1,108 Illinois parolees of 1939 and 1940 and compared these results with the rates as projected from the 1938 Illinois Experience Table. His results were negative in that the observed rates were consistently smaller than the expected rates, the average difference being approximately 13 per cent. The experience table, equipped with memory but not foresight, reacted as if the violation rates would maintain themselves indefinitely, while in fact there was a marked decline in score-specific rates throughout the table. Therefore, even had the parole board selected only the most favorable parole risks, the estimated number of violators would still have been excessive since, as previously noted, score-specific rates were dropping over the entire table.

In a study of greater scope and refinement, but similar in orientation, Ohlin compared the parole experience of 8,013 consecutive parolees from 1936 to 1944 with the rates predicted by the 1925-1935 sample on which the 1928 Illinois Table was based. His major result, anticipated by Hakeem's earlier finding, was that the 1938 experience table was outmoded, as the observed rates were significantly lower than the expected rates. To meet this serious difficulty, Ohlin devised an ingenious method for adjusting the experience table on an annual basis, utilizing the parole experience of persons who had completed the first year of their five-year parole period. This procedure utilizes the constant relationship, as it has been observed, between the number of parole violators in the first year and the total number who will violate in the entire five-year period. Application of this procedure to the

1925-1944 Illinois State Prison series revealed that an experience table, if made to eliminate outmoded information, can be made to predict violation rates with reasonable accuracy, although such revisions in no way guarantee that an experience table is performing more efficiently than the overall rate. The significance of these two validation studies seems to consist in their demonstration that an experience table may be outdated in a short period of time, due to major social changes which facilitate or hinder adjustment on parole, and that provision must be made therefore to keep the table up to date by continuous feedback of the latest parole experience.

By 1950, it was possible to compare the inmate hunches solicited by Laune in 1934 with actual parole behavior of 110 of the 150 inmates who had been rated. This comparison, undertaken by Ohlin and Lawrence, revealed that the hunch method was not quite as efficient as the Burgess method, although neither method predicted much better than the overall rate.

Another recent study by Ohlin has demonstrated that an experience table based on twelve items performs just as efficiently for prediction purposes as a table based on the twenty-one items originally used by Burgess. As a result of this analysis, the experience table now in use at the Illinois State Prison is based on twelve items. This type of analysis, although designed primarily to eliminate useless items, has a certain theoretical significance in that it directs attention to basic variables, presumably most influential in regard to parole success. Ohlin discovered, for example, that the six most efficient items defined an area of personal and group attitudes toward criminality. It is to be anticipated that the question whether several prediction items reflect the influence of a single common factor will be approached next by factor analysis, as this method seems especially appropriate.

Kirby has recently completed an investigation of the efficiency of an experience table based on items selected and weighted in accordance with the principle of least squares. His table, representing the experience of 455 federal parolees, was slightly more efficient than a comparable table based on arbitrary weights, but not much more efficient (10%) than a blanket prediction based on the overall rate. Although an important demonstration of the power and advantages of the least squares method, this study nevertheless underscores the need in parole prediction for more meaningful data.

The research of Glaser represents an exception to the main trend of recent methodological studies in that his search for factors was guided by a theoretical concept. He hypothesized that degree of identification with criminality as a way of life would distinguish prospective violators and nonviolators, and, in accordance with this idea, scored persons on seven items thought to be indicative of "differential identification" with criminality. The resulting experience table was somewhat superior in efficiency to the twelve-factor table prepared by Ohlin, tending to uphold the claim for theoretically oriented research as opposed to the statistical manipulation of available material.

Conclusion

It is evident from the foregoing review that parole prediction as a research movement has centered in the Midwest and that this activity has been pursued mainly by Burgess and other sociologists in the Chicago area. Illinois is the only state that has thus far made provision for the tabulation of actuarial data and its continuous utilization in connection with selection for parole. That this method has not diffused rapidly to other states is due, as is true of most social inventions, to a wide variety of complex social circumstances: political, legal, economic, and ideological. Whatever social conditions have impeded its spread, it must be acknowledged on the basis of this review that the application of actuarial methods to parole experience has thus far not provided data that greatly reduce the uncertainty attached to forecasting individual behavior on parole. The reasons for this seem to lie, not in the actuarial method itself (which is indifferent to the nature of the data) but rather in the unavailability of items that sharply differentiate outcome groups and in the apparent sensitivity of parole adjustment to abrupt social changes which militate either for or against a good parole adjustment. The significance of parole research to date, therefore, seems to consist not so much in the actuarial data produced but rather in its delineation of the most troublesome problems in this field. These problems, as mentioned before, embody as their major theme, the need for improved knowledge concerning the conditions, both personal and situational, which determine outcome on parole.

PERSONAL CHARACTERISTICS AND PAROLE OUTCOME*

The first information available on prisoners is that which most immediately identifies them. This comprises facts which generally can be learned quickly, such as sex, race, age, offense, prior criminal record, intelligence, and body dimensions. Some of these attributes, for example, the offense and criminal record, may actually have intricate variations. However, we shall first consider them as broad categories into which inmates may be classified soon after they reach the prison. This section is concerned with the parole prognosis value of this gross information by which prisoners may be divided into the young and the old, the thieves and the murderers, the first offenders and the repeaters, and so forth.

Age

One of the most firmly established pieces of statistical knowledge about criminals is that the older a man is when he is released from prison, the less likely he is to return to crime. By no means should it be inferred that all old prisoners are good risks or all youngsters poor risks. Nevertheless, as Table 10-I shows, for all parolees taken collectively, the older they are at release the less likely they are to fail on parole.

Table 10-I indicates that the parole violation rate predominantly decreases as the age at parole increases, although there is some deviation from perfect consistency in this relationship. Such findings have been reported for many decades, and in numerous jurisdictions both in the United States and abroad. A related finding is that, as age at release increases, it is increasingly likely that, if any further criminality occurs, it will be a misdemeanor rather than a felony.

---

* Reprinted in part from Daniel Glaser and Vincent O'Leary: *Personal Characteristics and Parole Outcome.* Washington, U.S. Government Printing Office, 1966, pp. 5-24. (Parole Decision Making Series.)

The easiest interpretation of this finding is that people become less criminal as they become more mature. Such an interpretation only has much validity if the word "mature" is used primarily in a nonbiological sense. Criminals generally are at least as well-developed physically as the average person of the same age. They can only be considered immature by defining normal maturation as change from delinquent youth to noncriminal adulthood.

It will suffice at this point to observe that the age group which

TABLE 10-I

POSTRELEASE VIOLATION RATES IN RELATION TO AGE AT RELEASE

Wisconsin Parolees					
	Juvenile			*Adult*	
Age at Release	*Males (%)*	*Females (%)*	*Age at Release*	*Males (%)*	*Females (%)*
12 to 13	78	67	Under 20	31	40
14	54	58	20 to 24	37	26
15	58	40	25 to 29	41	13
16	50	33	30 to 34	40	23
17	44	40	35 to 39	34	29
18 and over	41	34	40 to 49	29	14
Rates for			50 to 59	28	50
all cases	50	39	60 and over	21	
Number				36	23
of cases	1,037	453		2,255	206

New York Adult Parolees			Federal Adult Male Releasees	
Age at Release	*Males (%)*	*Females (%)*	*Age at Release*	*Failure Rate (%)*
20 years or less	36	43	18 to 19	51
21 to 25	38	54	20 to 21	46
26 to 30	41	48	22 to 23	42
31 to 35	39	41	24 to 25	38
36 to 40	38	26	26 to 30	36
41 to 45	29	22	31 to 35	30
46 to 50	32		36 to 40	28
51 to 55	25	17	41 to 49	25
55 and over	18	9	50 and over	29
Rates for				
all cases	37	43		35
Number				
of cases	7,626	738		1,015

Note: The violation rates shown in this table, as in all other tables, are based on the number of "failures on parole" for all reasons. For example, the following are included in these rates: new commitments, serious violations of parole rules such as absconding, and preventive actions on the part of parole authorities such as warrants issued for failure by individuals to abide by stipulated parole conditions.

has the highest crime rates in most industrialized societies is the vaguely defined one which is in transition between childhood and adulthood. These are the people we call "adolescents." For them to become adults, in the sense that others treat them as adults, requires not just physical maturation but the acquisition of a self-sufficient position in the adult economic and social world. Prisoners tend to be persons who have failed in the past and may be handicapped in the future in achieving this transition, although most of them eventually do become self-sufficient in a legitimate adult life.

These data have two important general implications for parole policy in dealing with youthful offenders.

First is the emphasis on change. It is the consensus of both satistical analysis and personal impressions of experienced officials that youths are the least predictable of all prisoners. Although they have high rates of return to crime, this rate diminishes as they mature, and it is hard to predict when their criminal careers may end. They are in a period in which old associates and points of view may suddenly be dropped and new ones gained. Innumerable cases can be cited where marriage, new employment, or other incidents marked a turning point which was followed by the complete metamorphosis of such offenders. Many individuals with long histories of juvenile crime, including acts of violence and drug addiction, are now leading respectable and law-abiding lives.

The second implication is that youths are particularly in need of new paths to follow toward a secure and satisfying life. Frequently, they have only had gratification in delinquent pursuits and have only felt at ease and important in a delinquent social world. Simply to release such a youth unconditionally, to give him "another chance" with no prospect that he will enter a new social and occupational world, is likely to be futile. Placing such a youth where he may have new and satisfying legitimate achievements which contribute to his self-sufficiency, and new types of contacts among his peers, is more preferable to merely "giving him a buck" by parole. A feasible school or work program, or a combination of the two, and a home in which the youth feels "at home," are ideal ingredients for rehabilitating a youthful criminal. While it is easy to state these desirable resources, their procurement is difficult. Frequently, relatives of youths make rash promises for parole placement which they do not intend to keep, or for which neither they nor the youth are adequately prepared. This includes both home and job arrangement.

Even where ideal placement seems to be guaranteed, success is never certain. Invariably, some youths will not perceive a work or school program as feasible for them, in comparison to illegal pursuits with which they are familiar, or about which they have illusions. Similarly, new homes which seem ideal to officials may be distinctly uncomfortable or even frightening to a youth from another background who has had little gratifying personal experience in new relationships. For these reasons, testing parole placement in advance of complete release is particularly desirable for the youth. Both for staff information and to aid the youth's adjustment, intensive counseling should be concomitant with the early placement experience. Minimal tests of a prospective parole home may be provided by furloughs the institution in advance of parole. An optimum program involves transfer of the youth, several months before parole, to a release guidance center in the community where parole will occur.

The Criminal Record

The extent to which a person has devoted himself to crime is not easily measured. We only know of the offenses for which he was apprehended, or which he will admit, and he may have been involved in considerable criminality not revealed to us. Nevertheless, that which can be learned about prior criminality often is the most valuable information that a parole board has about a prisoner.

At first inspection of a man's file, we usually learn only the events which appear on the FBI's list of his fingerprint reports. This is sometimes called his "rap sheet." It has a wealth of valuable information but is often difficult to interpret. One problem in using these records is that a criminal commonly is fingerprinted several times on each major offense, and each fingerprinting leads to a new line on this report. First, the prisoner may be reported by the police who arrested him, then by the sheriff who operated the jail in which the prisoner was confined, then by each prison to which he may have been committed. Each of these separate lines on the FBI sheet should not be confused with those for a new offense. Of course, this problem will not confront a parole board if it receives a casework report which summarizes the criminal record in a simpler and clearer manner than that of the original record.

During the intervals in which he was free, between his major offenses, a prisoner often will have had numerous arrests not resulting in conviction. While a man must legally be presumed innocent of any charge for which he was not convicted, such arrests suggest that the person with whom we are dealing frequented places, had associates, or kept hours which got him into difficulties with the law. These could also interfere with his fulfillment of parole requirements. Minimally, these arrests may suggest that the prisoner's reputation with the police in his home community is not conducive to his parole success there. Even where there is a possibility that this was police harassment due to his earlier behavior, the prospect of its continuing should be taken into account.

Ideally, inquiry and investigation of gaps in the criminal record and of other matters should begin in the presentence study by the probation officer. Of course, such studies are not always made, or are not reported to the board. Remaining issues should be probed by the prison caseworker, by interview and by correspondence, so that adequate information is available when the parole board member confronts the prisoner. By directing appropriate questions to the caseworkers on gaps or errors in information available at the parole board hearing, the parole board may promote improvements in the material prepared for its case.

There are so many standpoints from which criminal records can be analyzed that we cannot exhaust all of the possibilities here. Instead, we shall focus on three principal types of information for which this record is our primary or our initial source. These are the *duration* of the prisoner's prior involvement in crime, his *prior experience with government agencies dealing with crime* (police, courts, prisons, etc.), *and the types of offenses* he has committed.

Duration of Prior Criminality

The duration of prior criminality can be estimated imperfectly from several types of evidence. For example, offenders can be differentiated according to the age at which they were first arrested, first adjudicated, first committed to a correctional institution, or first reported in any type of difficulty for delinquent activity. Presumably, among offenders of approximately the same age, the earlier they first have any of these experiences, the longer is the span of their prior involvement in crime, and the more likely they are to continue in crime. This is indicated by Table 10-II.

The foregoing conclusion has occasionally been challenged by a theory that all offenders have approximately the same period of delinquency and crime to go through, so that the earlier they start this period, the younger they will be when they conclude it. This is suggested by the finding that many older chronic offenders have no record of juvenile delinquency or youth crime.

Nevertheless, the predominance of evidence is against this conclusion. Despite some deviations, the overall generalization indicated by Table 10-II is that at any age, the longer the span of prior criminality, the more likely it is that it will be extended in the future. Unfortunately, not many cross-tabulations of violation rates are available which relate age at release to age of first arrest or other index of first criminality, as does Table 10-II.

The few rather persistent types of crime, characteristically starting at a later age than the majority of offenses, provide exceptions to the foregoing generalization that early onset means more persistence in crime. These late-starting offenses consist of some crimes associated with alcoholism, especially check forgery, and some offenses that also seem to occur as an abnormal adjustment to senility. These include a petty theft and vagrancy combination, and certain sexual indecency offenses. The old and persistent criminals who do not have a criminal record which goes back to juvenile days, or have a long gap between youth and old-age offenses, are not sufficiently numerous to contradict the overall

TABLE 10-II

POSTRELEASE FAILURE RATES OF FEDERAL ADULT MALE PRISONERS ACCORDING TO BOTH AGE AT RELEASE AND INDICES OF DURATION OF PRIOR CRIMINALITY

(Number of cases is indicated in parentheses)

Index of Duration of Prior Involvement in Crime	*Age at Release from Prison*				
	All Cases	*18 to 21*	*22 to 25*	*26 to 35*	*36 and over*
Age at first arrest (%)					
16 and under	46	53	43	43	40
	(304)	(94)	(68)	(106)	(35)
17 to 20	38	37	45	41	28
	(316)	(49)	(73)	(116)	(78)
21 and over	24		24	24	24
	(395)		(37)	(184)	(174)
Number of Prior Sentences for Felony-like Offenses (%)					
None	25	44	31	21	11
	(423)	(78)	(98)	(151)	(96)
1	37	52	46	34	25
	(221)	(31)	(37)	(105)	(48)
2	44	57	52	45	28
	(154)	(23)	(27)	(64)	(40)
3 or more	46	45	63	48	42
	(217)	(11)	(16)	(86)	(104)
All cases	35	48	40	34	27
	(1,015)	(143)	(178)	(406)	(288)

generalization that the younger a person was when his crime began, the more likely he is to persist in it.

The number of prior felony convictions is only a rough indication of the duration of prior criminality. Of course, what we know about a man's criminal record generally is limited to that which was recorded by government agencies which dealt with him. Therefore, the duration of past criminality often can be roughly estimated from many types of available records on a person's experience with agents of the law.

Prior Police, Court, and Correctional Experience

Since there are many ways of classifying a criminal's record of previous experience with government agencies, it is often difficult to compare statistical tabulations from different jurisdictions. A variety of ways of classifying the data are illustrated in Table 10-III.

TABLE 10-III (Part 1)

POSTRELEASE VIOLATION RATES IN RELATION TO VARIOUS CLASSIFICATIONS OF PRIOR CONTACT WITH AGENCIES OF THE LAW

California Youth Authority Male Parolees

Prior Contacts	*Violation Rate (%)*
None	24
1 or 2 contacts for delinquency, no commitment	37
3, 4, or 5 contacts for delinquency, no commitment	44
6 or more contacts for delinquency, no commitment	44
1 or 2 contacts and 1 commitment	49
3, 4, or 5 contacts and 1 commitment	46
6 or more contacts and 1 commitment	45
2 or more prior commitments	50
Violation rate for all cases	44
Number of cases	3,046

New York Adult Parolees

Number of Prior Arrests	*Violation Rate (%) Males*	*Females*
None	21	36
1	27	45
2	35	50
3	35	53
4 or more	46	46
Rates for all cases	37	43
Number of cases	7,636	738

Washington Adult Parolees

Prior Felony Conviction	*Violation Rate (%)*
None	23
1	33
2	40
3 or more	50
Rates for all cases	38
Number of cases	1,731

These tabulations indicate, on the whole, that no matter how one counts the volume of previous experience with police, court, or correctional agencies, the overall trend is for the parole failure rate to increase as the magnitude of this prior experience increases. This trend, however, is offset by the influence of age: one or more commitments as a juvenile seems to be more unfavorable as a prognostic sign than the same number of commitments later. In general, the increase in violation rate with increasing number of prior commitments becomes progressively less, or halts completely, after a few terms of imprisonment, or even of successive felony convictions. However, Table 10-II indicated quite clearly that this decrease in failure rate simply reflects the crime-diminishing effect of older age at release for those with three or more prior felony convictions. Possibly the reduced rate of return to crime with each successive commitment also reflects some rehabilitative or deterrent influence of imprisonment. It is clear, at any rate, that we cannot conclude with certainty that everyone in any category of prior criminal record will persist in crime indefinitely into the future.

The Wisconsin data in Table 10-III show that prison commitments alone may not be as unfavorable for parole prognosis as combinations of prison and lesser commitments. This unfavorable prognosis is in terms of overall violation rate only; it ignores type of violation. Persons habitually in minor difficulty with the law,

TABLE 10-III (Part 2)

POSTRELEASE VIOLATION RATES IN RELATION TO VARIOUS CLASSIFICATIONS OF PRIOR CONTACT WITH AGENCIES OF THE LAW

Federal Adult Male Releasees		Illinois Youthful Male Parolees	
Most Serious Prior Contact	*Violation Rate (%)*	*Most Serious Prior Contact*	*Violation Rate (%)*
No prior contact	15	No prior contact	24
Arrests or fines only	25	Arrests or fines only	35
Jail and/or probation	31	Jail and/or probation	40
Training, reform, or industrial school	55	Training, reform, or industrial school	54
Reformatory or prison	43	Reformatory or prison	39
Rates for all cases	35	*Rates for all cases*	39
Number of cases	1,015	*Number of cases*	2,693

	Wisconsin Parolees			
	Juveniles		*Adults*	
Types of Prior Contacts	*Males (%)*	*Females (%)*	*Males (%)*	*Females (%)*
Most serious prior commitments				
No prior commitment	46	40	27	13
Juvenile detention, jail, or probation	61	41	42	26
1 prison only			45	50
Prison plus lesser commitments			59	33
2 prison only			36	
2 prison plus lesser commitments			53	
3 prison			50	
4 or more prison			70	
Prior releases on present commitment				
None	48	38	34	23
1	53	41	51	25
2 or more	52	41	55	40
Rates for all cases	50	39	36	23
Number of cases	1,037	453	2,255	206

such as drunks and vagrants, may not be as serious a problem to parole boards as persons less likely to violate, but more likely to commit serious new offenses if they do. This observation, of course, brings out the oversimplification we are employing in most of this discussion by not distinguishing different types of violations. Some correction of this deficiency will be made in considering offense as a factor in parole prognosis.

Types of Offenses

Still another aspect of the vital information provided to parole boards by the criminal record is the type of offense for which a prisoner is currently committed, or in which he was previously involved. It is appropriate therefore to provide an overall view of the many types of offenses, and to compare their significance in predicting continuation of criminality.

The most persistent types of common crimes are those in which offenders obtain someone else's money without use of violence. These crimes can be divided into two major categories: illegal service and predatory crimes.

Illegal service crimes consist of economically motivated offenses in which there is no person who clearly considers himself a victim; instead, the persons with whom the criminals deal are his customers. Examples of such crimes are the sale of illicit alcoholic beverages ("moonshine"), narcotics and stolen goods, and the provision of illegal gambling and prostitution services. Only a minute proportion of these offenses lead to arrest and prosecution. Also, conviction on some of these charges such as gambling and prostitution seldom leads to imprisonment, so parole boards seldom confront such criminals. Because these criminal services are both more profitable and safer than most other offenses, one can reasonably speculate that they may be the most frequently committed clearly criminal acts, even though this is not confirmed by complaint or arrest statistics.

The crimes usually encountered by parole boards are predatory crimes. As indicated in Table 10-IV (Parts 1 and 2), on the whole, these offenses usually fall into three main clusters from the standpoint of violation rates. The offenses usually associated with the highest violation rates involve taking somebody else's property by stealth or by deceit. Notable here are the crimes of theft, burglary, and forgery.

Theft, which older criminal codes usually call "larceny," consists simply of taking somebody else's property. Both in the law and in statistical tabulations, the crime of auto theft usually is treated separately. Auto thieves have the highest rates of parole violation in most jurisdictions, possibly because they generally are the youngest parolees. Their crime usually is committed for the temporary enjoyment of transportation rather than for long-term economic gains. For this reason, in approximately 90 per cent of auto thefts the vehicle is recovered intact, even though the thieves usually are not caught. However, in some auto thefts the cars are

TABLE 10-IV (Part 1)

POSTRELEASE VIOLATION RATES IN RELATION TO OFFENSE

Offense	*Wisconsin Parolees* *Juveniles** *Males* (%)	*Females* (%)	*Adults* *Males* (%)	*Females* (%)	*New York Adult Parolees* *Males* (%)	*Females* (%)
Highest violations						
Auto theft	50	20	47	60		
Other theft	51	42	34	25		27‡
Burglary			39	20	42	36
Forgery and fraud			48	32	46	5
Intermediate and inconsistent						
Robbery			38	12	37	38
Narcotics						
Lowest violations						
Rape and assault to rape			31		19	
Other sex offenses	33	37	21	16	24	
Felonious assault			31	17	33	29
Homicide			16	20	19	28
All others	44	41	35	25	38	19
Rates for all cases	50	39	36	23	38	36
Number of cases	1,037	453	2,255	206	5,929†	329†

* Offenses for juveniles were tabulated by Wisconsin officials separately for three major offenses—theft, auto theft, and sex offenses—plus purely juvenile offenses like truancy, plus all combinations of these several categories. The above tabulations are based on all parolees charged with any of these three offenses, alone or in combination. The few multiple-major-offense cases are included under each of their offenses.

† Felonies only; excludes cases tabulated as "misdemeanors" and "youthful adjudications."

‡ Auto theft and all other thefts are compiled as one offense, grand larceny, in New York.

TABLE 10-IV (Part 2)
POSTRELEASE VIOLATION RATES IN RETURN TO OFFENSE

Offense	*Minnesota Adult Male Parolees (%)*	*California Youth Authority Parolees (%)*	*Federal Adult Male Releasees (%)*	*Illinois Adult Male Parolees (%)*	*Illinois Youthful Male Parolees (%)*	*Washington Adult Parolees (%)*
Highest violations						
Auto theft	58	49	47		50	52
Other theft	57	54	38	36‡	39	40
Burglary	41	42		42	48	38
Forgery and fraud	54	43	30	55	42	50
Intermediates and inconsistent						
Robbery	47	29	28	42	31	31
Narcotics		41	30	14		
Lowest violations						
Rape and assault to rape		41				21
Other sex offenses	22	32		14*	13*	16
Felonious assault	41	28	18*†			36
Homicide	21	18		14	20§	21
All others	38	48	25	44	35	34
Rates for all cases	44	44	35	37	39	38
Number of offenses	525	3,046	1,015	955	2,693	1,731

* Includes "rape."
† Includes "homicide."
‡ Includes "auto and stolen property."
§ Includes "assault."

stripped; some older auto thieves work in gangs and falsify ownership papers to sell stolen cars.

Other types of theft include shoplifting, removing objects from parked cars, picking pockets, taking goods from places of employment, and many more varieties of "stealing." Most of the separate crimes are small, frequently they are not immediately discovered by the victim, and probably a majority are never reported to the police. Only a small proportion of theft reported to the police, other than auto theft, is solved by recovery of the stolen goods or conviction of the offenders. Furthermore, the small value of the property taken in separate offenses frequently results in a convicted person receiving only a minor penalty, so that most of the time he will never go to prison or will receive only a short sentence. Probably the persistence of these criminals is due in large part to the fact that they cannot readily be given certain or severe penalties.

Burglary consists of breaking and entering for the purpose of committing a felonious act, and it sometimes is designated in the law as "breaking" or "breaking and entering." Usually it is committed in conjunction with larceny at the place entered. However, burglary almost always causes a more severe penalty than larceny alone, so the offenders usually are prosecuted only for burglary. However, some state laws make "burglary and larceny" a single compound offense. A majority of persons arrested for burglary are under nineteen years of age, but an appreciable number of the burglars who are encountered in prison populations are older. These often include those for whom burglary has become a profession in which they work closely with dealers in stolen goods ("fences").

Another kind of recurrent economic offense not involving violence is the crime of forgery. Forgers differ from most criminals in the extent to which they commit their crimes alone and in being relatively older. Petty or naive forgery is notably associated with chronic alcoholism. Perhaps because cashing a fraudulent check requires a certain amount of facility at writing and an appearance of success, forgers are also distinctive in generally having more education and less often coming from an impoverished home than most prisoners. Other types of fraud, often called "confidence games" or "bunko games," are less often associated with alcoholism than simple check forgery and are more frequently persistent criminal professions. Embezzlement is a special kind of fraud, frequently involving violation of trust by a prominent and presumably trustworthy citizen so that he is placed in a government or business position where he handles much money. These offenders generally are good risks as far as prospects for violation are concerned, but their parole poses special public relations problems.

The selling of narcotics has already been mentioned as an illegal service crime. Other narcotic offenses include illegal possession, use, and purchase of narcotic drugs. Evidence on the relative risk of these narcotic offenders as parolees is inconsistent. There is some indication that they have very high violation rates when they are paroled to neighborhoods where narcotics usage is extensive, but that they have average or below average violation rates elsewhere.

Robbery is different from the economically motivated crimes described earlier in that robbery involves the use or threat of violence in order to procure someone else's property. Like narcotics offenses, it is associated with diverse violation or recidivism rates in different jurisdictions, but robbers generally seem to have about the average violation rate for their age group. However, they are of concern to parole boards because of the serious injury or death which they may cause. Robbers vary tremendously in character. They include groups of adolescents in slum areas who "roll" drunks coming from taverns in the late hours of night, naive individuals who make a foolhardy effort to solve economic crises by trying to hold up a large bank (often without a working weapon), and some highly dangerous individuals who have a psychological drive to hurt their victims.

The cluster of offenses associated with the lowest violation rates on parole comprises crimes which least often serve as vocations. These include homicide and rape. However, the strong public demand for punishment as an expression of revenge against such offenders, plus the extreme importance of preventing recurrence of these crimes, makes parole boards exceptionally cautious in paroling those who commit these offenses.

One of the least favorable crimes, from the standpoint of parole violation probability, is the crime of escape from prison. In some states, notably California, offenders sentenced for this offense have the highest violation rate of any offense category, even higher than auto thieves. However, escapees do not constitute a large proportion of prisoners.

Thus far, this discussion has dealt only with gross violation rates, although it has been noted that the nature of the probable parole violation may be a crucial consideration in parole decisions. The type of violation likely to be committed, if any, is a concern especially in the forefront of a parole board member's thoughts when he considers the type of offense for which a prisoner was last convicted. William L. Jacks, statistician of the Pennsylvania Board of Parole, has made one of the few studies on type of violation in relation to type of offense. This is summarized in Table 10-V.

Table 10-V indicates, first, that in Pennsylvania the offenses fell into three main clusters in terms of prospects of committing a new crime on parole, and these three clusters were much like those for overall violation rates shown in Table 10-IV. However, larceny and narcotics offenses are ranked somewhat differently in these two compilations. Burglars, forgers, and narcotic drug offenders were most likely to commit the same offenses, while larceny and robbery comprise an intermediate cluster, followed by felonious assault and sex offenses. Homicides were lowest, only about 1 in 250 committed a homicide on parole after being imprisoned for homicide. The gravity of this offense, of course, still makes any repetition a crucial concern.

A California tabulation of adult male parolees returned to prison for a new offense in 1959, 1960, and 1961 concluded: 26 per cent are returned for a more serious offense than that on which they were paroled, 38 per cent are returned for an offense of similar seriousness to that on which they were paroled, and 37 per cent are returned for a less serious offense. Seriousness was measured by the length of the statutory maximum sentence for the offense in California, except that narcotics offenses were classified as more serious than property offenses with higher maximum sentences.

Intelligence

Intelligence tests are almost invariably administered to the inmates of correctional institutions today. They are used to determine the appropriate education, work, and treatment of each prisoner, and the test results also are reported to the parole board. Despite the convenient availability of this information, it has been found to have only a slight relationship to parole outcome. As Table 10-VI shows, in the several jurisdictions for which we have procured statistics, there was little consistent pattern of violation rate according to intelligence. Generally, the most mentally deficient inmates did not do as well on parole as most prisoners, but usually their violation rates were not extremely different from many with above average intelligence scores.

TABLE 10-V

TYPE OF OFFENSE FOR WHICH COMMITTED AS A FACTOR IN TYPE OF OFFENSE, IF ANY COMMITTED ON PAROLE (FOR PENNSYLVANIA ONLY)

(All parolees, 1946-61)*

Offense for Which Imprisoned	*Per Cent Committing New Crimes on Parole*	*Per Cent Repeating on Parole the Crime for Which Imprisoned*
Auto larceny†		
Larceny	22.5	6.4
Burglary	23.4	11.1
Forgery	22.3	10.2
Robbery	19.5	5.1
Narcotics	15.9	10.1
Sex offenders	8.8	2.9
Assault and battery	12.3	3.6
Homicide	5.7	0.4
Other offenses	10.2	3.1
Rates for all cases	18.4	6.8
Number of cases	29,346	29,346

* *From* Pennsylvania Board of Parole: *A Comparison of Releases and Recidivists from June 1, 1946, to May 31, 1961.* Harrisburg, The Board, Dec. 20, 1961.

† Included in Larceny.

A prisoner's intelligence test score, of course, can reflect his capacity for both legal and illegal types of behavior. It may be significant information for the parole board as an indication of whether an expected parole job is within a parolee's capacity. It may also be the basis for speculation that certain inmates would be particularly dangerous if they returned to crime. However, it is surprising how often crimes reflect emotional behavior not guided by much apparent intelligent thinking, even when the offender has considerable mental capacity.

An additional consideration which parole board members should keep in mind is that intelligence tests are never perfectly accurate, and those given in a prison or other correctional institutions are often exceptionally unreliable. Although the test scores theoretically reflect an inherited mental capacity, it is well known that performance on many of these tests is greatly affected

TABLE 10-VI

POSTRELEASE VIOLATION RATES IN RELATION TO INTELLIGENCE

Minnesota Adult Male Parolees		*California Youth Authority Male Parolees*		*Illinois Youthful Male Parolees*		*Washington Adult Parolees*	
Intelligence quotient	Violation rate (%)	Intelligence classification	Violation rate (%)	Intelligence classification	Violation rate (%)	Intelligence classification	Violation rate (%)
145 and over	33	Very superior	0	Very superior	16		
135 to 144	53	Superior	43	Superior	39		
125 to 134	42	High average	48	High average	33	Above average	27
115 to 124	49	Bright normal	37				
105 to 114	57	Normal	40	Average	41	Average	32
95 to 104	42	Dull normal	46	Low average	39		
85 to 94	46	Borderline	49	Dull	38	Below average	39
75 to 84	49	Moron	55	Borderline	45		
65 to 74	51			Mentally deficient	47		
Rates for all cases	44		44		39		32
Number of cases	525		3,046		2,689		809

by exposure to schooling, by the type of vocabulary which an individual needed in his social environment, by experience in using the type of arithmetic and mathematics included in the test, and especially, by motivation to perform well. These tests often underrate a prison inmate's intelligence because he is indifferent or hostile to taking the test at the time it is administered, usually when he is new to the prison and because he has not been involved in school for some time. Frequently, the scores on these tests increase if they are administered again after the inmates have attended a prison school for an extended period. It should also be noted that intelligence scores sometimes are erroneously high in some correctional institutions because of lax control in administering the tests or in recording their results.

Race and Nationality

Although Negroes in the United States have a higher rate of arrest, conviction, and imprisonment for crimes than whites, most tabulations we have encountered find little marked or consistent difference in the parole violation rates of the two groups. This is indicated in Table 10-VII. It is probable that the higher crime rates among Negroes occur largely because Negroes, more often than whites, experience conditions associated with high crime rates in all racial groups. These conditions include low income, high unemployment, low level of education, and residence in slum areas which have long had high crime rates.

These conditions conducive to high crime rates usually are also associated with high parole violation rates. The fact that Negro parole violation rates are not higher than those of whites, therefore, is somewhat puzzling. It may reflect more careful selection of Negroes for parole than of whites, or more frequent institutionalization of unadvanced offenders among Negroes than among whites. There is some evidence that the latter occurs with juvenile delinquents, but evidence as to its occurrence in prison is conflicting.

TABLE 10-VII

POSTRELEASE VIOLATION RATES IN RELATION TO RACIAL OR NATIONAL DESCENT

	Wisconsin Parolees			
	Juveniles		*Adults*	
Ethnic Classification	*Males (%)*	*Females (%)*	*Males (%)*	*Females (%)*
White	49	37	36	21
Negro	57	49	35	23
American Indian	48	59	37	40
Mexican	71		19	
Mongoloid				
Other				
Rates for all cases	50	39	36	23
Number of cases	1,037	453	2,255	206

Ethnic Classification	*Minnesota Adult Male Parolees (%)*	*California Youth Authority Parolees (%)*	*Washington Adult Parolees (%)*
White	46	41	38
Negro	35	49	34
American Indian	56		47
Mexican		44	
Mongoloid			
Other		43	
Rates for all cases	44	44	38
Number of cases	525	3,046	1,731

In the southwestern portion of the United States, the largest ethnic minority comprises persons of Mexican descent. In California, where they are most numerous, they have a parole violation rate about the same as that of whites and Negroes. American Indians generally have an average or somewhat higher than average rate of parole violation.

The differences in crime or parole violation rates for various ethnic groups could readily develop as a consequence of police or parole officers not treating every person in the same fashion for a given type of behavior, regardless of the person's ethnic descent. Statistics to assess whether or not this occurs are not available on a widespread and recent basis. A common impression is that officials tend to overlook infractions committed by minority group members in their own community and tend to be unusually severe in dealing with infractions which members of minorities commit elsewhere. This, of course, could be conducive to the habituation of minority group members to criminal behavior, which they might engage in wherever they encounter an opportunity.

Japanese and Chinese are infrequent in correctional institution populations. In California, where they are most numerous, they have a lower violation rate than other parolees. This probably reflects the close-knit community and family support which they receive.

In a few portions of the country, notably New York, persons of Puerto Rican descent are a new and extensive component of the prison population. Experience with them as parolees has been too brief for confident conclusions as to how their violation rates compare with those of other ancestry.

TABLE 10-VIII

POSTRELEASE VIOLATION RATES IN RELATION TO SEX OF PAROLEE

Sex	*Wisconsin Parolees*		*New York Adult*	*Washington Adult*
	Juvenile (%)	*Adult (%)*	*Parolees (%)*	*Parolees (%)*
Male	50	36	37	38
Female	39	23	43	25
Rates for all cases	47	35	37	38
Number of cases	1,490	2,461	8,364	1,731

In general, the evidence on race and nationality as a factor in the evaluation of parolees suggests that it is not of much predictive utility in itself. However, an understanding of the different social and cultural worlds from which members of some minorities come, and to which they return, may be useful in understanding their offenses and in evaluating their parole plans.

Sex

Males coming before parole boards in most states outnumber females in a ratio of about 20 to 1. This probably occurs both because females in our society commit felonies less often than males do, and because those females who are convicted of felonies are less likely to receive a sentence of imprisonment than are males. Table 10-VIII suggests that female parolees violate less often than males, but the differences are not always marked.

Body Characteristics

In the nineteenth century, there was much effort to explain crime as the expression of an inherited characteristic that could be identified by a person's physical appearance. One still frequently hears people say that somebody looks like a criminal, or that someone else looks like he could not possibly be a criminal. However, parole board members often observe a fine appearance in some individuals who have shocking criminal records.

There have been popular experiments to investigate the ability to predict criminality from physical appearance. The most useless efforts involved asking people to judge character from photographs of criminals mixed with photographs of highly respected noncriminal persons when all persons portrayed were of about the same age and wore similar apparel. These studies demonstrated almost complete failure of this approach to character judgment.

Years ago, a study found that height and weight had no relationship to parole violation. Classification of people by their general physical condition has not uncovered clear and consistent findings of marked deviation from average violation rates. Some studies find those in poor health or having a handicap with slightly higher than average violation rates, while others found these individuals slightly more successful on parole than the average.

The most recent extensive research in this field has been that of the Gluecks, which compared the overall body dimensions of delinquents with those of nondelinquents from the same high-delinquency neighborhoods. The delinquents were huskier (mesomorphic) in body build than the nondelinquents. It has not yet been demonstrated that this is not simply the result of the huskier youth in high-delinquency areas being more readily accepted in delinquent street gang activity (and perhaps, also, more readily picked up by the police), than the slender (ectomorphic) or paunchy (endomorphic) youth.

Conclusion

Of the gross characteristics readily available for the classification of prisoners, those most closely related to parole outcome were age and criminal record. On the whole, younger prisoners were shown to have the highest violation rates. However, the extent to which violation rate decreased with age was not uniform for all populations for which this information was available. Some sources of variation in this relationship were discussed.

The criminal record was found to have a wealth of information closely related to parole outcome, but capable of classification in many ways. Of course, an individual's prior criminality is only known from the crimes for which he was apprehended and his offenses recorded, and this record is often incomplete. Nevertheless, lower parole violation rates were consistently found for those with no prior criminal record. However, the violation rate for younger first offenders was much higher than that for older first- or second-felony offenders. The figures predominantly support a conclusion that the lower a prisoner's age at first arrest, the higher his parole violation rate is likely to be at any subsequent age, but some types of late-starting persistent offenders were noted.

Although persons with little or no prior contact with police, courts, or correctional institutions have a much better record on parole than those who have been in institutions before, the rate of violation does not always increase markedly with each increase in the number of convictions or commitments. This may partially reflect the crime diminution generally occurring with older age at release; the extent to which it can be credited to rehabilitative or deterrent effects of prior imprisonment cannot readily be determined.

Offenses were found to fall into three main clusters as far as parole violation rates are concerned. Those for which the prospect of violation is greatest are crimes involving the taking of someone's property by stealth or deception without the use of force. Notable here are theft, burglary, and forgery. Narcotic offenses and robbery generally are associated with violation rates near the average for all parolees, but they were inconsistent in this respect from one jurisdiction to the next. On the whole, the lowest parole violation rates were associated with crimes of violence including rape, assault, and homicide.

A Pennsylvania study was cited on the extent to which persons who violate parole by committing a new offense repeat the offense for which they previously were imprisoned. Burglars, forgers, and narcotic users were found most likely to repeat their previous offenses if they committed a new offense. Sex offenders tabulated collectively were relatively low in rate of repeating the same crime, while those convicted of homicide showed the lowest rate of repeating the same offense while on parole of any category.

Intelligence, race, nationality, sex, and body build were found not to have sufficiently marked or consistent relationships to parole outcome for large numbers of offenders to be very useful in evaluating parolees.

Appendix I

Correctional Standards

Selected by the
SPECIAL TASK FORCE ON CORRECTIONAL STANDARDS

IN November 1965, a Special Task Force on Correctional Standards was appointed by the staff of the President's Commission on Law Enforcement and Administration of Justice. Its purpose was to select, from the correctional standards already published by authoritative bodies,* those that (1) would be useful to the President's Commission and the survey of correction in the United States to be made by the National Council on Crime and Delinquency in 1966 and (2) were susceptible to measurement.

Correctional standards are defined as the best professional thought concerning the organization and function of a correctional system. Few of those that state a numerical ratio, such as the number of personnel in proportion to the correctional population, have been tested by rigorous research and are, therefore, tentative and subject to change as means for validation become available.

The members of the Special Task Force were John A. Wallace (Chairman), Office of Probation for the Courts of New York City; Kenneth S. Carpenter, Children's Bureau, U.S. Department of Health, Education, and Welfare; Fred Fant, Division of Probation, New York State Department of Correction; Benjamin Frank, Bureau of Prisons, U.S. Department of Justice (Ret.); Abraham G. Novick, Berkshire Farms School, New York; and E. Preston Sharp, American Correction Association.

The standards finally selected by the Special Task Force were reviewed by a committee consisting of Walter Dunbar, American Correctional Association; Philip Green, U.S. Children's Bureau,

---

* A list of the source material from which the selected standards were derived can be obtained from the Library of the National Council on Crime and Delinquency, 44 East 23 St., New York 10010.

Department of Health, Education, and Welfare; Milton G. Rector, National Council on Crime and Delinquency; and Heman G. Stark, Governor's Conference Committee on Juvenile Delinquency.

I. General Standards

1. Though parts of the correctional system may be operated by local jurisdictions, the state government should be responsible for the quality of all correctional systems and programs within the state.
2. If local jurisdictions operate parts of the correctional program, the state should clearly designate a parent agency responsible for consultation, standard setting, research, training, and financing of or subsidy to local programs.
3. All correctional systems should have a statement of objectives, policies, and general plans governing their organization and function.
4. Specific rules and regulations setting forth the delegation of authority to subordinate executives as well as the limitations of that authority should be compiled in all systems.
5. Every correctional system requires a staff of administrative and supervisory personnel commensurate with the size and extent of the system. The staff should be so organized that all important functions in the total administrative process are represented and an adequate span of control is maintained.
6. A structured program of on-the-job training is essential for every correctional agency. Its elements are (a) an orientation period for new workers, geared especially to acquainting them with the agency and its rules, procedures, and policies; (b) a continual in-service program designed to meet the needs of all personnel, including administrators and supervisors, through the agency directly and by participation in seminars, workshops, and institutes; (c) educational-leave programs with provision for part-time and full-time salaried leave, with financial assistance for educational costs, to achieve preferred qualifications and to improve professional competence.
7. Besides the appropriate educational qualifications for his position, each correctional employee should have good health, emotional maturity, integrity, interest in the welfare of human

beings, ability to establish interpersonal relationships and to work with aggressive persons, belief in the capacity of people to change, recognition of the dignity and value of the individual, resourcefulness, patience, ability to use authority responsibly, and a continuing interest in professional development.

8. Personnel should be covered by a merit or civil service system. They should serve a probationary period of at least six months before attaining permanent status. When permanent status has been achieved, dismissal should be for cause only, and the discharged employee should have the right to a hearing before an appropriate body.

9. Appointment should be based on the educational and personal qualifications set forth in the job description of each class of position.

10. Salaries should be adequate and commensurate with the qualifications, high trust, and responsibility involved. Salaries should have minimum and maximum levels with provision for regular increments based on merit performance evaluations.

11. There should be provisions for sick leave, annual leave, hospital and medical care, insurance, disability, retirement benefits, and other accepted employee benefits compatible with the best practices of public and private agencies.

12. An adequate research, evaluation, and statistical reporting program should be maintained. All correctional data should be uniformly and routinely reported to a central state agency. The statistical reporting system should provide for the collection, storage, and analysis of information, and its dissemination to local jurisdictions within the state, to other states, and to national agencies.

13. Citizen committees should be developed to serve state correctional agencies and institutions in an advisory capacity. Similar advisory committees should serve local agencies operating parts of the correctional system.

II. Standards for Probation

Definitions

Probation: A legal status granted by a court whereby a convicted person is permitted to remain in the community subject to conditions specified by the court.

Probation agency: The organization that conducts prehearing or presentence investigations, supervises probationers, and makes recommendations regarding modifications of probation conditions, revocation, and discharge.

A. Statutory Provisions

1. The statute should require that a paid, full-time probation service be made uniformly available to all courts needing the service. It should prescribe how the service is to be established, financed, and administered, and it should state the qualifications of staff, methods of staffing, and the duties and functions to be performed.
2. The statute should authorize the court to use probation at its discretion, following adjudication or conviction, for the best interest of the offender and society.
3. The statute should require that a probation investigation be completed in all juvenile and adult cases, as an aid to the court in making an appropriate disposition, and it should require the court to consider the investigation report and give due weight to the findings before making a decision.
4. The statute should prohibit indiscriminate scrutiny of the probation investigation report and improper disclosure of information contained in the report and other probation records to unauthorized persons, and it should authorize the court to make such information available to persons and agencies having a legitimate and proper interest in the case.
5. The statute should authorize the court to determine the conditions of probation, and it should prohibit incarceration as one of the conditions.
6. The statute should provide that, for juvenile offenders, the period of probation supervision be indeterminate but be terminated before the twenty-first birthday.
7. The statute should provide that, for adult felony offenders, the period of probation supervision be fixed by the sentencing judge at not less than one year and not more than five years.
8. The statute should authorize the court to discharge persons from probation at any time when supervision is no longer needed and to revoke probation for sufficient cause after a hearing.
9. The statute should provide that the discharge of adult offend-

ers from probation has the effect of restoring all civil rights that may have been lost as a result of conviction.

10. The statute should provide for the transfer of probationers under the Interstate Compact for the Supervision of Parolees and Probationers and the Interstate Compact on Juveniles.

B. Organization

While there is as yet no discernible authoritative consensus on the best organizational structure, it is clear that a sound probation system should conform to either of these two structures:

1. A centralized statewide system providing, to all courts, state-administered, state-controlled, and state-financed service through (a) a board, commission, or department, (b) a department of which probation is a bureau or division, or (c) a department of probation and parole.

2. A centralized county or city system locally administered by the court or a nonjudicial body, with state responsibility for supervision, consultation, standard setting, training, and research, with financing or subsidy through (a) a board, commission, or department or (b) a department of which probation is a bureau or division.

C. Personnel

1. *Probation Officer Qualifications*

a) Preferred: Possession of a master's degree from an accredited school of social work or comparable study in correction, criminology, psychology, sociology, or a related field of social science.

b) Minimum: Possession of a bachelor's degree from an accredited college, with a major in the social or behavioral sciences and one of the following: (1) one year of graduate study in an accredited school of social work or comparable study in correction, criminology, psychology, sociology, or a related field of social science or (2) one year of paid full-time casework experience under professional supervision in a recognized social agency.

2. *Supervisor Qualifications.* Possession of at least the probation officer's minimum educational qualifications listed above, and two years of paid full-time casework experience under professional supervision in a recognized social agency.

3. *Administrator Qualifications.* Possession of the educational and experience qualifications required for a supervisor and, in addition, three years of paid full-time experience in a supervisory capacity in a recognized social agency maintaining acceptable standards.

4. A probation officer's workload should not exceed fifty units a month. (Each case under active continuing supervision is rated as one unit; each regular probation investigation that is completed and written is rated as five units.)

5. One full-time supervisor should be assigned for every six full-time probation officers.

6. A minimum of one supporting position (stenographer, clerk, or receptionist) should be provided for every three probation officers.

D. Clientele

1. For juveniles a procedure should be established that provides for screening and possible adjustment of complaints before a petition is filed.

2. No juvenile or adult offender should be placed on probation until a probation investigation has been completed.

3. Where probation is used as a disposition, a probation agency should be available to provide service and exercise supervision.

4. A written copy of the conditions of probation should be given to each offender placed on probation (or the parents when the offender is a child). The offender (or, in the case of a child, his parents) should acknowledge by signature that the conditions have been discussed, are understood, and are accepted.

5. Probation may be revoked only after the probationer has had an opportunity to be heard.

6. At a hearing held to consider revocation of probation, charges alleging violation of the conditions of probation and a summary statement of the probationer's adjustment should be prepared in writing and submitted to the court.

7. New infractions of the law by a probationer should be reported to the court.

8. Each probationer should be given a copy of his discharge when probation is terminated prior to, or at the expiration of, the maximum period of probation supervision.

9. When an adult is discharged from probation, instruction and help should be given for expunging the record.

III. Standards for Parole and Aftercare

Definitions

Parole: A method of releasing an offender from an institution prior to the completion of his maximum sentence, subject to conditions specified by the paroling authority.

Aftercare: The term equivalent to *parole* when applied to a juvenile.

Mandatory or conditional release: The release, as prescribed by law, of a prisoner who has served his term of commitment less "good time" or "work time" credits, under parole conditions and under supervision until the expiration of the maximum term for which he was sentenced.

Paroling authority: The body authorized by statute to grant or revoke parole or aftercare status.

Parole agency: The organization that completes preparole investigations, supervises parolees, and makes recommendations regarding modifications of conditions of parole, revocation, and discharge.

A. Statutory Provisions

1. *Sentencing*

a) The court should select and impose a maximum sentence within the maximum sentence prescribed by law.

b) The law should not establish a mandatory minimum sentence. However, if the court is authorized to impose a minimum sentence, the law should provide for a broad spread between the minimum and the maximum.

2. *Parole Laws*

a) The law should empower the paroling authority to consider all prisoners for parole, regardless of the nature of the offense committed, to establish the time when a prisoner is eligible for parole, and to exercise full discretion in determining the time at which parole should be granted to any eligible person.

b) The law should empower the paroling authority to establish rules of operation, to establish conditions of parole, to revoke parole for the violation thereof, and to discharge a person from parole when it determines that supervision is no longer needed.

c) The law should provide for the establishment of a parole agency which should have supervision of all persons paroled or discharged from a correctional institution by mandatory release.

d) The law should provide that proper notification be given to the paroling authority regarding violations of any of the conditions fixed by the authority.

e) The law should provide that discharge from parole has the effect of restoring all rights that may have been lost as a result of conviction and that the certificate of discharge should so state.

f) The law should provide for the transfer of parolees for supervision under the Interstate Compact for the Supervision of Parolees and Probationers.

3. *Disposition for Juveniles*

a) When a child is committed to a state institution, the court having jurisdiction should vest legal custody of the child in the appropriate central agency of state government responsible for administering state institutions for delinquent children.

b) Legal custody in such commitments should be vested for an indefinite period of up to three years.

4. *Aftercare Laws*

a) The law should provide that commitment to a training school is for an indefinite period (i.e. the child shall not be required to serve a specified minimum length of time before being released on aftercare).

b) The law should give the agency granted legal custody the right to determine when the child shall leave a training school.

B. Organization

1. *Parole*

a) The authority to release on parole should be placed in a centralized board whose members are appointed by the governor through a merit system or regular civil service procedure, or from a list of candidates who meet the minimum requirements of education and experience. None of the parole board's members should be a person who is already a state official, such as the commissioner of correction, or any other state official serving ex officio.

b) The parole board should bear full responsibility for all

parole decisions. It should not serve as a hearing and advisory board with parole decisions being made by the governor, the director of correction, or any other state administrative officer, and it should not have the pardoning function.

c) Whenever possible, members of the parole board should serve full-time and be paid salaries comparable to those for judges of courts of general jurisdiction.

2. *Aftercare*

a) Responsibility for aftercare should be vested in the state agency that is responsible for administering institutional and related services for delinquent children.

b) The authority to approve release should be vested in the parent state agency. The aftercare decision should be based on an appropriate training school staff committee's opinion of the child's readiness for release.

C. Personnel

1. *Parole Officer Qualifications*

a) Preferred: Possession of a master's degree from an accredited school of social work or comparable study in correction, criminology, psychology, sociology, or a related field of social science.

b) Minimum: Possession of a bachelor's degree from an accredited college, with a major in the social or behavioral sciences and one of the following: (1) one year of graduate study in an accredited school of social work or comparable study in correction, criminology, psychology, sociology, or a related field of social science or (2) one year of paid full-time casework experience under professional supervision in a recognized social agency.

2. *Supervisor Qualifications.* Possession of at least the parole officer's minimum educational qualifications listed above, and two years of paid full-time casework experience under professional supervision in a recognized social agency.

3. *Administrator Qualifications.* Possession of the educational and experience qualifications required for a supervisor and, in addition, three years of paid full-time experience in a supervisory

capacity in a recognized social agency maintaining acceptable standards.

4. A parole officer's work load should not exceed fifty units a month. (Each case under active continuing supervision is rated as one unit; each preparole or pre-aftercare investigation is rated as three units.)

5. One full-time supervisor should be assigned for every six full-time parole officers.

6. A minimum of one supporting position (stenographer, clerk, or receptionist) should be provided for every three parole officers.

7. An employment specialist should be on the staff of the adult parole agency to serve as liaison between the agency and outside employment agencies, union officials, and employer organizations.

D. Clientele

1. *Adult*

a) The prisoner should be present at his hearing when the granting or revoking of parole is being considered.

b) A prisoner should not have to apply for parole.

c) Attendance at parole hearings should be restricted to members of the releasing authority, a recorder, a professional staff member responsible for preparing the case, the prisoner himself, and persons invited by the paroling authority for purposes of public education.

d) Prisoners being considered for parole should be assisted by staff in developing parole plans. A staff member, sometimes called an institutional parole officer, should serve in a liaison capacity between the classification department of the institution and the paroling authority.

e) Basic information regarding the offender that should be available to the parole board at any hearing for parole should include (1) a report on the inmate's prior history, (2) a report on his adjustment in the institution, and (3) a preparole investigation report from the community.

f) Every offender eligible for parole should be involved in a program of prerelease preparation.

g) Supervision of parolees should be carried out by full-time paid staff. Supervision should not consist entirely of written reports; home and community contacts should be made.

2. *Juvenile*

a) Diversified aftercare services and facilities should be available for children returning to the community from a training school. They should include foster homes, foster-group homes, and group resident homes for older youths who are unable to return to their own homes or the homes of relatives or foster families. Such group homes should be under the supervision of the parent agency or the training school.

b) The program of the training school should include the preparation and counseling of youths for their return to the community.

c) Every child entering a training school should be released under an aftercare program.

IV. Standards for Institutions for Felony Offenders

Definition

Institutions for felony offenders: Residential facilities, generally called reformatories, prisons, penitentiaries, or correctional institutions, for the confinement and treatment of adult offenders under felony sentences.

A. Statutory Provisions

1. The administration of the state correctional institution system for adults should be vested in a separate state department of correction or its equivalent.

2. The institutional system should be headed by a single administrator.

3. The law should specify the minimum qualifications for the state institution administrator in terms of general education and progressive administrative experience.

B. Organization

1. The central office staff should be commensurate with the size and extent of the institution system and should be so organized that all the important functions represented in the total operation receive central supervision and guidance.

2. The state institutions system should demonstrate evidence of its leadership in the treatment and control of offenders through its annual reports and other publications, by services performed for local communities and other units of government, and through its consultation and advisory services to legislative committees.

C. Personnel

1. The warden and all other employees of correctional institutions should be appointed through the competitive selection process of a merit system.

2. In each institution, staff should be assigned for establishing and directing a personnel training program. Assignment of a full-time central staff person responsible for staff development should be made where it is justified by the size of the institutional system.

3. Training of personnel should be considered of sufficient importance to warrant the inclusion of budgeted funds for this purpose. Fifty-two hours of annual training time should be budgeted for each custodial position.

4. All correctional institutions should have on staff, in addition to correctional officers and operations personnel, the following employees: medical staff, social caseworkers, chaplains, vocational counselors, psychologists, academic and vocational teachers, librarians, and recreational supervisors. The number of employees and their qualifications and experience should satisfy the requirements established by standard-setting agencies for the various positions.

D. Clientele

1. *Custodial Supervision and Discipline*

a) A system of correctional institutions should have facilities for diversification of custody and program by age, sex, custodial requirements, types of inmates, and program needs. The system should include such facilities as camps, residential centers, halfway houses, and work-furlough or work-release programs.

b) The classification procedure within a state system and in each institution should provide for at least an annual review of the treatment program of each prisoner.

c) Every institution should have predetermined and well-defined plans for civil defense and for coping with emergencies such as fire, disorder, escape, and power failure.

d) The types of disciplinary measures authorized should be set forth in writing and strictly controlled by the central office or governing body of the correctional system.

e) Hearings on discipline should be conducted, and disciplinary measures should be imposed not by a single official but by a disciplinary committee.

f) Confinement to disciplinary quarters should be for short periods and should not exceed thirty days. Inmates in disciplinary confinement should be visited daily by a supervisory officer of the institution and by the medical officer. They should be given a daily exercise period and a regular diet with a minimum of 2,100 calories per day. No inmates should be placed on a restricted diet without the approval of the medical officer.

g) Corporal punishment should never be used under any circumstances. Physical force may be used only when necessary to protect one's self or others from injury, to prevent escape, and to prevent serious injury to property. Officers should not be permitted to carry clubs.

h) Useless made-work for purposes of punishment or humiliation should be prohibited.

2. *Classification*

a) Every state correctional department should have on its central staff a qualified person responsible for supervising classification procedures in the institutional system and for coordinating the institutional program with training, treatment, and parole planning.

b) An essential element in the classification process is a reception program for individual diagnosis, evaluation, and orientation of the newly admitted prisoner.

c) Cumulative case histories of all inmates should be maintained and conveniently located in a records office not open to inmates.

3. *Counseling, Casework, and Clinical*

a) The maximum work load for a caseworker assigned exclusively to the reception process is thirty cases per month. In general institution programs, there should be one counselor for every 150 inmates.

b) Clinical services (psychiatric, psychological, and counseling) for a general institution with a population of six hundred inmates should include a minimum of one psychiatrist, three clinical psychologists, and three specialized counselors.

c) There should be at least one professionally qualified vocational counselor having a work load of forty cases per month in the reception process and one vocational counselor to every three hundred inmates in general institution programs.

4. *Other Services*

a) All inmates and employees should be provided with a wholesome and adequate diet conforming to the daily dietary allowances recommended by the Food and Nutrition Board of the National Research Council.

b) The institution's medical services should be directed and supervised by a qualified medical officer, and there should be a medical director for the institutional system where its size warrants this position. The medical services program should include immediate access to various medical specialists as the need arises.

c) Suitable screening programs should be developed to insure that all prisoners are given the medical attention and treatment indicated. Provision should be made for the care of inmates with chronic illnesses such as tuberculosis, heart disease, and diabetes. Complete dental care should be provided.

d) An adequate medical staff for an institution of five hundred inmates should include a doctor, an assistant medical officer, a dentist, five medical technicians, and a suitable complement of consultants including psychologists and psychiatrists.

e) All employable prisoners should have the opportunity to work. Their assignments should be closely related to their ability, interests, training needs, and custodial requirements. Prisoners should be paid for their work.

f) The central office of the institutional system should be responsible for planning, administering, and supervising all aspects of the educational program.

g) The library collection within an institution should consist of not less than six thousand well-selected volumes, with at least ten books per inmate. Institutions with large groups of long-term prisoners should provide a minimum of fifteen to twenty volumes per inmate.

h) For the average correctional institution, recreation programs should be directed by a fully qualified recreation supervisor (a college graduate with a major in recreation or physical education) assisted by an arts-and-crafts teacher, a music teacher, two physical education or recreation teachers, and four correctional officers.

i) There should be one clinically trained chaplain for each major faith group in an institution having fifty or more communicants.

V. Standards for Juvenile Detention

Definition

Juvenile detention: The temporary care of children in physically restricted facilities pending court disposition or transfer to another jurisdiction or agency.

A. Statutory Provisions

1. No child of juvenile court age should be admitted to a jail or police lockup. Local or regional detention homes for children should be provided.

2. No child should be placed in any detention facility unless he is a delinquent or alleged delinquent and there is a substantial probability that he will commit an offense dangerous to himself or the community or will run away pending court disposition. He should not be detained for punishment or for someone's convenience.

3. When the child denies the offense or when parents question the need for detention, a court hearing on detention should be held forthwith.

4. The release of a child should depend, not on his family's ability to secure a bail bond, but on the personal recognizance of the parent, guardian, relative, or attorney or other responsible person.

5. Delinquent or allegedly delinquent children who must be

removed from their homes temporarily but do not require secure custody should be placed in shelter care.

B. Organization

1. An appropriate state agency should be given statutory responsibility for statewide detention planning and the operation of regional detention homes.

2. The juvenile court is responsible for providing the policies and procedures governing conditions under which a child may be placed into temporary care (detention or shelter). Such policies and procedures provide the necessary legal safeguards for police, parents, and child regarding admission, case processing, and release from temporary care. They should be set forth clearly in writing, with specific delegation to appropriate personnel for implementing them at all times.

3. Detention construction requires complete separation from jail or any place of adult confinement, foolproof security features (psychiatrically secure and nonjail-like), provisions for auditory and visual control, fireproof materials, and 100 square feet of living area and program space per child in addition to individual sleeping rooms.

4. Sleeping rooms in detention should be individually occupied, should have a minimum floor dimension of 8 by 10 feet and be provided with toilets and lavatories protected by semi-partitions.

5. Sleeping units and activity groups should be of a size that encourages individual attention within one person's ability to supervise. Under no circumstances should groups exceed fifteen children under one employee's supervision.

C. Personnel

1. Group workers in direct contact with children should possess physical stamina, personality, and resourcefulness to conduct programs and relate constructively to detained children. They should have sufficient intelligence and education (B.A. degree in one of the social sciences) to participate effectively in the process of helping the child.

2. Staff members should preferably work an eight-hour day and a forty-hour week.

3. Provisions should be made for medical, religious, and clinical services to meet needs promptly and competently to avoid prolonging detention.

D. Clientele

1. Detention should provide care that will offset the danger inherent in confinement, enable observation and study, and enhance any later treatment.
2. Children in detention should be under direct supervision at all times to assure their own safety, protect them from one another, and minimize further delinquency contagion.
3. Constructive activity should be provided to meet individual and group needs, including a full school program, preferably on a twelve-month basis, and a balance of quiet and vigorous recreation, creative crafts, and work details.
4. Length of stay should be as short as possible, consistent with prompt processing of the case.
5. Children, including those committed to institutions or ordered placed in foster care, should be removed from detention immediately upon court disposition.

VI. Standards for Juvenile Institutions

Definition

Juvenile institution: A residential facility, often called a training school, for treatment of delinquent youth.

A. Statutory Provisions

1. Legal custody of a child should be vested in the parent state agency administering the state's delinquency program rather than in the individual institution. Custody should be for an indeterminate period not to exceed three years.
2. The state agency as the legal custodian should be permitted to select the type of care and treatment which most closely meets an individual child's needs.
3. No child committed under noncriminal proceedings should be housed in institutions with those convicted under criminal proceedings.
4. The parent agency should not be permitted to place a child

for long-term care in a facility which requires special admission proceedings, such as an institution for the mentally retarded or mentally ill.

5. Use of institutions for the mentally retarded or mentally ill for observation and diagnosis should be temporary and should not exceed ninety days.

6. Dependent and neglected children should not be committed to or placed in training schools or other facilities for delinquents.

7. Training schools should not be used as detention centers for the temporary care of children pending court decision.

B. Organization

1. The parent state agency administering the state delinquency program should have the control, supervisory consultation, data collection, and research functions to discharge its statutory obligations.

2. The parent state agency should have inspection and subsidy authority for juvenile detention and other local services dealing with delinquency treatment.

C. Personnel

1. All positions in the juvenile institution, including that of superintendent, should be covered by an adequate merit or civil service system. The forty-hour week should prevail for all employees.

2. The institution administrator should have training in social work, clinical or social psychology, psychiatry, education, or a related field of child development.

3. The following staff ratios should be met:

a) A minimum of one full-time psychiatrist for each 150 children.

b) A minimum of one full-time psychologist for each 150 children.

c) A minimum of one social caseworker for every thirty children.

d) One trained recreation person for each fifty children.

e) A minimum of one supervisor for eight or ten cottage staff, or one supervisor for two or three living units.

f) A minimum of one registered nurse during the working hours.

g) A minimum of one teacher to fifteen youngsters with sixth-grade reading ability and above.

h) A minimum of one teacher to ten youngsters with third- to fifth-grade reading ability.

i) Individual teaching staff for each youngster with less than third-grade reading ability.

j) A full-time librarian for each institution.

4. Major religious faiths represented in a training school population should be served by chaplains on the training school staff.

D. Clientele

1. A state should have diversified services and institutions for delinquent youth. These should include, in addition to basic child welfare services, detention facilities, diagnostic study centers, small residential treatment centers for seriously disturbed children, facilities for various age and coeducational groupings, foster homes, group homes, forestry camps, and other community-based facilities.

2. The capacity of a training school should be limited to 150 children.

3. Living groups in a training school should consist of not more than twenty children. Forestry camp populations should total no more than forty to fifty.

4. Corporal punishment should not be tolerated in any form in a training school program.

5. Confinement of children for prolonged periods in segregation rooms as a disciplinary measure should be prohibited. Children in segregation should be constantly supervised.

6. Each child should have a complete physical examination by a physician upon admission or within twenty-four hours. He should have a complete physical examination just prior to his release from the training school.

7. A twelve-month school program is recommended. The entire educational program within a training shool should be administered within the institution's administrative structure. All youth in the training school who can benefit from an education should have access to participation in a complete educational program.

Selected Bibliography

Note: The following abbreviations are used:

ACA, APA	Proceedings of the Annual Congress of Corrections (formerly American Prison Assoc.) American Correctional Assoc.
Annals	Annals of the American Academy of Political and Social Science.
JNPPA	Journal of the National Probation and Parole Association (discontinued).
Focus	Journal of the National Probation and Parole Association (discontinued).
JCLC	Journal of Criminal Law, Criminology, and Police Science.
Fed. Prob.	Federal Probation Quarterly.
NPPA	Yearbook of the National Probation and Parole Association (discontinued).

ADAMS, STUART: The value of research in probation. *Fed Prob,* Sept. 1965.

AMERICAN CORRECTIONAL ASSOCIATION: *Correctional Officers Training Guide,* 1962.

AMERICAN CORRECTIONAL ASSOCIATION: *A Manual of Correctional Standards,* 1966.

AMERICAN CORRECTIONAL ASSOCIATION (formerly American Prison Assoc.): *Handbook on Pre-release Preparation in Correctional Institutions,* 1948.

ANTOLINA, CHARLES S.: Principles of intake control. *NPPA,* 1952.

ARLUKE, N.R.: A summary of parole rules. *JNPPA,* Jan. 1956.

ASHLEY, P.D.: Group work in the probation setting. *Probation* (Great Britain), Mar. 1962.

BARNETT, JACOB B., and GRONEWOLD, DAVID H.: Confidentiality of the presentence report. *Fed Prob,* Mar. 1962.

BARRY, J.V.: An Australian experiment in probation and parole. *Probation* (Great Britain), Mar. 1961.

BARTOO, CHESTER H.: Interviewing candidates for probation. *Fed Prob,* Mar. 1961.

BARTOO, CHESTER H.: Some hidden factors behind a probation officer's recommendations. *Crime Delinq,* July 1963.

BATES, JEROME E.: Presentence investigation in abortion cases. *Crime Delinq,* July 1963.

BEATTIE, R.N.: Measuring the effectiveness of probation. *Calif Youth Authority Q,* Summer 1957.

BISSELL, D.: Group work in the probation setting. *British J Crim,* Jan. 1962.

BIXBY, F. LOVELL: New Jersey's consultation system for improved probation services. *State Govt,* Spring 1965.

BOTKA, JOSEPH J.: The importance of pre-trial investigation and study. *Child Welfare*, June 1959.

BRESLIN, MAURICE A., and CROSSWHITE, ROBERT G.: Residential aftercare: An intermediate step in the correctional process. *Fed Prob*, Mar. 1963.

BRILLINGER, ROY: The role of the probation officer with the alcoholic. *Canad J Corr*, Apr. 1963.

CAILLIET, ANDRE: Treatment of a juvenile delinquent: A probation officer's view. *Fed Prob*, Sept. 1964.

CALIFORNIA STATE BOARD OF CORRECTIONS: *The Treatment of Delinquents in the Community: Variations in Treatment Approaches.* (I) July 1960.

CALIFORNIA STATE BOARD OF CORRECTIONS: *Correction in the Community: Alternative to Incarceration.* (IV) June 1964.

CALIFORNIA YOUTH AUTHORITY: *Standards for the Performance of Probation Duties.* rev. ed., Sacramento, 1962.

CAMPBELL, JAY: A strict accountability approach to criminal responsibility. *Fed Prob*, Dec. 1965.

CHAPPELL, RICHARD A.: The lawyer's role in the administration of probation and parole. *Amer Bar Assoc*, Aug. 1962.

CHEW, CHARLES: Parole of lifers in Virginia. *Univ Va News Letter*, Nov. 1960.

CHUTE, C.L., and BELL, MARJORIE: *Crime, Courts and Probation.* New York, Macmillan, 1956.

CLARK, R.E.: Size of the parole community as related to parole outcome. *Amer J Sociol*, 1951, vol. 57.

CLASS, N.E.: Qualifications: A realistic approach to personnel requirements. *JNPPA*, Apr. 1957.

CLEGG, REED K.: *Probation and Parole: Principles and Practices.* Springfield, Thomas, 1964.

CLOWARD, RICHARD A., and OHLIN, LLOYD E.: *Delinquency and Opportunity.* Free Press, 1960.

COHEN, IRVING E.: Twilight zones in probation (with reference to restitution). *J Criminal Law*, Nov.-Dec. 1946.

COHN, YONA: Criteria for the probation officer's recommendations to the juvenile court judge. *Crime Delinq*, July 1963.

CONRAD, JOHN P.: *Crime and Its Correction.* Berkeley, U. of Calif., 1965.

COUNCIL OF STATE GOVERNMENTS: *Suggested State Legislation Program*, especially materials on detainers, 1957.

CRAIN, WILLIAM W.: Indeterminate and determinate time in the treatment of the adolescent delinquent. *Fed Prob*, Sept. 1962.

CRAIN, WILLIAM W.: The chronic "Mess-Up" and his changing character. *Fed Prob*, June 1964.

Crime and Delinquency. Issue devoted to parole prediction tables. July 1962.

CUNNINGHAM, GLORIA: Supervision of the female offender. *Fed Prob*, Dec. 1963.

CZAJKOSKI, EUGENE H.: The need for philosophical direction in probation and parole. *Fed Prob,* Sept. 1965.

DAVIS, GEORGE F.: A study of adult probation violation rates by means of the cohort approach. *JCLC,* Mar. 1964.

DIANA, LEWIS: Is casework in probation necessary? *Focus,* Jan. 1955.

DIANA, LEWIS: What is probation? *JCLC,* July-Aug. 1960.

DICERBO, EUGENE C.: When should probation be revoked? *Fed Prob,* June 1966.

DISKIND, MEYER H., and KLONSKY, GEORGE: A second look at the New York State parole drug experiment. *Fed Prob,* Mar. 1965.

DONOHUE, JOHN K.: *Baffling Eyes of Youth.* Assoc. Press, 1957.

DRESSLER, D.: *Parole Chief.* New York, Viking, 1951.

DRESSLER, D.: *Probation and Parole.* New York, Columbia, 1951.

DRESSLER, D.: *Practice and Theory of Probation and Parole.* New York, Columbia, 1959.

DUPREE, HARRY C.: The U.S. Army and Air Force clemency and parole board. *Amer J Corr,* Nov.-Dec. 1959.

DWOSKIN, S.I.: Jail as a condition of probation. *Calif Youth Authority Q,* Summer 1962.

ELIASBERG, W.G.: Group treatment of homosexuals on probation. *Group Psychother,* Dec. 1954.

ELLIOTT, ARTHUR E.: Parole readiness: An institutional dilemma. *Fed Prob,* Mar. 1964.

ENGLAND, RALPH W., JR.: What is responsible for satisfactory probation and post-probation outcome? *JCLC,* Mar. 1957.

EVANS, WALTER: The probationer's job: An essential factor in his rehabilitation. *Fed Prob,* June 1961.

EVJEN, V.H.: Continuance of services following termination of probation. *APA,* 1951.

EVJEN, V.H.: Current thinking on parole prediction tables. *Crime Delinq,* July 1962.

FARROW, R.G.: The give and take of parole supervision. *Focus,* Jan. 1953.

FARROW, R.G., and GIARDINI, G.I.: The paroling of capital offenders. *Annals,* Nov. 1952.

FENTON, NORMAN: The psychological preparation of inmates for release. *APA,* 1949.

FENTON, NORMAN: *Prisoner's Family; A Study of Family Counseling in an Adult Correctional System.* Palo Alto, Pacific Books, 1959.

FISHMAN, J.F., and PERLMAN, V.: In the name of parole. *Yale Rev,* 1939, vol. 28.

FITZGERALD, E.: A critical review of probation and parole. *NPPA,* 1953.

FITZGERALD, E.: The presentence investigation. *JNPPA,* Oct. 1956.

FLOCH, M.: Mental hygiene in parole work. *Focus,* Jan. 1955.

Fox, Vernon: Probation and parole: Theory versus practice. *JCLC,* May-June 1959.

Frisbie, Louise Viets: Treated sex offenders who reverted to sexually deviant behavior. *Fed Prob,* June 1965.

Fuller, J.K.: Extension of group therapy to parolees. *Prison World,* July 1952.

Galvin, J.: Planning a pre-release unit program. *APA,* 1950.

Garrett, Edward W.: Improvement of officer performance through supervision. *Fed Prob,* Sept. 1963.

Gary, Holland M.: Division of responsibilities between the juvenile court and welfare agencies. *Fed Prob,* June 1961.

Geis, Gilbert, and Woodson, F.W.: Matching probation officer and delinquent. *JNPPA,* Jan. 1956.

Gernert, Paul J.: Interstate compact for parolees and probationers. *Pa Chiefs of Police Assoc,* Summer 1958.

Giardini, G.I.: Evaluating the work of parole officers. *NPPA,* 1953.

Giardini, G.I.: *The Parole Process.* Springfield, Thomas, 1959.

Gibbons, Don C.: Probation: Theory and reality. *Canad J Corr,* Jan. 1959.

Gibbons, Don C.: Some notes on treatment theory in corrections. *Social Service Rev,* Sept. 1962.

Gibbons, Don C.: *Society, Crime, and Criminal Careers.* Englewood Cliffs, Prentice-Hall, 1968.

Gillin, J.S.: Parole prediction in Wisconsin. *Sociol Soc Res,* 1950, vol. 34.

Glaser, D.: The efficacy of alternative approaches to parole prediction. *Amer Sociol Rev,* June 1955.

Glaser, D.: *The Effectiveness of a Prison and Parole System.* Indianapolis, Bobbs, 1964.

Glover, E.: *Probation and Re-education.* London, Routledge & K. Paul, 1949.

Glueck, S.: *Probation and Criminal Justice.* New York, Macmillan, 1933.

Goodman, L.A.: The use and validity of a prediction instrument. *Amer J Sociol,* 1953, vol. 58.

Gottesman, Michael, and Hecker, Lewis J.: Parole: A critique of its legal foundations and conditions. *NYU Law Rev,* June 1963.

Gottfredson, Don M., and Ballard, K.B.: Differences in decisions associated with decision makers. *J Res Crime Delinq,* July 1966.

Gronewold, David H.: Supervision practices in the federal probation system. *Fed Prob,* Sept. 1964.

Gronewold, David H.: Casework in probation. *Prison J* (Philadelphia), Oct. 1959.

Gross, Seymour Z.: Biographical characteristics of juvenile probation officers. *Crime Delinq,* Apr. 1966.

Gruenhut, Max: *The Selection of Offenders for Probation.* United Nations Secretariat, 1959.

GRUENHUT, MAX: *Probation and Mental Treatment.* London, Tavistock, 1963.

GRUPP, STANLEY E.: Work release and the misdemeanant. *Fed Prob,* June 1965.

GRYGIER, T.: A research scheme into personality interaction in probation. *Canad J Corr,* Apr. 1961.

GRYGIER, T.: Education for correctional workers. *Canad J Corr,* 1962, vol. 4.

GRYGIER, T.: The chronic petty offender. *J Res Crime Delinq,* 1964, vol. 1.

GURMAN, I.: The relationships that should exist between prisoner aid societies and probation and parole department. *APA,* 1952.

GURMAN, I.: Community discrimination against the parolee. *Focus,* Nov. 1953.

HAKEEM, M.: Glueck method of parole prediction applied to 1861 cases of burglars. *JCLC,* 1945, vol. 36.

HAKEEM, M.: The validity of the Burgess method of parole prediction. *Amer J Sociol,* 1948, vol. 53.

HALLECK, SEYMOUR L.: The initial interview with the offender. *Fed Prob,* Mar. 1961.

HALLECK, SEYMOUR L.: The impact of professional dishonesty on behavior of disturbed adolescents. *Soc Work,* Apr. 1963.

HARDMAN, DALE: The function of the probation officer. *Fed Prob,* Sept. 1960.

HARTMAN, HENRY L.: Interviewing techniques in probation and parole—Building the relationship. *Fed Prob,* Mar. 1963.

HARTMAN, HENRY L.: Interviewing techniques in probation and parole—The art of listening. *Fed Prob,* June 1963.

HARTMAN, HENRY L.: Interviewing techniques in probation and parole—The initial interview (Part 1). *Fed Prob,* Sept. 1963.

HARTMAN, HENRY L.: Interviewing techniques in probation and parole—The initial interview (Part 2). *Fed Prob,* Dec. 1963.

HARVARD LAW REVIEW ASSOCIATION: Parole revocation procedures. *Harvard Law Rev,* 1951, vol. 65.

HAVEL, J.: Special intensive parole unit reports on Phase III, Calif. Dept. of Corrections. *Res Newsletter,* Mar. 1962.

HENDRICK, E.J.: Basic concepts of conditions and violations. *JNPPA,* Jan. 1956.

HERMON, ZVI: Pre-sentence investigations and the development of probation legislation in Israel. *Int Rev Criminal Policy,* Apr. 1962.

HINK, H.R.: Application of constitutional standards of protection to probation. *Univ Chicago Law Rev,* Spring 1962.

HOUTS, MARSHALL: *From Arrest to Release; An Analysis of the Administration of Criminal Justice.* Springfield, Thomas, 1958.

HYMAN, E.C.: Holding the promiscuous girl accountable for her own behavior. *NPPA,* 1948.

IRWIN, OLIVE T.: Group reporting in juvenile probation. *Crime Delinq,* Oct. 1965.

IVES, JANE K.: The essential task of the probation-parole officer. *Fed Prob,* Mar. 1962.

JACKS, W.L.: *A Comparison of Parole Agents' Salaries, Caseloads, and Supervision Duties.* Pa. Board of Parole, 1957.

JOHNSON, A.R.: Recent developments in the law of probation. *JCLC,* June 1962.

JONES, M.: The treatment of character disorders. *British J Crim,* 1963, vol. 3.

KAY, BARBARA A., and VEDDER, CLYDE B. (Eds.): *Probation and Parole.* Springfield, Thomas, 1963.

KEVE, PAUL W.: *Prison, Probation, or Parole?* Minneapolis, U. of Minn., 1954.

KEVE, PAUL W.: *The Probation Officer Investigates.* Minneapolis, U. of Minn., 1962.

KEVE, PAUL W.: *The Probation Officer Investigates; A Guide to the Presentence Report.* Minneapolis, U. of Minn., 1960.

KEVE, PAUL W.: *Imaginative Programming in Probation and Parole.* U. of Minn., Minneapolis, 1967.

KILLINGER, G.: The functions and responsibilities of parole boards. *NPPA,* 1950.

KIRBY, B.C.: Parole prediction using multiple correlation. *Amer J Sociol,* May 1954.

KLONSKY, GEORGE: Extended supervision for discharged addict-parolees. *Fed Prob,* Mar. 1965.

LEENHOUTS, KEITH J.: The volunteer's role in municipal court probation. *Crime Delinq,* Jan. 1964.

LEJINS, P.: Criminology for probation and parole officers. *JNPPA,* July 1956.

LEJINS, P.: Parole prediction—an introductory statement. *Crime Delinq,* July 1962.

LOPEZ-REY, MANUEL: United Nations activities and international trends in probation. *Howard J* (London), 1957.

LYKKE, ARTHUR F.: *Parolees and Payrolls.* Springfield, Thomas, 1957.

MANDEL, NATHAN G., and PARSONAGE, WILLIAM H.: An experiment in adult "group-parole" supervision. *Crime Delinq,* Oct. 1965.

MARTIN, JOHN B.: The Saginaw Project. *Crime Delinq,* Oct. 1960.

MARTINSON, ROBERT M.; KASSEBAUM, GENE G., and WARD, DAVID A.: A critique of research in parole. *Fed Prob,* Sept. 1964.

MCCORD, W.; MCCORD, J., and VERDEN, P.: Family relationships and sexual deviance in lower class adolescents. *Int J Soc Psychiat,* 1962, vol. 83.

MCMINN, E.: The institutional parole officer. *Focus,* Jan. 1954.

MEEKER, B.S.: Federal Probation Training Center exemplifies agency responsibility for training. *Social Work Ed,* Sept. 1962.

MEEKER, B.S.: Relationships of probation staff and the guidance center. *Progress Report,* July-Sept. 1962.

MEEKER, B.S., and BLAKE, MARILYN A.: Probation is casework; probation is not casework. *Fed Prob,* June 1948.

MEINERS, ROBERT G.: A halfway house for parolees. *Fed Prob,* June 1965.

MEYER, CHARLES H.Z.: The "Brooklyn" plan of deferred prosecution of juvenile offenders. *J Criminal Law,* Mar.-Apr. 1947.

MILES, ARTHUR P.: The reality of the probation officer's dilemma. *Fed Prob,* Mar. 1965.

MONACHESI, E.D.: American studies in the prediction of recidivism. *JCLC,* 1951, vol. 41.

MONGER, MARK: Referral and the probation service. *Social Work* (London), Apr. 1963.

MONGER, MARK: Marital problems and the probation officer. *Probation,* Mar. 1963.

MONGER, MARK: *Casework in Probation.* Great Britain, Butterworth.

NATIONAL COUNCIL ON CRIME AND DELINQUENCY: *Int Bibliography on Crime Delinq* (periodical).

NATIONAL COUNCIL ON CRIME AND DELINQUENCY: *Current Research Projects Reported to Natl Research and Information Center* (periodical).

NATIONAL COUNCIL ON CRIME AND DELINQUENCY: *Crime Delinq* (periodical).

NATIONAL COUNCIL ON CRIME AND DELINQUENCY: *NCCD NEWS* (periodical); Employment Bull.

NATIONAL COUNCIL ON CRIME AND DELINQUENCY: *Standard Probation and Parole Act.*

NATIONAL COUNCIL ON CRIME AND DELINQUENCY: *John Augustus, First Probation Officer.* (Reprint of the original with an introduction by Sheldon Glueck.)

NATIONAL COUNCIL ON CRIME AND DELINQUENCY: *Guides for Sentencing.*

NATIONAL COUNCIL ON CRIME AND DELINQUENCY: *Standards and Guides for Adult Probation.*

NATIONAL COUNCIL ON CRIME AND DELINQUENCY: *Standards for Selection of Probation and Parole Personnel.* 1962.

NATIONAL COUNCIL ON CRIME AND DELINQUENCY: *Annulment of Conviction of Crime—A Model Act.* 1962.

NATIONAL COUNCIL ON CRIME AND DELINQUENCY: Guides for Juvenile Court *Judges.* 1963.

NATIONAL PAROLE INSTITUTES: *A Survey of the Organization of Parole Systems.* Publication III, NCCD, Dec. 1963.

NEWMAN, CHARLES L.: Let's "sell" corrections: A straight talk to probation officers. *Fed Prob,* June 1955.

NEWMAN, CHARLES L.: Casework in adult probation and parole. *Indian J Social Work* (Bombay), Mar. 1959.

NEWMAN, CHARLES L.: Re-establishment of the adult probationer and parolee in the family and in the community. *Police,* Jan.-Feb. 1960.

NEWMAN, CHARLES L.: Concepts of treatment in probation parole supervision. *Fed Prob*, Mar. 1961.

NEWMAN, CHARLES L.: The sexual offender: Criminological enigma. *Ala Corr J*, Nov. 1962.

NEWMAN, CHARLES L.: Foster care in the treatment of juvenile delinquency. *Quart J Pa Prob Parole Assoc*, Feb. 1963.

NEWMAN, CHARLES L.: Education and training for the field of corrections. *Quart J Pa Prob Parole Assoc*, 1967.

NEW YORK STATE, DIVISION OF PAROLE: *Parole Officers Manual.*

NEW YORK STATE, DIVISION OF PAROLE: An approach to the study of delinquency among parolees. *Correction*, New York, Nov. 1953.

NEW YORK STATE, DIVISION OF PROBATION: *Manual for Probation Officers.*

OHLIN, L.E.: *Selection for Parole.* Russell Sage Foundation, 1951.

OHLIN, L.E.: The routinization of correctional change. *JCLC*, 1954, vol. 45.

OHLIN, L.E.: *Sociology and the Field of Corrections.* Russell Sage Foundation, 1956.

OHLIN, L.E.: Major dilemmas of the social worker in probation and parole. *JNPPA*, July 1956.

OHLIN, L.E., and DUNCAN, O.D.: The efficiency of prediction in criminology. *Amer J Sociol*, 1949, vol. 54.

OSWALD, R.D.: Community discrimination against the parolee—a second look. *Focus*, May 1954.

OUTERBRIDGE, WILLIAM: Authority—its use or misuse in probation. *Canad J Corr*, July 1960.

OUTERBRIDGE, WILLIAM: Staff development in the Ontario provincial probation services. *Canad J Corr*, Oct. 1963.

OVERTON, ALICE: Establishing the relationship. *Crime Delinq*, July 1965.

PANAKAL, J.J., and DIGHE, K.G.: Probation. *Indian J Soc Work* (Bombay), Sept. 1961.

PIGEON, H.D.: *Probation and Parole in Theory and Practice.* National Probation and Parole Assoc., 1942. (now, the National Council on Crime and Delinq.)

PRESIDENT'S COMMISSION ON LAW ENFORCEMENT AND ADMINISTRATION OF JUSTICE: *The Challenge of Crime in a Free Society.* USGPO, 1967.

PRESIDENT'S COMMISSION ON LAW ENFORCEMENT AND ADMINISTRATION OF JUSTICE: *Task Force Report: Corrections.*

PRESIDENT'S COMMISSION ON LAW ENFORCEMENT AND ADMINISTRATION OF JUSTICE: *Task Force Report: Juvenile Delinquency and Youth Crime.*

PRESIDENT'S COMMISSION ON LAW ENFORCEMENT AND ADMINISTRATION OF JUSTICE: *Task Force Report: The Courts.*

PRESIDENT'S COMMISSION ON LAW ENFORCEMENT AND ADMINISTRATION OF JUSTICE: *Task Force Report: The Police.*

PRIGMORE, C.S.: Surveillance or treatment—the supervisor's decision. *Focus*, Jan. 1955.

PRIGMORE, C.S.: The role of the supervisor in achieving a balance between surveillance and treatment in probation and parole. *APA,* 1954.

PRIGMORE, C.S. (Ed.): *Manpower and Training for Corrections.* Council on Social Work Ed., 1966.

PRINS, HERSCHEL A.: Training for probation work in England and Wales. *Fed Prob,* Dec. 1964.

RAY, J.M.: Scientific parole—a proposal. *JCLC,* 1947, vol. 37.

REED, GEORGE J.: Due process in parole violation hearings. *Fed Prob,* June 1963.

REINEMANN, J.O.: *Parole and Probation.* Phila. Jr. Chamber of Commerce, 1953.

RESKO, J.: *Reprieve.* Garden City, Doubleday, 1956.

ROOT, MANLY G.: What the probation officer can do for special types of offenders. *Fed Prob,* Dec. 1949.

ROSENGARTEN, LEONARD: Intensive probation supervision for juveniles. *Amer J Corr,* Nov.-Dec. 1963.

ROSENGARTEN, LEONARD: Volunteer support of probation services. *Crime Delinq,* Jan. 1964.

ROSENHEIM, MARGARET K. (Ed.): *Justice for the Child.* Free Press, 1962.

RUBIN, SOL: A legal view of probation and parole conditions. *JNPPA,* Jan. 1956.

RUBIN, SOL: Due process is required in parole revocation proceedings. *Fed Prob,* June 1963.

RUBIN, SOL, and others: *The Law of Criminal Correction.* West Pub. Co., 1963.

RUMNEY, J., and MURPHY, J.P.: *Probation and Social Adjustment.* New Brunswick, Rutgers, 1952.

SANSON, D.R.: Probation and parole for misdemeanants. *NPPA,* 1949.

SCHNUR, A.C.: The validity of parole selection. *Social Forces,* 1951, vol. 29.

SCHUESSLER, K.F.: Parole prediction: Its history and status. *JCLC,* 1954, vol. 45.

SCOTT, A.W., JR.: The pardoning power. *Annals,* Nov. 1952.

SELLIN, THORSTEN: Adult probation and the conditional sentence. *JCLC,* Mar.-Apr. 1959.

SHAH, SALEEM A.: Changing attitudes and behavior of offenders. *Fed Prob,* Mar. 1963.

SHELLY, JOSEPH A., and BASSIN, ALEXANDER: Daytop Lodge: A halfway house for drug addicts. *Fed Prob,* Dec. 1964.

SHIREMAN, CHARLES H.: Casework in probation and parole: Some considerations in diagnosis and treatment. *Fed Prob,* June 1963.

SILVER, ALBERT W.: Operating a psychiatric clinic in a juvenile court. *Fed Prob,* Sept. 1962.

SILVERMAN, E.: Surveillance, treatment, and casework supervision. *JNPPA,* Jan. 1956.

Sims, Leon J.: Pre-arraignment investigations: A partial solution to the time problem. *Fed Prob,* Mar. 1964.

Singh, S.D.: Law of probation in India. *Indian J Soc Work,* June 1959.

Skolnick, Jerome H.: Toward a developmental theory of parole. *Amer Sociol Rev,* Aug. 1960.

Smith, A.B., and Bassin, A.: Research in a probation department. *Crime Delinq,* Jan. 1962.

Smith, Charles E.: Observation and study of defendants prior to sentence. *Fed Prob,* June 1962.

Stanton, John M.: The typical parolee. *Amer J Corr,* May-June 1963.

Stanton, John M.: Is it safe to parole inmates without jobs? *Crime Delinq,* Apr. 1966.

Stone, W.T.: Administrative aspects of the special intensive parole program. *ACA,* 1956.

Street, T.G.: Canada's parole system. *Amer J Corr,* Mar.-Apr. 1962.

Sullivan, K.: *Girls on Parole.* Boston, Houghton, 1955.

Studt, E.: An outline for the study of social authority factors in casework. *Soc Casework,* 1954, vol. 35.

Studt, E.: *Education for Social Workers in the Correctional Field.* Council on Social Work Ed., 1959.

Studt, E.: Worker-client authority relationships in social work. *Social Work,* Jan. 1959.

Tappan, P.W.: *Juvenile Delinquency.* New York, McGraw, 1949.

Tappan, P.W.: *Contemporary Correction.* New York, McGraw, 1951.

Tappan, P.W.: The legal rights of prisoners. *Annals,* May, 1954.

Tappan, P.W.: *Crime, Justice, and Correction.* New York, McGraw, 1960.

Terwilliger, Carl: The nonprofessional in correction. *Crime Delinq,* July 1966.

Thomsen, Roszel C.: Confidentiality of the pre-sentence report: A middle position. *Fed Prob,* Mar. 1964.

Timasheff, N.S.: *One Hundred Years of Probation.* Bronx, Fordham, 1941.

Timasheff, N.S.: *Probation in the Light of Criminal Statistics.* Declan X McMullen, 1949.

Tinsley, Henry C., and Grout, Edward W.: Colorado's pre-parole release center. *State Govt,* Spring 1960.

Tompkins, Dorothy C.: Administration of criminal justice, 1949-1956; A selected bibliography. *Calif Bd Corr,* Nov. 1956.

Tompkins, Dorothy C.: *The Offender—A Bibliography.* Inst. Govt. Studies, Berkeley, U. of Calif., 1963.

Tompkins, Dorothy C.: *Probation Since World War II—A Bibliography.* Inst. Govt. Studies, Berkeley, U. of Calif., 1964.

Tracey, Gerald A.: A social worker's perspective on social work in probation. *Crime Delinq,* Apr. 1961.

TRAVERS, P.: Experiment in the supervision of paroled offenders addicted to narcotic drugs. *Amer J Corr,* Mar.-Apr. 1957.

UNITED NATIONS: *Probation and Related Measures.* Dept. of Social Affairs, 1951.

UNITED NATIONS: *Practical Results and Financial Aspects of Adult Probation in Selected Countries.* Dept. of Social Affairs, 1954.

UNITED NATIONS: *Parole and Aftercare.* Dept. of Social Affairs, 1954.

UNITED NATIONS: International Review of Criminal Policy, periodical (Extensive bibliographies in most issues).

UNITED STATES, ATTORNEY GENERAL: *Survey of Release Procedures.* vol. 2, Probation; vol. 3, Pardons; vol. 4, Parole. USGPO, 1939-1940.

VAN WEST, ALEXANDER: Cultural background and treatment of the persistent offender. *Fed Prob,* June 1964.

VOGT, HERBERT: Group counseling in probation. *Fed Prob,* Sept. 1961.

VOLD, G.B.: *Prediction Methods and Parole.* Sociol. Press, 1931.

WALLACE, JOHN A.: The casework approach to rules. *JNPPA,* Jan. 1956.

WALLACE, JOHN A.: A fresh look at old probation standards. *Crime Delinq,* Apr. 1964.

WEINBERG, S.K.: Theories of criminality and problems of prediction. *JCLC,* Nov. 1954.

WILKINS, LESLIE T.: *Social Deviance and Prediction Methods.* Englewood Cliffs, Prentice-Hall, 1964.

WILLIAMS, M.E.: Developing employment opportunities for parolees. *Focus,* Mar. 1952.

YABLONSKY, LEWIS: *The Tunnel Back: Synanon.* New York, Macmillan, 1965.

YOUNG, PAULINE V.: *Social Treatment in Probation and Delinquency.* New York, McGraw, 1952.

YOUNGHUSBAND, E.: Report on a survey of social work in the field of corrections. *Soc Work Ed,* Aug. 1960.

Index

Q

R

S